Rudolph Wagner, John Hunter

The anthropological treatises of Johann Friedrich Blumenbach

Rudolph Wagner, John Hunter

The anthropological treatises of Johann Friedrich Blumenbach

ISBN/EAN: 9783742818737

Manufactured in Europe, USA, Canada, Australia, Japa

Cover: Foto ©Thomas Meinert / pixelio.de

Manufactured and distributed by brebook publishing software (www.brebook.com)

Rudolph Wagner, John Hunter

The anthropological treatises of Johann Friedrich Blumenbach

Publications of the
Anthropological Society of London.

THE ANTHROPOLOGICAL TREATISES OF
BLUMENBACH
AND
HUNTER.

THE ANTHROPOLOGICAL TREATISES

OF

JOHANN FRIEDRICH BLUMENBACH,

LATE PROFESSOR AT GÖTTINGEN AND COURT PHYSICIAN
TO THE KING OF GREAT BRITAIN.

WITH MEMOIRS OF HIM BY MARX AND FLOURENS,
AND AN ACCOUNT OF HIS ANTHROPOLOGICAL MUSEUM BY
PROFESSOR R. WAGNER,

AND

THE INAUGURAL DISSERTATION OF JOHN HUNTER, M.D.

ON THE VARIETIES OF MAN.

TRANSLATED AND EDITED

FROM THE LATIN, GERMAN, AND FRENCH ORIGINALS,

BY

THOMAS BENDYSHE, M.A., V.P.A.S.L.

FELLOW OF KING'S COLLEGE, CAMBRIDGE.

LONDON:
PUBLISHED FOR THE ANTHROPOLOGICAL SOCIETY, BY
LONGMAN, GREEN, LONGMAN, ROBERTS, & GREEN.
1865.

EDITOR'S PREFACE.

THE Works of Blumenbach edited in this volume are the first and third or last edition of his famous Treatise *On the Natural Variety of Mankind;* which were published in 1775 and 1795 respectively: the *Contributions to Natural History*, in two parts; and a slight notice of three skulls which appeared in the *Göttingische gelehrte Anzeigen* of Nov. 1833, only remarkable for being the last printed utterance of the author. Two Memoirs of Blumenbach have been prefixed, which contain together almost everything of interest concerning the circumstances of his life. I have also added an account of his once famous anthropological collection, written by his successor, now himself lately deceased, Professor Rudolph Wagner, one of the original Honorary Fellows of the Anthropological Society, London.

Blumenbach has related in the little autobiographical fragment, which has been incorporated by Marx in his memoir, the causes which led to his selection of an anthropological subject as the thesis for his doctoral dissertation. It was delivered in 1775, and reprinted word for word in 1776. A second edition, enlarged by as much as would make about fifteen printed pages uniform with this translation, was issued in 1781; and finally a third in 1795, which in arrangement and matter was almost a new work. I hesitated some time as to which of the two first editions it would be most satisfactory to give to the public; for, on the one hand, the first is obviously most interesting for the history of the science, and the additional matter contained in the second has scarce any intrinsic value in the present day; but, on the other hand, in the first mankind is divided into four races only, and the now famous division of the Caucasian, Asiatic, American, Ethiopian, and Malay races, occurs for the first time in the edition of 1781.

To give them both in their entirety would have perhaps been less troublesome to myself, but certainly tedious to the reader, for not only are the Plates the same, but much the greater part of the second edition is a mere repetition. At last I determined to use the first as my text, and appended in a note the important pentagenist arrangement. Accordingly the translation has been made from the reprint of 1776, which differs in the title-page alone, and that I have taken from the copy in the British Museum. The preface *To the Reader* has been omitted as of no value. But this is not the case with the Letter to Sir Joseph Banks, which forms the preface to the third edition of 1795, and contains a system of natural history, with appendices giving an account of Blumenbach's Collection as it then was.

The *Contributions to Natural History* consists of two parts; the first of which went through two editions. The first in 1790, and the second, from which the translation is made, in 1806. The second part appeared in 1811. That part in the original is composed of two sections; the first upon Peter, the Wild Boy, and wild boys in general: and the second on Egyptian mummies. This latter essay, as may be supposed, is considerably behind the knowledge of the present day, and though in it, as well as in that written by Blumenbach in English and printed in the *Philosophical Transactions* of 1794, he had observed the varieties in the national character of the Egyptian mummies and artistic representations, yet the whole essay has been pronounced lately by a competent writer to be "in some sort not worthy of that great authority[1]." The fact that the incisors of the mummies resembled in shape the molar teeth was thought by Blumenbach to be a discovery of much greater importance than modern writers are willing to allow. I have therefore come to the conclusion that it is not worth while to edit this part of the *Contributions*, especially as it is quite distinct by itself, and has no immediate bearing on general anthropology.

The treatise *On the Natural Variety of Mankind* cannot be considered obsolete even at the present day. All subsequent writers, including Lawrence, Prichard, Waitz, &c., have acknowledged their obligations and proved them, especially Lawrence, by borrowing largely from it. "Blumenbach may still be considered a chief authority," says Waitz[2]. And his classification of mankind, though avowedly neither final nor rigidly scientific, has survived a very considerable number of pretentious improvements, and still holds its ground in the latest elementary text-books of ethnology[3]. "The illustrious naturalist, in whom, after Buffon, we ought to acknowledge the father of anthropology, has made two important advances in

---

[1] Perier (J. A. N.), *Sur l'ethnogenie Egyptienne*. *Mém. de la Soc. de l'Anthropologie de Paris*, Tom. I. p. 443.

[2] p. 29. Eng. Trl. by J. F. Collingwood. 8vo. Lond. 1863.

[3] See Page D. *Introductory Text Book of Physical Geography*, p. 178, Edinb. and Lond. 1865, 12mo.

that science, in his views on the classification of races. Although he continued to place at the head of all the characteristics that derived from colour, Blumenbach is the first who founded his classification in great part on those presented by the general conformation of the head, so different in different races, as to the proportion of the skull to the face, and of the encephalon to the organs of sense and the jaws. This progress led also to a second. It is because Blumenbach attributed a great importance to that order of characteristics; it is because he was the first who devoted himself to determine exactly, by the assistance of a great number of observations, the essential elements which distinguished the types of man that he was also the first who made a very clear distinction of several races in which it is impossible to fail of recognizing so many natural groups. Thus it has happened that these races, after having been once introduced into science by Blumenbach, have been retained there; and we may assert that they will always be retained, with some rectifications in their characteristics and in their several boundaries. But are the five races of Blumenbach the only ones possible to distinguish in mankind? And if all the five must be considered as natural groups, is it proper to place them in the same rank, and allow them all the same zoological value? Blumenbach himself did not think this.

"In the first place his five races are not the only ones whose existence he is disposed to admit; but what is very different, the five *principal* ones. *Varietates quinæ principes*, says Blumenbach in his treatise *On the Varieties of Mankind*. He uses the same expression in his *Representations*. The unequal importance of these races in a zoological point of view, is also, at least by implication, admitted by Blumenbach. Of the five races there are three which he considers above all as the principal races; and therefore he deals with those first. These are the Caucasian, which is not only for Blumenbach the most beautiful, and that to which the pre-eminence belongs, but the primitive race; then, the Mongolian and Ethiopian, in which the author sees the extreme degenerations of the human species. As to the other races, they are only for Blumenbach, transitional: that is, the American is the passage from the Caucasian to the Mongolian; and the Malay, from the Caucasian to the Ethiopian. These two races are put off till the last, instead of being treated of intermediately, as they ought to be, if they were not considered as divisions of an inferior rank.

"It is apparent that Blumenbach was more or less aware of three truths whose importance no one can dispute in anthropological taxinomy, that is to say, The plurality of races of man; the importance of the characteristics deduced from the conformation of the head; and the necessity of not placing in the same rank all the divisions of mankind, which bear the common title of races, in spite of the unequal importance of their anatomical, physiological, and let us also add, psychological characteristics[1]."

This criticism taken from one of the latest essays of a most distinguished modern naturalist and anthropologist will relieve me from the arduous task of passing this work of Blumenbach in review. The *Contributions* as is pointed out by M. Flourens is altogether a production of a lighter kind. It contains many curious observations, and though its geological theories are long since obsolete, the chapters on anthropological collections and on the Negro may still be read with considerable interest. Lawrence has largely borrowed from the last in his lectures on

---

[1] Is. Geoffroy-Saint-Hilaire, *Classification Anthropologique. Mém. de la Soc. d'Anthrop. de Paris*, Tom. 1. p. 119. sq.

the Natural History of Man. The history of Peter the Wild Boy has, so far as I know, never been translated into English in its entirety, but all that has been said of him and the other wild men there mentioned has been borrowed from Blumenbach.

I had at one time intended to edit the *Decades Craniorum*, a book now become somewhat scarce. Inquiries were made by the President and Publishing Committee of the Anthropological Society as to the probable expense which would be incurred in reproducing the 63 plates of which that work is composed. The results showed that such an undertaking would be beyond the present means of the Society; and an opinion was also expressed by some who are worthy of all attention in such a matter that more typical, characteristic, and hitherto undelineated skulls scattered about in the different English Museums should have a preference, in case such an outlay as the publication of so many crania with their descriptions should at any time be seriously contemplated. Whilst I do not for a moment doubt the wisdom of the decision, or deny the expediency of preferring hitherto inedited materials, I still think that if the present possessors of the Blumenbachian Collection could be induced to join not only in furnishing entirely fresh drawings of the skulls contained in it, but also in publishing the very minute and accurate descriptions, certificates, and documents relating to each particular one, which form by no means the least instructive portion of the inedited remains of Blumenbach, the result would not only be a great stimulus to those international exertions without which the science of Anthropology cannot hope to make the progress so much to be desired for it, but would also confer the greatest credit on the Societies which might be principally concerned in carrying out such an undertaking. With respect to the last utterance of Blumenbach, which has been extracted from the Göttingen Magazine, I am indebted to Professor

Marx for the following information. "The *Spicilegium* was not printed. It had been the intention of Blumenbach to work out in greater detail the short lecture which was read at the session of the 3rd August, 1833, but he did not fulfil it. Therefore the short notice in the 177th number of the *Göttingische Gelehrte Anzeigen*, for 1833, is the only communication on that point that we have of his."

The Memoir of Prof. Marx has been previously translated in the Edinburgh *New Philosophical Magazine*, but many interesting details about the life and habits of Blumenbach were omitted. It was made great use of by M. Flourens, as he acknowledges; but since his own memoir contains many original details and remarks from an independent point of view, I have thought it would be equally acceptable.

A singular mistake has however been made by M. Flourens, both in this memoir, and in his larger book[1] on Buffon, which I cannot help pointing out. The reader will probably observe that he gives as the title of Blumenbach's book *The Unity of the Human Genus*, which is obviously wrong. This would be of no importance; but in the work above referred to we have this reflexion: "Nothing promotes clearness of ideas so much as precision in the use of words. Blumenbach wrote a book to prove the unity of the human species[2], and entitled it *On the Unity of the Human Genus*; now, a genus is made up of species, a species only of varieties. Buffon writing on the same subject, and putting before himself the same object, said excellently, *Varieties in the Human Species*."

Blumenbach never once gave as a title, *The Unity*, &c.; and

---

[1] *Hist. des travaux et des idées de Buffon*, p. 169, second ed. Paris, 1850, 12mo.
[2] *De l'unité du genre humain et de ses variétés*, Trad. Franc. Paris, 1804.

notwithstanding the elaborate ingenuity of M. Flourens as to the word *genus*, I have preferred to translate the Latin words *humanum genus*, by the ambiguous, and as I believe correct expression, *mankind*.

I have thought the reader would prefer for many reasons to find each of the several treatises in this volume with an exact copy of its original title-page prefixed. Those which had no title-page have still one made up of that of the periodical, and the heading prefixed to each in its original form of publication.

M. Flourens had appended to his Memoir a list of some of Blumenbach's works. A much more perfect one, with notices of many of their translations, and of the different portraits and engravings taken of Blumenbach at various periods of his life, is to be found in Callisen (A. C. P. von), *Medicinisches Schriftsteller-Lexicon*, B. II. pp. 346—356. 1830. Copenhagen, 12mo. As will be observed it occupies ten pages, and therefore is far too long for insertion here, yet is still neither quite complete nor quite correct.

The treatise of John Hunter, delivered in June 1775, has been added. It will be interesting to compare it with the contemporaneous effort of Blumenbach. But to enter into the question why the study of anthropology never became popular in Edinburgh, whilst it continued to be cultivated in Göttingen, would carry us beyond the limits of a Preface.

KING'S COLLEGE, CAMBRIDGE.
Jan. 1, 1865.

CONTENTS.

Monstrosity

	PAGE
Editor's Preface	xii
Memoir of J. F. Blumenbach by Prof. Marx .	1
" " " M. Flourens .	47
On the Natural Variety of Mankind, ed. 1775 .	65
" " " Third ed. 1795 .	145
Contributions to Natural History, Part I. .	277
" " " " Part II. .	323
Remarks on an Hippocratic Macrocephalus .	341
An Account of the Blumenbachian Museum by Prof. Rudolph Wagner	345
Inaugural Disputation on the Varieties of Man, by John Hunter, June, 1775	357
Index of Subjects . . .	395
Index of Authors . .	399

ERRATA.

For Jesus Sirach, p. 35, read Jesus the son of Sirach.
... Mongos Lemur, p. 90, read Lemur Mongos.

ZUM ANDENKEN

AN

JOHANN FRIEDRICH BLUMENBACH.

EINE GEDÄCHTNISS-REDE

GEHALTEN IN DER SITZUNG DER KÖNIGLICHEN SOCIETÄT
DER WISSENSCHAFTEN DEN 8 FEBRUAR, 1840.

VON

K. F. H. MARX.

GÖTTINGEN:
DRUCK UND VERLAG DER DIETERICHSCHEN BUCHHANDLUNG.
1840.

LIFE OF BLUMENBACH

BY

K. F. H. MARX.

———

Though a very vivid and uneffaceable recollection of the man, who has lately departed from our circle, can never cease to dwell in us, still I may be permitted to sketch with a few strokes a picture of his occupations and his personality, and in that way to strew a flower upon the grave of him who in life was honoured by all of us, but was especially dear to myself.

It was his happy lot to fulfil the office of instructor far beyond the limits of the ordinary age of man, and to direct the affairs of our society for a longer time than any one of those here present can remember. For more than half a century the most important events of this University are bound up with his memory and his name; and the development of one of the greatest and most important branches of science is essentially involved with his undertakings, his accomplishments, and the efforts he made to advance it.

He stood at last like a solitary column from out the ranks of those who had shared his struggles and his enterprises, and had trodden in the same path, or as an old-world pyramid, a stimulating example to us juniors, how nature will sometimes stamp her crowning seal on high mental powers, by adding to them the firmness and long continuance of the outer form.

John Frederick Blumenbach was born at Gotha on the 11th May 1752. His father was a zealous admirer of geography and natural history, and lost no time in arousing a love for them in his son. It will be convenient to insert here a note in his own handwriting, which I owe to the kindness of the departed, upon the earliest incidents which happened to him while still under the paternal roof, and his earliest promotion on his first entrance into the great world; for it will tell a clearer tale than if I were to turn it into an historical form.

"My father was born at Leipsig, and died at Gotha in 1787, proctor and professor of the gymnasium[1]. He owed his scientific culture to two men especially, Menz and Christ, two Leipsig professors of philosophy, and so, indirectly through him, they contributed a great deal to my own. Amongst other things, he owed to the first his love for the history of literature and for the natural sciences, to the second his antiquarian and artistic tastes. And so in this way I also acquired a taste and a love for these branches of knowledge, which I never found to stand in the way of my medical studies, to which in very early days I had addicted myself from natural inclination, and sometimes they were even in that way of great service.

"I began my academical career at Jena, and there I derived nourishment for literature and book-lore from Baldinger, whilst my relation, J. E. I. Walch, the professor of rhetoric, performed the same office for me as to natural history and the so-called archæology. I went from there to Göttingen to fill up some remaining gaps in my medical studies; and my old rector at Gotha, the church-councillor Geisler, gave me a letter for Heyne. As I was giving it to him, I showed him at the same time an antique signet-ring, which I had bought when at school from a goldsmith. Such a taste in a medical student attracted his attention, and this little gem was the first step to the intimate acquaintance which I subsequently enjoyed in so many ways with that illustrious man.

"There resided then at Göttingen professor Chr. W. Büttner,

---

[1] Besides the more considerable communication in the text Blumenbach has left only a few scattered notices of his life. So far as these have come to my knowledge, I have made good use of them. He had an idea of composing his own biography, and two passages, written by him in his pocket-book, seem to point to this intention. "Many have written their own lives from feelings of sincerity rather than of conceit."—"Without favour or ambition, but induced by the reward of a good conscience."

an extraordinary man, of singularly extensive learning. He had at one time been famous for the great number of languages he was skilled in, but had for many years given up delivering lectures, and was then quite unknown to the students. Just, however, about the time I came, the oldest son of his friend and great admirer, our orientalist, Michaelis, had then begun to study medicine; and his father had enjoined him to do his best and get Büttner to deliver a lecture upon natural history, which in old days he could do very well, and for which he had a celebrated collection. Immediately on my arrival I also was invited to the course, and as the hour was one I had at my disposal, I put my name down, and so came to know the whimsical but remarkable Büttner. The so-called lecture became a mere conversation, where for weeks together not a word was said of natural history. Still he had appointed as a text-book the twelfth edition of the *System of Nature;* though in the whole six months we did not get beyond the mammalia, because of the hundred-and-one foreign matters he used to introduce.

"He began with man, who had been passed over unnoticed in his readings by Walch of Jena, and illustrated the subject with a quantity of books of voyages and travels, and pictures of foreign nations, out of his extensive library. It was thus I was led to write as the dissertation for my doctorate, *On the natural variety of mankind;* and the further prosecution of this interesting subject laid the foundation of my anthropological collection, which has in process of time become everywhere quite famous for its completeness in its way.

"In that very first winter, through Heyne's arrangement, the University undertook the purchase of Büttner's collection of coins and natural history. But in consequence of the unexampled disorder, in which the natural objects had been let lie utterly undistinguished from each other by this most unhandy of men, he was first of all in want of an assistant to arrange and got them ready for delivery. So Heyne said to him, 'Don't you give lectures on natural history? and haven't you got any one among your pupils whom you can employ for that?'

'That I have,' said Büttner, and named me. 'Ah, I know him too;' so the office of assistant was offered to me, and I gladly undertook it without any fee, and found it most instructive.

"Sometime after, when everything had been handed over, and the collection had found a temporary home in the former medical lecture-room, the honourable minister and curator of the University, von Lenthe, came to visit our institute, so these things too had to be shown him, and as the worthy Büttner did not seem quite fit to do it, I was hastily summoned, and acquitted myself so well, that the minister directly he got out took Heyne aside, and said, 'We must not let this young man go.' I took my degree in the autumn of '75, on the anniversary day of the University, and directly afterwards in the ensuing winter I commenced, as private tutor, my first readings on natural history, and during the same term, in February '76, was nominated extraordinary, and afterwards in November '78, ordinary professor of medicine."

Such was Blumenbach's very promising beginning. How he progressed onwards in his scientific and municipal career, how he became in 1784 member of this society, in 1788 aulic councillor, in 1812 perpetual secretary of the physical and mathematical class of this society, in 1815 member of the library committee, in 1816 knight of the Order of the Guelph, and in the same year chief medical councillor, and in 1822 commander of the Order, all that is so well known and so fresh in everybody's recollection, that I need make no further mention of any of those particulars.

Much more appropriate will it be to describe here the direction he followed himself and also imparted to the sciences, his activity as teacher, his relations to the exterior world, and, in a few characteristic outlines, the principal features of his personal appearance and character.

First of all it may fairly be asserted of Blumenbach, that he it was especially, who in Germany drew the natural sciences out of the narrow circle of books and museums, into the wide cheerful stream of life. He made the results of his own persevering researches intelligible and agreeable to every educated

person who was anxious for instruction, and understood very
well how to interest the upper classes of society in them, and
even to excite them. Taking a comprehensive view over the
whole domain of the exertions of natural science, he knew how
to select whatever could arouse or sharpen observation, to give
a clear prospect of what was in the distance, and to clothe the
practical necessities in a pleasing dress. This feeling and tact
for the common interest, this inclination for popular exposition
and easy comprehension was meantime no obstacle to his solid
progress. He laboured away on the most diverse departments
of his science with single and earnest application, and arrived at
results, which threw light on the darkest corners.

Equipped with classical knowledge, perpetually sharpening
and enriching his intellect with continuous reading, and kept in
lively intercourse with the first men of his day, he knew how
not only to look at the subjects of his attention from new points
of view, but also how to invest them with a worthy form of
expression and representation.

Besides, he looked upon every result either of his own
researches, or those of other people, as seed-corn for better
and greater disclosures. He busied himself unceasingly by
writing, conversation, and instruction in disseminating them,
and endeavouring to fix them in a productive soil. Thus it
came to pass, that he soon came to be regarded as the supporter
and representative of natural science, and collected crowds of
young men about him, and by words as well as deeds continued
to exercise an increasing influence upon the entire circle of
study for many decades of years.

Blumenbach soon became known to the Society of Sciences
as an industrious student of physic, and in the meeting of
the 15th January, 1774, he communicated[1] the remarkable discovery he had made (which had been already done by Braun in
1759 at St. Petersburg) of how to freeze quicksilver.

---

[1] *Götting. gel. Anzeigen*, 1774, st. 13, s. 105—7. Blumenbach himself set little
store by this experiment; for he suspected that his friends might be too hasty in
considering the fact to be proved.

In 1784 he became member of this Society, and immediately afterwards read his first paper *On the eyes of the Leucæthiopians and the movement of the iris*[1].

It was a happy chance, that his first literary work was concerned with the races of men, and thus physical Anthropology became the centre of the crystallization of his activity.

Few dissertations have passed through so many editions, or procured their author such a wide recognition, as that *On the natural variety of mankind*[2]. It operated as an introduction to the subsequent intermittent publication of the *Decades*[3], on the forms of the skull of different people and nations, as well as the foundation of a private collection[4]. This was unique in its way; and princes and the learned alike contributed to its formation by giving everything which could characterize the corporeal formation and the shape of the skull in man. Blumenbach used to call it his "Golgotha," and though they do not often go to a place of skulls, still the curious and the inquisitive of both sexes came there to wonder and reflect.

Perhaps it is worth while remarking that the theme of this earliest work of his youth was likewise that of his last scientific writing, for after the 3rd August, 1833, on the exhibition of an Hippocratic Macrocephalus before the Society, when he communicated his remarks[5] thereon, he came no more before the public except to read a memoir upon Stromeyer, and to say a few never-to-be-forgotten words at the festival meeting of the centenarian foundation feast.

One of Blumenbach's great endeavours was to illustrate the difference between man and beast; and he insisted particularly

---

[1] *De oculis Leucæthiopum et iridis motu.* Comment. Soc. R. Gött. Vol. vii. p. 19—62.

[2] *De generis humani nativa varietate.* 1st ed. 1775.

[3] The first decade of his collection of skulls of different nations with illustrations appeared in 1790 in Vol. x. of the Comment. Soc. &c. The last under the title, *Nova Pentas collectionis suæ craniorum diversarum gentium tamquam complementum priorum decadum exhibita in consensu societatis 8 Jul. 1826.* Comment. recentior. Vol. vi. p. 141—8. Comp. Gött. gel. Anz. 1826. st. 121, s. 1201—6.

[4] Comp. his paper *On anthropological collections* in the second edition of his *Beiträge zur Naturgeschichte* 1806. Th. 1. s. 55—66.

[5] Gött. gel. Anz. 1833, st. 177, s. 1761. [Edited in this volume. ED.]

upon the importance of the upright walk of man, and the vertical line. He asserted the claims of human nature, as such, to all the privileges and rights of humanity, for, without denying altogether the influence of climate, soil, and heredity, he regarded them in their progressive development, as the immediate consequences of civilization and cultivation. Man was to him "the most perfect of all domesticated animals." What he might become by himself in his natural condition, without the assistance of society, and what would be the condition of his innate conceptions, he showed in his unsurpassable description of the wild or savage Peter von Hameln[1]. How the osseous structure of the skull will approximate nearer and nearer to the form of the beast, when unfortunate exterior circumstances and inferior relations have stood in the way of the development of the higher faculties, might be seen in his collection from the cretin's skull, which, not without meaning, lay side by side by that of the orang-utan; whilst, at a little distance off, the surpassingly beautiful shape of that of a female Georgian attracted every one's attention.

At the time when the negroes and the savages were still considered as half animals, and no one had yet conceived the idea of the emancipation of the slaves, Blumenbach raised his voice, and showed that their psychical qualities were not inferior to those of the European, that even amongst the latter themselves the greatest possible differences existed, and that opportunity alone was wanting for the development of their higher faculties[2].

Blumenbach had no objection to a joke, especially when it injured no one, or when the subject in hand could be elucidated thereby, and with this view he wrote a paper on *Human and Porcine Races*[3].

---

[1] *Beitr. zur Naturg.* Th. II. s. 1—44.
[2] *Götting. Magazin,* 1781, st. 6, s. 409—425. *On the capacities and manners of the Savages.*
[3] Lichtenberg and Voigt, *Magazin für das neueste aus der Physik,* B. VI. Gotha, 1789, st. 1. s. 1.

Man always was and continued to be his chief subject, not from a transcendental point of view, which he gave up to the philosophers and theologians, but man as he stands in the visible world. Not only did he contribute essentially to his better comprehension and treatment, but it was not very easy for any one to surpass him in practical knowledge of men.

Natural history, not the description of nature, was the aim he placed before him. With Bacon he considered that as the first subject of philosophy. He understood how to indicate the peculiarity of the subject with a few characteristic strokes; and showed also how the inner properties, relations, and attributes of the individual were connected with each other, and their connexion and position to the whole. With this view he busied himself actively on organic and also on animal nature. Nor was he a stranger to the study of geology and mineralogy, as is clear from De Luc's letters[1] to Blumenbach, besides what he himself communicated about Hutton's theory of the earth, and his paper on the impressions in the bituminous marl-slates at Riegelsdorf[2].

The name of Blumenbach must certainly be recorded amongst those who have signally contributed through the research and discovery of the traces of the old world to the history of the condition of our earth and of its earliest inhabitants. He, too, it was who, long before any others, prepared a collection of fossils for the illustration and systematic knowledge of the remains of the preadamite times[4].

---

[1] He worked long at a *History of Natural History*, but he never gave any of it to the public. That he had reflected on the possibility of a *Philosophy of Natural History* may be seen, amongst other proofs, by a letter to Moll in his Communications, Abth. 1, 1819, s. 60.

[2] *Magaz. für das neu. aus der Physik*, B. VIII. st. 4. 1793. Comp. *Gött. gel. Anz.* 1799, st. 135, s. 1348.

[3] In Köhler's *berymannisch. Journ.* Freyberg. 1791, *Jahrg.* IV. B. t. s. 131—6. Blumenbach proved that though they were the marks of a mammal, they were not those of a child, and therefore no anthropoliths.

[4] The fossil genus Oxyporus, which is found in amber, and was represented by Gravenhorst in *Monographia Coleopterorum Micropterorum*, Gotting. 1806, 8vo. p. 235, exists also in Blumenbach's collection. Speaking of the last, that author says, "I wish Blumenbach would give us a description of the numerous insects preserved in amber, which he possesses, and compare them with the allied insects of the present day. His well-known genius for natural history, so long and so

In 1790 he wrote *Contributions to the Natural History of the Primitive World*¹. He devoted two papers before the society to the remains with which he was acquainted of that oldest epoch, principally from the neighbouring country². He also expressed an opinion upon the connection of the knowledge of petrifactions with that of geology, thinking by that means a more accurate knowledge of the relative age of the different strata of the earth's crust might be obtained³, and he was the first who set this branch of study going. On the occasion of a Swiss journey, he drew particular attention to those fossils, whose living representatives are still to be found in the same country, to those whose representatives exist, but in very distant regions of the earth, and to those of which no true representative has yet been found in the existing creation⁴. Later on he elucidated the so-called fossil human bones in Guadaloupe⁵.

His views on opinions of that kind, as also on more comprehensive considerations, such as *On the gradation in nature*⁶, or, *On the so-called proofs of design*⁷, generally like to abide within the limits of experience, and the conclusions which may fairly

---

justly famous, might furnish us with some well-weighed and sound hypothesis on the origin and formation of amber."

¹ *Magaz.* ib., B. VI. st. 4, s. 1—17.
² *Specimen archæologiæ telluris terrarumque imprimis Hannoveranarum*, 1801. In den *Comment.* Vol. XV. p. 132—156. Spec. alterum 1813. Vol. III. recent. p. 3—24.
³ *On the recreation in time of the different Earth-catastrophes*, Beitr. zur *Naturg*. 2nd ed. 1806, Th. I. s. 113—123. One of the most competent judges on this subject, namely, Link, in his work *The Primeval World and Antiquity elucidated by Natural Science*, which he dedicates to *his teacher*, says in the preface, that the representation of the primeval world, as quite different from that of the present, is due to the science of Blumenbach and Cuvier. To the same effect Von Hoff, who is well entitled to a voice in this matter, expresses himself (*Thoughts on Blumenbach's Services to Geology*. Gotha, 1861, s. 3.): "Amongst naturalists Blumenbach is the first who assigned to a knowledge of petrifactions its true position in the foundation of Geology. He considered them as the most necessary helps to that study. He asserted with determination, that from a knowledge of petrifactions, and especially from an acquaintance with the different position of fossils, the most important results for the cosmogonical part of mineralogy might be expected."
⁴ Lichtenberg and Voigt's *Mag.* &c. 1788, B. v. s. 13—24.
⁵ *Gött. gel. Anz.* 1815, st. 177, s. 1753.
⁶ *Beitr. zur Naturg.* 2nd ed. 1806, Th. I. s. 106—112.
⁷ Ib. s. 123.

be deduced therefrom. Brilliant hypotheses, subtle and imaginary combinations, phantastic analogies, were not to his taste.

If it can be said of any scientific work of modern times, that its utility has been incalculable, such a sentence must be pronounced on Blumenbach's *Handbook of Natural History*[1]. Few cultivated circles or countries are ignorant of it. It contains in a small space a marvellous quantity of well-arranged material, and every fresh edition[2] announced the progress of its author. Still in spite of the effort after a certain grade of perfection the skill is unmistakeable, with which only the actual is set forth; and with which by a word, or a remark, attention is directed to what is truly interesting, agreeable, and useful, and an incentive given to further study.

Not only did Blumenbach well know how to set out the whole domain of this study in a simple, easily comprehensible and transparent way, so as to utilize it for instruction; but he also, by bringing to its assistance allied occupations, obtained new points of view, and enlarged its boundaries.

His *Contributions to Natural History*[3], and his ten numbers of *Representations of Subjects of Natural History*[4], have by interesting translations, prudent selection, and accuracy in handling the subjects, done profitable service in the extension and foundation of this science. He took special pains to throw light on doubtful questions, and to clear up overshadowing and difficult undertakings in natural history from old monuments of art[5], and the traditions of the poets[6]. He looked on the migra-

---

[1] It appeared first in 1779.
[2] The publishers alone issued 12, the last in 1830, not including the re issues and the translations into almost all civilized languages.
[3] The first part appeared in 1790, the second in 1811. They contained the following essays: Part I. On variability in creation. A glance at the primæval world. On anthropological collections. On the division of mankind into five principal races. On the gradation in nature. On the so-called proofs of design. Part II. On the *homo sapiens ferus*. On the Egyptian mummies.
[4] 1796—1810.
[5] *Specimen hist. nat. antiquæ artis operibus illustr. cap. vicissim illustr.*, 1803. *Comment.* Vol. XVI. p. 169—198.
[6] *Sp. hist. nat. ex auctor. class. præsertim poëtis illustr. &c. vic. illustr.*, 1815. *Comm. recent.* Vol. III. p. 61—78. Comp. *Gött. gel. Anz.*, 1815, st. 205, s. 2033—1040.

tions of animals and their appearance at different times, and their wide dispersion in enormous numbers as a great, but not necessarily insoluble riddle; and he contributed his mite also to the future solution of this weighty question[1].

Blumenbach was blamed somewhat here and there for following with little divergence the artificial classification of Linnæus. But this conservatism was not the consequence either of convenience, or want of knowledge, but from the conviction that the time for a natural system was not yet come. That he felt the want of such a system is plain, because as early as 1775 he sketched out[2] an attempt at a natural arrangement of the mammalia, according to which attention is paid not to single, or a few, but to every outward mark of distinction, and the whole organization of the animals.

His communications, *On the Loves of Animals*[3], and *On the Natural History of Serpents*[4], display not only the critical, but the judicious observer. Manifold interest attaches to his remarks on the kangaroo[5], which he kept for a long time alive in his house, on the pipa[6], and on the tape-worm[7].

Blumenbach was thoroughly penetrated with the truth, that we are only then in a proper position to understand the appearances of the present, when we attempt to clear up as far as possible their condition in the beginning, and from early times down to the present. He considered archæology and history not only as the foundations of true knowledge, but also as the sources of the purest pleasures. He was not afraid of being reproached with encroaching upon foreign ground[8], for he knew his own moderation: nor did he shrink from the trouble of seeking and collecting, for he had too often had experience

---

[1] *De anim. roden. vivi sponte migr., sive rarum aut studio ab hom. aliors. transl.*, Comm. recent. Vol. V. p. 101—116. Comp. *Gött. gel. Anz.*, 1820, st. 57, s. 561—68.

[2] *Gött. gel. Anz.* st. 147, s. 1757—1759.

[3] *Gött. Magaz.* 1781, s. 93—107.

[4] *Magaz. für das n. aus der phys.*, B. V. st. 1, 1788, s. 1—13.

[5] Ib. 1791, B. VII. st. 4, s. 19—24.

[6] *Gött. gel. Anz.* 1784, st. 156, s. 1553—1555.

[7] Ib. 1774, st. 134, s. 1313—1386.

[8] He approved of Seneca; "I often pass into the enemy's camp, not as a deserter, but as a spy."

that though the roots of a solid undertaking may be bitter, the fruit may be sweet. Besides he knew well how, by keeping at a distance from useless distractions, and by internal collectiveness and regulated arrangement of work, to bring together in one much that lay widely separated.

Some years after he had written his paper *On the Teeth of the Old Egyptians, and on Mummies*[1], he had an opportunity during his stay in London on the 18th February, 1791, of opening six mummies, and derived considerable reputation from his communication[2] to Banks on the results he obtained therefrom. He took his part also in the opinion[3] pronounced by the Society of Sciences of that day on Sickler's new method of unfolding the Herculaneum manuscripts, which he had invented.

He showed that our granite answers to the syenite of Pliny[4]. He possessed a collection of ancient kinds of stone to illustrate the history of the art of antiquity, on which account his opinion was often consulted on the determination of doubtful antiques, for example, those given out as such made of soap-stone[5].

He had himself, principally with a view to natural history and the varieties of man, a collection of beautiful engravings and pictures, and set great store besides on the woodcuts in old works which give representations of animals[6], for in that way the proper position of observing the art of that time is easily arrived at. And so also he endeavoured to become better acquainted with "the first anatomical wood-cuts," and drew attention to them, when otherwise they would have remained quite unnoticed[7].

After a careful comparison of the objects of ancient art, with

---

[1] Gott. Mag. 1780, Jahrg. 1, s. 109—139.
[2] Philos. Trans. 1794. [The original MS. of this paper is in the Library of the Anthrop. Soc. of London. Ed.] His letter to Sir Joseph Banks was printed in the third edition of the *De Generis Hum. v. n.* 1795. The subject is thoroughly treated of by him in the *Beitr. zur Naturg.* Th. II. s. 45—144.
[3] Gött. gel. Anz. 1814. st. 100, s. 1993.
[4] Ib. 1819. s. 1108. Blumenbach gave his views before in the second part of the edition of *Natural History* in 1780, on the proper distinction of the kinds of stones employed by the ancients.
[5] Gott. gel. Anz. 1811. s. 2050.
[6] Gott. Mag. 1781. st. 4. s. 136—156.
[7] Baldinger, Neues Mag. für Aerzte, 1751, B. III. s. 123—140.

which he was acquainted, his opinion' was that we ought to be chary in our praise of the anatomical knowledge of the artists of antiquity, but that their accuracy in the representation of characteristic expression had not been sufficiently appreciated.

In the history of literature Blumenbach emulated his original and pattern, Albert Von Haller, whose acquaintance he had made when studying at Göttingen, by sending to him at Berne a book², on the suggestion of Heyne, which Haller had mentioned in one of his works as unknown to him, and which he had picked up at an auction³. Later in the day he often furnished him with many additions and supplements to the already published volumes of the *Practical Medical Library*⁴.

Among the bibliographical labours of that great writer Blumenbach esteemed most highly the *Bibliotheca Anatomica*. In his own pocket copy he wrote down especially all the volumes and editions of it which were at that time to be found in the royal library, and to the first volume he added a supplement.

He wrote a preface⁵ to Haller's *Journal of Medical Literature*, in which his services as critic received their due.

However little value the body of physicians generally attach to literary performances, still there is no doubt that most of them are acquainted with Blumenbach's *Introduction to the Literary History of Medicine*⁶. With a prudent selection, precision, and brevity the whole field of medicine, quite up to the end of the preceding century, is there described in a comprehensive survey⁷.

---

¹ *De veterum artificum anatomicæ peritia laude limitanda, celebranda vero in charactere gratilitio exprimendo accuratione.* The treatise itself was never printed, but on its contents comp. *Gött. gel. Anz.* 1813. st. 118. s. 1141.
² *Observationum anatomicarum collegii privati Amstelodamensis Pars altera.* Amst. 1673. 12mo.
³ Haller's answer is dated 28th March, 1775.
⁴ Baldinger's *N. Magaz. für Aerzte*, 1780, B. II. s. 33.
⁵ Besides this perhaps scarcely any one was so well acquainted with all the writings of that most famous of Göttingen teachers as Blumenbach. He learnt much from the collection of letters to and from Haller, for there he found, among many other remarkable observations for the history of medicine, the mode of curing deafness by piercing the tympanum. *Gött. gel. Anz.* 1806, st. 147, s. 1459.
⁶ Theil 2. Bern. 1792.
⁷ *Introductio in historiam medicinæ literariam*, 1786.

On the occasion of the fifty-year Jubilee of our University he brought together all the literary performances of the medical professors of Göttingen in a catalogue[1], which had equally the effect of serving as a memorial to them, and as a cause of emulation to their successors.

He frequently celebrated the memorials of distinguished men, especially in his *Medical Library*[2], that almost insurpassable journal, and then as secretary of our Society, in which capacity he worthily fulfilled this painful duty over his departed colleagues, in the memorial orations over Richter (1812), Crell (1816), Osiander (1822), Bouterwek (1828), Mayer (1831), Mende (1832), and Stromeyer (1835).

His *Honourable mention of Regimental-Surgeon Johann Ernst Wreden*[3] is so far of importance for the history of the career of medicine, as that long-forgotten surgeon was the first on the continent, and that in Hanover, to introduce inoculation for the small-pox.

The lover of literature should not pass unnoticed his *Notice of the Meibomian Collection of Medical MSS. preserved in the Göttingen Library*[4].

What has already been done goes some way to place Blumenbach's merits and excellence in a right light. But the most important of all have not been mentioned yet, and from their exposition it will be clear how many things were united in one man, of which each by itself would have gone far to confer reputation upon the possessor.

The branches of learning in which the name of Blumenbach shines forth without ceasing are physiology and comparative anatomy. What he performed both by word of mouth and by his writings in these departments, will all the less easily be

---

[1] *Synopsis systematica scriptorum, quibus inde ab inauguratione Academiæ Georgia Augusta usque ad solemnia istius inaugurationis semisæcularia disciplinam suam augere et ornare studuerunt professores medici Göttingensis*, 1788.
[2] B. I—III. 1783—1793.
[3] *Annalen der Braunschw. Lüneb. Churlande.* 1789, Jahrg. III. st. 2, s. 389—396.
[4] In his *Medicin. Biblioth.* B. 1, s. 368—377.

forgotten by his fatherland, because foreign countries first took a liking to these studies through him, and expressed their gratitude not only to him, but above all to German erudition.

The obscure learning of generation, nutrition, and reproduction received light and critical elucidation from him. If after the lapse of sixty years since he first strenuously employed his mind to sift the existing materials and make particular investigations, more comprehensive results than he expected have been obtained, still it is but just to observe, that his ideas have certainly been expanded and here and there connected, but have not in any way been controverted.

On the 9th of May, 1778, his observations upon green hydræ, then in the act of reproduction, first led him to the comprehension, and afterwards to the further investigation of the incredible activity of the powers of nature in the circle of organized life. In 1780 appeared his essay *On the Formative Force and its Influence on Generation and Reproduction*[1]; and the next year the monograph, *On the Formative Force and on the Operations of Generation*[2]. At the same time he expressed himself *On an uncommonly simple method of Propagation*[3],—namely, on that of the conferva in wells, whose mode of propagation he had discovered on the 18th of February, 1781.

He sent in on the 25th of May a short reply to the question proposed by the Academy of St. Petersburg, *On the Force of Nutrition*[4], which he wrote on the preceding day, and obtained half the prize. He wrote some remarks on Troja's experiments on the production of new bone[5]. On the occasion of

---

[1] *Gött. Mag.* 1780, s. 247—266.
[2] 1781. Then in the *Comment.* T. VIII. p. 48—68: *De vi sive formativa et generationis negotio.* 1785. In all living creatures there is a peculiar, inherent, live-long active energy, which first of all causes them to put on their definite appearance, them to preserve it, and if it should be disturbed, as far as possible to restore it. The theory of development from spermatic animalcule, or by means of panspermy, he showed is without foundation. [A translation of this treatise by Dr Crichton was published in 1792, London, 12mo. ED.]
[3] *Gött. Mag.* 1781, st. 1, s. 80—89.
[4] *De nutritione ultra vasa.* The prize was awarded Dec. 4, 1789. The essays sent in were 24. *Nova Acta &c. Petropol.* T. VI. 1790: *Histoire.* Comp. *Zerri abhandl. über die Nutritionskraft*, K. F. Wolf, St. Petersb. 1789. (The second is by C. F. Born.)
[5] Richter's *Chir. Bibliothek*, B. VI. st. 1, 1782, s. 107.

The Generation of the Eye of a Water-Lizard, he communicated in a sitting of this Society[1] the fact that he had amputated four-fifths of the apple of the eye, and a *new eye* had been produced.

With clear insight and unusual experience he distinguished the anomalous[2] and morbid aberrations of the formative force, and showed[3] how *The Artificial or Accidental Mutilations in Animals degenerate in Process of Time into Hereditary Marks*. His studies upon the formative force were taken up by great thinkers, and were made use of, though with alterations of expression and manner of representation, as foundations for further developments, by Kant[4] in his *Critique of the Understanding*, Fichte in the *System of Morality*, Schelling in the *Soul of the World*, and Goethe in the *Morphology*. From this he derived particular satisfaction, as it was a proof of their solidity and productiveness.

His *Elements of Physiology*[5] is remarkable not less for the elegance of its language, than, like all his books, for a well-selected display of reading, and the profusion of his own observations.

He busied himself much[6] with the investigation, whether a peculiar vital energy ought to be attributed to the blood, or not. And also with the origin of the black colour of the negroes[7]. He confirmed the principal discovery of Galvani,

---

[1] *Gött. gel. Anz.* 1789, st. 47, s. 465.
[2] *De anomalis et vitiosis quibusdam nisus formativi aberrationibus*, 1813. *Comment. recent.* Vol. II. p. 3—20.
[3] *Magazin für das N. aus der Physik.* 1789, B. VI. st. 1, s. 13.
[4] With reference to Kant's manner of expression, he remarked (*Gött. gel. Anz.* 1800, st. 61, s. 612), "that the ornithorynchus affords a striking example of the formative force, as showing the connection of these two principles, the mechanical and the teleological, in the exhibition of an end being also a product of nature."
[5] *Institutiones Physiologicæ*, 1787. Amongst the many editions and translations of this work, Blumenbach set the most value upon the edition of Elliotson's translation, published by Bentley, London, 1814; because this was the first book which was ever printed entirely by a machine. Comp. *Gött. gel. Anz.* 1818, st. 172, s. 1713.
[6] *De vi vitali sanguinis*, 1787. *Comment.* Vol. II. p. 1—13. And again on the appearance of the posthumous work of John Hunter *On the Blood*, on the occasion of the degree of seven candidates in 1795, the argument he gave was *De vi vitali sanguini deneganda, vita autem propria solidis quibusdam corp. hum. partibus adserenda cura iterata*.
[7] *De gen. hum. var. nat.* p. 122. ed. 3.

reposing on his own observations¹. With respect to the eyes of the Leucæthiopians² and the movement of the iris, he took great pains to ascertain their probable reasons by collecting and criticizing the experiences of others, and by personal observation. On the 23rd Aug. 1782, he examined two Albinos at Chamouni.

In 1784 he discovered³, during the dissection of the eye of a seal, the remarkable property by means of which these animals are enabled to shorten or lengthen the axis of the eyeball at pleasure, so that they can see clearly just as well under the water as in the air, two mediums of very different density. He was the first⁴ who accurately distinguished the nature and destination of the frontal sinuses, as also their condition in disease. He showed the intersection of the optic nerves to be a settled fact⁵. He would not adopt the belief in a muscular coat of the gall-bladder⁶. With regard to the protrusion of the eyes in the case of persons beheaded, he drew attention to the fact that the phenomenon was not, as in the case of those who have been hanged, caused entirely by congestion⁷. On the opportunity of a communication *On a ram which gives milk*⁸, he expressed himself on the presence of milk in the breasts of men, and attempted an explanation.

His *History and Description of the Bones of the Human Body*⁹, in which this naturally dry subject is treated in the most interesting way and from fresh points of view, will always retain an enduring value.

His *Handbook of Comparative Anatomy*¹⁰ was the first of its kind, not only in Germany but throughout the learned

---
¹ *Gött. gel. Anz.* 1793, st. 32, s. 320.
² *De oculis Leucæthiopum et irullis motu.* 1784. Comm. Vol. VII, pp. 19—61. Comp. *Bibl. gel. Anz.* 1784, st. 175. *Med. Bibliothek.* B. II. s. 537—47.
³ *Comment.* Vol. VII, 1784, p. 46. *Handbuch der vergl. Anat.* Aufl. 3, s. 501.
⁴ *Proleg. anat. de sinibus frontal.* 1779. His thesis on becoming ordinary Professor. Comp. *Gött. gel. Anz.* 1779, s. 913—916.
⁵ *Gött. gel. Anz.* 1793, st. 34, s. 334.
⁶ Ib. 1806, st. 135, s. 1352.
⁷ *Abhandl. der phys. med. societ. zu Erlangen.* 1810, Th. I. s. 471.
⁸ *Hannover Mag.* 1787, st. 48, s. 753—762.
⁹ First in 1786, then in 1806.
¹⁰ First in 1803.

world. Before his time there was no book on the totality of this branch of learning; he was the first to find a place for it in the circle of subjects of instruction. One of his earliest communications was upon *Alcyonellæ in the Göttingen ponds*[1]. Then he furnished a running comparison between the warm and cold-blooded animals[2], and afterwards between the warm-blooded viviparous and oviparous animals[3]. Nor can we pass over in silence his remarks upon the structure of the Ornithorynchus[4], on the bill[5] of the duck and toucan, and on the sack in the reindeer's neck[6].

Inasmuch as Blumenbach regarded physiology as the true foundation of the science of medicine, it is not difficult to perceive from what point of view his contributions to practical medicine are to be criticized: besides, he let slip no opportunity of proving his sympathy in that particular direction. Thus he gave his opinions on the frequency of ruptures in the Alps[7]; on nostalgia[8], on melancholy[9] and suicide in Switzerland; on the expulsion of a scolopendra electrica[10] from the nose; and on a case of water in the head of seventeen years' standing[11]. He also contributed to the extension of the science of medicine by experiments[12] with gases on live animals, and by the communication[13] of a new sort of dragon's blood from Botany Bay on

---

[1] *Gött. Mag.* 1780, s. 117—127.
[2] *Sperim. physiol. comp. inter animantia calidi et frigidi sanguinis*, 1786. *Comm.* Vol. VIII. pp. 69—100.
[3] *Spec. phys. comp. int. anim. cal. sang. vivip. et ovip.* 1788. *Comm.* Vol. IX. pp. 108—129. Comp. *Gött. gel. Anz.* 1789, st. 8, s. 73—77. In this treatise he also gave his views upon the appearance of yellow corpuscles in the unimpregnated ovum; on the formation of the double heart; on the period when the ribs are produced in the embryo.
[4] *De Ornithorynchi paradoxi fabrica observ. quædam anat., Mem. de la soc. méd. d'Emulation*, T. IV. Paris, 1779, pp. 310—313. *Gött. gel. Anz.* 1800, s. 609—612.
[5] *Spec. phys. comp. int. anim. cal. sang. vivip. et ovip.* 1789.
[6] *Gött. gel. Anz.* 1783, st. 7, s. 68.
[7] In his *Medic. Bibliothek.* B. I. s. 725.
[8] Ib. s. 731. Comp. Schlözer's *Correspondenz*, Th. III. 1778, s. 231.
[9] *Med. Bib.* B. II. s. 165—175.
[10] *Feuer-assel.* Comp. J. L. Welge, *Diss. de morbis nissum frontalium.* Göttingen. 1786, 4to. § IV. p. 10.
[11] "*Ueber den sogenannt Wagler'schen.*" *Med. Bibl.* B. III. s. 616—639.
[12] *Med. Bib.* B. I. s. 175.
[13] *Contributions to the Materia Medica from the University Museum of Göttingen.* Ib. B. I. s. 166—171.

the east coast of New Holland, and by a description of the true Winter's bark.

Blumenbach's reputation as a learned man was so great, that every hint of his was considered and followed up, as that *On the best methods of putting together collectanea and extracts*[1]; and his works, especially his handbooks, stood in such esteem, that authors and booksellers[2] alike considered a preface from him as the best recommendation for their works. In this way he introduced Cheselden's *Anatomy*[3], Neergard's[4] *Comparative Anatomy and Physiology of the Digestive Organs*, and Gilbert Blane's[5] *Elements of Medical Logic*.

I must take notice here of one branch of learning, in which Blumenbach had scarce his like, I mean his familiarity with voyages and travels. All the books of the sort in the library of this place he had read through over and over again, and made extracts of, and prepared a triple analysis, namely, one arranged geographically, a chronological and an alphabetical one. To this occupation, as he frequently took occasion to mention, he owed no small part of his knowledge; and for his researches in natural history and ethnography it was a most solid foundation.

He himself had made but few long journeys[6] in proportion, only through a part of Switzerland[7] and Holland to England, or rather to London[8], which afterwards he used to say was to the sixth part of the world; and a diplomatical one to Paris, in order, during the time of the kingdom of Westphalia, to

---

[1] Ib. B. III. s. 547.
[2] He wrote a preface to Gmelin's *Geschichte der thierisch. u. mineral. gifte.* Erfurt, 1805.
[3] German by A. F. Wolf. Götting. 1789.
[4] Berlin, 1806. In the preface Blumenbach speaks of the influence of Comparative Anatomy on the philosophic study of natural history in general, and on the physiology of the human body and the medical knowledge of beasts in particular.
[5] Göttingen, 1819.
[6] When he wanted to take a journey for recreation, he liked going to the widowed Princess Christiane von Waldeck at Arolsen, who had proved herself very useful to him; or to Pyrmont, or to Gotha, Rehburg, Weimar, and Dresden.
[7] In 1783.
[8] In 1791—92.

propitiate the good will of Napoleon for the University, on which occasion De Lacepede was his advocate and guide. He kept a journal on his travels, in which he made short notes of all that was worth noticing. Up to this time very few of these very multifarious remarks have been made public[1].

He published a translation of the medical observations in the second part of Ives' *Travels*[2]; he wrote a Preface to the first part of the *Collection of Rare Travels*[3], and a Preface and Remarks to Volkmann's translation of Bruce's *Travels*[4].

It is not perhaps too much to assert, what I may be allowed to say here, that the desire which was aroused in many most distinguished men to undertake great expeditions for the sake of natural history, and the results, which have accrued in consequence to the knowledge of the earth and of mankind, were particularly prompted through the medium of Blumenbach. Hornemann[5], Alex. von Humboldt, Langsdorf, Seetzen, Röntgen, Sibthorp, Prince Max von Nouwied, were and are his grateful pupils.

Amongst the unknown, or, at all events, the insufficiently appreciated services of Blumenbach to literature belong his beyond measure numerous reviews, which he continued to write for a long series of years, not only in the *Bibliothek*, which he edited himself, but also particularly in the *Göttingische gelehrte Anzeige*, on all the books in his various provinces. His first criticism was upon Xenocrates, *On the Aliment in Aquatic Animals*, in 1773, in Walch's *Philological Library*[6].

---

[1] Remarks on some travels in Waldeck collected in Schlözer's *Brief-wechsel*, Th. III. 1778, st. 16, s. 229—237. Then: *Some Remarks upon Natural History on the occasion of a Swiss journey*. In *Magaz. für das neueste aus der Physik*, B. IV. st. 3, 1787, s. 1; B. v. st. 1, 1778, s. 13.

[2] The remaining part of this *Voyage to India* was translated by Dohm. Leipz. 1777.

[3] Memmingen, 1789.

[4] Leipzig, 1790, in 5ve volumes.

[5] On July 2, 1794 Hornemann first of all expressed a wish to his teacher to travel into the interior of Africa. Zach's *Geogr. Ephem.* B. I. Weimar, 1798, s. 116—130, s. 368—371, and in B. III. s. 193. Blumenbach gave a public notice of this active young man and of the fortunate completion of his plan.

[6] B. II. st. 6, s. 533. Blumenbach corrected and added to the edition of Xenocrates περι της των ενυδρων τροφης by Franz.

He himself had in the beginning to experience how unfairly and carelessly reviews are often scribbled off[1]. He always adhered to the rule of separating the man from the thing, and tried to make his judgment as objective as possible, and not to pervert the scientific judgment-seat with which he was entrusted to gratifying his personal likes or dislikes. His reviews may be known by their convincing brevity, their clear exposition of the essential points, the witticisms scattered here and there, and the instructive observations and remarks of the writer.

One of his manuscript observations is worthy of notice, which I found in a pocket-book that he once allowed me to examine, because it explains to some extent how the facility and power of finishing off work of this kind became in a certain sense habitual to him. It is as follows: 'In church, which we continually attended, I was always obliged whilst at school to write down an abstract of the sermon. This has been since of the greatest utility to me in my reading, extracting, reviewing, and in many matters of business, &c., for it has enabled me to detect the essential point with rapidity, to exhibit it, and briefly to express it again.'

Although Blumenbach beyond all others was involved in few literary feuds[2], and it did not easily happen that any of his reviews occasioned him any complaint[3] or enmity, still he could not help frequently calling things by their right names, and displaying false celebrities in their nakedness[4].

And now we must turn our attention from Blumenbach the author, to the Göttingen professor, to whose lecture-rooms youth

---

[1] When his *Handbook of Natural History* had been not only awkwardly but inconsiderately criticised, he wrote his *On a literary incident worth notice, which unfortunately is no rarity* in *Gött. Mag.* 1780, s. 467—484.

[2] On one with his old colleague Meiners, comp. *Beitr. zur Naturg.* Aufl. I. 1790, Th. 1. s. 62.

[3] His criticism on Kampf's new method of curing the most obstinate disorders of the abdomen (*Med. Bibl.* B. II. st. 1), was however taken ill by him, but afterwards was the subject of open thanks to Blumenbach, in the second edition of that book, Leipz. 1786, s. 366.

[4] As in the review of Sander's *Travels. Gött. gel. Anz.* 1784, st. 17.

and age alike pressed, in order to receive words of lasting instruction from the wit and humour which overflowed from his mouth.

The undivided approval, which was paid to his discourses, underwent no diminution in his extreme old age, and he gave up teaching, not because either the wish or the power failed him, or because he suffered any diminution of audience or sympathy, but solely in accordance with the entreaties of his friends. He knew well how in a very singular and inimitable way to unite the valuable with the amusing, the relation of dry facts and scientific deductions with wit and humour, and to season them with keen well-pointed anecdotes. Every one enjoyed the lecture. Grave or gay, every one went away stimulated and the better for it.

As listeners came to him from all parts of the world and went home full of his praises, his name was carried into countries where previously German literati had been little thought of. With a letter of recommendation from Blumenbach, a man might have travelled in all the zones of the earth.

He had the art of never giving too much, of confining himself to the principal points, and of deeply impressing what was essential by well-varied repetitions. He assisted the comprehension by appealing to the senses in every way; by outlines which he drew with chalk on a board, by the exhibition of copies and preparations, by happy quotations of well-known sayings. He laid stress on the fact, that from him might be learnt the art of observing; but that it is necessary, according to circumstances, to listen, smell, and taste.

He made it plain, that he held no propositions such as could be written out prettily on law-paper; his subject was the entire man, his whole inner activity in representation, comparison, and connection.

The means he employed to obtain this result were indeed manifold, but it is very difficult to give a satisfactory account of them; they are too much bound up with his peculiar personal appearance. One must have heard him speak himself, with the expressive play of countenance, the remarkable tone of voice, which now fell upon the ear in sharp abrupt sentences, now carried your senses along with him in overwhelming cadences, and with the imposing effect with which he knew how, to some extent, to throw life into the natural objects before him and bring them into unexpected relations.

I could give many examples[1] of his numerous clever and

---

[1] For the sake of example I will give an inkling of them. He wished people would accustom themselves to get a clear and definite notion of subjects, and to reproduce the whole from a part, for, said he, "I cannot bring everything into the lecture, as the elephant or rhinoceros."

He tried also to prevent people from deriving false ideas from their impressions and observations; viz. "If you wish to form an idea of the lowest depth to which men have descended in the interior of the earth, pile up your library at home, your Corpus Juris, your ecclesiastical history, and medical books, until you have put 12,000 leaves, that is, 24,000 pages one upon the other. And how far do you think we have got into the heart of the earth? just so far as the first and second leaf in thickness. And yet people are not ashamed to speak of the kernel of the earth. When the poet speaks of the bowels of the earth, we ought to translate 'the epidermis of the earth.'"

He knew his audience so well, that if he wanted to get anything, he felt no necessity for making long manœuvres, still less for finding fault. He appealed to the sense of what was right and proper, not with pathetic demonstrations, but cursorily, as by an electric shock. If, for instance, he saw that his subjects were handled rudely as they went round, he called out with an intelligible gesture; "They are best laid on your coat-lappet or on cotton; but I know one word is better than an hundred-weight of cotton."

Sometimes he was fond of speaking in aphorisms, leaving the connecting links to be made out by his attentive hearers, though he always stirred up and set in motion the most apathetic by his overflowing humour. Once, for instance, when lecturing on natural history, he told the story how they shaved a bear, and gave him out as a new sort of man. "A beast in Göttingen, in whom Buffon would have discovered a good deal that was human:—it showed one particular trait of modesty, because it would not allow its stockings to be taken off. Behind the stove in the Golden Angel was the creature in question to be found, clad in a Hussar's coat with an over-cloak. The breast was visible—of a most inviting colour. The mouth was silent; large claws with long ruffles—a Hussar with ruffles.—That was something to think of.—Now I'm the man who gives the lectures here on natural history, the lecture-room is gone mad;—you show me this evening the beast as God created it, or rather as you have shaved it, or I shall stand for nothing, for it is no laughing matter to play with the Professor in his lecture-room. The man's hair stood up with fright, like spikes: later in the day Blumenbach was present at its evening toilette. The waistcoat had been nailed to it."

Sometimes he did not disdain to say a word of fun to the students; viz. "Many exegetists think that the whale cast out the prophet Jonah, because where a bonus can find a place, a prophet might do so too. Blumenbach however stands rather by the opinion of Hermann von der Hardt in Helmstedt, who has written a very nasty commentary on that man of God; that he lodged in Nineveh at the Whale; that his cash ran out; the landlord would give him no more credit—he was turned out of the club; or—the Whale cast him out."

Or; "John Hunter used to inquire whether it was not possible for men to be thrown into the chrysalis state:—that would be good for the conscription, forced loans, or when the student is summoned; 'No, no, says the chambermaid, our master is become a chrysalis.'"

humorous illustrations, but I should be afraid, that deprived of the spirit of his pantomimic representation, and unsupported by his cheerful but still highly imposing delivery, they might easily appear in a false light.

It might sometimes have seemed that Blumenbach attached too much value to the singular and the curious, but when any one came to look into the matter more closely, he soon became convinced, that though what was extraordinary attracted him above all things, still, it was principally because it had remained unnoticed by others, or because it served him as a means, through which he could direct the attention to what was truly worth knowing. His business was with knowledge and explanation; yet he knew too well that the majority of men must have miracles to make them believe.

In literature he sometimes mentioned long-forgotten and obsolete works, and noticed with particular emphasis such as were not to be found in the royal library; but all that was only to excite the love of learning, and keep it at full stretch. Perhaps no teacher understood so well as he how to instil by the way a lasting interest in literature, and to accompany the acquaintance with the best and most select with opportune remarks.

The extraordinary reputation which remained to the famous teacher in full strength for more than half a century may partly be attributed to the influence of authority, which was then of more weight than it is now; partly perhaps to the more comprehensive view that though the University was in other ways crowded with teachers, he had no rival in his particular province; partly that he in all his outward circumstances and through his continuous good health was in a position to concentrate on his immediate objects all the materials which stood in his power; still we cannot help always admiring the greatness of his personality, and the wonderful insight and consistency with which he knew how to keep all this together. For a long period of time he continued to be the chief centre of instruction at Göttingen.

Not only did fathers send their sons, but grandfathers their grandchildren, in order that these might hear Blumenbach as they had done themselves, and so participate in that particular kind of learning, which had remained so singularly indelible in their recollection. Many first heard of Göttingen through its connection with Blumenbach, and lighted by his star, journeyed to the place of his operations.

In the summer of 1776 he arranged for the public vivisections and physiological experiments on living animals in the great theatre. Also in 1777 he gave there public readings on the natural history of mankind. In the same year he gave lectures on the dissection of the domestic animals of the country. Though he began very early to treat upon comparative osteology, it was not till after 1785 that he gave lessons on comparative anatomy in general. For a long time he delivered lectures on pathology, after Gaub, on the history of authorities on medicine and physiology, and at last in the winter term of 1836-37 on natural history, which he read 118 times.

The three English princes, who had arrived here on the 6th July 1785, attended the course on natural history in the winter of 1786[1]. Nor did the present king of Bavaria, then crown-prince, disdain to take his seat on the allotted benches, and in August, 1803, Blumenbach was his companion in the Harz as far as Magdeburg. This same royal patron of the sciences never forgot his student's time, or his teacher individually, as he proved not only by sending him valuable presents, especially the skull of an ancient Greek and his order of merit, but particularly by this, that he despatched in 1829 the present Crown-prince to be the alumnus of the Georgia Augusta and of Blumenbach. When our king, on the occasion of the hundred-year jubilee feast of the University, honoured us with his illustrious presence, he did not omit to visit his old preceptor in the house which he had so often entered as a student.

Blumenbach was a born professor; in this occupation he sought and found his satisfaction and his pride. What he

---

[1] With which agrees the passage of Heyne (*Opusc.* Vol. IV. p. 243). "the royal princes of Great Britain attended the lectures of some of the Professors, and were seen on the benches of the audience."

prompted and accomplished in that capacity is seen from the history of the literati of later years; innumerable are those who prize him as their teacher, benefactor, and friend. Who can enumerate the dedications in great and small books which were offered to him from far and near, partly out of gratitude, partly as expressions of praise and recognition? Out of all the great number of dissertations which have appeared here, the best have been accomplished with and through him. Read the words of affection and love in the elder Sömmerring's inaugural dissertation on Blumenbach[1], which has since become so famous, and you will want nothing more.

When his pupil Rudolphi, in conjunction with Stieglitz and Lodemann, who had equally been instructed by him in science, canvassed the German physicians, in order to celebrate the doctor's jubilee of their great teacher in a worthy manner, all to whom he had been a leader either by speech or writing rose like one man, and perpetuated the recollection of the event with a medal[2], and by the foundation of a travelling scholarship[3].

The naturalists of his day endeavoured to recognize the services of the Nestor of their science by naming after him plants, animals, and stones. It was for him a particular pleasure, that on the morning of the day of his doctor's jubilee (Sept. 18, 1825), his colleague Schrader showed him a drawing of the new kind of plant, *Blumenbachia insignis*[4].

---

[1] *De basi Encephali*. Gött. 1778, 4to. And Baldinger's title to it: *Epitome nosologiæ physiologico-pathologicæ*, and in the *Curriculum vitæ Sömmerring*, p. 15: "Exc. Blumenbach was not only my most desirable instructor in general zoology, mineralogy, physiology, pathology, the particular history of man, and in relating the traditions of medicine, but also a distinguished patron, who deigned to treat me as a friend. Such was his kindness that he not only often took me as his companion in his zoological and mineralogical excursions, but also in his vivisections and experiments, which he carried on at his own expense in order to illustrate publickly the physiological part of natural history; he permitted me most kindly to give him my personal and manual assistance."

The dedication runs: Viro illustri Germaniæ decori diem semisæcularem Physiophili Germaniei læte gratulantur. On the medal are drawn an European, Ethiopian, and Mongolian skull with the legend: Naturæ interpreti, cum haud jubenti Physiophili Germanici. d. 19 Sept. 1825. [Wood-cuts from this medal have been given on the title-page. Ed.]

[2] The value of the travelling scholarship was 600 gold thalers. Comp. *Gött. gel. Ann.* 1829, st. 73, s. 721.

[3] Comp. *Comment. Soc. R. Sc. Gött.* Vol. VI. 1818, p. 91—138.—A *Blumen-*

Although the confidence of the world in the learning of the aged veteran rested on firm foundations, still notwithstanding that he never left off continually improving it, for he was always putting fresh life into what he knew, and endeavouring to add new matter to his acquisitions. In his pocket-book we find the following remark made in later days. "Although I have been many years now delivering lectures, still up to this time I have never once been into the lecture-room without having prepared myself afresh, and specially for every particular hour, because I know from experience how much injury many teachers have done to themselves, by considering as unnecessary these perpetual preparations for lectures, which they have read already twenty times and more."

Blumenbach never, above all, allowed himself to repose upon his happy natural advantages, but was always endeavouring without ceasing to procure for them the greatest possible development. Only I may remark here, that his manner of speaking and writing never grew old, but on the contrary remained interesting and in many respects masterly, and was such as to fix the attention of hearer and reader in a remarkable way.

It is worth while to bring into notice the following extract from his note-book, which is intimately connected with the solidity and repose of his delivery. "Amongst the rules on which my father most strongly insisted in our education, was one especially, that when we had once commenced a sentence with a certain form of construction we must go on with it, and try to carry it out completely, and we were never allowed to begin over again, and join another construction on to the first. This was afterwards of great assistance to me towards an easy delivery."

Blumenbach not only developed himself into a most superior teacher by natural talent, reflection and experience, but he also possessed both by practice and by natural advantages the gift, in ordinary conversation, of bringing out the main points in his

---

Iach is multifido is drawn and described in Curtis' *Botanical Magazine*, Vol. 64, 1837. Pl. 3599.

answers and stories, partly by short terse sentences, partly by unexpected hints. He was always lucky enough to hit the nail on the head, to bring the subject into a fresh position, and to attack it in new and interesting ways. He would sometimes describe reason as "the desire of perfecting oneself, or the determination to accommodate oneself to circumstances," and his manner both of address and of doing business was a standing commentary on this definition.

Generally he preferred listening to speaking; frequently he would only let fall isolated sentences, leaving people to guess at the connection; he avoided direct contradiction, and was pleased when his meaning was understood, without his having been obliged to express himself in so many words. In this way he spared the personal feelings of others, gladly recognized assistance from without, and was tender to human weaknesses, especially the vanity of authorship[1].

Grammar had sometimes to give way in his cursory discourse for his immediate objects. In other respects his talk, just like above all his style and delivery, was the result of conscious deliberation. In his note-book I find written down the following remark: "In the delivery of my lectures, as in my writings, I have always endeavoured to follow Quintilian's pattern[2]. This is it. 'I' tried to throw in some brilliancy, not for the sake of displaying my genius, but that in this way I might more readily attract youth to the acquaintance of those things which are considered necessary for study. For it seemed probable that if the lecture had anything pleasant in it they

---

[1] He was of opinion that this in respect of opinions upon it, might fairly stand upon the same footing as personal beauty. Hence he used to remark on the latter: "If a toad could speak and were asked which was the loveliest creature upon God's earth, it would say simpering, that modesty forbad it to give a real opinion on that point."

In his pronunciation he followed ordinary usage, quoting Horace, 'quem penes arbitrium est, et jus, et norma loquendi.' He used Adelung as a decisive authority, and that dictionary always lay by the side of his table. Purists were a nuisance to him. To call granite *wrmsteis*, he said, made him shudder.

He always tried to correct the improper use of definite words, especially with a view to the language of natural history: viz. 'My canary bird sings beautifully.' 'To hear a canary bird *sing* I would go ten miles; but perhaps it *pipes*.' 'Yes, pipes, sings.' 'Ah, ah, now we understand each other.'

[2] *Instit. orator.* l. III. c. 1. Lodg. list. 1770, p. 211.

would be more glad to learn; whereas a dry and barren mode of teaching would probably turn their minds away, and grate rudely against ears tender by nature.'"

After what has been said already about Blumenbach's relations to the outer world, it seems almost superfluous to go on mentioning in detail how numerous and honourable his connections with that world became.

It might be sufficient to mention, that 78 learned societies elected him as a member. There was scarcely any scientific body of reputation in the wide extent of cultivated nations which did not send him its diploma by way of testifying their respect.

One of the necessary consequences of this was a very extensive correspondence, and though much of the correspondence between him and distinguished persons has already been printed[1], there must still remain, on the other hand, a great deal, which will one day be made public. Blumenbach himself laid the greatest stress upon his correspondence with Haller, Camper and Bonnet, and considered these as amongst the fortunate incidents of his life[2].

He was made Secretary to the Physical and Mathematical branches of our Society in 1812, and in 1814 General Secretary. In this capacity, it was his duty to keep up the connection between it and allied institutions, as well as with the individuals who belonged to it, both at home and abroad; to prepare the memorials of deceased members, and to compose the introductions to the printed volumes of our Society. We are all witnesses of the zeal and devotion with which he fulfilled these

---

[1] Viz. with Zach, to whom particularly he gave information about distant travellers. *Allgem. Geogr. Ephem.* B. II, s. 66, 158. B. III. s. 101. With Carl Erenbert von Moll in his *Mittheil. aus mein. briefwechsel*, 1829, Abthl. I. s. 56—61, on general subjects of natural history. With Johann Heinrich Merk in his *Briefen*, published by K. Wagner, Darmstadt, 1835, Nos. 197, 218, 250, principally on primeval bones.

[2] *Medic. Bibl.* B. III. s. 734. These entries are to be found in his journal: "1775, Nov. 1, My first acquaintance with De Luc; 1777, Nov. 21, with G. Forster, 1778, in summer, with Camper. In the same year my correspondence with Baron Asch began, 1781 with R. Forster in Halle; in Bern, 1782, my acquaintance and subsequent correspondence with Bonnet; in 1786 my correspondence with Banks."

honourable duties. He had laid down himself the 84th year[1] as the natural termination of human life, and so it might be regarded as one of his many peculiarities, that it was not till his 68th year that he expressed a wish, in a higher quarter, to be relieved of that office.

There are still some of his official relations to be noticed, which brought him into manifold connection with others, and into business transactions with colleagues and magistrates, namely, his position towards the Faculty, the Library, and the public Natural History Collections. In all these different circles it may be said, that he conducted himself to universal satisfaction, and gave proofs in every detail of his knowledge, his experience, his forbearance and good feeling.

As member of the Faculty of Honours[2], he distinguished himself throughout by conscientiousness in delivering the judgments demanded of him, by giving out his individual statements of the prizes, by mild and moderate examinations. He did neither too little nor too much. During his decanate in 1818 he created 76 doctors, the greatest number since the foundation of the University. He fulfilled that office with all its obligations up to 1835. On the 20th Feb. 1826, his Professor's jubilee was celebrated. Blumenbach himself considered it a remarkable occurrence, that he in his 60th year[3] should be already not only the senior of the medical faculty, but also that of the whole Senate. He showed that the case had now really occurred which Michaelis[4] had declared was scarcely possible.

As member of the Library Committee he was always ready to give his advice and influence for the improvement of an institution he held so dear. He arranged[5], as its Director, the

---

[1] *Medic. Bibl.* D. III. s. 181. "The goal which many old people arrive at, but few pass by."

[2] In 1783 he was assessor; in 1791 he shared the post with Gmelin, and in 1803, after his death, held it alone.

[3] When Richter, July 23, 1812, had died, 71 years old.

[4] In his *Raisonnement über die protest. Universit.* Th. II. s. 343: "The senior of a whole University can hardly be a man of sixty years, but generally somewhat younger or older than 80."

[5] *Gött. gel. Anz.* 1778, st. 172, s. 986.

University Museum, and continued to overlook it to extreme old age, when he could no more attend to it personally. To his name also it was owing that many presents were sent to it from far and near[1].

Blumenbach never undertook the office of Proctor of the University, although he knew as well as anybody else how to deal properly with the students, and to remain in the best understanding possible with older persons and with his superiors. Very early in the day he had asked it as a favour of the Curator, that he might never be chosen for that office. His familiarity with the older conditions of discipline, and the then unavoidable disturbances which agitated the University, and his fear[2] of being withdrawn from pure scientific activity by this official business determined him to come to this conclusion.

But this refusal did not prevent him from doing all the services in his power, both to the University and the town, by deputations of all kinds. On the 10th June, 1802, he went with Martens to Hanover, and on the 5th Nov. 1805, to Cassel, in the same company, to visit Mortier. On the part of the higher authorities such a value was set upon these two organs of the University, that it was made its duty never to put them aside on any important occasion[3].

---

[1] Comp. *Some Notices of the University Museum* in *Annalen der Braunschw. Länder. Churlande.* Jahrg. I. 1787, st. 3, s. 84—99. Jahrg. II. 1788, st. 2, s. 25—35. In his sketches of subjects of natural history, he always mentions where the examples quoted were to be found in our Museum.

[2] In his journal I find written with a lead pencil: "From the year when Ruhnken was made Rector Magnificus, says his biographer Wyttenbach (Ludg. B. 1799, 8vo. p. 141), he became lost to literary pursuits."

[3] In a P.M. of the University and School department at Hanover to the University d. 11 Jan. 1805: "In respect of the business which under the present circumstances are to be seen to by the Privy Councillor von Martens, which do not ordinarily belong to the duties of Proctor, it will continue to be the case, and so long as the condition of things renders it necessary, that all and every communication with the French generals, whatever name they may have, shall be conducted by Privy Councillor Martens, or, if he is unable, by Privy Councillor Blumenbach, since both are known to the French generals through the University deputations they have already been employed upon. In consequence, the rules hitherto attended to must be resumed, according to which, in all cases where it is necessary to send a deputation of honour, the Proctor of the day does not go himself, but must send a deputation, and that must consist, when there is no necessity for its being more numerous, of Privy Councillors von Martens and Blumenbach, and if a more numerous one be sent, then these two must always be members of it."

3

On the 28th Aug. 1800, Blumenbach and Martens set out for Paris: on the 28th Sept. they had an audience of the Emperor. On the 30th Oct. 1812, Blumenbach went, as deputy of the University, with Sartorius to Heiligenstadt, to the headquarters of Bernadotte, the subsequent King of Sweden.

In consequence of these important services, combined with his other academical exertions, the town-magistrates resolved to give him a most unusual proof of their recognition of them: namely, on the 1st March, 1824, the magistracy of the town decreed him a twenty years' exemption from the municipal taxes imposed upon his house.

With respect to the outer appearance and personal effect of the departed, they are undoubtedly still fresh in our memory. Still perhaps some outlines may be of use to preserve them fresh, especially since in his last years he lived very much retired in his apartments, and so many had very little opportunity of coming in contact with him.

No one who had once seen or conversed with Blumenbach could easily forget him; and he knew how to make himself valuable to every one who lived with him. Even in extreme old age, when the weight of years had bent even his resisting back, there he stood and sat, as if cast in bronze, in every look a man. Any one who heard the stout voice with which he answered, "Come in," to a knock at his door; or saw the wonderful play of muscles in his expressive face, and remarked in any interview his undisturbed equanimity and collectedness, and the freshness and cheerfulness of his spirit, soon knew with whom he had to do.

No one left his presence without receiving either an instructive narrative, a cheerful story of old times, or some weighty hint. He understood a joke, and knew how to return one. If any one let slip in conversation an expression, or a suggestion, which was wanting in due consideration or respect, or if any one appeared as if he wanted to impose upon the old man, he must have been wonderfully put down, when he snatched at his cap, and bared his snow-white head, with the words, "Old Blumenbach is obliged to you." I cannot leave untold how Astley Cooper, in 1839, said in a letter of recommendation, that King George IV. had declared that he had never seen so imposing a man as Blumenbach.

His health suffered on an average little disturbance. Blumenbach refused to be ill; he had no time for it. In his youth he was delicate, and was liable to violent bleedings at the nose, and even to spitting blood; but by taking the greatest care, and by regularity in his mode of life, he arrived in the course of years to a very sound state of health. He declared that the occupying himself with natural history had done him this good among others, that he could sleep like a marmot, and had acquired the digestion of an ostrich. Every now and then he suffered from dry coughs, inflammation of the eyes, or lumbago, which he called the thorn in the flesh. If he found it impossible to subdue or conceal the complaint, he went to a physician, and followed his prescriptions most punctually. Glad indeed was he when he found himself relieved of the inconvenience, and thankfully did he exclaim with Jesus Sirach, "A short madness is the best."

Extreme old age can scarcely avoid bringing with it some unpleasant consequences, but altogether the still intellectual old man enjoyed sound bodily health. After he had got over the cold days in the middle of the past January pretty well, he was seized at the commencement of the mild but stormy weather with his cough, which however left him again. Only the old annoyance, of not being able conveniently to void his phlegm, drew from him the remark, that in the pathology which he possessed, this chapter had not been satisfactorily accomplished.

On Saturday the 18th Jan. I was summoned between eight and nine o'clock in the morning from the lecture to visit him. He had chosen to get out of bed, but had been unable to walk or to stand. On the first seizure they had placed him in his armchair, close to the stove, and covered him with pillows. When I came I saw what I had never before remarked in him, and what immediately filled me with uneasiness; his body trembled all over, and was cold to the touch; his expression was altered; his pulse was irregular in the highest degree; nothing could enable him to throw off his dejection.

Still by good luck this threatening storm passed away. The remedies which were applied might congratulate themselves on a happy result. When I saw him again two hours afterwards, he gave me his hand, he had recovered his usual expression, and the natural motions seemed to have suffered no essential interference.

However tranquillizing this might appear, still there was the apprehension that so lamentable and powerful an accident, which had proceeded from the central organ of the nervous system, in an organism which had hitherto gone on working with such regularity, might only too easily occur again, and at last bring to a standstill the machine which was kept going by habit alone. When I saw him again at 5 o'clock in the evening, he stretched out his arms towards me, and spoke aloud; still I thought that he felt as if he must not consider the circumstances as so trivial. About 8 o'clock I found him in a sound sleep, which continued throughout the night.

Sunday and Monday passed off well enough, and he spent them, with the exception of his siesta, in his arm-chair. When I entered his room, he gave me so loud a "good day," that, according to his own expression, the angels in heaven might have heard him. When I asked him how he was, I received for answer, "Quite in the old way." He had books brought to him again, read them, had himself read to at intervals, and was particularly cheerful. But I could only share this happy tone of mind by constraint, for his pulse became more and more irregular, and fainter, and when he spoke I missed the old tone of voice.

On Tuesday one might still have been deceived as to his condition on the first glance, because when I asked to feel his pulse, he thrust out his arm with energy, in his usual way; and he showed by all his other motions that the power of the will over the body was yet entire. This was the first time that he spent the whole day in bed. Still in the evening I conversed with him upon subjects of natural history, and recounted to him some bygone passages of his life, at which the expression of his face, his cheerful humour, and many a subtle remark showed the clearness of his mind.

Wednesday morning, the 22nd, about 8 o'clock, contrary to his previous custom, he did not extend his hand to me; still he quickly recognized me, and was as friendly as usual. On my repeated inquiry whether he felt anywhere any pain, any oppression, or any anxiety, he answered straight and decided with "No, nowhere at all." The only thing which annoyed him was, that he could not expel the phlegm from the windpipe. He began to doze, and spoke at intervals a few words to himself; but when a question was put to him he always gave an answer. As I was going away he said, "Adieu, dear friend." These were the last words which I heard him speak plainly and connectedly. The tone of his voice remained good till midday. Dozing and feebleness increased; but his consciousness remained undisturbed till evening, and when I asked him several times if I should give him something stimulating, he opened his eyes readily, and fixed them hard. At half-past 8 I could feel no pulse, and the inspirations were numbered. I laid my hand upon him and said, "Adieu;" but the dear well-known voice, which had so often heartily responded to the greeting, was silent for ever. Five minutes afterwards he was in another world.

There still remain some isolated strokes to be given, which may help to the better comprehension of this generous and unusual character, who retained his innate harmony even in the very hour of departure.

Blumenbach never shed tears[1]. After a heavy domestic misfortune I found him collected, reading some travels of natu-

---

[1] "Look for the lachrymal gland after my death," he said sometimes, "you will find none," or "I must have nerves like cords, or none at all." The dissection never took place. It would have been most interesting in many respects for the more accurate knowledge of the particular parts of the brain, and their connection with each other, the comparison of the skull, the windpipe and the lungs, with the well-known symptoms which were seen during the life of the old man, who was remarkable even in a physical point of view. Still, with respect even to the

ral history, and calling my attention to the pictures in them. He suffered through his whole organization, yet he made no complaint, and shed no tear, but tried to occupy himself as far as he possibly could.

He never used spectacles, and in his 88th year read with ease the smallest letters and type. His handwriting changed remarkably according to the different epochs of his existence. In his youth and active manhood he wrote beautifully. Then he was afflicted with a difficulty of using his writing finger, and after he had tried hard to conquer it without success, he accustomed himself to write with the left hand, guiding the pen with the right. For this purpose he used a swan's quill, and the thickest lead-pencil. In his 87th year however he again attempted to write with the right hand, and the strokes by their firmness and clearness recalled the best performances of his earlier years. If you ever got him to talk on the chapter of writing, he took care never to forget to recommend the art of writing handily in your pocket, which had been of great service to him on diplomatic missions, through the agency of a short thick lead-pencil and strong parchment paper.

Blumenbach was a man of the watch, which always lay beside him. No one could be more punctual than he was. If any one expected anything from him to no purpose, he might be quite certain that it had not been forgotten, but that he had let it go, because he considered that the proper thing to do.

Immediately after he had got up in the morning he was frizzled and powdered, according to the old-fashioned style, and then put on his boots and kept them on till he went to bed. It took a great deal of trouble to get him at last to use slippers and a footstool. Even his physician scarcely ever saw him in his night-shirt. As he spent the whole day entirely in full dress, so also he scarcely in other ways indulged himself in the slightest relaxation. He had a sofa for visitors in his study,

---

peculiarities mentioned, it must be considered that the forms hinted at were easy to be seen, and as normal as might be; but long-continued design, iron will, and custom, which had almost become law, had made their influence distinctly tell upon them.

but he never made any use of it himself. Only on one single occasion, when he was ill and obliged to lay up, did I find him upon it. He pronounced against arm-chairs for a long time, and said there ought to be pricks in the back of them; and it was only by degrees that this position was made agreeable to him.

It was one of his principles never to sleep in the day-time; only in his very last years did he allow himself a siesta. It was his opinion that a man ought always to be wakeful, active, and cheerful, and on that account he was slow to understand how he sometimes in his 88th year went off into a doze in the day-time, in the absence of any outward excitements.

He kept himself free from every confining habit; after allowing himself to smoke for some time, he gave it up again, and did the same by snuff-taking too, which had occupied the place of the other. After his 86th year I saw his snuff-box no more.

Moderation at table was his habit; he always took exactly the same quantity. He used to tell of himself that he had never been drunk[1].

With respect to this unusual self-reliance which Blumenbach arrived at so early, and which he retained to the end, it will be interesting to hear his own account, to what influence he principally ascribed this important result. It stands written in his journal. "My parents, among other wise and serviceable principles of education, as I consider, never allowed us children to know that they had any possessions. All we knew was this, that everything which they had was entirely their own unencumbered property. That fortunate ignorance was for me a mainspring to more earnest exertion to help myself on alone, and it is that principally which has made of me an useful man. How many unhappy examples there are, on the other hand, of young people, who have neglected to cultivate their natural capacities solely for the reason, that their parents have too

---

[1] He used to say with Johnson, "Abstinence is an easy virtue, temperance a very difficult one."

early let them become acquainted with the lucrative inheritance which was awaiting them."

Blumenbach was economical, but he understood also how to give. He knew how to appreciate the value of money, without at the same time setting any higher consideration upon it. There was once a passage in his note-book which some time later was written down: "However singular it may appear to many, still it is literally true, that up to the date at which I am now writing, I have never once solicited any emolument, salary, or addition, or anything else of the kind concerning myself, but have received everything throughout from the Hanoverian government, from my first appointment up to the last addition allotted to me in the summer of 1813, entirely from free gifts, that is, without any exertion of my own; and so also under the kingdom of Westphalia."

As Blumenbach himself was beyond all things discreet, both in public and in private affairs, so also he expected the same from those he associated with. He had no objection to a piece of news, especially when it was of a piquant nature, but beyond that, he troubled himself little about the concerns of other people. He used to say, "De occultis non judicat ecclesia."

If any one complained to him of his position, and solicited his intercession, he would encourage him with the saying, "Lipsia vult expectari." If it appeared to him that the petitioner stepped beyond the proper bounds, he would exclaim, "I shall remember you," and with these words the negotiation would be closed.

Blumenbach was always himself, never distracted, never preoccupied. Had he been woke up in the middle of the night and questioned upon the most important subjects, he would certainly have given the same distinct answer as at midday. He acted according to definite inner determination. He acted or declined to do so according to certain rules of the understanding, which became at last a sort of machinery of his character.

He was never wanting in attention to others, and he had

the faculty of attaching to himself in a subtle way men of all classes, but especially superior men. It was his plan to bring up and, as it were, accidentally to allude to whatever must necessarily have an agreeable effect, and to stir beforehand all the strings in harmony; and in this way he won for himself many well-wishers, and knew how to keep them when they were won. Politeness he considered as a duty, and he knew very well how to use it, both to attract people and to keep them at a distance.

Not only did he closely adhere to what was demanded by custom, and all the observances of society and official relations, but his attention to these things put many younger men to the blush.

Blumenbach was always anxious to learn, and was never idle for a moment. He used to say, he only knew ennui by reputation. As he was reckoned the great curiosity of Göttingen, and scarcely any traveller omitted to visit him, he was kept continually on the stretch through the quantity of fresh information. To this also contributed his unceasing reading—in the evenings he preferred to be read to—and his unexampled memory, which he was always trying to strengthen by taking memoranda. He often used to laugh at the perverted manners of certain men who wanted to be taken for clever, and complained about their bad memory, when that was the very thing they could exercise a certain power over. One hears people say, "I have a most wretched memory," but never "What a miserable judgment I have."

It will serve to show how attentive he still was in extreme old age, that one Wednesday morning when the *Literary Notices* had been published, and in one of the Reviews, without naming him, I had hinted at something which concerned him, he greeted me with the words, "To-day old Blumenbach has been out-jockeyed."

He was not in the habit of speaking his opinion or his ideas straight out, but he left them to be seen through a hint, or only by a jest; any one who knew his way of speaking wanted no further explanation.

He was not one of those who received everything immediately as true and certain'; but he guarded himself and also warned others against carrying their scepticism too far. He said it would be a subject for a very acute head to decide, whether too much credulity or hyper-scepticism had done the most harm to science, and he inclined to the latter opinion. He considered it as above all necessary, on every assertion to keep in view the individual from whom it proceeded[1].

He always found fault when any one lost himself in common figures of speech, instead of seeing the way clearly to the foundation of appearances from the immediately connected facts. Thus he used to express himself: "The lament, that mankind is always growing weaker, is a miserable Jeremiad. Lay upon one of our horses the horse-trappings of the middle ages—it will be crushed under them as a pancake. Yet these drink no tea or coffee, and do not suffer from the evil, which has been given us by America. Habit does it all."

In his thought as in his action all was considerate, connected and moderate.

In what has been done already, an attempt has been made

---

[1] In his preface to the *Samml. Merkwürd. reisegesch.* Erst. Th., Memmingen, 1789, he gives some words of warning against too confident a belief in the accounts of travellers.

[2] This lay at the bottom of a playfully told story. "In Moravia on a sun-bright day there was a thunder-clap, and stones like pigeons' eggs fell from the sky. The testimony of those who heard it is remarkable, as a specimen of what often occurs in courts of law. 'Did you hear the noise! what did you think it was like?' 'Like platoon-firing.' 'What are you?' 'Musketeer.' 'Did you hear it?' 'Yes.' 'And what did you think of it?' 'It was like an old carriage rolling along the street.' 'What are you?' 'Postilion.' 'And you?' 'Yes.' 'What did you think it was like?' 'Janissary music.' 'Have you ever heard Janissary music?' 'Never in my life, but I think it must sound something like that.'"

He used to take opportunities of showing how people sometimes propagate an error from a self-pleasing delusion, viz.:—"The Hungarians boast that on their Tokay grapes you will often find grains of pure gold. All is not gold, which glitters. Looked at more closely it is no real gold, but glittering yellow caterpillars' eggs."

His criticism was intelligible, and yet was more subtle and instructive than the most elaborate exposition. Thus, "The Sloth can never be brought to move both feet at the same time. When it goes it moves first one foot, stops and sighs Ah! It could not have been in the universal menagerie of Mount Ararat, because it lives in Brasil only; if it had had to come from Ararat to Brasil, it would not have been there yet."

to throw off a silhouette of Blumenbach's exertions and personal appearance; in conclusion, I may be allowed to give some account of his nearest external connections.

His father, Henrich Blumenbach, was first of all private tutor in Leipzig, and in 1737 became tutor to the chancellor of Oppel in Gotha, and in the same year was made professor in the school there. He had a very choice library, and many engravings and maps. For Leipzig, the place of his birth, he had such a preference, that when his son went, against his wishes, to Göttingen, he alluded in a school prospectus to the new University as the *quasi modo genita;* but however at last he changed, and later in the day ceased to refuse it the well-merited honour of being the *optimo modo genita.*

His mother, Charlotte Elenore Hedwig, was the daughter of Buddeus, the Vice-Chancellor of Gotha, grand-daughter of the Jena theologian; she died in 1793, sixty-eight years old. The departed left behind him, in his journal, this remark upon her. "A woman full of great and at the same time domestic virtues, and perfectly faultless." He had a brother who died in the prime of life, in an employment at Gotha, and his sister was the wife of Professor Voigt, who afterwards came to Jena.

In 1759 Blumenbach went to the school of Michaelis. In 1768 he delivered an address on two occasions: on the Duke's birth-day, and the marriage of the then Crown-prince.

Amongst the interesting men in Gotha, to whom he often went, and who were glad to see him, was the Vice-President Klüppel, who took a great share in the Gotha *Literary Journal,* which began to appear in 1774.

On the 12th October, 1769, Blumenbach, then seventeen years old, went from school to Jena, where Baldinger was then Proctor, principally to attend the lectures of the then famous Kaltschmidt; but on the very day when his lectures commenced, he dropped down dead, from a stroke of apoplexy, at the wedding dance of one of his friends. In his place at Easter, 1770, Neubauer came to Jena, to whom Blumenbach took prodigiously, and to whom he was very grateful.

After he had studied there for three years, he felt the necessity of getting instruction from other teachers, and soon made his choice, in consequence of the renown Göttingen then enjoyed. On the 15th October, 1772, he arrived here; on the 16th September, 1775, a Sunday, he took his degree[1]; and on the 31st October he began to read his first lecture.

For his learned career he considered it the greatest of good luck that he came to Göttingen. He shared, as he often remarked, with regard to a learned life the saying of Schlözer[2]: "To live out of Göttingen is not to live at all."

Nor did he conceal from himself that the fact of his career coinciding with the necessities of that day, and his personal position to influential men, had had an important influence on the recognition of his labours[3].

By his marriage (on the 19th Oct. 1778) he became the brother-in-law of Heyne, and as his father-in-law George Brandes, and afterwards his brother-in-law Ernst Brandes, managed the affairs of the University, we can see partly at least how Blumenbach came to have so much influence in it.

---

[1] His sponsor was his old Jena tutor Baldinger, who in the meantime had been summoned here, and who on that occasion had written his thesis *De malignitate in morbis ex mente Hippocratis*, 1775, on which depended Blumenbach's career in life. According to him Blumenbach had attended the following lectures. In Jena: logic with Hennings; pure mathematics and physics with Succow; botany, physiology, pathology, and the history of medicine with Baldinger; anatomy, surgery, and midwifery with Nenbaner; practical medicine and pathology with Nicolai; natural history and archaeology with Waleh; German antiquities with Müller; English language with Tanner. In Göttingen: on the power of medicine, on the nature and cure of diseases with Vogel; pharmaceutical chemistry and the preparation of medicines, the art of prescribing and clinical lectures with Baldinger; botany and materia medica with Murray; anatomy and midwifery with Wrisberg; pathology and ocular diseases with Richter; mineralogy with Kästner; history of the mammalia with Erxleben; natural history with Büttner; on the odes of Horace with Heyne; the English language with Dietz; the Swedish with Schlözer.

On the occasion of that anniversary, Heyne said (*Opusc.* Vol. II. p. 215): "Blumenbach, from whose genius and learning we expect something very great."

[2] In his life written by Blumenbach himself. Götting. 1803, s. 197.

[3] He had early made a mark against the two following passages: "It makes a great difference on what times a man's peculiar virtues fall" (Plin. *Nat. Hist.* VII. 29). "Nor can any one have so splendid a genius that he can come to light without material, opportunity, or even a patron and some one to recommend him" (Plin. *Ep.* VI. 23).

What he was to this institution of learning in general, and our society in particular, that the world knows well, and history will not forget. In our tablets of memory his name will always endure, and his recollection will always renew in us the picture of a great and beautiful activity.

He who like him has satisfied the best of his time, he has lived for all time.

ÉLOGE HISTORIQUE

DE

JEAN-FRÉDÉRIC BLUMENBACH,

UN DES HUIT ASSOCIÉS ÉTRANGERS DE L'ACADÉMIE,

PAR M. FLOURENS,

SECRÉTAIRE PERPÉTUEL.

LU DANS LA SÉANCE PUBLIQUE DU 26 AVRIL 1847.

PARIS. 1847.

MEMOIR OF BLUMENBACH

BY

M. FLOURENS[1].

Some years since died at Göttingen a member of our Academy, whose great works have rendered him famous, and whose particular works, applied to the new study of man himself, have rendered dear to humanity. It is to M. Blumenbach that our age owes Anthropology. The history of mankind had been disfigured by errors of every kind, physical, social and moral. A sage appeared. He contended against the physical errors; and, by so doing, destroyed in the surest manner the foundation of all the others.

John Frederick Blumenbach was born at Gotha, in 1752. From his very birth nature seemed to devote him to education. His father was professor at Gotha; his mother belonged to a family at Jena, which was attached to the universities.

It was in one of those German interiors, where the love of retirement, the necessity of study, the habits of an honourable independence reign with such a charm, that the little Blumenbach first saw the light. A brother, a sister, a father studious and grave, a mother tender and enlightened, formed at first all his world. It was soon observed that this child, surrounded by such soft affections, was occupied by quite a dreamy curiosity. It played but little, and began to observe very early. It endeavoured, and sometimes with great ingenuity, to comprehend or to explain to itself the structure of a plant or an insect.

Everything is taken seriously in Germany, even the earliest education of the infant. The father of M. Blumenbach, who

---

[1] *Mémoires de l'Institut de France*, Tom. XXI. p. 1. Paris. 1847.

intended him for education, never permitted him, even from the most tender age, to break short a sentence badly commenced in order to put something else in its place. The sentence badly commenced had to be finished. The child had to get itself out of the little difficulty it had got into. In this way it learnt naturally, without effort, or rather by scarcely appreciable efforts, to think clearly and express itself with precision.

His mother, a woman of elevated spirit and noble heart, inspired him with ideas of glory. The soul of the mother is the destiny of her son. These first impressions have never ceased to influence the whole life of M. Blumenbach. Of his numerous writings there is only one which is foreign to the sciences, and that is the panegyric of his mother. He ends it by saying, "She had all, and knew how to cherish all the family virtues."

To return to the child. At ten years old he already took up the subject of comparative osteology, and this was the way. There was then but one solitary skeleton in the town of Gotha. This skeleton belonged to a doctor, who was the friend of the family of our little scholar, who often told afterwards the story of the many visits he used to make, during which he took no notice of the doctor, but a great deal of the skeleton. His visits became, by little and little, more assiduous and more frequent. He came, on purpose, when his old friend was out; and, under pretence of waiting for him, spent whole hours in looking at the skeleton. After having well fixed in his memory the form of the different bones and their relations, he conceived the bold idea of composing a copy. For this purpose he made frequent journeys in the night to the cemeteries. But, as he was determined to owe nothing except to chance, he soon found out that he would have to content himself with the bones of our domestic animals. In consequence, he directed his private researches in such a way as to provide himself with all sorts of that kind of bones. Then he carried them all to his bed-room, concealed them as well as he could, and shut himself too up there, in order to give himself up at his leisure, and with an enthusiasm beyond his age, to the studies he had marked out for himself.

Unfortunately, at last a servant discovered the child's secret treasure; she saw that ingenious commencement of a *human skeleton*, and cried out sacrilege and scandal. Young Blumenbach, all in tears, ran to his mother; and she, under the advice of the good doctor, prudently decided that the precious collection should be removed into one of the lofts. Such was the modest beginning of the famous collection whose reputation has become universal.

At seventeen, young Blumenbach quitted his family for the University of Jena. There he found Sömmerring: the same age, the same tastes, the same passion for study, which already concealed another, that for fame. They soon became friends; and for these two friends everything was in common, library and laboratory. Blumenbach lent his books; Sömmerring lent his anatomical preparations. In their confidential intimacies they often allowed themselves to give way to their illusions, predicting for one another the first rank in the sciences they cultivated. Nor were they deceived; the one became the first naturalist, the other the first anatomist of Germany.

After spending three years at Jena, Blumenbach went to the university of Göttingen, then famous for the residence of a great man, the great Haller, one of the grandest geniuses science has ever had; a first-rate author, poet, profound anatomist, a botanist equal to Linnæus in his way, a physiologist without parallel, and of an erudition almost unlimited. Haller indeed had left the place; but his reputation was everywhere. At the sight of reputation the cry of genius is always the same; and Blumenbach said with Correggio, "I too am a painter."

There lived then, at Göttingen, an old professor, forgotten by the students and very oblivious himself of delivering lectures, but in other respects very learned, and, besides, the possessor of an immense collection, remarkable for its books of geography, philology, voyages, and pictures of distant nations. Young Blumenbach, who was already dreaming of a history of man, was delighted at finding materials of this kind, so laboriously and diligently brought together. He foresaw with a singular clearness all the advantages that might be got from it.

He listened to and admired the old professor; and let him go on talking for a whole twelvemonth; then, rich with these treasures of erudition, of history, and continuous studies of the physiognomy of peoples, he wrote his doctor's dissertation on *The Unity of Mankind*.

This was quite a new way of opening the science which he was destined to found and to render attractive. He commenced from that time his anthropological collection. He did more; he got the University to buy the collections of his old master, he became their conservator, he arranged them; and very soon brought them into notice by the great instruction in natural history he added to them. His teaching in this way marks quite an epoch in the studies of Germany.

The peculiar genius of that nation is well known; the genius of thought governed by imagination; devoted at once to truth and to systems; brilliant, and rejoicing in elevated combinations, bold, surprising, and, if I may use the expression, given up to the adventures of thought. M. Blumenbach was no exception to this genius; but he developed, with a wonderful good nature, all the wisest points of it.

The fifty years during which he was professor, and, if I may say so, a kind of sovereign, was, for natural history in Germany, the time of the most positive and the soundest study. The day of systems did not re-appear till he was gone; and when they did, although recalled to life by a man of astonishing vigour of mind[1], they never could regain the empire they had lost. They had to deal with an entirely new power. The *experimental method* had been established. The great revolution which has made the modern human intellect what it is had been effected.

M. Blumenbach has published four works which give us pretty well the whole of his great course of instruction: the first, on *The Human Species*[2]; the second, on *Natural History*;

---

[1] M. Oken. I speak here of systems, and especially of the philosophy of nature, only in reference to the study of the Animal Kingdom.
[2] I include, under this head, his dissertation, *De Generis Humani varietate nativa*, &c., and his *Decades craniorum*, &c.

the third, on *Physiology;* and the fourth, on *Comparative Anatomy.*

To form a proper opinion of these works, it is necessary to consider the time when they appeared. About the middle of the eighteenth century, Buffon, Linnæus and Haller had founded modern natural history. Towards the end of the century, at the very moment when science lost these three great men, M. Blumenbach wrote his first work[1].

The glory of M. Blumenbach is that he preceded Cuvier. There was indeed between these two famous men more than one relation; both introduced *Comparative Anatomy* into their own country, both created a new science; the one, Anthropology; the other, the science of Fossil Anatomy: both conceived the science of Animal Organization in its entirety; but G. Cuvier, impelled by a greater bias towards abstract combinations, did more to display a method; whilst Blumenbach, guided by a most delicate sensibility, did more to elucidate physiology.

Everything belonging to method was neglected by Blumenbach; he confined himself to following Linnæus; he adopted from him almost all his *divisions* with whatever advantages they had, and also with all their defects, their narrowness of study, and their caprice.

In Germany, where they will not easily admit that M. Blumenbach was deficient in anything, this kind of forgetfulness with which that great intellect treated method is explained and excused by his deference for Linnæus, the master, in that way, of a whole century. In France, where greater liberty of speech is allowed, without going beyond the bounds of respect, we say, plainly enough, that Blumenbach had not the genius of *method;* a genius so rare, that Aristotle alone, of antiquity, possessed it; and only three or four men in modern times have

---

[1] His dissertation, *De Generis humani varietate nativa,* is of 1775; his *Manuel d'Histoire Naturelle* is of 1779; his *Manuel de Physiologie,* of 1787; his works on the *Animaux à sang chaud et à sang froid,* on the *Animaux à sang chaud vivipares et ovipares,* are of 1786 and 1789; his first *Decas craniorum,* of 1790; his *Anatomia comparée,* of 1805.

had it in so high a degree, Linnæus, the two Jussieu and G. Cuvier.

All the writings of M. Blumenbach indicate the character and, if I may say so, the stamp of the physiologist. In his *Comparative Anatomy* he arranges his facts according to the organs, which is pre-eminently the physiological order. In the Physiology, properly so called, he first of all considers the *forces of life*, which is the point of view at once the most elevated and the most essentially peculiar to that science. His works on the cold-blooded and hot-blooded animals, and on the hot-blooded viviparous and oviparous animals are a true Comparative Physiology, and that too at an epoch when the very name of that science was unknown[1]. He has submitted the great question of the *formation of beings* to the most profound researches[2], and always as a physiologist. Facts were his study; and from facts he tried to mount up to the force which produced them. Nothing is more famous than the formative force of M. Blumenbach[3].

Three principal ideas about the formation of beings have been successively in vogue; the idea of *spontaneous generation*, which was the idea, or rather the error, of all antiquity; the idea of the *pre-existence of germs*, conceived by Leibnitz, and popularized by Bonnet; and the idea of the formative force of M. Blumenbach. No doubt the new idea does not clear up the difficulty any more than the two others; but at least it does not add to it. It does not contradict the facts, like the idea of spontaneous generation; nor does it exact of the mind all that mob of suppositions and concessions which is demanded by the idea of the pre-existence of germs[4].

The *formative force* of M. Blumenbach is only a mode of expressing a fact, like *irritability* or *sensibility*; and whatever

---

[1] I consider him to be the first who employed in his works the terms "cold-blooded" and "hot-blooded animals."
[2] And through them he made the beautiful discovery of the umbilical membrane of the mammals.
[3] His *Nisus formativus*.
[4] The *Molecules organiques* of Buffon are only the pre-existing germs in another form. See my *Hist. des travaux et des idées de Buffon*, pp. 64, 72.

may be said of it, is not more obscure. Every *original force* is
obscure for the very reason that it is *original.* "The first
veil," says Fontenelle, "which covered the Isis of the Egyptians
has been lifted a long time; a second, if you please, has been so
in our time; a third never will be, if it is really the last[1]."

Great studies absorb those who pursue them. Blumenbach
travelled little. His labours were only interrupted by some
journeys in the interior of his country; and what was remarkable, these very journeys were of just as much use to natural
history as his works. The old Germany, with its old chateaux,
seemed to pay no homage to science; still the lords of these
ancient and noble mansions had long since made it a business,
and almost a point of honour, to form with care what were
called Cabinets of Curiosities. Their successors, attracted by
the warlike tastes of the great Frederick, had forgotten these
collections. Blumenbach came and reclaimed these treasures
in the name of science, and everything was granted to him.
Natural history began everywhere to have its museums, and so
had civil history; and all this was due to what Blumenbach
used to call, laughingly, his *Voyages of Discovery.*

Of all these collections, the most peculiar to Blumenbach,
the most important, the most precious at least for its object,
was his collection of human skulls; an admirable monument of
sagacity, labour and patience, and the best established and
surest foundation of the new science, which interests us all
to-day, of Anthropology. Anthropology sprung from a great
thought of Buffon. Up to his time man had never been
studied, except as an individual; Buffon was the first who,
in man, studied the species[2].

After Buffon came Camper. Buffon had only considered
the colour, the physiognomy, the exterior traits, the *superficial
characteristics* of peoples; Camper, more of an anatomist, considered the more real characteristics. With Camper began the
study of skulls. Camper had a quick apprehension, and was as

---

[1] Panegyric of Ruysch.
[2] See *Hist. des travaux et des idées de Buffon*, p. 16.

ready at seizing a happy view as prompt to abandon it. He compared the skull of the European with that of the negro; the skull of the negro with that of the orang-utan; he struck out the idea of his facial angle, and very soon greatly exaggerated its importance.

Blumenbach has pointed out what a very unsatisfactory and incomplete characteristic the facial angle is; he has shown that we must compare all the skull and all the face; he has laid down rules for that learned and perfect comparison, and was the first to deduce that division which is almost everywhere now adopted, of the human species into five races; the European, or white race; the Asiatic, or yellow; the African, or black; the American, or red; and the Malay.

I confess at once, and without difficulty, that this division of races is not perfect. The division of races is the real difficulty of the day, the obscure problem of Anthropology, and will be so for a long time. The Malay race is not a simple or a single race[1]. Precise characteristics have been sought, but not yet found, by which to describe the American race. There are three principal races, of which all the others are only *varieties*, or *sub-races*; I mean the three races of Europe, Asia and Africa. But the idea, the grand idea, which reigns and rules and predominates throughout in the admirable studies of Blumenbach is the idea of the unity of the human species, or, as it has also been expressed, of the human genus. Blumenbach was the first who wrote a book under the express title of the *Unity of the Human Genus*[2].

The *Unity of Mankind* is the great result of the science of Blumenbach, and the great result of all natural history. Antiquity never had any but the most confused ideas on the physical constitution of man. Pliny talks seriously of peoples with only one leg, of others whose eyes were on their shoulders,

---

[1] But a mixture of two others, the Caucasian and the Mongol.
[2] Blumenbach says Human Genus. We now say, what is much preferable, the Human Species. The use of these two words is no longer arbitrary. The characteristic of genus is limited fecundity; the characteristic of species is unlimited fecundity. See *Hist. des t. et des i. de Buffon*, p. 177.

or who had no head, &c. In the sixteenth century, Rondelet, an excellent naturalist, gravely describes sea-men, who live in the water, and have scales and an oozy beard. In the eighteenth century Maupertuis describes the Patagonians, as giants whose ideas ought to correspond to their stature; but as a compensation, for the credit of the century, Voltaire laughed at Maupertuis. Finally, what speaks volumes, Linnæus, the great Linnæus, puts into the same family man and the orangutan. The *homo nocturnus*, the *homo troglodytes*, the *homo sylvestris* of Linnæus is, in fact, the orang-utan.

To raise the science out of this chaos, Blumenbach laid down first of all three rules. The first is, to draw a distinction everywhere between what belongs to the brute and what belongs to man. A profound interval, without connexion, without passage, separates the human species from all others. No other species comes near the human species; no genus even, or family. The human species stands alone. Guided by his facial angle, Camper approximated the orang-utan to the negro. He saw the shape of the skull[1], which gives an apparent resemblance; he failed to see the capacity of the skull, which makes the real difference. In form nearly, the skull of the negro is as the skull of the European; the capacity of the two skulls is the same. And what is much more essential, their brain is absolutely the same. And, besides, what has the brain to do with the matter? The human mind is one. The soul is one. In spite of its misfortunes, the African race has had heroes of all kinds. Blumenbach, who has collected everything in its favour, reckons among it the most humane and the bravest men; authors, learned men and poets. He had a library entirely composed of books written by negroes. Our age will doubtless witness the end of an odious traffic. Philanthropy, science, politics, that is true politics, all join in attacking it; humanity will not be without its crusades. The second rule of Blumenbach is, not to admit any fact except when supported

---

[1] Or, more precisely, the form and prominence of the upper jaw. See *Hist. des t. à das i. de Buffon*, p. 183.

by trustworthy documents; and in this way, everything which is puerile and exaggerated, everything which is legend, will be excluded from science. The third rule is the very basis of science. Once nothing but extremes were compared; Blumenbach laid down the rule not to pass from one extreme to the other, except by all the intermediate terms and all the shades possible. The extreme cases seem to separate the human species into decided races; the graduated shades, the continuous intermediate terms make all men to form but one mankind.

There never was a scholar, author or philosopher, who seemed more adapted to endow us with the admirable science of Anthropology. Blumenbach joined to vast knowledge a power of criticism still rarer than the most unbounded erudition, and much more precious; he had that art which discriminates and judges; he had a clear sweep of view, a sure tact, and a good sense not easily deceived. He knew everything, and had read everything; histories, chronicles, relations, travels, &c.; and he took pleasure in saying, that it was from travels that he had received the most instruction.' The study of man is founded on three sciences, besides anthropology properly so called: geography, philology and history. Geography gives us the relations of races to climates; history teaches us to follow the migrations of peoples and their intermixtures; and when once they have been mixed, it is philology which teaches us how to separate them again. But whatever be the progress which these three sciences have made in our days, none has yet arrived at the original and certain unity of man; each foresees it and prophesies it; all tend in that direction; thanks to Blumenbach, that unity, which these sciences still are in search of, has been demonstrated by natural history. And here let me speak out, without being afraid of exaggeration. Voltaire says of Montesquieu, that he restored its lost rights to the human race. The human race had forgotten its original unity, and Blumenbach restored it.

I have examined the principal works of Blumenbach; I mean those works which have made him famous; but there is another I cannot omit, a work very different from those, at least, in the form; a work full of ideas, and one of the most intellectual, the most discriminating, or, to speak like Descartes, the most sensible that have ever been written on the sciences. That work is composed of two little volumes. The title is very simple, that is, *Contributions to Natural History*[1]. The true title should be, *The Philosophy of Natural History*. There Blumenbach passes in review all the philosophical questions of his science; the question of the original unity of man, the question of the scale of beings, that of innate ideas, that of the so-called man of nature, and the others. The author's object is to point out, in each instance, where the truth ends and system commences. And to get to that point, there is no apparatus of learning, no long ratiocination, no phrases; a word, a witty sally, an anecdote are enough. As to the original unity of man, he says it was an honest German doctor, who not being able to reconcile the different colour of men with the fact of their single origin, imagined, in order to settle the question, that God had created two Adams, one white and the other black. As to the scale of beings, it was the opinion of an English naturalist, who proposed to establish two, in order to place in the second everything that could find no place in the first. As to innate ideas and the man of nature, the following are the facts. Towards the middle of the year 1724, there was found, in the north of Germany, near a village called Hameln, a young boy quite naked, who could not speak, but eagerly devoured all the fruits he could get hold of. At that time the dispute about innate ideas was at its highest. Immediately the imagination of the philosophers was excited. The man that had been found was no doubt the wild man, the man of nature; and the man of nature would finally resolve the problem of innate ideas. The Count de Zinzendorf, who was afterwards the founder of the Moravian brothers, hastened to ask him of the Elector of Hanover. The Elector of Hanover sent him to England. In England the curiosity was as great as in Germany. Peter de Hameln, as the young savage was

---

[1] [Edited in this volume. ED.]

called, became famous. Dr Arbuthnot wrote his life. After him Lord Monboddo wrote it again; and, with his usual enthusiasm, proclaimed the young savage as the most important discovery of the age. At last, M. Blumenbach wished in his turn to see what it all was; he undertook the examination of the facts as a philosopher, but as a calm and judicious one; and he found that the wild man, the so-called man of nature, the most important discovery of the age, was only a poor child, born dumb, and driven from the paternal roof by a step-mother.

It will be seen what sort of book it is I am speaking about. The tone is that of learned and delicate raillery. The author rallies, but so as to make you think. It is the ironical philosophy of Socrates, or at least what Socrates is said to have had, and what Voltaire really possessed. He who has read that book has the whole key to Blumenbach's character. He will understand the charm of his conversations, the success of his lessons, and his vast renown, so dear to all those who approached him. Above all, he will have the secret of his soul, born essentially for that general virtue defined by Montesquieu, *the love of all*. Even in this book, where however raillery predominates, as soon as Blumenbach touches on the great question of the unity of men, he jokes no more; his language immediately alters, and takes naturally the tone of the truest sensibility. He never speaks of men, or of any men, but with affection. According indeed to his doctrine, all men are born, or might have been born, from the same man. He calls the negroes *our black brothers*. It is an admirable thing that science seems to add to Christian charity, or, at all events, to extend it, and invent what may be called *human charity*. The word Humanity has its whole effect in Blumenbach alone.

I have already said that Blumenbach, always wrapped up in his great works, had seldom quitted Germany. Still he made two journeys, one to England and one to France. In these two journeys he observed everything, but all as a naturalist. This man, who had passed so many years in meditating on the most important questions, on the highest problems of natural history, had at last only one idea, one object, one all-powerful pre-occupation; a pre-occupation so strong as to be sometimes quite ludicrous, as we may judge from the two instances he used to relate himself.

Being entertained in London by all the English professors, they one evening took him to the theatre. The actor Kemble played the part of the Moor of Venice. Some days after, Kemble met Blumenbach at a party, and said, "M. Blumenbach, how did you think I succeeded in representing the character of a negro?" "Well enough, as far as the moral character goes," said our naturalist, and then added, "but all the illusion was destroyed for me the moment you opened your hand; for you had on black gloves, and the negroes have the inside of the hand of a flesh-colour." Every one laughed except Blumenbach; he had spoken quite in earnest.

After the peace of Tilsit, the town of Göttingen was included in the kingdom of Westphalia, and the University thought it necessary to solicit the protection of the great Emperor. Blumenbach was chosen as a deputy. "I found," said he, "all the French men of letters as eager to support me as if the question had been the preservation of a French institution; I owed to that generous zeal the success of my mission." Admitted, at last, to take leave in solemn audience, he attended in an antechamber with many of the foreign ambassadors. Napoleon appeared; all turned their attention to him except Blumenbach; for how could he? "I had," said he, "before me the ambassadors of Persia and Marocco, of two nations whom I had never yet seen."

To his passion for natural history Blumenbach joined a passion for all the great studies. Erudition, philosophy, letters had a share of his attention, but did not exhaust it. He was a good man of business. He had, in a high degree, that delicate and calm judgment which business demands. More than once, when charged with important missions, he brought them to an end with singular good fortune. In fact, the town of Göttingen decreed, in consideration of his services, that his property should be exempted from taxes. Göttingen indeed ought to have been grateful to him in every way. During sixty years the celebrity of the man of learning and the professor was the cause of its prosperity. His name alone brought there a crowd of pupils; a population brilliant, moving, always being changed, always young and always learned. Nothing could equal the veneration all that population had for him. Almost all those of his pupils who became famous dedicated their works to him; and these dedications were not the mere homage of admiration. A touching and higher sentiment is found in them, and what indeed is better still, an affection almost filial. What more can I say? M. de Humboldt was a pupil of his[1], and the highest intellects of Germany, the Fichtes, the Kants, the Schellings have interpreted his ideas[2].

In private life Blumenbach was a thorough German, good-natured, frank, open and mild in manner. In him an honest character shone throughout. Essentially a man of good sense, after more than forty years spent in education, he wrote these words: "I never enter the amphitheatre without having particularly prepared each lesson, for I know that many professors have lost reputation by thinking that they know well enough a course they have delivered twenty times." He worked up to the end of his life. "I only know satiety by reputation," said he. It is said also that he preferred listening to speaking. He was prudent in everything. As La Fontaine says,

"The wise know how to manage time and words."

He had a maxim which displays his character: "One must know how to attract and retain by indulgence."

All happiness was his; a great reputation, a quiet life, a family tenderly beloved, illustrious pupils, a son worthy of his name. His long and beautiful old age was surrounded with the most touching homages. Every anniversary, which still preserved him to science, was celebrated as a festival. Seventy-eight learned societies elected him an associate. Medals were struck in his honour. Prizes were instituted in his

---

[1] In 1786 he had the honour to see the British Princes attend his lectures; and in 1803, the King of Bavaria; and in 1830, his son, the now Prince Royal.
[2] Particularly his idea of a *formative force*.

name; useful foundations still exist which perpetuate his memory by benefactions[1]. This universal enthusiasm made no difference in him; he remained always good, simple, even familiar; everything in him was natural; no pretension, no affectation; nothing by which he tried to distinguish himself from others. "When one has a great deal of merit," says Fontenelle, "it is the crown of all to be like the rest of the world."

Blumenbach died on the 22nd Jan. 1840, being nearly a century old;- a man of a high intellect, an almost universal scholar, philosopher and sage; a naturalist, who had the glory, or rather the good fortune, of making natural history the means of proclaiming the noblest and, without doubt, the highest truth that natural history ever had proclaimed, *The Physical Unity*, and through the *physical unity* the *moral unity*, of the human race.

---

[1] In 1830, the friends of Blumenbach, when they met to celebrate the fiftieth anniversary of his doctorate, conceived the idea of perpetuating the recollection of the day so memorable for science, by making up a purse of 5,000 dollars, about £800, of which the interest should be adjudged every three years by way of prize, to a young doctor, to be both physician and naturalist, who must have taken his degree in a German university, and be, says the deed, *young, poor, but fit*. Blumenbach himself gave out the prize twice, in 1833 and in 1836; after his death, it is to be adjudged alternately by the faculties of medicine at Göttingen and Berlin.

DE GENERIS HUMANI VARIETATE
NATIVA

ILLUSTRIS FACULTATIS MEDICÆ CONSENSU

PRO

GRADU DOCTORIS MEDICINÆ

DISPUTAVIT

D. XVI SEPT. M.DCC.LXXV

H. L. Q. S.

JOANN. FRIDER. BLUMENBACH,
GOTHANUS.

GOETTINGAE:
TYPIS FRID. ANDR. ROSENBUSCHII.

NATURÆ SPECIES, RATIOQUE.

CONTENTS.

INTRODUCTION; generation; climate; mode of life and aliment; hybrid generation; fertile hybrids; sterile hybrids; copulation of animals of different species, barren; on Jumars; no human hybrids; difference between man and other animals; mental endowments; instincts of man very few and very simple; reason the property of man alone; speech the same; properties of the human body; erect position; two hands; the human body naked and defenceless; laughter and tears; hymen; menstruation; other differences falsely supposed; internal structure of the human body; the brain of the *papio mandril;* intermaxillary bone; *membrana nictitans;* the suspensory ligament of the neck; orang-utan and other anthropomorphous apes; is there one or more species of mankind? one species alone; the varieties very arbitrary; division of mankind into *four* varieties; [note from edition of 1781, containing the division into *five*]; observations on national differences; variety of the human stature; causes of this variety, climate, food, &c.; colour of man; causes of its variety; effect of climate; examples from other organic bodies; effect of mode of life; various colour of the reticulum in apes; black men become white; white men black; mulattoes, &c.; spotted skin; different shape of skulls; examples of the first variety; the second, third, and fourth; conclusion; physiognomy; examples of the first, second, third, and fourth variety; difference in hair, teeth, feet, breasts; singularities of pronunciation; artificial varieties; circumcision; castration; beardless Americans; other mutilations; monstrous ears; other deformities; paintings; conclusion; digression on *albinism;* white rabbits; white mice; diseased whiteness in other animals; human albinism; symptoms of the disease; unhealthy whiteness; affection of the eyes; remaining conditions of body; mental condition; disease known to the ancients; recent examples from the world at large; stories of the ancients about men with tails; fictitious *rentrals* of the Hottentot women.

5—2

EXPLANATION OF THE PLATES.

PLATE I. Fig. 1. *Base of the skull of a Papio mandril.*

A. Posterior lobes of the brain. B. Anterior lobes of the brain. C. Fossa Sylvii. D. Cerebellum. E. Commencement of the spinal marrow. F. Region where in man the pyramidal and olivary bodies are inserted. G. Place where in the human brain the pons Varolii is divided by a fissure from the medulla oblongata. H. Pons Varolii.

1, 2, 3, 4, 5, 6, 7, 8, 9. Pairs of the nerves of the brain. The mammillary eminences, infundibulum, &c. cannot be seen in consequence of the size of the junction of the optic nerves.

Plate II. Fig. 1. *Vertebræ of the neck of the same Papio.* The bodies of the vertebræ descend by a kind of scaly processes in front downwards, and stand upon each other like tiles.

Fig. 2. *Fifth and sixth vertebræ of the neck of an adult man.* In these the bodies are parallel, smooth, and disciform.

Fig. 3. *Skin from the forehead of the Papio mandril.* The varieties and diminution of the blackness in the reticulum are here shown.

Fig. 4. *The clitoris of an Arabian girl, circumcised.*

Fig. 5. *A callitrix, or some other tailed ape copied from Dreydenbach's Travels.* This has been made more and more human by successive copyings till at last it has come out [in Martini's Buffon] a tailed man.

ON THE NATURAL VARIETY

OF

MANKIND.

As I am going to write about the natural variety of mankind, I think it worth while to begin from the beginning, that is, with the process of generation itself. I do not intend to put forth a system, or frame hypotheses, or enter into the intricacies of a labyrinth, out of which I should scarce find an exit; or, lastly, stir up cud already chewed a thousand times. Nor am I one to write the Iliad after Homer, that is to say, the universal history of generation after the immortal labours of the great Haller; but to spend only a few words upon a matter, which may be considered as demonstrated from the repeated observations and profound judgment of the most learned men, and which will throw some light on my subject.

The part which each sex takes in the generation of the fœtus, and which of the two has the greatest influence has occupied the principal philosophers and physicians for many thousand years. It was reserved at last for the profound sagacity of Haller, to be the first who was bold enough to break open the bars of nature's doors, and to unfold, from observing the incubation of eggs, so often investigated before by eminent men, that great mystery, which it was thought could be explained by nature alone; and in the fewest possible words I must here give his account of the matter[1]. A close dissection of impreg-

---

[1] I use almost the exact words of the illustrious discoverer. *Opusc. min.* II. p. 418. *Physiol.* T. VIII. See also Bonnet, *Corps Organisés*, T. p. 107.

nated eggs shows that the intestine of the chick is so of a piece with the envelopes of the yolk that the first envelope forms the skin of the fœtus; the second envelope forms the exterior lining of the intestine jointly with the mesentery and the peritonæum of the fœtus; the third is the covering of the interior intestine, and is produced from the same membrane as the ventricle, the œsophagus, the throat and the mouth, from what is in fact the skin and the epidermis of the fœtus: that the yolk takes up the arteries from the mesenteries of the chicken itself. It follows from this, that the whole egg is part of the mother, in whom the ovarium lies with all its eggs quite perfect, before any contact with the male has taken place. Then, that the fœtus is part of the egg, or at all events is joined to the egg by an inseparable bond, for the yolk (and that alone) constitutes the egg, together with its envelope, whilst it is in the mother, but that yoke is so united with the fœtus by its duct, that it forms but one continuous body. Hence it is proved, by direct demonstration, that the embryo is contained in the maternal egg, and that the female supplies the true stamina of the future fœtus. That primeval germ would lie buried as it were in eternal slumber, were it not aroused by the access and stimulus of the fertilizing seed of the male, and particularly by the subtle odour of his parts, which are particularly adapted for causing irritation; and then it breaks forth from the Graafian follicle in which it was shut up, runs through the canal, and in this way comes into the womb; there again it is finally unfolded and developed, and changed in some of its parts by the influence of the male, comes out like its parents. It leaves a manifest trace of its former habitation in the ovarium, in the shape of an opaque body, which takes its place[1]. The offspring at last brought to light, and in the process of time become adult, can produce like with the other sex of its species, whose posterity ought to go on for ever like their first parents. What then are the causes of the

---

[1] As to this little body, which was also illustrated by the labours of the great Haller, see *Hist. de l'Acad. des Sc. de Paris.* 1753, No. VII., and *Physiol.* T. VIII. p. 30. It is well delineated from dissected bodies by W. Hunter, *Anatomia Uteri Humani Gravidi.* Birm. 1774, Tab. 15, 29, 31.

contrary event? What is it which changes the course of generation, and now produces a worse and now a better progeny, at all events widely different from its original progenitors? This it will be our business to answer in the course of this dissertation. But in order not to break the thread of the discussion, it will be better to make a few preliminary observations.

First of all I will say a few words about the influence of climate, whose effects seem so great that distinguished men have thought that on this alone depended the different shapes, colour, manners and institutions of men[1]. There are, however, two ways, in which men may gather experience of a change of climate, both of which are to our purpose. They may emigrate and so change the climate, and also it may happen that the climate of their native country may sensibly become more mild or more severe, and so the inhabitants may degenerate. Several examples of each kind will be given in the proper place. It will be sufficient to say here that there is no diversity of habit, which may not be produced by varieties of climate; which is extremely apparent, even from the history of brute animals. If European horses are transported towards the east, as to Siberia, China, &c., in process of time they, as it were, dwindle, and become much smaller in body, so that at last you would scarcely recognize them as being of the same species. Cattle, on the contrary, whether they are sent to the Yakutan peninsula, or Kamtshatka, or Archangel, turn out taller and more robust, and the same thing has been experienced with English sheep in Sweden.

The squirrels on the river Obi are larger by one third than those which are found at Obdorsk[2], &c., to say nothing of the difference in colour, which observation shows to vary with still greater facility. But that the climate of the same country may

---

[1] Polyb. T. 1. p. 461, ed. Ernesti: "for through this cause and no other we differ most from each other in our ethnical and universal distinctions, in customs, in shape, and colour, and in most of our institutions." Comp. besides, Cardan in Hipp. *De aer. aq. et loc.* p. 218, who goes at length into the effects of climate on human bodies.

[2] Steller, von sondert. *Meerthieren*, p. 41 sqq.

undergo a change, no one can doubt, who will only compare this very Germany of to-day with ancient Germany, or our own contemporaries with our ancestors[1]. There was a time when the elk, now only an inhabitant of the extreme north, was common on the banks of the Rhine, and when that very river was so often frozen that the Gauls themselves used to offer sacrifices to prevent its affording a passage to our ancestors, their neighbours; when the most prodigious forest covered almost the whole country, and when there were no vintages, and other very good reasons of the same kind, which will account for our being unable to find the huge bodies of our ancestors, powerful only for attack, their firm limbs, threatening countenances, and fierce eyes, in the Germans of our age.

Besides the climate there are other causes, which have indeed an influence in altering bodies; many of those you might say depended, however, upon the climate themselves, but there are others which it is very clear have nothing to do with it. Amongst these influences above all we must set down the mode of life and of bringing up. The examples of domestic animals are trite, which manifestly have diverged into astonishing varieties, and almost put off their original nature. I have mentioned the effect climate has upon horses, and we shall now see how they are affected by mode of life. It is quite astonishing how wild horses[2] differ from our geldings by their small stature, their large heads, their murrey colour, their shaggy coats, and by a ferocity of disposition, which is almost untameable, so that they seem to approach almost nearer to the ass than to our domestic horses. Indeed, the famous Gmelin had scarcely any hesitation in believing that the tame horse, the wild horse, and the ass, were all of the same species, and that the latter had by circumstances alone degenerated from the tame horse; but this is going too far, because the ass has

---

[1] Conring. *De Germaniæ. corp. habitus antiqui ac novi ratiois*, learnedly according to his wont.
[2] Encyunkl, A. s. *Pol.* p. 117. Pallas, *Reise*, i p. 111. S. C. Gmelin, *Reis.* I. p. 44 sq. *fg.*

certain interior organs which are wanting in the horse[1], and the reverse also is true. However, among horses certainly wild, and also among our own, we may perceive a great difference in strength between those which feed upon natural pastures[2], and those which are kept in stables. For example, it is known that a colt, if it is born in a feeding-ground of the former kind, within half-an-hour after its birth will run after its dam seeking food, but if it is born in a stable, it will frequently lie for twenty-four hours and more on the ground, before it dares to stand on its feet.

As yet I have touched on two causes which change the form of animals, climate and mode of life. It remains to speak of the third, namely, the conjunction of different species, and the hybrid animals thence produced. It is a difficult subject, although after the labours of recent authors[3] I may treat it briefly.

There are three cases in the discussion about hybridity which ought to be clearly distinguished. First, the mere copulation of different animals; secondly, the birth of offspring from such copulation; and, thirdly, the fertility of such offspring and their capacity for propagation.

The latter case, although rare, (and that by the providence of the Supreme Being, lest new species should be multiplied indefinitely,) I would admit of in beings closely allied. At all events there are many testimonies to the fertility of mules[4]. There is no reason for doubting that hybrids have sprung from the union of the fox and the dog, and those too capable of generation, as the Spartan dogs or alopekides of the ancients.

---

[1] On the organs of the voice, Herissant, *Mém. de l'Acad. des Sciences de Paris*, 1753. Tab. 9 sq.
[2] As the *Lipprsers*. Comp. J. G. Prizelius, *Vom Sauer grosse*, 1771, 8vo.
[3] Buffon frequently but especially on the degeneration of animals, xiv. p. 248, and *Suppl.* T. III. p. 1. I. S. Reimar, *Naterl. Religion*, p. 411. Gleichen, *Enemerationes*, p. 24; and above all Haller, *Physiol.* viii. pp. 8, 100.
[4] Aristot. *De gen. an.* ii. 8, says they can only be conceived at a certain time. Varro, *De re rust.* ii. 1, 17. Columella, vi. 37. J. Plin. viii. 44, and Hardouinus. Bartlii *Adversus*. 42. Bochart, *Hieroz.* l. 2, 20. Recently Roxier, *Obs. sur la phys.* 1772. Comp. Gleichen, *l. c.* p. 75. Such things are often mentioned among the prodigies related by Livy and Obsequens.

There is still at Göttingen the daughter of a fox (from which many children have been born) which was impregnated by a domestic dog; and in it you may still recognize the smooth forehead and other marks of the ancestral form. The experiments of Sprenger[1] prove the prolificacy of hybrid birds.

The number of infertile hybrids is so copious as to be tiresome to count. Of all these, mules, so far as we know, are the most ancient. For although we may doubt their being antediluvian[2], nor dare ascribe their discovery to Anah[3], yet their extreme antiquity appears even from profane authors[4], and almost the first monuments of art[5]. To these rarer hybrids may be added the one Linnæus saw from the copulation of the *Capra reversa* with the *Capra depressa*[6]. But I do not quite trust Hesychius, when he says that the jackal comes from the union of the hyæna and the common wolf[7]. With respect to the union of dogs and apes[8], and the hybrids so born, I still remain in doubt. The animals seem too different; still I have known two instances, where bitches are said to have been impregnated by male apes, to which I should think it wrong to refuse credit. One took place in the territory of Schwartzburg; and a picture of this hybrid, carefully drawn, is in the possession of Büttner, who very kindly lent it to me. It represents a dog, of smaller size than the domestic dog, and of a dirty yellow colour; its eyes, ears, and hairy collar differed from the common dog, but it is said were very like those parts in the father. The other instance is related by an eye-witness, worthy of all belief, to have occurred about three years ago at Frankfort-on-the-Maine; that a bitch brought forth offspring by the *Simia Diana* of Linnæus, in ferocity, disposition, and in its gibbous habit

---

[1] *Opusc. Physico-math.* Hannov. 1753, p. 27.
[2] Pererius, on *Genesis*, T. II. p. 185, discusses at length the question if the mule entered Noah's ark or not?
[3] *Genes.* c. 36, v. 24. Bochart, *l. c.* at length.
[4] Hom. II. B. 852, who derives them from Enea.
[5] On the coffer of Cypselis. Heyne, *über den kasten des Cyps.* p. 58, circ. p. c. 660.
[6] In the Clifford menagerie. *Syst. Nat.* ed. XII. p. 96.
[7] Bochart, *Hieroz.* 1. p. 832.
[8] Osbeck, *Ostindisk Resa.* p. 99.

and long tail, exactly like its father. I leave this business to
be investigated by those who, perhaps, may have an opportunity
of more accurately observing it; for the difficulties are well
known which occur in experiments of this kind. It is very
hard to prevent the animals upon whom the experiment is to
be made from consorting with others, and at the same time not
to destroy the desire of copulation: moreover, if offspring have
anything peculiar by accident, it is instantly attributed to a
diversity of parentage. And what makes me suspicious about
these things is this especially, that I have seen many apes of
both sexes and different species constantly living for many
years in the midst of dogs, also of different sexes, and yet never
saw anything of the kind. On the other hand, instances of
false reports are very common, as that of a cat, born together
with two puppies, the report of which reached this neighbourhood a few years ago; but when it was properly examined, the
little creature which they called a cat, was easily recognized by
the more sagacious as a puppy slightly deformed, and the whole
prodigy became a joke. Nor can I otherwise interpret
Clauder's account[1] of a cat being impregnated by a squirrel, of
whose litter one is said to have been like the father, and the
rest like the mother; and other stories of the same kind.

From all this we must carefully separate the plainly fruitless
unions of animals of different species. I will allow that male
brutes when burning with desire, and unable to obtain females
of their own species, may sometimes be so excited by others,
whom they come in contact with, as perchance to copulate with
them; but I think that with very few, and those only very
nearly allied, is this actually successful, and in most cases the
attempt is ineffectual. There are, however, good reasons for
refusing to believe that from any incongruous attempt of this
kind, offspring can be born or even conceived. Here let us
consider the unequal proportions of the genital organs in many[2];
which parts are providently and carefully adapted for copulation

---

[1] Eph. N. C. dec. 2. ann. IX. p. 371.
[2] Haller, Physiol. VIII. p. 9.

in either sex of the same species; but in distant genera render the whole thing impossible, or at all events very difficult, and certainly unfit for the purposes of conception. Besides, I do not see according to what laws the offspring of this kind, coming from diverse parents, is to be formed in the womb, since in each species of animals there are certain and very definite periods for the gestation and pregnancy of the mother, the formation and progressive development of the fœtus. It will, however, be worth while to relate some instances of connexions of this kind which have been formed contrary to nature.

Of all these the most paradoxical seems to be the union of a rabbit with a hen, so celebrated by Reaumur[1]; but on which doubt has been thrown by his own pupil Buffon[2], Haller[3], and others; indeed, Buffon could not even succeed in raising a progeny from the hare and the rabbit, animals so nearly allied, although he suspected copulation took place. That illustrious philosopher seems, therefore, correct in supposing that if the rabbit of Reaumur ever did tread the hen, it must have been done from extreme lasciviousness, and had there been no hen the animal would have made use of something else for the same purpose. Meanwhile there are other evidences to this remarkable fact. Thus my revered tutor Büttner, himself, often saw rabbits treading hens, and they afterwards laid empty eggs (*hyponemia* or *zephyrea* as the ancients called them).

I have often seen a rabbit running about alone amongst broods of fowls, and playing with and imitating them, but I never could observe that it attempted anything more, or really had connexion with them. I have been told the same story about a house dog of Matthew Gesner, who they say also used to tread hens. I am not much surprised at this, since it is well known that dogs, when in heat, make use of inanimate things sometimes in order to effect their purpose. It is said that the *Gallus calecuticus* has been known to tread the duck, and in the

---

[1] *Art de faire eclorre les poulets*, T. II. p. 340.
[2] *Hid. Nat.* VI. p. 303.
[3] *l. c.* and in Bonnet, *Corps Organ.* II. p. 214.

same way that the drake treads the hen, and that chickens of wonderful forms are the result[1]. They have often been observed to copulate. There is still in the town a drake which treads the hens, but they are barren. But I will pass over many instances of this sort of monstrous and fruitless copulation, since I wish to say a little about the jumars, those famous hybrids from two clearly different species, the bovine and the equine.

I do not know whence Buffon[2] took it, that Columella had mentioned jumars, and that he had been quoted by Conrad Gesner. I cannot find either the mention in the one, or the quotation in the other. On the contrary, I think Gesner was the first to mention jumars[3]. For I cannot take notice here of the filly born from a cow at Sinuessa in Livy[4], since he speaks of it as a most unheard-of prodigy. But Tigurinus Polyhistor says "that he once heard that a particular kind of mule was to be found in Gaul, near Grenoble, which was sprung from an ass and a bull, and called in the vulgar tongue *Jumar*. And in the Swiss Alps near Coire, in the Splugen country, he had heard on credible testimony, that a horse had been born from a bull and a mare[5]." Jerome Cardan, a contemporary of Gesner, has also mentioned jumars, and says they have superior teeth[6], and are very strong and bold[7]. After him Joh. Baptist Porta reports that he himself had seen at Ferrara an animal of this kind, in shape like a mule, with a calf's head, two protuberances in the place of horns, black in colour, and with the eyes of a bull[8]. Things of this kind are repeated down to the time of John Leger, who discourses at great length[9] about them, and also gives a print of them[10]. He says "that jumars

---

[1] *Physiv. Belustig.* p. 392. Spal'anzani in *Memorie sopra i muli,* p. 18.
[2] T. xiv. p. 248.
[3] *Hist. quadrup. vivip.* pp. 19, 106, and 799.
[4] *Dec.* iii. L 3.
[5] Comp. Jac. Rueff, *De conceptu.* p. 48 a, in the history of monsters.
[6] *Contradic. Medic.* L. ii. tr. vi. Contrad. 18, p. 444.
[7] *Ib.* p. 448.
[8] *Mag. Nat.* L. i. c. 9. He adds that they were common in some parts of France, although he did not see one when he passed through.
[9] P. Zacchias, *Quæst. med. legal.* T. i. p. 533, from a mare and bull.
[10] *Hist. generale des Eglises evangeliques des vallées de Piémont* ou *Vaudoises,* Leyde, 1669, p. 7, and in *Almanach de Gotha,* 1767, p. 63.

are born from the union either of a bull and a mare, or a bull and an ass: the former are taller, and called *Baf*; the latter smaller, and *Bif*; that the former have the upper jaw evidently much shorter than the lower, like swine; that the upper teeth are placed further back than the lower, to the distance of a thumb, or two fingers. In the latter, the *Bif*, the lower jaw is shorter than the upper, as is the case in hares, and the upper teeth project beyond the lower. So that neither kind can graze in the fields, unless the grass is so long, that they can crop it with the tongue. These hybrids are exactly like an ox in the head and tail, and the places for horns are marked by small protuberances. As to the rest, they are exactly like an ass or horse. Their strength is wonderful, especially compared with their small body; they are smaller than common mules; they eat little and are swift; that he himself went in one day 18 miles among the mountains with a jumar of this kind, and that much more comfortably than he could have done with a horse."

After this account more recent[1] authorities have received others in good faith, and report that jumars are to be found elsewhere besides in Piedmont; according to Shaw[2] at Tunis and Algiers, according to Merolla[3] at Cape Verde, and by others in Languedoc[4].

Naturalists gradually became more sceptical of the fact and were disposed to dissect this kind of hybrid. Reaumur[5] met with a disappointment and so did Albinus, who had ordered one from Africa, which perished on the way. Bourgelat, the veterinary surgeon, was afterwards fortunate enough to be able to dissect a jumar in the theatre of Lyons[6], but the results

---
[1] Venette, p. 314, from a horse and cow. It was reported that the offspring of an ass and a cow had cloven hoofs. Bourguet, *Lettres philosophiques*, IV. p. 160, and from a bull and an ass *Nouveau Lexique*, Paris, 1755. *Encyclop. Paris.* T. IX. p. 57. B. S. Albinus in *Prælec. physiol. Meptis.* Still more recently the author of the book *Cours d'hist. nat. ou tableau de la nature*, T. I. Paris, 1770, 12mo. See Gleichen, loc. cit. p. 19.
[2] *Travels*, p. 239, ed. Oxf., 1738, there called *Kwarah*.
[3] *Voyage au Congo* in Churchill's *Collect.* T. 1. p. 653.
[4] *Diction. Languedocien François*, par M. l'Abbé de S... à Nimes, 1756, 8vo. p. 256.
[5] *Mem. sopra i muli*, p. 6.
[6] *Avant-coureur*, 1767, No. 50 sq.

of his labours are not satisfactory, because he seems to have trusted too much to report. "The ventricle was in shape like that of the horse, but much larger. The jumar had altogether much more of the mare than of the bull, both as to its external form, and its interior constitution, especially as regards the ventricle, whose singular structure in the bovine genus, on account of their rumination, is well known. And thus the observation of those physicians stands confirmed, who assert that the mother has a larger share in the formation of the fœtus than the father." The consequence therefore of this investigation was that the learned knew less what to think than ever[1]. Afterwards Buffon had two jumars dissected; one from the Pyrenees, the other from Dauphiné. In neither of them was any trace of a bull to be found[2].

All this however was not enough for inquirers into natural history. And at last, at the request of some men of great note, Bonnet, namely, and Spallanzani, Cardinal delle Lanze had two jumars[3] dissected by a skilful hand, and ordered anatomical plates of them to be engraved. It is very clear from these efforts that the pretended jumar is nothing more than a mere hinny[4] (*bardeau*). The larynx, glottis, ventricle, biliary ducts, are all specifically equine and not bovine.

Thus was finally proved what was suspected from the first by the great Haller[5]. I myself have lately seen at Cassel quite closely two hinnies, which report asserted to be jumars. They were of the size of a large ass, and very like one in shape,

---

[1] *Dictionn. des animaux*, T. II. p. 555. Bomare, *Dict. Nat.* T. VI. p. 174.
[2] *l. c.*
[3] Bonnet on Spallanz. op. *Mem. sopra i muli*, p. 11. *Encyclop. par De Felice*, T. XXV. p. 242.
[4] From the stallion and the-ass. Varro, *De re rust.* II. 8, 1. Columella, VI. 37, 5. Plin. VIII. c. XLIV. 5. Hesych. "Hinny, of which the father is a horse, and the mother an ass." Smaller than the mule, very patient of labour, tall like an ass, &c. Linnæus evidently transposed the terms of hinny and mule in *A mœn. Acad.* VI. p. 12, *pro. ambig.*
[5] *l. c.* p. 9. "This seems to me too much, nor is there any proportion between the pizzle of the bull and the vagina of the mare." The same difficulty which I suggested above occurs here, if we compare the novimestral pregnancy of the cow with the undecimestral of the mare.

black in colour, with horses' teeth in each jaw[1]; no vestige of rumination, &c.

But to return from this digression. What has already been said serves partly to show the difficulty of dealing with the accounts of hybrids of species very different from each other, and partly as some sort of proof of development; and will afterwards be of use to us when in varieties alone it will help to show that the greater part of the form in animals is derived from the mother, and very little from the father.

Let me say only a very few words about those human hybrids which credulous antiquity so frequently declared to be born or generated from brutes[2], but to which not only physical arguments but also moral ones of the greatest importance forbid us to attach the slightest faith; so that it seems extremely likely that the Supreme Being foresaw these disgusting kind of unions and took care to render them futile.

Those points which ought to be carefully attended to in any discussion upon hybrids, and which I took notice of above[3], must not be neglected here.

That men have very wickedly had connexion with beasts seems to be proved by several passages both in ancient[4] and modern writers[5]. That however such a monstrous connexion

---

[1] Comp. also *Remark. einer reisend. durch Deutschland, Frenkr. Engl. s. Holl.* 2 Th. p. 60 sq.

[2] Jac. Rueff, Parous, Aldrovandus, Schenk, Licetus, and other compilers of prodigies. On the Swedish girl ravished by a bear, and the hero she gave birth to, see Sax. Gramm. and Olaus Magnus. (The rage of bears against pregnant women and the singular remedy for it perhaps occasioned this fable.) A similar story occurs in Vinc. le Blanc, *Voyages*, p. 119 sq. The instances in the writings of the ancients have been studiously collected by Fortun. Fidelis, *De relat. Medic.* p. 493 sq. Storch, *Kinderkrankh.* I. p. 16, relates some more recent ones.

[3] P. 73.

[4] Plutarch in several places in the *Symposia* and the *Parallels*. Virgil, *Eclog.* III. 8. That Semiramis carried her passion for a horse to that point is asserted by Juba, in Pliny, VIII. c. 42.

[5] On the 3000 Italian auxiliaries to the Duc de Nemours, in 1562, who were sent into Dauphiné, and who ravished the she-goats, see Bayle, *Dict.*, Art. *Buthyl-lus*, T. 1. p. 469. Th. Warton on Theocr. *Idyll.* (Oxford, 1770, 4to.), 1. 88. p. 19. "I have heard from a learned friend, that when he was travelling in Sicily, and was accurately investigating the ancient monuments and the manners of the people, that one of the usual points of confession which the priests were in the habit of

MENTAL ENDOWMENTS.

has any where ever been fruitful there is no well-established instance to prove. Indeed those things which are related of the intercourse of Indian women with the larger apes and of their anthropomorphous offspring[1] seem dubious and fabulous even to James Bontius[2], who is in other respects sufficiently credulous. And even if it be granted that the lascivious male apes attack women, any idea of progeny resulting cannot be entertained for a moment, since those very travellers relate that the women perish miserably in the brutal embraces of their ravishers[3].

I now leave this disgusting theme, and all the more willingly, because I must draw near our goal; but still a few words must be said upon the actual ways in which man differs from other animals, before we investigate the varieties of men amongst themselves. The theme is indeed a most fruitful and admirable one, but the narrow limits of this book do not permit me to linger long over it, and it is necessary in this place to dismiss it in a few words; although the slender matter which I have got together on this interesting subject, I will gladly promise to give elsewhere to the public.

I think I shall here perform my duty best, if I first say a little about the endowments of the mind, and then about the bodily structure. Not indeed that these two points have apparently the slightest relation to each other. For it would clearly be impossible to draw any inference from comparing the organic structure of animals with the human body, as to their respective mental faculties: which will easily appear to any one who compares an elephant or a horse with an ape (which Reines[4] calls the copy of a man, or even a man as

---

examining the Sicilian herdsmen who spent a solitary life upon the mountains about, was whether they had anything to do with their sows."

It is said that the organs of the Manatis are so like those of women that the Arabs copulate with them. Comp. Michaelis, *Frag. on die nach Arab. reisenden*, p. 115.

[1] See Zucchelli, *Relat. di Congo*, p. 148.
[2] *Hist. Nat. et Med. Ind.* v. c. 32. "Let boys believe who have not yet to shave."
[3] Comp. Wieland's elegant dissertation on this point against Rousseau, *Beytr. zur ph. gesch. des M. V. a. II.* II. p. 50.
[4] *Var. lect.* p. 69.

regards the structure of the face, the φοράν and the motions of the limbs).

As to the discussions, which in this age particularly, have stirred up so many barren disputes about the mind, the reason, and the speech, &c. of brutes, they do not seem to me to be really so difficult or confused, if a man have only a moderate familiarity with the habits of animals, some knowledge of the physiology of the human body, and be sufficiently free from prejudices.

Man then alone is destitute of what are called *instincts*, that is, certain congenital faculties for protecting himself from external injury, and for seeking nutritious food, &c. All his instincts are artificial (*kunst-triebe*), and of the others there are only the smallest traces to be seen. Mankind therefore would be very wretched were it not preserved by the use of *reason*, of which other animals are plainly destitute. I am sure they are only endowed with innate or common and truly material sense (which is not wanting either to man), especially after comparing everything which I have read[1] upon the rational mind of animals with their mode of life and actions, and what perhaps is the most important speculation, and demands most attention, with the phenomena of death, which are very much like both in animals and men[2]. Instinct always remains the same, and is not advanced by cultivation, nor is it smaller or weaker in the young animal than in the adult. Reason, on the contrary, may be compared to a developing germ, which in the process of time, and by the accession of a social life and other external circumstances, is as it were developed, formed, and cultivated. The bullock feels its strength so much as to threaten, though its weapons of offence do not yet exist;

> Before his horns adorn the calf, they're there,
> All weaponless he butts, and furious beats the air[3];

---

[1] Very recently in *Deutsch. Merkur*, 1773, September, October.
[2] Carlsan, *In subtil.* l. xi. p. 551, T. iii. *Oper.* "Man is no more an animal, than an animal is a plant. For if an animal, although it is nourished and lives, does not deserve the name of a plant, nor is entirely a plant, because it has a life which feels over and above the plant, since man has a mind over and above the animal, he ceases to be an animal," &c.
[3] Lucret. v. 1033. Comp. Reimar, *Trieb. der th.* p. 101.

whence unless from some interior sensation? To man, on the contrary, nothing of the kind happens. He is born naked and weaponless, furnished with no instinct, entirely dependent on society and education. This excites the flame of reason by degrees, which at last shows itself capable of happily supplying, by itself, all the defects in which animals seem to have the advantage over men. Man brought up amongst the beasts, destitute of intercourse with man, comes out a beast. The contrary however never occurs to beasts which live with man. Neither the beavers, nor the seals, who live in company, nor the domestic animals who enjoy our familiar society, come out endowed with reason.

From what has been said, the direct difference between the voice and speech of animals is plain[1], since we consider that man alone ought to be held to possess *speech*[2], or the voice of reason, and beasts only the language of the affections. In process of time, the mind becomes developed, and finds out how to express its ideas with the tongue. Young children give names to those they love, which is the case with no animal, although they can distinguish their master and those familiar to them well enough. Those stories are utterly undeserving of attention which the old travellers related about the language of certain distant nations, who they said were endowed with nothing but an inarticulate and, as it were, brutish voice. It is indeed beyond all doubt that the fiercest nations, the Californians, the inhabitants of the Cape of Good Hope, &c. have a peculiar sort of speech, and plenty of definite words, and that animals on the contrary, whether they be like man in structure, as the famous orangutan is[3], or approach man in intelligence, to use the words of Pliny about the elephant, are destitute of speech, and can only

---

[1] Count de Gebelin says elegantly in *Plan général du monde primitif*, p. 10, "Language is twofold: that of the sentiments and of the ideas. The first is common both to man and the animals, though much more perfect in the former. The second is absolutely peculiar to man, for it can only be adapted to him, inasmuch as it answers to the operations to which he alone of all the beings who inhabit the earth can elevate himself."

[2] Hence some of the Rabbins not inaptly call man *the speaking animal*.

[3] Th. Bowrey, *Malayo Dictionary*, London, 1701, 4to. Ott. Fr. v. d. Gröben, *Guineische reisebeschr.* p. 31.

emit a few and those equivocal sounds. That speech is the work of reason alone, appears from this, that other animals, although they have nearly the same organs of voice as man, are entirely destitute of it[1].

If now any one casts an eye on the human body, it would certainly be more easy to distinguish man from every other animal at the very first glance, than to lay down any fixed criterion[2] by which he differs from the rest. It would seem as if the Supreme Power had avoided giving any distinct and persistent characters to the human body, just in exactly the same proportion as this its highest master-piece far excels all other animals in its noblest part, which is reason.

But it will be worth while to reckon up, one by one, a few of those things which seem peculiar to our bodies. First of all I would speak of the erect position of man, which I cannot leave untouched because of the recent paradoxes of P. Moscati[3]; although it is very tedious to serve up, and as it were to chew over again a matter which has been most thoroughly investigated, and is clearer than the noon-day sun. It is true, I can believe that this elegant author, who is in other ways worthy of all praise, composed this book as an attempt and not quite seriously, partly because he has made use of arguments which you would scarcely expect to find from a man not only acquainted with human and comparative anatomy, but from one who constantly appeals to both; and partly because he leaves quite unnoticed points of indisputably great importance as to the bipedal structure of man, which have already been most diligently handled by the great Galen[4], and the immortal Barth. Eustachius[5]. I could easily allow our author[6] that there is little

---

[1] I have myself found the uvula in apes, and the other parts of the larynx exactly like those in man. See on the Pygmy, Tyson, p. 51.
[2] Linnaeus could discover no point by which man could be distinguished from the ape. *Praef. ad Faun. Suecic.*
[3] *Delle corporee differenze essenziali, che passano fra la struttura de' bruti, e la umana.* Milano, 1770.
[4] Especially in his precious books *De usu partium*, l. III. c. 1. p. 123 sqq., c. 16. p. 193; l. XIII. c. 11. p. 765, ed. Lagd. 1550, 16mo.
[5] Throughout the *Ossium examen*, pp. 175—182, ed. Venet. 1564, 4to.
[6] P. 34.

weight in those common arguments for the erect position of man, deduced from the position of the great occipital foramen[1], the proportion of the feet to the hands, the mammae, the chest[2], and the shape of the shoulder-blade; although there remain the greater difficulties of the parts which so wonderfully prove that the walk should be bipedal. I say nothing of the apex of the heart and its direction in the embryos of man and the brutes; this indeed our author[3] mentions, but yet explains in such a way that he seems to give a handle to the opposite opinion. I say nothing of that powerful argument deduced from the movement of the head and its connexion with the first cervical vertebræ, and I omit it the more readily, because of that elaborate work of Eustachius on the point[4], which I should have to transcribe almost in its integrity. The pelvis alone, and the construction of the feet would easily bring over to my view those in other respects acquainted with anatomy, if they would compare even cursorily the composition of the bones of the quadrupeds with those of man. Let any one look at the broad flanks of the human skeleton, ending below in a narrow hip, the short pelvis largely dilated above but narrowed below so as to open an escape for the fœtus, yet carefully provide for the prolapsus of the womb, and then compare these things with the oblong right-angled and almost cylindrical pelvis of quadrupeds with their wide hip, and their outwardly curved ischiatic prominences; lastly, let him observe the construction of the glutei muscles, and the connexion of the muscles of the leg in man and the brutes, and then let him say if he thinks it probable that they can have the same mode of locomotion. Let any one make the experiment on some fresh animal skeleton, or at least let him look at Coiter's picture[5] of the erect skeleton of a fox, going along in the most ridiculous manner on its hind-feet, and then let him imagine a human skeleton resting upon its arms and feet, and

---

[1] Daubenton, *Sur les différences de la situation du grand trou occipital dans l'homme et dans les animaux.* *Mém. de l'Acad. des Sc. de Paris*, 1764, p. 568.
[2] See Eustach. *l. c.* p. 173.
[3] P. 26.
[4] *l. c.* p. 234 sq.
[5] Scalet. animal. Norib. 1575, fol. mag. Tab. II.

he will not but see that a bipedal brute and a quadrupedal man would equally pass for prodigies. Inseparable also from the general consideration of the pelvis is that other proof derived from the *acetabulum*, and the head and neck of the thigh-bone. And that this neck is oblong in man, and goes downwards with a sensible obliquity, but is short in brutes, even in apes, and nearly horizontal; and the head more obliquely articulated with the hip; so the whole structure of the bones of the feet, the thick calcaneum of man, the juncture of the ancle with the sole of the foot, which in man too is oblong and broader, and many other things of the kind which point in this direction, disagreeably trite and too well known to students of anatomy, but difficult to be understood by those unacquainted with medicine. For which reason I think it would be foolish to say much about them, especially as I have indicated the sources to which those should go who want still more proofs of so easy a matter.

Another property of man comes directly from the foregoing, namely, his two hands, which I consider belong to mankind alone; whereas apes, on the contrary, must either have four or none at all, of which the great toe being separated from the other fingers of the feet serves the same purposes which the thumbs do in the hands. This is so certain, that on that account alone the fœtus said by Robinet[1] to be that of a pongo, must certainly be considered a human embryo, even if no notice be taken of the other proportions of the bodily parts, and the whole structure which is entirely human. Hahn[2] besides Galen[3] has written expressly on the admirable formation of the human hand.

All these things therefore being duly weighed, I am induced to consider even that famous animal the orang-utan as a quadruped. I know indeed that several authors of voyages have said a good deal about him, and given him out as a biped. The reasons which induce me to come to a different conclusion, besides the tendency of many travellers to exaggerate a little what is extra-

---

[1] *Essai de la nature qui apprend à faire l'homme*, Tab. IX. p. 155.
[2] J. F. Hahn, *De manu hominem a brutis distinguente*, Lips. 1719, 8vo.
[3] l. c.

ordinary, are the following; in the first place, some who have described these animals have said only that it *frequently*[1] goes on its hinder feet, which at least excites a suspicion, that they do go on all fours like other animals: moreover, many are depicted in the plates as leaning upon a club, after the fashion of dancing bears[2]. The palm of their hands is as deeply furrowed, and marked with folds and slits as the soles of their feet[3]. The depressed and receding heel-bones prevent their walking firmly. If you examine them more closely, the elongated pelvis, and especially the muscle called *elevator claviculæ*[4], make it highly probable that a quadrupedal gait is natural to this animal. The instance of the long-armed ape is favourable to the same opinion[5]. Man therefore is the only biped, unless any one likes to put forward the manati, birds, (especially penguins,) or the lizard *Siren*. The example of those unfortunate creatures who, according to accounts, have been here and there brought up amongst wild beasts, goes no way to show that the erect position is not natural to man. Hard necessity, perhaps too imitation, taught these wretches to go on their hands and feet at the same time that they were obliged to creep through woods and fruit-bearing copses, and even into the dens and receptacles of wild beasts; nor is it quite certain that it was the case with all. The Hessian boy[6] found amongst the wolves *sometimes* only walked as a quadruped; the girl of Zell[7], and the girl of Champagne[8], and the boy of Hameln[9] went upright. And the argument deduced from the first crawlings of infants is much weaker still, since it must be very well known to any one who has observed them, that they scarcely ever crawl as quadrupeds, but rather squat upon their buttocks, rest upon their

---

[1] Leguat, T. II. p. 93—*sourent*—Tulp. l. III. c. 56 — *multoties*.
[2] Tyson, Edwards, Buffon. The orang-utan which I saw myself alive at Jena in 1770 could not go on its hinder feet without the assistance of a stick, nor walk about easily at all.
[3] Le Cat, *Traité du mouvement musculaire*, Tab. I.
[4] Tyson, *Anat. of a pygmy*, figs. 3, 12, p. 87. *Opusc.* London, 1751.
[5] *Homo lar*, Linn.
[6] Dilich. *Hessische Chronick.* P. II. p. 187.
[7] *Bresl. Samml.* January 1718, August and October 1731.
[8] *Hist. d'une fille sauvage*, &c. Paris, 1761, 12mo.
[9] *Bresl. Samml.* December 1725.

hands¹, and as it were row with their feet. Pliny² therefore was not quite correct when he said that the first promise of strength and the first gift of life was to make a man like a quadruped.

As to those who make out the erect position to be the fomenter of disorders, they must forget both veterinary practice and the diseases³ which we find afflict both wretched men and fierce quadrupeds.

Besides his erect position and his two hands there are some other things to be considered which also seem peculiar to man. Of all animals he alone seems to be placed on the earth *altogether naked and defenceless*, since he has neither powerful teeth, nor horns, nor talons, nor a shaggy hide, nor any other protection. It is no use objecting that there are other animals equally unprovided; something will always be found which keeps them protected to some extent⁴. He is usually without hair, whereas the quadrupeds which expose their body to the heavens and the seasons are provided either with a shaggy hide, or a thick skin, or shells, or scales, or spikes. Few parts of a man's body can be called hairy⁵, and his back is nearly bare, which is certainly another argument for the erect position of *man*. His teeth all on a level, round, smooth, and perfectly regular, are in one word so constructed, that it is clear from the first glance, they were given to man principally to chew his food with, partly also for speech, and in no wise as weapons of attack⁶. Even the teeth of apes differ greatly in form from those of men. Their canines are longer, sharper, and more dis-

---

¹ Thus the boy of Hameln. *Bresl. Sammt. l. c.*
² VII. I. T. I. p. 369, ed. Hard.
³ See the hypochondriac tumors of the *juvenis Hibernus* in Tulp. IV. 10.
⁴ The polypus has scarcely any enemies, and when it is accidentally wounded fresh animals of its own species are the result of the excrescence.
⁵ The instances of hairy men are no objection, and I am inclined to consider them as prodigies. The hairy family of the Canary Islands, in Aldrovandus, *Monstr. Hist.* p. 16 sqq., even if we can trust a generally credulous author, are no more to be wondered at than the six-fingered families. Comp. Zahn, *Specul. physico-math. Hist.* T. III. p. 70. I recollect myself that the back of that man-eating shepherd, who was executed in 1772, at Herea, near Jena, when he had been a fastened to the wheel for some weeks and exposed to the weather, and his clothes fell off, appeared completely covered with shaggy hair.
⁶ Man is an animal mild and soft, whose strength and power consist more in wisdom than in force of body. Eustach. *De dentibus*, p. m. 85.

tant from their neighbours: the molars deeply incisive, bristling as it were with enormous tusks. Besides the teeth, man is marked out as a gentle and unarmed being, by the small bone which is covered by the lips, by which also he is distinguished from the apes and the other beasts like him.

It has been disputed whether brutes have the same affections[1] of the mind as man. This is a very difficult question, if we examine the ways in which men express joy and sorrow, and especially laughter and tears. That animals can cry is certain, since they have organs[2] exactly like those in man for weeping; but we must go deeper and enquire whether they do so in consequence of feeling sorrow. It is said to be so with some animals, as the orang-utan[3], the sloth[4], seals[5], the horse[6], the stag[7], the turtle[8], the tortoise[9], &c. The narrative of Steller, amongst others, deserves certainly great credit; so that it is probable that weeping from sadness is common to animals and man. About laughter as the effect of joy there seems more doubt. Some animals have peculiar ways of expressing[10] tranquillity or joy, but I do not think that a change in the muscles of the face[11], or the utterance of cacchination, has been observed in any other animal but man. The croaking of apes, or the cries of the sloth, have no more to do with this than the barking of dogs, or the songs of birds, as the indications of joy.

Women have something peculiar, which seems to be denied to all other animals, even if they remain untouched; I mean the hymen, which has been granted to woman-kind perhaps much more for moral reasons[12], than because it has any physical uses.

---

[1] On this point, see Moscati, l. c. p. 38.
[2] Bertin, *Sur le sac nasal ou lacrymal de plusieurs espèces d'animaux.* Mém. de Par. 1766, p. 281.
[3] Bontius, l. v. c. 32. Le Cat, l. c. p. 35. But this good man seems to allow too much to the ape, in his endeavour to make out that there is an almost imperceptible transition from man to the rest of the animals.
[4] Artedi in descr. Mus. Seba, 1. p. 53.
[5] Steller, v. wunderb. meerth. p. 140.
[6] Schneider, de Catarrho, p. 371.
[7] Some look on these tears as dirt, osseous concretion, &c.
[8] Quiqueran, Laud. provinc. p. 36.
[9] Ligon, Barbad. p. 36.
[10] The wagging of the dog's tail, the peculiar purring of cats, &c.
[11] James Parson, *Human Physiognomy explained*, p. 73.
[12] Read the great Haller, Physiol. L. XXVIII. p. 97.

MENSTRUATION.

I am inclined to allow the *menstrual* flux to the females of human kind alone[1]. There are some who say that some other animals of that sex have also their menstrual excretions[1], and Buffon[2] has particularly asserted this of many apes. The whole point depends upon the notion of a *periodic* flux, which, if properly considered, will scarcely be allowed to apes. I have carefully observed many female apes of more than one species, and that for many years, in the menagerie of Büttner, yet I cannot undertake to say that they have menstrual excretions. Meanwhile it is certain that they are afflicted with hæmorrhages of the womb, which however do not occur at any fixed period, but sometimes after one week, and sometimes after three or more, return in the same ape, which otherwise is enjoying good health; in some however it never appears at all.

These two things then, the hymen and periodical menstruation, I consider as peculiar to mankind[4]. As to the *clitoris* and the nymphæ[5], there is no doubt that other animals also have them too; and in some the clitoris appears very large and almost enormous. The hymen, the guardian of chastity, is adapted to man who is alone endowed with reason; but the clitoris, the obscene organ of brute pleasure, is given to beasts also. A few examples are enough: in the papio mandril (*Simia maimonides* Linn.) which I dissected last winter, I observed the clitoris of half-an-ounce in weight, swelling, wrapped in a loose prepuce, and so prominent that it might easily have made an incautious observer think the animal was an hermaphrodite, and all the more because a little fold, which was visible in the apex of the member and impervious, increased the general resemblance to the virile gland. The *nymphæ* seemed worn down, or had coalesced with the callous and gaping lips of the pudendum. And I have observed those as well as the clitoris distinctly in a *Mongoz Lemur*, which I myself saw alive last summer at Göttin-

---
[1] Thus Plinius, vii. 15. p. m. T. i. p. 382. Solinus *ex Democrito*, i. p. m. 6.
[2] See in Haller, *l. c.* p. 137.
[3] T. xiv. xv. frequently.
[4] As to some of the old wives' stories about some nations of America, who are said not to menstruate, at this time of day they want no refutation.
[5] It is doubted by Linnæus, *Syst. Nat.* ed. xii. p. 33.

gen. The *Didactylus ignavus* of the Royal Museum has a very round clitoris between the swelling lips of the pudendum. But the great Haller has collected many instances[1]. These therefore are some of the points which are peculiar to mankind and which can be easily distinguished without any very delicate anatomy. I leave out others, as the immobility of the ears[2], or the hairs of either eye-brow[3], which were formerly attributed to man alone.

A very extensive and at the same time a very pleasant field would be open to us, if we could now investigate the internal structure of the human body, in so far as it differs plainly from the structure of other animals. But the limits of this our book do not allow us to wander so far. It is therefore the business of those who want information on these points to go to the authors of comparative anatomy, and, above all, to those who have dissected carefully the animals which are most like man; amongst whom it will be sufficient to mention Eustachius[4], Coiter[5], Riolani[6], and Tyson[7]. Let them study those who think that perhaps the orang-utan and some other apes are not so much unlike man, but that they may be considered as of the same species, or, at all events, as animals very closely allied to man. It is now my present intention to select a few points from many, and reckon them up briefly.

As the brain, the most noble entrail of the animal body, for numberless reasons which everybody knows, demands particular attention beyond all other parts, men of the greatest reputation have laboured[8] on its comparative anatomy and have stirred up others[9], when there was an opportunity, to similar labours.

---

[1] *L. c.* p. 80. Besides these is the perforated clitoris leading in the urinal bladder of the *Coccyyx Lemur* (*tardigrad* Linn. But it seems best with Parkinson to give it the name of its country) in Daubenton, T. XIII. p. 317; Tab. XLII. fig. 4. Can it be likely that this was an abnormal accident?

[2] Aristot. *De part. anim.* II. ii.

[3] Perrault. *Hist. des anim.* P. III. p. 112. ed. Paris, 1733. He saw it in the elephant, the ostrich, the vulture. I have seen things very like the human ones in many apes.

[4] Frequently. [5] *Principal. corp. h. part. tab.* Norib. 1575. fol. maj.

[6] Jo. Riol. Jo. fil. *Osteologia simiæ*, Par. 1614. 8vo. [7] *Op. cit.*

[8] Sam. Collin's *Comparative Anatomy*. Haller, *Physiol.* T. IV. and *Op. Minor.* T. III.

[9] Haller, *Physiol.* T. V. p. 579.

Recollecting this, as I have been fortunate enough to dissect apes, last winter, of more than one kind, I have, above all, investigated their brains, and I exhibit as a specimen the base of one[1]. It is the brain of that very mandril I was just speaking of. Cut off at the great occipital foramen, and taken out of the skull, it weighed three ounces and one drachm, whilst the rest of the body of the ape weighed eight common pounds and a half. The principal points in which its base differs from the human organ are these. The two anterior lobes of the brain are almost entirely unified. The cerebellum is large in proportion to the brain, more than is the case with the pygmy. The *pons varolii* is separated from the *medulla oblongata* by no apparent fissure, but is joined on, and down continuously with it. Not a vestige of the pyramidal or olivary bodies, as is also the case in the pygmy. The *medulla oblongata* much thicker than in the man or the pygmy. The second pair of nerves which were united in one great mass and then again divided at the very entrance of the orbits, was cut off before the separation. No *rete mirabile*. I omit other things of less importance, which any one who is skilled in anatomy will easily recognize; and I can assure such an one that the figure is most accurately drawn[2].

I have subjoined to the brain the skull of the same *papio*, in which, besides the deeper orbits, the thickness of the zygomata, the widely divergent teeth, the immense canines, and other things of smaller importance, that peculiar bone in which the incisors are set deserves particular attention. This man is without, although all the apes and most of the other mammals[3] have it. I doubted whether it was to be found in the orang-utan; since in the figures of Tyson[4] and Daubenton[5] the skulls were not drawn in such a way that the sutures could be well distin-

---

[1] Pl. 1. fig. 1.
[2] Compare with my figure the brain of Tyson's pygmy, fig. 13, and that most elegant chart by Haller of the base of the human brain, Fasc. VII. Tab. 1. To make the comparison easier, I have preserved the same lettering, by which in Haller's chart the parts of the brain are marked.
[3] The *Myrmecophaga didactyla*, whose skull I have, does not possess it.
[4] l. c. fig. 5.
[5] *Mém. de Par.* 1764. Tab. XVI. fig. 2.

guished¹: nor did the English author speak precisely about it²: but Fr. Gabr. Sulzer has settled the point, for he kindly writes me word that Camper, a great authority, has dissected animals of this kind, and found this bone in them. Another difference flows from this singular structure, namely, in the bone of the nose, which is double in the human head, and nearly of a rhomboidal figure, whereas it is seen to be single in the apes, and also triangular, which however, like the other things which may be observed in this figure, are very patent, and will easily be seen by those who know anything of osteology, and therefore do not want any further explanation.

Amongst other differences between the human body and that of the beasts there are some which are better known, and may be briefly touched upon. As, for example, the *membrana nictitans, periophthalmium*, or third eyelid, which Haller³ says is in man a very slight imitation of the organ in animals, although in animals also according to their class and order, their mode of life, and their size, it differs much in position and constitution⁴.

Besides this, the bulbous or suspensory muscle of the eye is common to nearly all⁵ quadrupeds, and so is the suspensory ligament of the neck, which is said to be wanting in man and the apes alone⁶. This white and tendonous part which is known to

---

¹ The figure of the skeleton of the long-handed ape in Buffon, T. xiv. Tab. vi, has the same fault; and even Coiter, who is famous in other things, has omitted to mark this bone in the skeleton of the tailed ape, the figure of which is added to in the book and place already quoted. Still it is most distinctly visible in the skulls of five different kinds of apes which I have before me.

² P. 65. "In a monkey I observed that peculiar suture Riolan mentions, but did not find it in the Pygmie, only in the palate of the Pygmie I observed a suture, not from the *dens caninus*, as was in the monkey, but from the second of the *dentes incisores*."

³ *Physiol*. T. v. p. 378, where there are a good many interesting things about this membrane. There is a good deal about it also in Peter Tarrarumi, *Osc anatomiche in Atti de' Saico-critici di Siena*, T. iii. p. 115. De Pauw, *Recherch. philos. sur les Americ*. T. ii p. 70 n.

⁴ In some I certainly found a few traces, as in the *Lemur Mongoz*. It is small too in the apes.

⁵ It is wanting in Tyson's orang-utan, p. 85. Andr. Vesalius had falsely and obstinately assigned it to man. Comp. Haller, *l. c.* p. 411. Douglass Schreiberi, p. 40.

⁶ Linnæus, *Syst. Nat.* ed. xii. T. 1. p. 48.

everybody, and is called by my countrymen, *haarwachs*; by the English[1], *packwax, taxwax, fixfax* and *whiteleather*; by the Belgians[2], *vast*, &c. is inserted for the purpose of sustaining the head and neck of quadrupeds[3]. But although man shares the absence of this with the apes, yet it by no means follows that apes are meant to walk upright, since in them the subtle structure of the vertebræ of the neck, and in man the peculiar bipedal walk, supply the defect of this ligament. The whole point about the bodies of these vertebræ is best explained by a comparison of these bones themselves, as they appear in the skeleton of the man and the ape, and for this reason I have had engraved the whole construction of the vertebræ of the neck in the same papio[4] (Pl. II. fig. 1), the base of whose brain and whose skull we have just seen, because in that it may be seen as clearly as possible why he scarcely ever goes on two feet. I have subjoined the fifth and sixth vertebræ of the human neck (Pl. II. fig. 2). In these the bodies are nearly parallel, and almost disciform, whereas in the ape they descend by a sort of scaly process in front, and one is placed upon and dove-tailed into the other. So it can easily be made plain by experiment that the vertebræ in these animals support each other, and serve to sustain the head, which could not be done with man if placed in a quadrupedal position, on account of the smooth surfaces of the body of the vertebræ, for so it would be excessively difficult to sustain the mass of the very heavy human head, which would more and more collapse and subside by its own weight.

I have selected a few out of many points in which man differs most clearly from the other animals. I have said that there are many which go to demonstrate his natural position to be an erect one, and to separate him fairly from the apes, especially from the *orang-utan*. I have been induced to do this because of the

---

[1] Allen Mullen, *Anatomical Account of the Eleph.* p. 14. Ray, *Wisdom of God*, pp. 261, 338, and *Synops. quadrupedum*, p. 136. Derham, *Physico-theol.* p. 324.
[2] Vesal. *De corp. hum. fabr.* p. 361.
[3] La Fosse, *Cours d'Hippiatrique*, Tab. xi a.
[4] It would have been tedious to transcribe from Eustachius and Coiter all the other points in which the vertebræ of the apes diverge from those of man.

opinions lately expressed by some famous men[1], who however are ill-instructed in natural history and anatomy, but who are not ashamed to say that this ape is very nearly allied, and indeed of the same species with themselves.

I do not think this opinion deserves any lengthened refutation for those who are adepts in the matter; but it will clearly not be foreign to our purpose if I say a few words about the orang-utan himself. After the labours of Buffon and others it is not worth while to spend any time on his habits and mode of life[1]. But it would be worth while if the species were a little more accurately defined. For although this remarkable animal has very seldom been seen in Europe, and few authentic representations of it exist, still such as they are they differ so much from each other that they can in no way be considered as belonging to one and the same species. I shall pass by the delineations which are manifestly fictitious, or carelessly drawn, such as those of Bontius, Neuhof, Jürgen Andersen, Ja. Jac. Saar, and Franc. Leguat; and examine more closely the authentic ones alone. These are those of Tulp, Tyson, Edwards, Scotin[3], Le Cat, and Buffon, which when they are compared together manifestly differ very much both in form and size. Recent authors have deduced from this a variety of species, and have called one the larger, and the other the smaller orang-utan. I do not however place much trust in this distinction. Some of the specimens which have been brought to Europe were very young, and there were indications which, considering that they all died prematurely[4], forbid us to come to any conclusion as to their size. Still

---

[1] *Cours d'hist. nat.* T. 1. That good citizen of Geneva *Sur l'inégalité parmi les hommes*, p. 157 D. *The Origin and Progress of Language*, Vol. 1. pp. 175, 189. *Hist. of Jamaica*, Vol. II. p. 363, Lond. 1774, 4to.

[2] I shall only remark on the name *orang-utan*, that it is incorrectly translated "wild man," *homo sylvestris*. Man in Malay is *Manusia*, but the word *oran* is applied not only to man, but also to the elephant, whom the Indians think is sensible. Buttner, to whom I am indebted for this observation, translates it *intelligent being*.

[3] Scotin's animal, Chimpansi, brought by H. Howe, master of the ship *Speaker*, from Angola to London, in Aug. 1738, was figured separately by Sloane, and repeated in *Nord acta erud.* Lips. Sept. 1739, Tab. v. p. 564. Linn. *Anthrop. dm. ac.* Vol. VI. Haubes, *Bibl. magica*, s. 35. Le Cat, above. The others are well known.

[4] The one Buffon saw was two years old. Tyson's had not yet cut all its teeth.

the habit of their whole body and the conformation of its parts seem to me much more justly to constitute them into species. I may be allowed therefore to admit at least two species, and in order that names may not be unnecessarily multiplied, I shall give them some which occur in Linnaeus, one which has been improperly appended to man by that illustrious author, the other to the first species of apes. Let there be then,—

1. *Simia troglodytes* or *Chimpansi*; represented by Tulp and Scotin, macrocephalous, sinewy, hairy on the back of its body alone; the front, except the shoulders, being bare.

2. *Satyrus* or *Orang-utan* of Tyson, Edwards, Le Cat, and Buffon; rather slender, with small head, clothed with thick hair, the hairs of the arm and fore-arm being in opposite directions. Such was the male which I mentioned having seen alive at Jena. It came very near to the figure of Tyson, and at the first glance was most unmistakeably different from the *Simia sylvanus*, &c. I made a drawing at that time of this rare animal, but I regret that I neglected to measure its parts more accurately.

These are the observations made partly by myself, and partly by my first preceptor in natural history, I. E. Im. Walch. The stature was that of a boy about ten years old, colour brown, face sufficiently human, the fingers of the hands and feet rather long, the thumb widely separated, the calves more fleshy than in other apes, the scrotum pendulous almost square, rather white, the penis small like Tyson's figure. It was so much in the habit of leaning on a stick, that though it could stand and walk on two feet, most persons would attribute that way of walking to the effect of education. The same might be said of his way of drinking and eating, in which actions he used spoon and cup. He showed a great desire for the other sex.

Linnæus doubted whether the animals which we have divided into two species, but which in his opinion were only varieties, differed in anything more than in sex. It is quite true that those represented by Tulp and Scotin were females, and the others males; but still the silence of travellers and eye-witnesses like Bontius and Th. Bowrey, on any different form in the sexes, convinces me that besides the difference of sex there must also be a variety of species. I cannot dismiss these animals without mentioning two points, of which one is concerned with a singular character of them which has been generally neglected, and the other regards their native country. I owe the knowledge of the former character to my great friend Sulzer, who repeated to me the words of Camper, who, I just mentioned, dissected these *Satyri* himself, "that in the front hands of these animals the nails of the thumbs were wanting." There are indeed nails in the plates of Tyson, Edwards, and Le Cat; but that singular and paradoxical character might very easily have been unnoticed; nor did I pay any attention myself to the nails of the Jena satyr. Was this a third species? that I cannot decide. The other point that remains to be mentioned is as to the native country of both species (chimpansi and orang-utan). By almost all zoological writers the torrid zone *of the ancient world* is given out as their native country. Bancroft[1] however relates a report of the inhabitants, that the orang-utan may also be found in the thick woods of Guiana. This account deserves further attention, but there is this against it, that the author adds that the animal has not yet been seen by Europeans resident there.

There is another animal nearly allied to the Troglodyte and the Satyr, which is the *Simia longimana* (*Homo Lar*, Linn., Gibbon, Buff.), an animal exactly like man, if you look at its face: but differing from almost all other animals if you consider the enormous length of its anterior feet. They are indeed represented as somewhat shorter in the figure of the Bengalese ape, which is inserted in the Philosophical Transactions[2], and taken for the *S. longimana*, which however is clearly drawn by the hand of no artist, as is shown by the unequal length of either fore arm, and by other particulars.

Enough then has been said about the Troglodyte and Satyr. And now we must come more closely to the principal argument of our dissertation, which is concerned with this question; *Are*

---

[1] *Nat. Hist. of Guiana*, p. 130.
[2] Vol. LIX. P. 1. for 1769, p. 71, Tab. III., of either sex. The female is repeated in *Gent. Mag.* 1770, September, p. 402. Comp. Pennant, *Synops. of Quadr.* p. 100.

men, and have the men of all times and of every race been of one and the same, or clearly of more than one species? A question much discussed in these days, but so far as I know, seldom expressly treated of.

Ill-feeling, negligence, and the love of novelty have induced persons to take up the latter opinion. The idea of the plurality of human species has found particular favour[1] with those who made it their business to throw doubt on the accuracy of Scripture. For on the first discovery of the Ethiopians, or the beardless inhabitants of America, it was much easier to pronounce them different species[2] than to inquire into the structure of the human body, to consult the numerous anatomical authors and travellers, and carefully to weigh their good faith or carelessness, to compare parallel examples from the universal circuit of natural history, and then at last to come to an opinion, and investigate the causes of the variety. For such is the subtlety of the human intellect, and such the rush for novelty, that many would rather accept a new, though insufficiently considered opinion, than subscribe to ancient truths which have been commonly accepted for thousands of years.

I have endeavoured to keep free of all these mistakes; I have written this book quite unprejudiced, and I have desired nothing so much as that the arguments which I have brought forward for the unity of the human species, and for its mere varieties, may seem as satisfactory to my learned and candid readers as they do to myself.

For although there seems to be so great a difference between widely separate nations, that you might easily take the inhabitants of the Cape of Good Hope, the Greenlanders, and the Circassians for so many different species of man, yet when the matter is thoroughly considered, you see that all do so run into one another, and that one variety of mankind does so sensibly

---

[1] Simon Tyssot de Patot, *Voyages et aventures de Jaques Massé*, T. 1. p. 36. Bazin (Voltaire), *Philosophie de l'histoire*, p. 45. Idem in *Quest. sur l'Encyclop.* T. IV. p. 112, T. VII. p. 98, 179, is completely refuted by Haller. *Briefen über einige Einwürfe noch lebend. Freygeister wider die Offenb.* 1. Th. pp. 101, 184, 196.
[2] Of this opinion were Griffith Hughes, *Nat. Hist. of Barbadoes*, p. 14. Henry Home, *Sketches of the History of Man*, Vol. I. p. 12.

pass into the other, that you cannot mark out the limits between them.

Very arbitrary indeed both in number and definition have been the varieties of mankind accepted by eminent men. Linnæus[1] allotted four classes of inhabitants to the four quarters of the globe respectively. Oliver Goldsmith[2] reckons six. I have followed Linnæus in the number, but have defined my varieties by other boundaries. The first and most important to us (which is also the primitive one) is that of Europe, Asia this side of the Ganges, and all the country situated to the north of the Amoor, together with that part of North America, which is nearest both in position[3] and character of the inhabitants. Though the men of these countries seem to differ very much amongst each other in form and colour, still when they are looked at as a whole they seem to agree in many things with ourselves. The second includes that part of Asia beyond the Ganges, and below the river Amoor, which looks towards the south, together with the islands, and the greater part of those countries which are now called Australian. Men of dark colour, snub noses, with winking eyelids drawn outwards at the corners, scanty, and stiff hair. Africa makes up the third. There remains finally, for the fourth, the rest of America, except so much of the North as was included in the first variety[4].

It will easily appear from the progress of this dissertation in

---

[1] *Syst. Nat.* p. 29.   [2] *Hist. of the Earth*, Vol. II. p. 211.

[3] Comp. besides the English terraqueous globes, which by the liberality of our queen the university library possesses, and the Swedish ones of Akerman, a copy of which is due to the kindness of J. Andr. Murray, the maps of D'Anville, Hasilin, and Engel, and the more recent labours of de Vaugondy, *Ser les pays de l'Asie et de l'Amérique situés au Nord de la mer du Sud.* Par. 1774, 4to.

[4] [3.] *Mankind divided into five varieties.* Formerly in the first edition of this work I divided all mankind into four varieties; but after I had more accurately investigated the different nations of Eastern Asia and America, and, so to speak, looked at them more closely, I was compelled to give up that division, and to place in its stead the following five varieties, as more consonant to nature.

The first of these and the largest, which is also the primeval one, embraces the whole of Europe, including the Lapps, whom I cannot in any way separate from the rest of the Europeans, when their appearance and their language bear such testimony to their Finnish origin; and that western part of Asia which lies towards us, this side of the Obi, the Caspian sea, mount Taurus and the Ganges; also northern Africa, and lastly, in America, the Greenlanders and the Esquimaux, for I see in these people a wonderful difference from the other inhabitants of America; and, unless I am altogether deceived, I think they must be derived from

which of the four varieties most discrepancies are still to be found, and on the contrary, that many in other varieties have some points in common, or in some anomalous way differ from the rest of their neighbours. Still it will be found serviceable to the memory to have constituted certain classes into which the men of our planet may be divided; and this I hope I have not altogether failed in doing, since for the reason I have given before I have tried this and that, but found them less satisfactory. Now I mean to go over one by one the points in which man seems to differ from man by the natural conformation of his body and in appearance, and I will investigate as far as I can the causes which tend to produce that variety.

First of all I shall speak of the whole bodily constitution, stature, and colour, and then I shall go on to the particular structure and proportion of individual parts. It will then be necessary carefully to distinguish those points which are due to art alone, and finally, though with reluctance, I shall touch upon

the Finns. All these nations regarded as a whole are white in colour, and, if compared with the rest, beautiful in form.

The second variety comprises that of the rest of Asia, which lies beyond the Ganges, and the part lying beyond the Caspian Sea and the river Obi towards Nova Zembla. The inhabitants of this country are distinguished by being of brownish colour, more or less verging to the olive, straight face, narrow eye-lids, and scanty hair. This whole variety may be sub-divided into two races, northern and southern; of which one may embrace China, the Corea, the kingdoms of Tonkin, Pegu, Siam, and Ava, using rather monosyllabic languages, and distinguished for depravity and perfidiousness of spirit and of manners; and the other the nations of northern Asia, the Ostiaks, and the other Siberians, the Tungueses, the Mantchoos, the Tartars, the Calmucks, and the Japanese.

The third variety comprises what remains of Africa, besides that northern part which I have already mentioned. Black men, muscular, with prominent upper jaws, swelling lips, turned up nose, very black curly hair.

The fourth comprises the rest of America, whose inhabitants are distinguished by their copper colour, their thin habit of body, and scanty hair.

Finally, the new southern world makes up the fifth, with which, unless I am mistaken, the Sunda, the Moluccas, and the Philippine Islands should be reckoned; the men throughout being of a very deep brown colour, with broad nose, and thick hair. Those who inhabit the Pacific Archipelago are divided again by John Reinh. Forster[1] into two tribes. One made up of the Otaheitans, the New Zealanders, and the inhabitants of the Friendly Isles, the Society, Easter Island, and the Marquesas, &c., men of elegant appearance and mild disposition; whereas the others who inhabit New Caledonia, Tanna, and the New Hebrides, &c., are blacker, more curly, and in disposition more distrustful and ferocious. Edit. 1781, pp. 51, 52.—This is the first sketch of the still famous division of mankind by Blumenbach; the well-known terms Caucasian, &c. will be found in the third ed. below.—Ed.)

[1] *Observations*, p. 228.

nosology and practical medicine, both, which chapters recent authors have tried to obtrude into natural history, but which I shall endeavour to vindicate for and restore to pathology.

The first three things I mean to discuss, the whole bodily constitution, the stature, and the colour, are owing almost entirely to climate alone. I must be brief on the first of these points, since I have had no opportunity of exercising my personal observation on the matter, and but few and scanty traces are to be gathered from authors. That in hot countries bodies become drier and heavier; in cold and wet ones softer, more full of juice and spongy, is easily noticed. It has long since been noticed by W. Cavendish, Marquis of Newcastle, that the bones of the wild horse have very small cavities, and those of the Frisian horses much larger ones[1], &c. This was confirmed by the elegant experiments of Kersting, a physician of Cassel, and a most skilled in the treatment of animals. He observed[2], amongst other things, that the bones of an Arab horse, of six years old, when subjected to the same degree of heat, were dissolved with much more difficulty in the machine of Papinus than those of a Frisian of the same age. It is very likely that similar differences would be observed in the bones of men born in different countries, although observations are wanting, and conclusions drawn from a few facts are unsatisfactory. Here and there indeed we find bones of Ethiopians[3] which are thick, compact, and hard; but I should be unwilling to attribute these properties to every skeleton coming from hot countries, since other instances occur of skulls of Ethiopians, about which the same remark has not been made[4]. The differences moreover are very great between the skulls of Europeans of the same country and the same age, which seem to depend, amongst other things,

---

[1] *Gen. Syst. of Horsemanship.* [The passage alluded to stands thus in the edition of 1743, Vol. I. p. 31. "I have experienced this difference between the bone of the leg of a Barbary horse, and one from Flanders, that the cavity of the bone in the one shall hardly admit of a straw whilst you may thrust your finger into that of the other."—ED.]

[2] Horses' bones are much more easily dissolved than those of mules, and asses' with still greater difficulty.

[3] B. S. Albini, *Suppl. Rar.* n. XIII. P. Paaw, *Prim. Anat.* p. 19.

[4] In the *Leg. Res.* n. XIII, and n. XLI, it is said that the bones of the Malabar women are very thin. See also J. Benj. de Fischer, *De modo quo ossa e vicin. accres. part.*, L.B. 1743, Tab. III.

principally upon the make of life[1]. Perhaps the same is the case as to the sutures, which Arrian[2] says the heads of the Ethiopians are without, and Herodotus[3] says the same of the Persian skulls after the battle of Plataea. The observation about the whole habit of the body, that the northern[4] nations are more sinewy and square, and the southern[5] more elegant, seems more reliable.

I go on to the human stature. It is an old opinion, that in very ancient times men were much larger and taller, and that they degenerate and diminish in size even now, that children are now born smaller than their parents, and all the things of this kind which the old poets[6] and philosophers[7] have said to discredit their own times.

But although this may be going too far, still we must allow something to climate, so far as that itself is altered by the lapse of time. The soil itself becomes milder, so that it may at last make its men less gigantic and less fierce. We have already spoken of an example of this change in our own Germany. But the idea that these differences of bodies in ancient and modern times have been enormous, is refuted by the mummies of Egypt, the fossil human skeletons[8], the sarcophagi, and a thousand other proofs.

Nor do a few skulls conspicuous for their age and size[9], scat-

---

[1] J. B. Com. a Covolo, *De act. duor. ess. ped. in quad. aliquot*, Bonan. 1765, p. 7.
[2] ἀρραφεῖς κεφάλαι. Arato.
[3] Cal. Rhodig. *Lect. Ant.* XIII. 28, p. 301. ed. Froben.
[4] For the *Lapps and Finns*, Loem, *Lules*, Högström, Calmucks, Pallas, *Greenlanders*, Crantz, &c.
[5] For New Zealand, New Holland, &c. see S. Parkinson. The inhabitants of the island of Mallicolo, lately visited by Forster, are remarkable for their slender arms and feet, as I have been kindly told by G. C. Lichtenberg since his return from England.
[6] Homer says repeatedly that Tydides, Hector, Ajax, Telamon, &c. (whose gigantic knee-cap Pausanias describes as being shown long afterwards) were much more strong and large than the men of his day, οἷοι νῦν βροτοί εἰσί. And he has been imitated in this by Virgil, who represents Turnus as equally large, not to be compared with 'Such human forms as earth produces now.'
[7] Plin. VII. c. 16. Solin. v. Comp. more upon this point J. S. Elsholtz, *Anthropom.* p. 31, ed. 1663.
[8] There is in the Museum of our University a fossil skull tolerably complete, of the greatest antiquity, the bones of the head very thick, but neither in magnitude nor form differing from a common skull.
[9] Fabricius Hildan, *Fürtreffl. nutz und nothw. d. anat.* Bern. 1614, p. 209. Head of March. Dietzmann killed at Leipzig, 1307. Glasey, Sacchs. *Kernhist.* Head

tered about here and there, prove anything more than those solid ones destitute of sutures, about which I was lately speaking. Some, it is clear, are diseased[1]. But as to the bones which credulous antiquity showed as those of giants, they have long since been restored to elephants and whales[2]. The investigation of the causes which in our days make the men of one country tall and another short is more subtle. The principal one seems to be the degree of cold or heat. The latter obstructs the increase of organic bodies, whilst the former adds to them and promotes their growth. It would be tedious even to touch upon a thing so well known and so much confirmed in both kingdoms, were it not that in our time men have come forward, and with the greatest confidence have presumed to think otherwise[3]. Experience teaches that both plants and animals are smaller in northern countries than in southern; why should not the same law hold good as to mankind? Linnæus long ago remarked in his *Flora Lapponica*[4], that alpine plants commonly reached twice as great an altitude out of the Alps. And the same thing may be observed frequently in those plants, some specimens of which are kept in a conservatory, while others stand out in a garden, of which the former come out much larger and taller than the others.

I have before me the most splendid specimens in a collection of plants from Labrador and Greenland, chosen by Brasen[5], which I owe to the liberality of my great friend, J. Sam. Lieberkühn, in which the common ones are almost all smaller than those which are obtained in Germany; and in some, as the

---

of Henry of Austria in the famous burying-place of Kœnigsfeld. Fassi, *Erdb. der eidgen.* I.

[1] Fossil head of Rhelms. Dargenville, *Oryct.* T. 17, f. 3, two osseous heads *Leg. rer. in Albin.* p. 4.

[2] J. Wallis, *Antiq. of Northumberland.* Dom. Gagliardi, *An. Oss.* p. 103. Even Felix Plater, who was the best lecturer of his day in all Europe, suffered himself to be led into error by the bones dug up at Lucerne in 1577, and after careful comparison gave them out as those of a human giant, *Obs. Med.* L. III. Wagner, *Hist. Nat. Helv.* p. 149: but they have lately been proved to be elephant's bones. *Erkl. der Gemälde auf die Kapellbr. zu Lucern.* This is also the case with the ribs of the Hun in the church of Göttingen.

[3] As Henr. Home, *loc. cit.* p. 11. *It is in vain to ascribe to the climate the low stature of the Esquimaux*, &c.

[4] *Prolegom.* 2 v. 1. 8. Comp. Arwid Ehrenmalm, *Awhle*, p. 386.

[5] The same observation has been made by Haller, *Hist. Stirp. Helv.* II. p. 317.

104   EXAMPLES.

Rhodiola rosea, which are common to both those regions of America, although their native soil is so near, yet the same difference is observed that the specimens from Labrador are somewhat larger than those from Greenland.

The same is the case with animals. The Greenland foxes are smaller than those of the temperate zone[1]. The Swedish and Scotch horses are low and small, and in the coldest part of North Wales so little as scarcely to exceed dogs in size[2]. It is however useless to bring a long string of examples about a thing so evident, when the difference of a few degrees in so many countries exhibits clearly the same difference. Thus, Henry Ellis[3] observed in Hudson's Strait, on its southern coasts, trees and men of fair size; at 61° shrubs only, and that the men became smaller by little and little, and at last at 67° that not a vestige of either was to be seen. And likewise Murray, within the limits of a few degrees, and in Gotha alone, declared he could observe so well, that whilst he was travelling, although he took no notice of the mile-stones, yet he could easily distinguish the different provinces by the difference of the inhabitants and of the animals. In Scania[4] the men are tall of stature and bony, the horses and cattle large, &c.: in Smaland they become sensibly smaller, and the cattle are active but little, which at last in Ostrogothia strikes the eye more and more.

The same thing may be observed in the opposite part of the world, almost under the same degrees, towards the antarctic circle. One example will suffice, taken from the most southern part of America, and compared with those European nations we have just been speaking of. The bodies of the notorious Patagonians answer to the lofty stature of the Scandinavians. A credulous antiquity indeed invented fabulous stories of their enormous size[5]. But in the progress of time, after Patagonia

---

[1] Crantz, *Hist. v. Gr.* p. 97.   [3] Th. Birch, *Hist. of the Royal Soc.* III. p. 171.
[2] *Voy. to Hudson's Bay*, p. 256.   [4] Comp. Linn. *Fauna Suecica*, p. 1.
[5] Comp. de Brosses, I. p. 193; II. beg. &c. De Pauw, *l. c.* I. p. 281, and *Hist. gén. de l'As. Afr. et Amér.* par M. L. A. R. Vol. XIII. Par. 1755. p. 50. Tom. Falkner, *Descr. of Patagonia*, p. 116, "The Patagonians, or Puelches, are a large-bodied people; but I never heard of that gigantic race, which others have mentioned, though I have seen persons of all the different tribes of southern Indians."

had often been visited by Europeans, the inhabitants, like that famous dog of Gellert, became sensibly smaller, until at last in our own days they retained indeed a sufficiently large stature, but were happily deprived of their gigantic form. If you go down from them towards the south, you will find much smaller men in the cold land of Terra del Fuego[1], who must be compared to the Smalands and the Ostrogoths, and by that example you will again see how nature is always like itself even in the most widely separated regions.

But besides the climate, there are other causes which exercise influence upon stature. Already, at first, I alluded to the mode of life[2], and it would be easy to bring here copious examples taken from the vegetable and animal kingdoms, in which the difference of nutrition may be detected by the greater or smaller stature. But these things are too well known already, and so many experiments of the kind have been made on Swiss cows, Frisian horses, &c., that I may easily pass over any proofs of this point. I omit also the causes of smaller importance which change the stature of organic bodies, which have been already most diligently handled by Haller[3], and I hasten to the last of those things which must be considered in the variety of mankind, that is, colour.

There seems to be so great a difference between the Ethiopian, the white, and the red American, that it is not wonderful, if men even of great reputation have considered them as forming different species of mankind. But although the discussion of this subject seems particularly to belong to our business, still so many important things have been said about the seat and the causes of this diversity of colour, by eminent men, that a good-sized volume would scarcely contain them; so that it is necessary for me to be brief in this matter, and only to mention those things which the industry of learned men has placed beyond all doubt. The skin of man and of most animals consists of

---

[1] Sydney Parkinson, p. 7, Pl. 1. 11. "None of them seemed above five feet ten inches high."
[2] p. 73.
[3] *Physiol.* L. xxx. s. 1, § 16.

three parts; the external epidermis, or cuticle; the *reticulum mucosum*, called from its discoverer the Malphigian; and lastly, the inner, or *corium*. The middle of these, which very much resembles the external, so that by many it is considered as another scale of it, is evidently more spongy, thick, and black in the Ethiopians; and in them, as in the rest of men, is the primary seat of the diversity of colour. For in all the *corium* is white, excepting where, here and there, it is slightly coloured by the adhering reticulum; but the epidermis seems to shade off into the same colour as the reticulum, yet still so, that being diaphanous[1] like a plate of horn, it appears even in black men, if properly separated, to be scarcely grey; and therefore can have little if any influence on the diversity of the colour of men.

The seat of colour is pretty clear, but for a very long time back there have been many and great disputes about the causes of it, especially in the Ethiopians. Some think it to be a sign of the curse of Cain[2] or Cham[3], and their posterity; others[4] have brought forward other hypotheses, amongst which the bile played the most prominent part, and this was particularly advocated by Peter Barrere[5], following D. Santorini[6]. Although this view has been opposed by many[7], I do not think it ought altogether to be neglected. The instances of persons affected with jaundice, or chlorosis, of the fish mullet[8], and moreover the black bile[9] of the Ethiopians, are all the less open to doubt, since more recent authors[10] have observed the blood to be black, and the brain and the spinal marrow to be of an ashy colour; and the phlegm of

---

[1] If the epidermis were less thin and not so transparent, perhaps it would seem just as dark as the reticulum; Jo. Fanton, *Diss. VII. Anat. pr. rraor.* Taurini, 1741, 8vo. p. 27.
[2] A recent supporter of this opinion is the learned Sam. Engel in *Ess. sur cette question quand et comm. l'Amér. a. t. été été peuplée*, T. IV. p. 96.
[3] *Mém. de Trevoux*, T. LXXIV. p. 1135.
[4] B. S. Albinus has collected many in *De sede et causa color. æth. et cet. hom.* L. B. 1737, with the beautifully coloured plates of that capital artist, J. Ladmiral.
[5] *Diss. sur la cause phys. de la couleur des nègres.* Paris, 1741, 12mo. Comp. *Dict. Encycl.* by De Felice, T. XXX. p. 199.
[6] *Obs. Anat.* p. 1.   [7] Le Cat, *De la coul. de la peau hum.* p. 72.
[8] Santorini, *l. c.*   [9] Barrere, *l. c.*
[10] Meckel, *Mém. de Berl.* 1753, 1757. The lice of the negroes are black, Long. II. p. 352.

the northern nations and other things of this kind seem to add weight to this opinion. But amongst all other causes of their blackness, climate, and the influence of the soil, and the temperature, together with the mode of life, have the greatest influence. This is the old opinion of Aristotle, Alexander, Strabo, and others[1], and one which we will try and confirm by instances and arguments brought forward separately.

In the first place, then, there is an almost insensible and indefinable transition from the pure white skin of the German lady through the yellow, the red, and the dark nations, to the Ethiopian of the very deepest black, and we may observe this, as we said just now in the case of stature, in the space of a few degrees of latitude. Spain offers some trite examples; it is well known that the Biscayan women are a shining white, the inhabitants of Granada on the contrary dark, to such an extent that in this region the pictures of the Blessed Virgin and other saints are painted of the same colour[2]. Those who live upon the northern bank of the river Senegal are of ashy colour and small body; but those beyond are black, of tall stature and robust, as if in that part of the world one district was green, and the other burnt up[3]. And the same thing was observed by some learned Frenchmen on the Cordilleras, that those who live immediately under the mountains towards the west, and exposed to the Pacific Ocean, seem almost as white as Europeans, whereas on the contrary, the inhabitants of the opposite side, who are exposed to constant burning winds, are like the rest of the Americans, copper-coloured[4].

It is an old observation of Vitruvius[5] and Pliny[6] that the northern nations are white, and this is clearly enough shown by many instances of other animals and plants. For partly the

---

[1] Cæl. Rhodig. *Lect. Ant.* IX. 15, p. 439, ed. Ald. Comp. Macrob. *in Somn. Scip.* p. 178, ed. H. Steph. αιδωψ εξ αιθω αι ωψ.
[2] Comp. a scale of colour in *Mém. de Trev. l. c.* p. 1190.
[3] Hist. Cardanes, *De subtilit.* L. XI. T. III. Oper. p. 555.
[4] Bouguer, *Voyage à Perou. Mém. de l'Acad. des Sc. de Paris*, 1744, p. 274.
[5] In the north are to be found nations of white colour, p. 104, ed. De Laert.
[6] On the opposite and icy side of the world are nations of white skin, T. I. p. 111, ed. Hard.

flowers[1] of plants, like the animals of the northern regions, are white, though they produce other colours in more southern latitudes; and partly in the more temperate zones animals only become white in winter, and in spring put on again their own natural colour. Of the former we have instances in the wolves[2], dogs[3], hares[4], cattle[5], crows[6], the chaffinch[7], &c., of the latter in the ermines[8], the squirrels[9], hares[10], the ptarmigan[11], the Corsican dog[12]. All of us are born nearly red, and at last in progress of time the skin of the Ethiopian infants turns to black[13], and ours to white, whereas in the American the primitive red colour remains, excepting so far as that by change of climate and the effects of their mode of life those colours sensibly change, and as it were degenerate.

It is scarce worth while to notice the well-known difference which occurs in the inhabitants of one and the same country, whose skin varies wonderfully in colour, according to the kind of life that they lead. The face of the working man or the artizan, exposed to the force of the sun and the weather, differs as much from the cheeks of a delicate female, as the man himself does from the dark American, and he again from the Ethiopian. Anatomists not unfrequently fall in with the corpses of the lowest sort of men, whose reticulum comes much nearer to the blackness of the Ethiopians than to the brilliancy of the higher class of Europeans. Such an European, blacker than an Ethiop, was dissected by Chr. Gottl. Ludwig[14]; a very dark reticulum has been observed by Günz[15], and very frequently by many others[16];

---

[1] Comp. Murray, *Prodr. Stirp. Gotti.* p. 18, who instances the *Campanula decurrens*, the common primrose, &c.
[2] Cranz, *Grœnl.* p. 97.   [3] Ib. p. 100.   [4] Ib. p. 95.
[5] Ehrenmalm, *l. c.* p. 349, "The further you go towards the north, the more frequently do animals of that kind occur."
[6] Jo. Nich. Pechlin, *De habitu et colore Æthiopum.* Kilon. 1677, 8vo. p. 141.
[7] Frisch, *Gesch. der Vogel.* Fasc. I.
[8] Wagner, *Hist. nat. Helv.* p. 180. Linn. *Faun. Suec.* p. 7. I myself have seen specimens in our own neighbourhood.
[9] Linn. l. c. p. 13. I have known too some caught near Jena.
[10] Ib. p. 10. Jetze, *Monogr. Lith.* 1749, 8vo.
[11] Cranz, l. c. p. 101.   [12] Linn. *Syst. Nat. Append.*
[13] Albinus, l. c. p. 12. Comp. Camper, *Dem. Anat. Path.* I. p. 1.
[14] *Ep. ad Haller.* Script. Vol. I. p. 393.   [15] On Hippoc. *De humor.* p. 140.
[16] Franc. de Rist, *De tact. org. in coll.* Haller, T. IV. p. 10. See Haller, *Physiol.* T. v. p. 18.

and I recollect that I myself dissected at Jena a man's corpse of this kind, whose whole skin was brown, and in some parts, as in the scrotum, almost black; for it is well known that some parts of the human body become more black than others, as, for example, the genitals of either sex, the tips of the breasts, and other parts which easily verge towards a dark colour. Haller observed in the groin of a woman the reticulum so black[1] that it did not seem to differ much from that of an Ethiopian; one as dark in the groin of a man was in the possession of B. S. Albinus; and it is so common an occurrence in a woman's breast, that I cannot be enough astonished that eminent men have been found to reckon the dark teats of the Samoyeds as prodigies[2], and therefore to consider that nation as a particular species of man[3].

Such a diversity of the reticulum is seen in other animals also, and especially in the face of the *Papio mandril*, a part of which I have therefore had engraved, (Pl. II. fig. 3.) There is a region of the upper part of the eyelids, of the root of the nose, and of the eye-brows, in which you may observe almost every variety of reticulum; the nose is plainly black, and also the part where the eye-brows are inserted; but that part which is lower and more on the outside is sensibly brown, and at length towards the outer corners of the eyes becomes pale. Not indeed that I have found this blackness of the nose equally intense in all the specimens of this ape which I have seen, since in apes, as in man and in other animals, the greatest variety of colour occurs in the reticulum. In two specimens of the *Simia cynomolgus* the tint of the face was not very different from that of an Ethiopian or a dark European; and this difference is so well known and so common throughout the animal kingdom, especially in the domestic quadrupeds, but above all in the vegetable[4]

---

[1] *L. c.* Alr. Kaav. Doerh. *Perspir.* Hipp. p. 21; so dark in the pudenda, that you would not believe the skin to be that of an European.
[2] *Mém. sur les Samojèdes et les Lappons*, 1762, 8vo. p. 44.
[3] Lord Kames, *l. c.*
[4] Two hundred years ago it was only the yellow tulip which was known in Europe; but what a variety of different coloured ones horticulturists are now acquainted with! See Haller, on the subject of the varieties of man. *Bibl. raisonnée*, 1744.

kingdom, that I can scarcely take notice of it, but prefer to return at once to man.

We see white men in a lower class rendered brown by a hard life; and it is equally certain that men of southern regions become whiter when they are less exposed to the effects of the weather and the sun. We have the most copious accounts by travellers of the inhabitants of Guzerat[1], of the Malabar coast[2], of the Caffres[3], of the Canadians[4], and the Otaheitans[5]. But besides their mode of life, old age and the change of country have an influence in making the Ethiopians more white. For when the Ethiopians begin to approach their seventieth year, the reticulum sensibly loses its dark colour, so that at last the bulbs come out yellow[6], and the hair and beard are grey like other nations; and if the young Ethiopian infants are brought into colder climates, it is certain that they lose a sensible quantity of their blackness[7], and their colour begins to verge more and more towards brown.

On the other hand, it is apparent that when white men reside a considerable time in the torrid zones they become brown, and sensibly verge towards black with much greater facility.

---

[1] J. Schreyer, Ostind. reis. p. 121.
[2] Tranquebar Miss. Ber. 27. Contin. p. 896. The more they dwell towards the north, and the more agreeable the race is, the more their black colour changes into brown, red, and yellow. The people of Harar are for the most part very black, and for the whole day long they work and are burnt up in sweat and dust by the rays of the sun. The better class of people do not go so much into the sun, and consequently they are not so black, &c. Comp. 30. Contin. p. 660.
[3] Müller. Linn. Syst. Nat. I. p. 95.
[4] Sir Francis Roberval in Hakluyt, Vol. III. p. 242. "The savages of Canada are very white, but they are all naked, and if they were apparelled as the French are they would be white and as fayre. But they paint themselves for feare of heat and sunne burning." "Those who are painted and who wear clothes, become so delicate in colour that they would be more readily taken for Spaniards than for Indians." La Hontan, t. sp. 16.
[5] Hawkesworth, II. p. 187.
[6] Wilh. J. Müller, Petu, p. 279. Mich. Hemmersam, Westind. Reisen. p. 38.
[7] The Colchians in the time of Herodotus were still black and had curly hair, p. 125, ed. Gronov. Leo Afric. P. 1. s. 3. L. M. A. a most competent judge, says in his Instit. Physiolog. Patav. 1773. 8vo. p. 194: "A cobbler of this nation is still living at Venice, whose blackness after a long lapse of years (for he came a boy to this country) has so sensibly diminished that he looks as if suffering slightly from jaundice." And I myself have seen a mulatto woman born from an Ethiopian father and a white mother near Gotha, who in her very earliest infancy was sufficiently dark; but in progress of time has so degenerated from her native colour, that she now only retains a sort of cherry or yellow tint of skin.

COLOUR.   111

The Spaniards who dwell under the equator in the new world have so much degenerated towards the native colour of the soil, that it has seemed very probable to eminent men[1], that had they not taken care to preserve their paternal constitution by intermarrying with Europeans, but had chosen to follow the same kind of life as the American nations, in a short time they would have fallen into almost the same coloration, which we see in the natives of South America. An Englishman who had spent only three years with the Virginians, became exactly like them in colour, and Smith[2], his countryman, could only recognize him by his language. A colony of Portuguese, who were carried to Africa[3] in the fifteenth century, can scarcely now be distinguished from the aborigines. The French, whether they emigrate to Africa or America, are invariably tinged with the brown colour of those countries[4]. I do not adduce here the numerous examples of Europeans who have become unnaturally black in their own country[5], or have brought forth black children[6], nor of Ethiopians who have been, at all events in some parts of their bodies, suddenly turned white[7], since all these cases seem to include something diseased or morbid.

As by the climate so also by the mode of life the colours of the body are seen to be changed. And this appears most clearly in the unions of people of different tints, in which cases the most distinct and contrary colours so degenerate, that white men may sensibly pass and be changed into black, and the contrary. The hybrid offspring (if we may use that word) are distinguished by particular names; in using which, however, the authors of travels vary so much, that it seemed to me worth while to collect as many of these synonyms as I could, to reduce them into grades of descending affinity, and exhibit them in a synoptic form.

---

[1] Mitchell, Philos. Transact. n. 474.   [2] Hist. Virgin. p. 116.
[3] Rech. sur les Amérie. L p. 186.   [4] Mém. de Trevoux, l. c. p. 1169.
[5] Many instances are collected by Le Cat, Conf. de la peau, p. 130.
[6] Cal. Rhedig. l. c. p. 776. Pichero, Le Cat, p. 109. A black princess was born to the queen of Louis XIV. Mém. de Trevoux, l. c. p. 1168. Abr. Kaav. Boerh. impet. fac. p. 354.
[7] Le Cat, p. 100. Frank, Philos. Tr. Vol. LI. Part L p. 176.

1. The offspring of a black man and a white woman, or the reverse, is called *Mulatto*[1], *Mollaka*[2], *Melatta*; by the Italians, *Bertin*, *Creole* and *Criole*[3]; by the inhabitants of Malabar, *Mestiço*[4]. The offspring of an American man and an European woman, *Mameluck*[5], and *Metif*[6].

2. The offspring of an European male with a Mulatto female is called *Terceron*[7], *Castiço*[8]. The son of an European female from a *Metif* is called a *Quarteroon*[9]. The offspring of two Mulattoes is called *Casque*[10]; and of blacks and Mulattoes, *Griffs*[11].

3. A Terceron female and an European produce *quaterons*[12], *postiços*[13]. But the American quarteroon (who is of the same degree as the black Terceron) produces from an European *octavoons*[14].

4. The offspring of a quateroon male and a white female, a *quinteroon*[15]; the child of an European woman with an American octavoon is called by the Spaniards *Puchuela*[16].

It is plain therefore that the traces of blackness are propagated to great-grandchildren; but they do not keep completely

---

[1] *Hist. of Jamaica*, II. p. 260. Aublet, *Plantes de la Guiane Françoise*, T. II. p. 122, App.
[2] Hammersmn, *l. c.* p. 36.
[3] Thomas Hyde on Abr. Perizol. *Cosmograph.* p. 99, ed. Oxon. 1691, 4to.
[4] Christ. Langhan's *Ostind. Reise.* p. 216. Tranquebar Miss. Ber. Cont. 33, p. 919. *Mestiço Lusitan.* that is, of mixed race.
[5] *Hist. de l'Ac. des Sc. de Paris*, 1724, p. 18.
[6] Labat, *Voy. aux Isles de l'Amér.* II. p. 131. Recherch. sur les Amér. I. p. 199. Newly-born metifs are distinguished by the colour of the genitals from true blacks, for it is well known that those parts are black even in the Ethiopian fœtus. Phil. Femelle, *sur l'œconomie animale*, Part I. p. 180. This author calls the offspring of the black male and the Indian female *Kakowgle*, and the offspring of these and the whites *Mulattos*, p. 179.
[7] *Hist. of Jamaica*, *l. c.*
[8] Langhan's Tranqu. Ber. *l. c.* Castiço, de boa casta, of a good stock.
[9] De Pauw, *l. c.*   [10] *Commerc. Paris. l. c.*
[11] Ib. p. 17. It is plain that the offspring of a Mestiço and a Malabar woman are black. *Relat. Tranquerb. l. c.* Those from a Mulatto are called Sambo in *Hist. of Jamaica*, *l. c.* p. 261, and the offspring of these and blacks become blacks again.
[12] *Hist. of Jam.* L. c. p. 260.
[13] Langhan's *Rel. Tranq. l. c.* Postiço means *adopted*: thus *cabello postiço*, false hair.
[14] De Pauw, *l. c.* p. 120.
[15] *Hist. of Jam. l. c.* The children of Postiços and whites are clearly white. Tranqu. Ber. *l. c.* According to the author of the *Hist. of Jamaica* the children of a quinteroon and a white man become white.
[16] De Pauw, *l. c.*

the degrees we have just noticed, for twins sometimes are born of different colours; such as Fermin[1] says came from an Ethiopian woman, of which the male was a mulatto, but the female, like the mother, an intense black. And from all these cases, this is clearly proved, which I have been endeavouring by what has been said to demonstrate, that colour, whatever be its cause, be it bile, or the influence of the sun, the air, or the climate, is, at all events, an adventitious and easily changeable thing, and can never constitute a diversity of species.

A great deal of weight has attached to this opinion in consequence of the well-known examples of those men, whose reticulum has been conspicuously variegated and spotted with different colours. Lamothe[1] has described very carefully a boy of this kind from the Antilles. Labat[2] saw the wife of a Grifole like this, a native of Cayenne, and in other respects handsome. Chr. D. Schreber[4] has collected many examples; and I myself had lately an opportunity of seeing an instance of this sort of variegated skin. One of my friends, a physician, has a reticulum of almost a purple colour, and distinctly marked with very white spots, of different sizes, but equal in other respects, and similar to the most shining skin. And on the back of his right hand there were five white spots of the same kind, of which each was almost equal to a thumb's breadth in diameter, interspersed with numerous smaller ones. This phenomenon very seldom occurs in men; but is very common in animals, especially in the reticulum of quadrupeds. The throats of rams, for example, are frequently so variegated, that you may observe in them the greatest similarity, both to the black skin of the Ethiop and the white skin of the European. I have examined many flocks of sheep in their pastures with this object, and I think I have observed, that the greater or smaller number of black spots in the jaws answer to the greater or smaller quantity of black wool on the animals themselves.

---

[1] l. c. p. 178.   [2] Hamb. Mag. xix. p. 400.
[3] Voy. en Esp. et en Ital. 1. p. 176.
[4] Saeugthiere, p. 15. I shall speak below about the spotting of the skin from diseases, which must be clearly distinguished from the instances in the text.

I will say no more of colour; and now, having disposed of all the general varieties of the whole human body, I will go on to the diversity of the separate parts and members; and will make a beginning with the head and its conformation. In the same way that it is always the case that there is the greatest possible difference between the skeleton of the embryo and the adult, so above all, the bones of the skull differ to such an extent in both, that you would scarcely recognize them as parts of the same body. For the bones which, in the adult, constitute a very solid case, and the hardest possible receptacle of what is at once the softest and noblest entrail, in the embryo appear only as thin but broad scales, "which," to use the words of Coiter[1], "are just fastened together by soft, broad, loose and flaccid bonds, sutures and commissures." Now the skull of the infant is wet and soft clay, and fit to be moulded into many forms before it is perfectly solidified, so that if you consider the innumerable and simultaneous external and adventitious causes in operation, you will no longer be able to wonder that the forms of skulls in adults should be different. But since for a considerable period of time singular shapes of the head have belonged to particular nations, and peculiar skulls have been shaped out, in some of them certainly by artificial means, it will be our business to look at these things a little more carefully, and to consider how far they constitute different varieties of the human race. For, although I only intend to reckon up in a passing way those differences of the human body which are due to art alone, still I intend to treat now a little more at length upon that part of the argument which has to do with skulls, since things very nearly allied may be conveniently embraced and handled at the same time. Claudius Galen[2], besides the common and symmetrical skull[3], had already described other skulls, which in some of their parts manifestly differed

---

[1] *De foet. hum. et inf. oss.* p. 59.
[2] *De usu part.* L. IX. p. m. 544 and *De oss.* v. 1. Ph. Ingrassias in h. l. Comm. Panormi, 1603, fol. p. 68, fig. 1—4.
[3] See the dimensions and definitions of these in Alb. Dürer, von menschl. proport. Fol. P. and Q. ed. 1528. Elsholz l. c. p. 55. Petr. Laurembergs, Pasicompas, p. 62, ed. 1634.

from the common structure; and Andrew Vesalius' and Barth. Eustachius' endeavoured to draw figures of them. But the forms of these skulls seem to be so arbitrary and so monstrous, that they are of little or no use to us at present, and seem rather to belong to some morbid constitutions of the bones than to any natural varieties of heads. Let us follow nature herself, and we shall reckon up the various shapes of the head in the various nations, according to the four varieties of mankind which we constituted.

To begin with Germany itself, Vesalius[1] says that its inhabitants are generally remarkable for having the occiput compressed and the head wide; and gives as a reason that infants in their cradles generally sleep on their backs, and besides being wrapped in swaddling-clothes, generally have their hands tied to their sides. This author also saw in the cemeteries of Styria and Carinthia wonderfully different skulls, which from their extraordinary shape seemed to be sports of nature[2]. Lauremberg[3] says the female inhabitants of Hamburg of his day were long-headed, because they by ligaments and a foolish practice were accustomed to elongate the head from the birth. The Belgians are said to have their skulls more oblong[4] than other nations, because the mothers permit their infants to sleep wrapped up in swaddling-clothes very much on the side and the temples[5]; but however the description of a Batavian skull by De Fischer does not answer to this[6], who praises in it the bones of the skull for being but little depressed around the sides, and making there almost an equal arch. Albinus[7] declares that the skulls of the

---

[1] *De corp. hum. fabr.* p. 21, ed. 1555.
[2] Tab. XLVI. f. 10, 15, 17, a little less monstrous than the figures of Vesalius and Ingrassias. The worst of all are in Maith. Merian, *Viv. ic. part. corp. hum.* in C. Bauhin, *Th. Anat.* L. III. T. I. Comp. Bertici, *Osteolog.* at the end of Part II.
[3] *l. c.* p. 23, and in Pet. Apol. exas. (Gabr. Cuneus), p. 838, *Opera.* Insfeldt says the shape of the German skull is half-way between the oblong of the Belgians and the round skull of the Turks. *De lus. nat.* L. B. 1772, p. 20.
[4] *Observ. Fallop. exam.* p. 768, ed. B. S. Albini.
[5] *l. c.* p. 63. [6] Insfeldt, *l. c.* [7] Vesalius, *l. c.*
[8] J. B. de Fischer, *De modo quo sunt a ricinis accommodant partibus.* L. B. 1743. 4to. Tab. III. A reversed copy is given by J. Casp. Lavater, *Physiognom. Progr.* Vol. II. p. 159, Tab. B. fig. I.
[9] *Ind. leg. Rar.* p. 2.

English, the Spanish, and French, are without any peculiarity of structure at all; and he is in most respects a very accurate observer of varieties of that kind. Christopher Pflug informed Vesalius that the skulls of the inhabitants of the Styrian Alps were of a singular shape. The same Vesalius is of opinion that the heads of the Genoese, and still more of the Greeks and the Turks, are nearly of the shape of a sphere, and that it is done through the care of the midwives when they bring their assistance, and sometimes through the great solicitude of the mothers[1].

There is a passage in Hippocrates[2] about the skulls of the Scythians, which is most worthy of notice. He says that after they had applied artificial means for a very long period in shaping their heads, at last a kind of natural degeneration had taken place, so that in his day there was no more necessity for manual pressure to arrive at the end in view, but that the skulls grew up to be elongated of their own accord. And this kind of thing should be examined in other varieties of mankind, especially as to form and colour, and their various causes, climate, &c., which in the progress of time become hereditary and constant, although they may have owed their first origin to adventitious causes. The nations towards our north have generally flatter faces[3]. Eber. Rosen is, so far as I know, the only writer who says that the Lapps of Lulah can, for the most part by the face being broad above[4], attenuated below, with the cheeks falling in, and terminated in a long chin, be distinguished from the other Scandinavians[5]. J. B. de Fischer[6] has published a drawing of a Calmuck's skull, and it is ugly, and nearly ap-

---

[1] l. c. But I do not see how Winkelmann (*Gesch. der Kunst des Alterth.* T. 1, p. 74) can use this passage of Vesalius to prove the influence of a more favourable climate and sky, when the Brussels anatomist attributes it to art alone. Moreover those skulls of the Turks which are preserved in the Royal Museum are much less oval, and of much less elegant shape than the common heads of our countrymen: and therefore a man so learned in his art ought to have said less about their beauty.

[2] *De aër. aqu. et loc.* 35.

[3] Goldsmith, *l. c.* p. 214.

[4] The jaws of the skull of a Malabar woman are also narrow. *Lay. Rav.* p. 3.

[5] *De Medic. Lappon. Luleus.* Lond. Goth. 1751. Engraved in Hall. *Coll. disp. pract.* 1v.

[6] l. c. p. 14, Tab. 1. Ixufeldt, l. c. also calls the head of the Calmuck square.

proaches a square in shape, and in many ways testifies to barbarism. But this single example shows how unfair it is to draw conclusions as to the conformation of a whole race from one or two specimens. For Pallas[1] describes the Calmucks as men of a symmetrical, beautiful, and even round appearance, so that he says their girls would find admirers in cultivated Europe. Nor do the said skulls answer to the two very accurate representations of that Calmuck, a boy of eleven years old, who lately came from Russia with the court of Darmstadt, drawings of whom I received from Carlsruhe. They represent a young man of handsome shape, lofty forehead and eye-brows; and whose face agrees in this respect with the description of Pallas, and diverges from the skull in question, that the mouth makes nearly an equilateral triangle with the eyes furthest from it, which brings out the head round instead of square. Passing from the most north-easterly part of Asia by the Anadirski Archipelago into North America, we come to the tribes whose name is derived from the singular form of their heads[2]. Either I am very much mistaken, or it is a skull of this sort which has been described by Winslow[3], and engraved by him. With its very protracted occiput, its somewhat flat forehead, the shape of the orbits, and other aberrations of that sort from the common structure, it seems to present some similarity to the skull of a dog. We know at present too little of the history of that country and its inhabitants to be able to add the cause of that singular conformation: but whatever it be, it seems that it must rather be in the mode of life, since the same peculiarity is observed sometimes in the skulls of Europeans. I myself have in my possession a skull, very ancient, dug out last summer from the city cemetery, which is as like that American in the points I have mentioned[4], and in every thing else, as one egg is to another.

---

[1] *Reis.* I. pp. 307, 311.
[2] *Tête-plaies*, or *plate ôtes de chiens*. De Vangondy, *l. c.* p. 27, lat. 65°, long. 175°. Engel, *Tab. & c. Borral.*
[3] *Mém. de l'Ac. des Sc. de Paris,* 1722, p. 323, Tab. 16. It is said to have been found in Hood-Eyland, lat. 78°, long. 310°.
[4] It measures six Paris inches and more from the apex of the nasal bone to the extreme bulging part of the occipital bone; but only four in diameter from the

Finally, as to the inhabitants of Greenland, and of Labrador, the former we are told by Cranz[1], and the latter by Henry Ellis[2], are longheaded and have flat faces. But I am afraid that the accounts of these most trustworthy men have been badly understood by many, who have thence come to the conclusion that these nations are badly formed and almost monstrous in shape[3]. Cranz himself says that a great many Greenlanders are to be found with faces so oblong that it is difficult to distinguish them from Europeans[4]; but as to the Esquimaux, I am led to a contrary opinion by some very accurate drawings of three inhabitants of Labrador, which have lately come into my possession, and are painted in colours with great care by that excellent artist J. Swertner, from copies sent by the Hernnhut Brothers, who have an establishment there. One is a male; and the two females, according to the custom of their nation, are clad with immense greaves, nearly reaching to their hips, and one of them carries a child in her right sandal[5]; all however are of a reasonably symmetrical and well-proportioned form. The face of the male is rather flat, and the nose but little prominent, though by no means turned up, the body square, and the head large, so as to be equal to the sixth part of his whole height; but the women are taller, and are seven of their own heads in length[6]; and if you except their colour[7], which verges towards brown, are in other respects of good appearance.

Let us turn to Asia, and look at our second variety, which dwells beyond the Ganges, and on the Islands, &c. The first

---

condyloid apophyses of the foramen magnum to the top of the head: the foramen magnum is placed rather towards the front, and so the occiput is longer, and the bones of the head descend in a more acute angle towards the base of the skull than in Winslow's example; and so in that it resembles the skull of Cowper's skeleton. *Myol. reform.* fig. XVIII.

[1] *Hist. of Greenl.* p. 179.
[2] *Voy. to Hudson's Bay*, p. 132.
[3] Henr. Home, *l. c.* Buffon, T. III. p. 485.
[4] This is confirmed by the pictures of the Greenlanders made after the life by Adam Olearius, *Gottorf. Kunstk.* Tab. III. F. 1—3.
[5] Cranz, *Portaits.* p. 310. Ellis, p. 136.
[6] They are placed by Alb. Dürer in his tables between A1 and B1.
[7] Which is caused by their mode of life. Cranz, *Portaits.* l. c. Comp. with *Hist.* p. 178.

thing we see are the Aracani on the Ganges, who flatten the foreheads of the newly-born with sheets of lead.

After these, going up to the Amur (Sahalien ula), the northern termination of this variety, come the Chinese, who, unless I am wrong, are less content than any other of the inhabitants of this world, with the natural conformation of their body, and therefore use so many artificial means to distort it, and squeeze it, that they differ from almost all other men in most parts of their bodies. Their heads are usually oval, their faces flat, their eyes narrow, drawn up towards the external corners, their noses small, and all their other peculiarities of this kind are well known from the numerous pictures of them, and from their china and pottery figures. Those Chinese whom Büttner saw at London were exactly of this kind, and so also was the great botanist Whang-at-tong *(the yellow man of the East)*, whose acquaintance was made there by Lichtenberg. But these artificial ways of moulding the head seem to have more to do with the soft parts of the face than the bony structure, for Daubenton[1] reckons up many skulls of the Chinese and Tartars, and declares that they differ in no way from the ordinary skulls of Europeans. The other nations of this variety looked at as a whole answer to those characters which I laid down above as belonging to them.

The New Hollanders make such a transition to the third variety, that we perceive a sensible progress in going from the New Zealanders through the Otaheitans to the fourth. The inhabitants of the Island Mallicolo[2], whom I was just speaking of, differ from their neighbours by the strange form of head, in which late travellers assure us they approach nearest to the figure of apes[3]. I do not see anything remarkable in the skulls

---

[1] *Descr. du Cab. du roi*, Vol. XIV. n. M.CCC.XXXIX.
[2] It is situated with Tanna and New Caledonia in 15° S. L., and is nearly as many degrees from the east coast of New Holland.
[3] I hope it will be agreeable to my readers if I append a short description of these men, taken from the account of the younger Forster, and communicated to me by Lichtenberg. "Contrary to all expectation, we found the inhabitants differing in everything from all the other people we had hitherto seen in the Southern Ocean. They were of small stature, rarely exceeding 5 ft. 4 in. Their limbs were slender, and ill-shaped; their colour blackish-brown, which was made more intense

of the remaining inhabitants of the Pacific Ocean; and so we will go on to the third variety of mankind, that is, the African nations, about whom we may be brief, since what there is to be said about their skulls is of small importance. Those skulls of mummies which I have seen are of round and spherical, but still of elegant and symmetrical form.

The head of an Ethiop from the southern part of Africa has been carefully described by J. Beni de Fischer, as I quoted above[1]. Broader in the upper region, suddenly narrowed, sharpened from the front towards the middle of the frontal bone and over the eyes, and widely stretched out below these, and very globular behind, he says that in its whole periphery it comes to be nearly of a triangular shape. And yet this description is scarcely satisfactory when I compare it with the Ethiopians that I have seen myself and carefully examined, or with that skull of Peter Pauw[2]; for this latter, if you except the large occiput and the narrow orbits, has very little resemblance to the description and very accurate engraving of Fischer.

There remains the fourth variety of the human race belonging to America[3], except that part we have just been speaking of. The same thing may be said of the inhabitants of this quarter, which I have just observed about the Chinese, that they take great pains, and employ artificial means, to distort the natural form of their bodies into some other. This is especially the case with the head; and the most numerous evidences of the wonderful ways in which they compress it are to be found in the stories of travellers; but still we are deficient in any accurate examina-

---

In the face, and the greater part of the body, by a black pigment. Their head was singularly formed, for it receded more from the root of the nose than other men's, and presented such a resemblance to that of the ape, that with one accord we all expressed our astonishment at it. Their noses and lips did not seem more misshapen than those of other nations of the Northern Ocean. The hair of their head was black, curly, and woolly; their beard thick and long, and less like wool. They gird the abdomen with a rope so tightly, that it seems nearly divided into two parts. So far as we saw they had no other covering, except in one place: but this had so little the effect of concealing what other nations try to hide, that it made it only still more conspicuous."

[1] *l. c.* Tab. III. pp. 14, 26. Is it the same in *Legal. Rav.* n. XIII. Isselidt *l. c.* The head of the Ethiopians approaches the triangular shape.

[2] *Primit. Anat.* p. 19.   [3] *Recherch. philos. sur les Amer.* t. p. 146.

tions of skulls of this kind, nor is it sufficiently clear in what parts of the head the greatest change takes place. J. Cardan[1] said that the heads of the inhabitants of the old Portus Provinciae were square, and deficient in the occiput. Hunauld[2] has exhibited the skull of a Carib, but it has been either so carelessly engraved, or is so misshapen, that I should prefer to consider it as a monstrosity, than to believe such to be the osseous conformation of a whole nation. The enormous bones of the nose, the little holes which give an exit to the nerves and arteries of the same size as the external auditory canal, the angular and large-lobed zygoma, the upper jaw deeply incised for the matrices of the teeth, and other things of this sort, excite a suspicion that this drawing was done in a hurry[3]. Finally, as to North America, Charlevoix describes the heads of one of the Canadian nations as globular, and the other as flat[4].

So much then about the shape of skulls. From what has been said I trust that it is more than sufficiently clear, that almost all the diversity of the form of the head in different nations is to be attributed to the mode of life and to art: although I should very willingly admit the position of Hippocrates, that with the progress of time art may degenerate into a second nature, since it has a very considerable influence in all the other variations of mankind.

The physiognomy and the peculiar lineaments of the whole countenance in different nations opens up a very vast and agreeable field. In many they are sufficiently settled, and are such faithful exponents of the climate and the mode of life, that even after many generations spent in a foreign climate they can still be recognized. But, besides other reasons, the want of sufficiently faithful and accurately delineated pictures forbids me to wander in that direction. I took a great deal of pains to compare pictures drawn from the life of more remote and, at present, little known nations; but I have been able to obtain very

---

[1] *De rer. variet.* L. VIII. c. XLIII. p. 163. T. III. *Oper.* Cap. Maragnon, Brasil.
[2] *Mem. de l'Ac. des Sc. de Paris,* 1740. p. 373. Tab. 16. fig. 1.
[3] *Hist. de la nouvelle France,* III. pp. 187, 314. Algonquins. Têtes de Boule.
[4] *Ib.* p. 373. Flat heads: each a work of art.

few; and there are not many authors of travels whose pictures, so far as regards the likenesses of nations, can be trusted. If you except the vast work of the brothers De Bry, the first editions of the travels of Cornelius Le Brun, the Tartary of Nic. Witsen, the diary of Sydney Parkinson, and the voyages of Cook himself, and except some genuine representations scattered about here and there in various books, especially in the work of S. R. Lavater on physiognomy, there are many nations of whom you can find no trustworthy pictures.

Meanwhile, it will be enough to bring forward a few examples, of which the Jewish race presents the most notorious and least deceptive, which can easily be recognized everywhere by their eyes alone, which breathe of the East. The Vallones, though they have lived among the Swedes for many years, still preserve the lineaments of the face, which are peculiar to them, and by which they can be distinguished at the first glance from the aborigines[1]. The clear and open countenance of the Swiss, the cheerful one of the young Savoyards, the manly and serious Turks[2], the simple and guileless look of the nations of the extreme north[3], can easily be distinguished, even by those least skilled in physiognomy.

The matter is a little more difficult in some nations of the south, especially in the west of Europe, who, it has been observed by some eminent men, from some reason or other, are cheerful and sanguine in youth, but, as manhood advances, become more morose, and inclined to be of a melancholy temperament[4]. In our other varieties the lineaments of the face are very much more persistent. To say nothing of the Chinese, who I have mentioned make their heads so much out of shape that it would be hazardous to say how much in them is to

---

[1] Clas Alströmer *Om den Ja-ulliga får-arela*. Stock. 1770. 8vo. p. 76.
[2] Russel, *Aleppo*. Niebuhr, *Reis. &c.*
[3] Samojed. Le Brun, *Voy. Amst.* 1718. f. n. 7, 8, and p. 9. The Tartars of Niberia, *ib.* p. 104. The Ostiaks, p. 112. The Greenlanders in Olear. *l. c.* The Esquimaux in our pictures approach very much to the Samojed. Le Brun, n. 7 and 8.
[4] Boerhaave, *Prael. in propr. inst.* s. 879. "The Italians, Portuguese, and Spanish are vivacious and playful up to the eighteenth year: after the thirtieth year they all become sad, morose, melancholy, and subject to hæmorrhages."

be referred to nature and how much to art, the inhabitants of
the Pacific Ocean retain evident examples of persistent physiognomy. Every one, for instance, will recognize the fierce and
savage countenance of the New-Hollanders and New-Zealanders
by looking at the magnificent plates of Parkinson[1], whereas the
Otaheitans, on the contrary, looked at as a whole, seem to be
of a milder disposition, as also the many pictures[2] of them by
the same well-known author testify[1].

Although almost all the nations of Africa are sufficiently distinguished by persistent and peculiar lineaments of face, still the
ancient Egyptians, and the inhabitants of the south of Africa,
differ very much by their singular physiognomy from the rest,
both of the Africans and of mankind. All the monuments of the
old art of the ancient Egyptians, from the statue of Memnon down
to the pottery scals which are found with the mummies, show
likenesses very similar, and all closely resembling each other.
The face is somewhat long, but by no means emaciated, the nose
prominent, broad towards the nostrils, and ending in a sharpish
lobe, and finally the mouth small, girdled with swelling lips, all of
which are most positive and unmistakeable signs of the Egyptian head. The appearance of the Ethiopians is so well known
that it would be superfluous to say much on that point. Their
depressed nose, which has been attributed by some to art[4], most
recent authors, and those eye-witnesses, have shown to be due
to nature[5], and the two Ethiopian fœtuses preserved in the
Royal Museum are exactly like the figures of Ruysch[6] and
Seba[7], and answer to this description. For although the nose
in almost all human embryos is depressed, still the Ethiopians

---

[1] Pl. xvii. xxiii. xxviii. &c.   [2] Pl. viii.
[3] When their faces are seen in profile, they are very distinct from the smooth
and equable countenance of the Chinese, through their distinctly prominent nose,
lips, and chin, &c. This was often observed in the men of both nations by Lichtenberg, who knew the Chinese I was speaking of and the Otaheitan O-mai (which
is commonly, but wrongly made a trisyllable O-mai-a) at London, and has often
wondered at the diversity of their faces.
[4] Hemmerman, p. 37.   [5] Müller, Fets, p. 31.
[6] Thes. Anat. III. t. 2. The forehead is more narrow than in any other fœtus,
as is shown by one of the specimens in the Royal Museum.
[7] Thes. T. i. Tab. cxi. f. 2.

of whom we are speaking have their noses, or interstices (to use the expression of Isidore, so expanded, that even setting aside the swelling lips, any one could tell the nation from them alone.

A few variations of the human body remain besides those which I think should be attributed to art alone, and which have to do with the peculiar formation of members and parts. The hair varies very much amongst most men, both in colour and form, but in some nations is of a constant character. And as it is said to be universal that white colours obtain more in the north, and brown in the south, so black hair and black eyes seem to be usual in the torrid zones, and light hair with blue eyes in the colder regions[1]. But, beyond all, the hair of the Ethiopians is conspicuous for its intense black and its singular woolliness, which however is no more congenital with them than the colour of their skin, but both have been contracted, as we have seen, by the progress of time and the heat of the sun[2]. For the Ethiopian fœtus, I mentioned, is covered with light brown straight hairs, which scarcely differ from the down of the European embryo; so that it is probable that the tint of the skin and the hair are changed sensibly at the same time. I have already observed that the Ethiopians get paler in old age, and that their hair also grows white; and it is a well-known thing, that in other men, in proportion as their skin is brown, so are the genitals covered with curly hair. We are also told in his last work, by D. Antonius de Ulloa[3], that the Ethiopians of Darien have hair, though black, still straight. Others too have declared, and I myself have often observed, that the structure of the Ethiopian hair is the same as that of other men, and the bulb of it as white.

Many authors tell us that the feet of the Ethiopians are badly formed, in more than one way. The author of the

---

[1] Avicenna, Canon. L. 1. Fen. L v. Haller, Elem. Physiol. T. v. p. 36.
[2] Carl Khrafigin. l. c. p. 440, ed. Ald. For dried-up hair is turned black and bent.
[3] Noticias Americanas. Madrid, 1772. 4to. Entretenim. XVII. p. 305.

Moretum (said to be Virgil) reckons up their many defects as follows[1]:

> With legs so thin, and feet so widely splayed,
> The wrinkled heels perpetual slits betrayed.

And Hier. Mercurialis agrees with him, for he says that these slits in the feet are endemic to the Ethiopians[2]. Another passage worthy of notice is to be found in Petronius[3], which, as Heyne[4] tells us, refers to the Ethiopian slaves, like those we call negroes. Cœl. Rhodiginus[5] says that the Egyptians and Ethiopians have splay feet, &c., which, however, do not seem to be by any means common to entire nations; for Albert Durer[6], after speaking of these deformities in the feet of the Ethiopians, adds that he has seen many well and symmetrically formed; nor was I able to observe anything of this kind in the Ethiopians I have seen myself.

That the breasts of the Ethiopian[7] and other[8] southern women are pendulous and contracted, from their mode of life and habits of lactation, wants scarcely any testimony adduced. To those mutations of the human body which are occasioned by the mode of life, we may also add those which owe their origin to the difference of languages, and which are sometimes to be found in the very organs of speech. To attribute this difference, with J. Senebier[9], to the influence of heat or cold, is forbidden by a slight comparison of neighbouring languages. Who could possibly attribute to the climate the fact that the Ephraimites said *Sibolet* instead of *Schibolet;* that the Chinese cannot pronounce the letters *R* and *D;* or the Spaniards the final *M,* or the inhabitants of the Marquesas and the Greenlanders of Kamtschadale *Tsch* and *ks.* But the prodigious labours of

---

[1] v. 35.   [2] *De decorat.* p. 103.
[3] c. 102. "Can we fill our lips with an ugly swelling? can we crisp our hair with an iron? and mark our forehead with scars? and distend our shanks into a curve? and draw our heels down to the earth? and change our beard into a foreign fashion?"
[4] Ad *Morell,* l. s.   [5] *l. c.* ed. Ald.
[6] *l. c.* Fol. T. 117.   [7] Fermin, *Œcon. Anim.* p. 117.
[8] Hottentots. Kolben, *V'oyrb. de p. H.* p. 474. The inhabitants of Horn Island in Le Maire, and Schouten in Dalrymple's *Collect.* T. II. p. 58.
[9] *L'Art d'observer.* Genev. 1775, 8vo. T. II. p. 237.

Büttner on this point forbid me to be more prolix on the matter, for he has collected with incredible labour all that relates to the subject, and will very soon give it to the press.

I pass on to those things which, besides the shape of the head, are apt to be changed by the aid of art in the other parts of the body amongst various nations. And first of all I mean to speak of mutilations, where members and parts of the body are cut or torn out, &c. The Scriptures, and the stories of Herodotus[1] about the Colchians, the Egyptians and the Ethiopians, and the wide extent of the practice[2], all prove that circumcision is exceedingly ancient. Nor is it confined entirely to the stronger sex, for amongst many oriental people it is applied to the weaker sex, and that part of their pudenda which answers[3] to the prepuce of the virile member is cut off; of which ceremony copious testimony both from ancient and modern writers has been collected by Mart. Schurigius[4] and Theod. Tronchin[5]. It will be enough for us at present to give our readers a drawing (Pl. II. fig. 4) of the genitals of a circumcised girl of eighteen years old, which I owe to the kindness of Niebuhr, who has also allowed me to give it to the public. When that famous company went to travel in Asia, one of the questions proposed to them was about this circumcision of both sexes[6]; and this illustrious man[7], who was the sole survivor of the expedition, settled this, as well as almost all the others; so much so as to bring back this drawing I am speaking of, which the great artist, G. W. Baurenfeind, had taken from the life. In it you can see the body itself of the clitoris, bare and deprived of its prepuce, hanging from the upper commissure of the labia,

---

[1] pp. 101. 125. ed. Grœn.
[2] The negroes of Angola. Hughes, Barbad. p. 14. The Otaheitans. Reinh. Forster, l. c. p. 169.
[3] So also P. Bellon, Obs. l. III. c. 28; although he adds obscurely, that the part which is in Greek called Aymnera is in Latin alas. Theraenot says they do not spare even these alæ or wings. Voy. l. n. c. 74. However the Greek words for these parts are often confounded: see their genuine explanations in H. Stephani Diction. Med. pp. 536, and 599, and Joach. Camerarius, Comment. utriusq. linguæ, p. 359.
[4] Muliebr. pp. 116, 141. Parthenol. p. 379.
[5] Diss. de Clitoride, p. m. 78.
[6] Michaelis, Fragm. p. 155.   [7] Bœckh. v. Arab. p. 77.

under the pubis, which is abraded, and below it lie the orifices of the urethra, and the vagina: if perchance some may think these things are not particularly well done, they must excuse the haste of the draughtsman[1].

Eunuchs have not so much to do with the matter in hand, as monorchides, one of whose testicles is extracted during infancy. First, this custom prevails amongst the Hottentots, who generally in the eighth, and sometimes, if we can trust Kolben[2], in the eighteenth year, are made monorchides. They suppose it makes them run quicker; but travellers remark that at the same time it affects their fertility[3]. The Swiss peasants not unfrequently undergo the like loss of a testicle, that being the way in which the neighbours used to cure ruptures[4].

To mutilations I refer the custom of eradicating the hair in different parts of the body practised by some nations. Thus the Burats keep only the hair below the chin, and pluck out the rest[5]; the Turks destroy[6] by various unguents the hair in every part of the body except on the head and the beard: the Otaheitans eradicate[7] the hairs under the armpit; and almost all the people of America extirpate the beard, which gave rise to the old idea[8], that the Americans were naturally beardless. But this story scarcely needs refutation. Lionel Wafer[9] expressly says about the inhabitants of Darien, that they would have beards if they did not pluck them out: and there is still a little beard in our picture of the male Esquimaux, though the rest of his face is smooth[10]. I say nothing of the artificial sharpening of the teeth[11] amongst others, and other mutilations

---

[1] *Beschr. v. Arab.* p. 80. Baurenfeind designed it after nature, but with an unsteady hand.
[2] p. 147.   [3] J. Schreyer, p. 34.
[4] See Haller, adv. Buff. *Opervm min.* T. III. p. 183.
[5] Le Brun, *Voy.* p. 110. *Mémoire sur les Samojedes*, p. 39.
[6] Leonh. Rauwolf, *Reis.* p. 31. Buff. T. III. p. 438.
[7] Hawkesworth, T. II. p. 188.
[8] Repeated lately in *Recherch. sur les Américains*, T. I. p. 37. *Quest. sur l'Encycl.* T. VII. p. 98.
[9] *Isthm. of Africa*, p. 106.
[10] The bearded race of the Esquimaux. Charlevoix, III. p. 179. A bearded inhabitant of Tierra del Fuego. Parkinson, Vol. I. Thus from all parts of America.
[11] *Ethiopisme.* Hammermann, p. 37.

of equally little importance. First of all, I refer to deformities those enormous and pendulous ears, which from a very long time have been so much in favour among many nations, so as to give a foundation to the old story about the Scythian populations in Pontus, that they have such large ears that they can cover their whole bodies with them[1]. We have certain information about the inhabitants of Malabar, of C. Comorin[2], Benares, the Moluccas[3], and Mallicolo[4], that they use various artifices to make their ears as large as possible, and truly monstrous. The picture of a man of the south in Corn. Le Brun represents them as disfigured in a wonderful way[5]. We are told by some English travellers in southern countries how the New Zealanders studiously prolong the prepuce of the penis[6]. The immense nails of the Chinese[7] are well known. The custom of making women thin by a particular diet is very ancient, and has prevailed amongst the most refined nations[8], so politeness and respect forbid us to class it, with Linnæus[9] amongst deformities. Though the use of pigments and different kinds of paint does not change the shapes of the members themselves, yet it is so constant in some nations, that it would clearly be wrong to leave it untouched. Some merely smear their skin with pigments, whilst others first of all prick it with a needle, and then rub the colours in, which in this way adhere most tenaciously. Both customs have prevailed amongst the most remote and different nations. The Kanagystæ[10], the Californians[11], the Turks[12], the inhabitants of the island of Santa Croce[13], and Mallicolo, of New Holland[14], and

---

[1] Plin. IV. 13, VII. 2. Pompon. Mela, L. III. de Hisp. et Sept. Insulis.
[2] Schreyer, p. 117.
[3] Maximil. Transylv. in Zahn, Spec. T. III. p. 69.
[4] They perforate them with reeds.   [5] 2. 197.
[6] Hawkesworth, Vol. III. p. 50.   [7] Ol. Toree, p. 69.
[8] Charca in Ternos, Ensuch. II. 3. 21.
[9] Syst. Nat. XII. 1. p. 29.
[10] In the Kad-jak islands of the Olutorian archipelago. Staehlin, l. c. p. 31.
[11] Bergert, p. 109.
[12] Rauwolf, Russel, Niebuhr, in either work.
[13] Intensely black. Alvaro Mendana de Neyra in Dalrymple, Vol. 1. p. 78.
[14] Parkinson, Pl. XXVII. The abdomen and the legs distinguished by white bands.

WILD MEN.   129

Cape Verde¹, paint themselves². We know that the Tungus³, the Tschuktschi⁴, the Arabians⁵, the Esquimaux⁶, the New-Zealanders⁷, the Otaheitans⁸, and many nations over all America⁹ draw designs in the skin with a needle, or what we call tattoo themselves.

And this is pretty well all that I have to tell about the variations of the human body and its members, whether occasioned by climate, or mode of life, or diverse unions, or finally, by artificial means. Any one will easily see that our discussion has been about the varieties of whole nations, and that we have nothing to do with those peculiarities which happen accidentally to one or two individuals; and therefore I am quite justified in making no mention here of those unfortunate children, who have been now and then found amongst wild beasts; and all the more because everything which is known of those instances has been diligently collected and dealt with in a regular way by the industry of some famous men¹⁰. Their more important, and more noble part, that is reason, remains uncultivated; but hard necessity has so perverted their human nature, that I should be inclined to refer these anthropomorphous creatures, who are so like beasts, to the *homines monstrosi* of Linnæus.

---

¹ In blue. Gröben, p. 19.
² On the ancient Picts, see Martini on Buff. *Allg. Nat. Gesch.* VI. p. 258.
³ *La Russie ouverte*, Petersb. 1774, fol. Fasc. 1. Tab. V. Coloured plates. Le Brun, p. 118. J. G. Gmelin, *Reis.* I. p. 77, II. p. 647.
⁴ Krascheninikof, *Kamtschatka*, Part II. p. 181.
⁵ Niebuhr, *Reis.* I. Tab. LIX. An Arabian woman of Tohâma.
⁶ The women in my plate are depicted with a double row of punctures on the frontal arch, and a single one under the lower lip.
⁷ Parkinson, Pl. XVI. XXI. XXIII.   ⁸ Ib. Pl. VII.
⁹ At length, John de Laet. edn. Hug. Grot. *de Orig. Gent. Americ.* Amst. 1643, 8vo. p. 224. Canadians in *Mus. Kirch.* ed. Bonanni. Rom. 1773, fol. Part I. Tab. I. II. col. plates. In Tierra del Fuego, Parkins. Pl. I. Instances of ancient tribes are collected by Ph. Cluver, *German. antiquæ*, p. 179.
¹⁰ For ancient instances see Ælian. v. h. l. XII. c. 42. Alex. ab Alex. *Genial. dier.* l. II. s. 31. Herodot. I. I. has doubts about Cyrus. Livy, l. I. c. 4, about Romulus and Remus. Pliny defends the story, VIII. 15, XV. 18, and Plutarch *Romul.* c. II. On the child of Gargoris by his daughter see Justin. l. XLIV. c. 4.
Among recent authors see for a well-written collection of histories, Hasse, Conr. König, *Sched. de hom. inter feras educat., statu nat. solitario*, Hanover, 1730, 4to. Ph. Hasse, Boncher, *de Statu Animair.* Hom. *fer.* Argent. 1756, 4to. Linn. *Anthropum.* T. VI. *Amœnit. ac.* p. 65, and *Syst. Nat. l. c.* p. 28, at length Martini, l. c. p. 263.

9

ALBINISM.

The diseases to which the human body is subject would appear to be much less to our purpose than even the wild state of these children; and yet I am unwillingly compelled to intrude here upon pathology, because of the recent mistakes of some famous men, who have not hesitated to consider the afflicted persons about whom I am going to speak, not only as a peculiar *species* of the human race, but even as the same with the apes. There is a disorder affecting both the skin and the eyes at the same time[1], which sometimes occurs amongst men of the most different nations, and amongst some kinds of quadrupeds, and birds. As we saw above that the whiteness of organized bodies was due to cold, so now we have to consider another kind of diseased whiteness which does not depend upon cold. It seems to be found in plants[2] also, but is more frequently observed, and appears with stronger and more remarkable symptoms in animals, whose skin and hair, or whose feathers and quills, become of an unnaturally chalky, or milky hair, and their eyes grey, or reddish. In some few genera this singular condition seems to become a second nature, so that they produce offspring like themselves, and the same colour is preserved to all generations; in most however instances of this sort seem scattered and anomalous; they spring from parents of the usual colour, and very often have offspring like them again, or at all events the case is confined within the limits of a few families.

Of the first sort the best known examples are white rabbits, which are called, not inaptly, by Nic. le Cat[3], the leucœthiops of their kind. Their fur is always a constant snowy white, whilst their eyes are rosy or red, but in other rabbits grey or black. They are deficient in that black pigment which lines internally

---

[1] I am surprised to see that some eminent men so far differ from me as to deny this leucœthiopia to be a disease, and go so far as to confound it with that natural whiteness which comes to animals in the winter; which I should scarcely have expected from men skilled in physiology, and who must be aware of the great importance of the black pigment which is drawn over the internal parts of the eye, and is entirely deficient in this disorder.

[2] Hyacinths, roses, &c. change anomalously their native colour into white.

[3] *Cual. de la peau*, p. 55.

the eyes of all the mammalia, the birds, the amphibious animals, many of the fishes, and even insects, and whose seat is to be found in the cellular web which lines the choroidal membrane, and the uvea, &c. That this blackness is of the greatest consequence towards sound and good vision is proved, besides other ways, by the weak eye-sight of those animals in whom, as in the white rabbit, that pigment is entirely wanting, or even in some considerable proportion[1]. For even those animals in whom the *tapetum* is blue or green are less able to bear a clear and noonday light, in proportion as they have that part larger or more conspicuous; as may be observed in the cat and other animals whose habits are nocturnal. But yet in them the external side of the choroid, and whatever internal part there is besides the tapetum, is covered with the usual blackness, of which however not a vestige appears in the rabbits we are speaking of. Hence an immense quantity of vessels, if they are turgid with blood, seem to be transparent with a sort of rosy or auburn colour through the pupil and in the iris; but this beautiful rosy hue perishes if the bulb of the eye is taken away from the orbit and the blood flows out; and it remains, if you first of all replenish the same vessels with dull-red suet. The pupil is, as in all the animals of which we shall speak, very large, even after death; the iris, if cut off from the vessels, white, and barely fibrous; which, if it is the case with the iris of other animals, clearly shows that the absence of circular fibres is connected with this deficiency of extraneous pigment: its vessels are beautifully curved; so also the folds of the ciliary processes, if the injection has been properly performed, &c. As this defect of the eyes is so common to this kind of rabbits, that their females, when embraced by black or grey males, produce offspring with white and red eyes, it is not to be wondered at if they become easily accustomed to the light, and able to endure the glare of day.

The nature of white mice is otherwise compounded, for although they preserve for many generations the snowy colour of their fur, and the red colour of their eyes, so far, like rabbits,

---

[1] The choroid grows pale in old men.

they still remain to an extreme degree avoiders of the light[1]. There is here at Göttingen a bakehouse, in which white mice are not unfrequently caught, many of which I have seen alive; and, if a light was brought to the hole, they would instantly hide themselves in the cotton which was put for them, but in the twilight, or when the season was cloudy, they used to run freely about.

Besides rabbits and mice there are other animals in which this variety of hair and feathers and eyes is sometimes, though rarely, to be seen. Amongst horses[2] such sometimes occur; which however must not be confounded with the breed peculiar to Denmark; for although these have white hair, yet their hoofs and eyes are black, and, according to the observations of Kersting, they have also the *rete Malpighianum* brown.

I myself have seen white dogs with red eyes; a hamster of the same sort I owe to the liberality of Sulz; and such a squirrel was kept living by J. J. Wagner[3].

Amongst birds, white varieties are known to occur in Canary-birds, parrots and cocks, and very seldom, but occasionally, in crows.

Finally, as to men who suffer from this defect, the accounts of them have been by some recent authors so deformed, and so mixed up with fables, that we may easily pardon those who have allowed themselves to be deceived, and have not hesitated to make out of them a particular species of mankind. It will therefore be our business to separate the stories from the truth, to show that the disease, so far from forming a species, does not even form a peculiar variety of mankind; to narrate its symptoms in detail; and to show that it was known to the ancients, and has spread over almost all the world.

The other immense merits of Linnæus, and my own respect for so great a man, forbid me to say much about his great mistake, repeated in so many editions[4] of his magnificent work, and which other learned men declare was put forth in all good

---

[1] *Physical. belustig.* 14 st. p. 439.
[2] Edm. Chapman, *de Leucæth.* in fine.
[3] *Hist. Nat. Helvet.* p. 184.
[4] *S. N.* xii. p. 35.

faith, especially after the severe censures of Buffon[1] and Pauw[2]. It will be sufficient to sum it up in a few words: that the attributes of apes are there mixed up with those of men—for a *body less than ours by half, eyes deep in their orbits*, joined to *the membrana nictitans*, and a *lateral vision at the same time on both sides*[3], *the fingers of the hand touching the knees when in an erect position, the wrinkled skin of the pubis*[4], and finally, *the whispering tongue* and *those arrogant conceits, the hope of future dominion, &c.* have nothing to do with the highest work of the Supreme Being, but must be relegated to the region of fable.

There is a disease of the human body, for the most part congenital, exactly like that which I have shown to attack certain animals; it is, however, different in this, that it plays with the symptoms, and now attacks man lightly, and now severely; in some countries it is rare, in others more frequent and endemic; here it is propagated in families, there it seizes people capriciously and individually. It affects the skin and the eyes at the same time, and therefore seems referable either to tetter or to *luscitio*[5]: that it is related to both, will be plain from an enumeration of the symptoms. As to the skin, or rather the cuticle, which is the principal seat of disease, in this disease it is affected in more than one way; it is indeed always of a diseased whiteness, and the hair[6] or groin are coloured in the same way; but the nature of the epiderm itself undergoes all sorts of mutations, though it is not always entirely

---

[1] T. xiv. [2] Rech. sur les Am. T. II. p. 69.
[3] Dalin. Am. dead. T. vi. p. 74. [4] Ib. p. 73.
[5] *Luscitio*; a complaint of the eyes, when the sight is better in the evening than at mid-day. Festus. In the same sense Hippocrates uses the ννκταλωπίαι. Prorrh. II. Galen, Isag. Plin. L. xxviii. c. 11, and Theod. Priscian, L. I. c. 10. Varro, on the contrary, calls those *luscitiosi* who cannot see in the evening: and Ælius, Paveus, Actuarius, and Orimasius call those νυκταλωπεῖς who see during the day, but not so well when the sun sets, and at night not at all. See more about this confusion of terms in H. Stephan. *Dict. Med.* p. 418. Ann. Foes, *Œcon. Hippocr.* p. 163. Tr. Taurmann on Plaut. *Mil.* III. 52, and Jo. Harduin on Plin. l. c. p. 471. R. Aug. Vogel follows Hippocr. *de cogn. et cur. c. A. aff.* p. 475, where the nyctalopia of the ancients is said to be blindness by day (*Hemeralopia* of the moderns), and the hemeralopia of the ancients (*nyctalopia* of the moderns) is said to be the periodical blindness which comes on at twilight.

[6] See Actuar. L. II., π. διαγν. πάθων, c. 23.

affected, but, in rare cases, the places are scattered over the surface of the body. Those, however, who are ill in this way must be carefully separated from those men who have the real parti-coloured, and of whom I have spoken above[1]. In the disease of which I am now speaking, it has been observed in the East Indies, by Rodolph[2], that the spots are rough and can be distinguished by the touch from the rest of the skin. Strahlenberg[3] and John Bell[4] report that parti-coloured persons of this kind are found amongst the Tartars; and the accounts of Hall[5] describe the Malabars as marked by large spots of the same kind, of a yellowish white, and make the disorder something like leprosy. Closely allied to this sort of disease is that in which the skin of the body becomes white, with spots of another colour, as yellow[6], scattered over it[7], or where the colour is a mixture of red and white[8], or where the face at least retains its natural redness[9].

In most cases however, the whole skin, though not in the same way, becomes white. For in many, little or nothing at all in the epidermis is changed, except the colour, so that in other respects there is no symptom of any disease at all. Such are many of the inhabitants of the isthmus of Darien, most carefully described by Lionel Wafer[10], who are said to be covered with a copious, though thin and snowy down. Like this also was a beautiful woman from the neighbouring island of Ternata, whom Le Brun[11] says was a concubine of the king of Bantam; and also a boy of five years old, shown to the Academy of Paris[12]. The English poet[13] speaks of another, lately shown in London,

---

[1] p. 5. [2] Schreber, Saeugth. p. 15.
[3] In Siberia, Nordostl. Eur. u. Asia, p. 121.
[4] Zullim. See Bell's Travels from Petersb. to divers parts of Asia, Glasg. 1763, 4to. T. I. p. 89. He attributes it to scurvy.
[5] Tranqueb. Miss. Ber. Contin. XLI. p. 741. So also borses may be seen spotted black and white.
[6] Like freckles. [7] Tranqueb. Ber. Contin. CVI. p. 1232.
[8] Ib. Contin. XLVI. p. 1239.
[9] Oliv. Goldsmith, Hist. of the Earth, T. II. p. 241. Whether the Otaheitan in Parkinson, p. 17, was of this kind I dare not decide.
[10] p. 107. [11] p. 353.
[12] Hist. de l'Ac. des Sci. 1744, D. V. p. 12. Voltaire, Mélang. T. III. p. 316. Maupertois, Venus physique, p. 147.
[13] Goldsmith, l. c.

with a skin like that of an European. In many, however, the epidermis too is scabby. I read the same about a Tamul schoolmaster, whose skin as it were came off in scales, and became almost of a red colour[1]. The disease is called the white leprosy, in Malabar *Wonkuschtam* or *Wenkuschtam*[2]. Allied to this also is the crusted leprosy of some inhabitants of Paraguay, recalling the scales of fish, painless, and in no ways affecting the general health[3]. The white Ethiopians too are made lepers by Ludolph[4], and so are the inhabitants of Guinea by Isaac Voss[5]. I myself have been acquainted for many years with a Saxon youth, whose whole skin, not excepting even his face and the palms of the hands, was rough with white, and as it were calcareous scales, which appeared red through the numerous interstices, and as it were fissures, of the crust. Sometimes these scales peeled off, and then the limbs looked redder; but new ones instantly grow up. The groin was white; the hair and the eye-brows, if I recollect right, of a mouse colour. For those hairs do not, like that on the groin, keep the same colour in this disease, but vary in the most capricious way. Most have white[6], soft hair, exactly like goats' wool[7]. Nor in these is the colour constant, but as they grow older is often changed into rosy[8]. Voss[9] attributes red and yellow hair to his Leucœthiopians: the hair was yellow in the Malabar family[10], golden in the Manilla girl of G. Jos. Camelli[11].

So much about one phase of our disorder, which occurs with tetter: the other phase, as I have said, affects the eyes, and belongs to *luscitio*, yet it is wonderful how the symptoms of it differ. In many the eyelids become turgid, winking[12]; the

---

[1] Gottl. Anast. Freylinghausen, *neuere Missions Geschichte*, 8 st. p. 1071.
[2] Tranqueb. *M. B. Cont.* CVI. p. 1253 not.
[3] *Lettres edifiantes*, Rec. XXV. p. 112.   [4] *Hist. Æthiopica*, l. c. 14 § 32.
[5] *De Nili et alior. flur. originæ*, p. 68.
[6] Bos. de Gruben, l. c. Wafer, p. 108. Tranqueb. *Miss. Ber. Contin.* XLII. c. VI. &c.
[7] *Ib.* Goldsmith, l. c. "The hair was white and woolly, and very unlike any thing I had seen before."
[8] *Tranqueb. M. B. Cont.* CVI. p. 1283 not.   [9] *l. c.*
[10] *Miss. Ber. Cont.* CIII. p. 637.
[11] *Philos. Trans.* n. 307. p. 2268.   [12] Le Brun, l. c.

eyes of the inhabitants of Darien open in a crescent shape¹; all blink during the day, which is also sometimes the case with people in good health and even with the fœtus, according to the observation of Wrisperg², when the light is too strong. It was also observed in that youth whose epidermis I lately described, that this monstrousness was with him at its height during winter, when he could not endure the brightness of the snow, so that he stood in fear even of ice. In some the iris is in perpetual motion, and the pupils so unquiet that they can never distinguish minute objects, as letters³. The colours of the iris and choroid are various, but all rather pale, so that less light is absorbed, and the retina all the more affected.

In some the eyes are rosy, as in the animals we mentioned. I have myself known such, two sons and the daughter of a French peasant⁴. Maupertuis and Voltaire differ in their description of the eyes of 1744 Leucœthiopians who were seen at Paris; for one calls them rosy, the other sky-coloured. They may however be reconciled if we follow Fontenelle⁵, who says that the iris, &c. appears red in a certain position of the eyes only. The man that Goldsmith saw had red eyes. Sky-coloured eyes are not however uncommon in this disease. For as this colour always denotes weak vision, according to Avicenna and Averroes, as quoted by Hermann Conring⁶, so especially it often occurs in our *nuctalopes*. The young man I knew had sky-coloured eyes. And those Malabars who suffer from white leprosy combined with luscitio, have eyes of a similar colour¹; and so also those who are said to exist in the kingdom of Loango⁷. Dapper says they have grey eyes. I am not quite sure whether this is the disease under which the family of Jerome Cardan

---

[1] Wafer, p. 108. "Their eyelids bend and open in an oblong figure, pointing downward at the corners, and forming an arch or figure of a crescent with the points downwards. From hence, and from their seeing so clear as they do in a moon-shiny night, we used to call them moon-eyed."
[2] *De usu fœt. hum. dijudic.* in *Nov. Comm. Soc. R. Sc. Götting.* T. III. p. 179.
[3] *Miss. Rev. Cont.* XLVI. p. 1240.
[4] In the parish of Champoises, one-and-a-half leagues from Civray, 1763, were still alive.
[5] *I. c. Hist. Ac. Par.*   [6] *De Lab. Germ.*
[7] *Tranq. Miss. Rev. Cont.* CII. p. 637, and CVI. p. 1283.
[8] Voss. l. c. p. 68.

laboured. For he says, in his own life¹, "my father was red, and had white eyes, and saw by night;" and again, "my eldest son had eyes exactly like him;" and again, about the same child², "like my father, with small, white eyes, which were never at rest;" and elsewhere about himself³: "In my early youth, immediately I awoke, though in extreme darkness, I saw everything exactly as if it had been bright day-light: but in a short time I lost this power. Even now I can see a little, but not so as to discern anything."

Let so much suffice about external condition of the skin and eyes in those suffering under this disorder. There is still a little to be said about the rest of the constitution of their body. In the first place, it does not follow that they all are either foul or dirty. We are told that many of them belong to the court of the king of Loango⁴. Certainly another was the mistress of the king of Bantam⁵, and such a woman of Malabar⁶ married an European soldier. She is described as of square body and round cheeks. And they seem at all events strong enough to do their business by night. In fact, it is said that they make hostile incursions into the neighbouring countries by night⁷, and that the Portuguese have carried off others from Guinea to Brazil, to make them work in the gold mines: this certainly would be a kind of life in which *nuctalopia* would be of some use.

Others seem to be of weak and feeble constitution. So Wafer speaks of the inhabitants of Darien⁸. The French of the parish of Champniers can scarcely stand being in the open air. The Malabars certainly cannot endure long journeys⁹, and are speedily fatigued¹⁰ with the wind and the heat¹¹. The brightness of the sun makes their eyes water¹², but they see pretty well in cloudy weather¹³.

---

¹ p. m. 7. ² p. 70.
³ *De rev. eurist.* l. VIII. c. XLIII. p. 161, T. III. *Operum.*
⁴ Vossius, *l. c.* ⁵ Le Brun, *l. c.*
⁶ *Miss. Rev. Cont.* CVI. p. 1185.
⁷ De Gröben, *l. c.* Georg. Agricola, *de Anim. subterr.* They are driven away by burning funeral piles, because they cannot bear the lights.
⁸ "A weak people in comparison of the other."
⁹ Freylinghausen, *l. c.* ¹⁰ *Miss. Rev. Cont.* XXVI. p. 151.
¹¹ *Ib.* and Freyligh. *l. c.* ¹² Wafer. ¹³ Freylinghausen.

Examples prove that the mind and the intellectual faculties are in no respect affected by this disorder, but may remain perfectly sound. The young man I have so often spoken of, was well instructed in more than one of what they call the polite sciences. I have mentioned the schoolmaster of Malabar, who was clever at writing poetry. And if you like, you may consider Cardan a great luminary of art.

These then are the phenomena and symptoms of the disease. It still remains to be proved that it attacks nations at all times and in all places, and that it partly belongs to the endemic, and partly to the sporadic diseases. In both ways it was long since known to the ancients. A sporadic instance of it gave a handle to the Roman story which, under the title of Ethiopics, has been handed down to us by Heliodorus. King Hydaspes, it appears, hesitates to acknowledge his daughter Charicles as his own, when she suddenly laid claim to him, because he and his wife were *Ethiopians*, whilst her skin was white. But Sisimithres, the advocate of Charicles, who had brought her up from infancy, explains the whole matter to the father: "she too was white," says he, "whom I brought up; besides, the lapse of time agrees with the present age of the girl, since she is seventeen years old, which is just the time the child was exposed. Moreover, the appearance of the eyes bears me out; and I recognize that the whole aspect of the countenance, and the beautiful figure which I now see, agrees with that which I then saw[1]." Perhaps also the story of the female child Aristotle[2] speaks of may be thus explained, which was born of the adulterous connexion of a Sicilian woman with an Æthiop, and did not have the colour of her father, but in process of time gave birth to a son, who was entirely black, like his grandfather. The ancients knew this disorder also as endemic, so that they gave names to whole nations and regions in consequence. It seems probable that Albania, on the confines of the Caucasian mountains and Armenia[3], had

---

[1] L. x. p. 477, ed. Bourdelot, Paris, 1619, 8vo.
[2] *Hist. Anim.* L. vii. c. 6.   [3] Plin. L. vi. c. 13, p. 311. Hard.

its name from this, about which Isigonus of Nice[1] speaks thus: "Some are born there with grey eyes, white from early childhood, who see better by night than by day". Another nation of this kind acquired the name of Leucœthiopes, hence transferred to all who suffer from this disease. They are mentioned by Pomponius Mela[2], Pliny[3], Ptolemy[4], and Agathemerus[5], but are not noticed by Strabo, Julius Honorius[6], later Æthicus[7], the anonymous writer of Ravenna, &c. They do not however agree as to the country which the Leucœthiopes are said to inhabit. Mela and Pliny place them with the Libyco-Egyptians, near the Libyan sea. Joh. Reinhold, in the plates to his edition of Mela, about long. 50° N. lat. 15°.[8] But Ptolemy says the Leucœthiopes live under Mount Ryssa, which, according to D'Anville, is the name for Capo Verde. However that may be, it is enough for our purpose, that this disease was not unknown to the ancients.

We have seen that there are modern instances in the most different and widely separated parts of the earth; and it will be worth our while to add a few more, and in a few words to reckon them up in the order of our four varieties. I have carefully described a youth of our own Germany. Edm. Chapman relates that instances have been known in Spain and France. Nic. Le Cat saw some children born at Ratisbon. I have already noticed the case of those in the parish of Champniers, and what Cardan says of his Italian family. G. Agricola and Olaus Magnus found men of this kind in Scandinavia. The accounts from Tranquebar tell us of many Malabars. They are contemptuously called there *kakerlacken*[10], from their resemblance to the eastern moth, which is a parti-coloured and nocturnal insect. And this disorder occurs in Labrador, if indeed

---

[1] Plin. l. VIII. c. 2, p. 371.
[2] Comp. Salmas. ad Solin. c. 15, and Gellius, *Noct. Att.* l. IX. c. 4.
[3] L. I. c. 4, p. 11, ed. L. B. 1743. On which see John de Watt. Thus they call some Ethiopians, who in comparison with others may be said to be whitish, neither altogether white, nor altogether black, p. 155, ed. Bas. 1543.
[4] L. V. c. 8, p. 152. Harl.
[5] L. IV. c. 6, p. 77, ed. Mich. Servetl, Lugd. 1541.
[6] *Georg.* l. I. c. 4.   [7] *Excerpt. cosmogr.*   [8] As is thought.
[9] Hardain on Plin. In the desert of Sahara.
[10] Calkalaken, *Miss. Ber. cont.* CVI. p. 1183. Kalkalatten, *cont.* CII. p. 637.

the Champagne girl, *Le Blanc*, belonged to the Esquimaux, as is most likely[1].

Leucœthiopians (if we may apply the old term to them also) of the second variety of mankind have been known in the islands of Java[2], Borneo[3], Manila[4], and others near Ternata, and in New Guinea[5] and Otaheite[6]. Of the third variety, are found instances to the south beyond the fountains of the Nile[7], and towards the river Senegal[8], whose mouth lies under the Ryssadian promontory, and still further south in Guinea[9], and its kingdom of Loango, and, finally, in the interior of Kaffraria[10] and the island of Madagascar[11]. The fourth variety can produce its *Blafards* on the isthmus of Darien, in the kingdom of Mexico[12], in Tucuman, and Paraguay.

But our digression from the subject of natural history and the varieties of mankind to pathology and diseases has been already too long. Those must bear the blame who have confounded men suffering under disease with the beasts, which the dignity of mankind demanded should be separated, and each referred to their own place.

It would be an immense and irrelevant labour, if I were to give an account of all the disorders which, according to the authors of medical observations, journals, &c., have occurred in the human body, in every quarter, contrary to nature. The transition from hence to monsters would be easy, and so on to general nosology; and thus the divine study of natural history would run up into a confused and formless mass. Let us leave therefore unnoticed, for physiologists and pathologists, the black and horny epidermis of the Italian boy[13], or the Englishman[14], and others, and similar peculiar aberrations from the natural condition. Nor have we anything to do with the dire disorder

---

[1] *Hist. d'une jeune fille sauvage*, &c. Par. 1761, 12mo. Her countrymen were nyctalopes, and did business by night, &c., and she had *lusciti̊o*, p. 56, &c.
[2] Legua. T. II. p. 136.   [3] Voss.   [4] Camelli, l. c.
[5] Voss.   [6] Hawkesworth, Vol. II. p. 188. Parkinson, p. 27.
[7] Voss.   [8] Chapman.   [9] Gröben, *Dondot. Portug. Africa.*
[10] Sim. v. d. Stel in Tachart, *Siam*, p. 110.
[11] De Cossigny in *Hist. de l'Ac. des Sci. l. c.*   [12] Ib.
[13] Half. v. d. Wiel, *Obs. cent.* II. p. 376, Tab. II. stab. 12, fig. 1, 2, 3.
[14] The porcupine man. G. Edwards, *Gleanings of Natural History*, Vol. I. p. 212.

of cretinism, which is by no means peculiar to the inhabitants of the Vallais, but has been noticed elsewhere[1], though distorted here and there by wonderful stories[2].

It seems almost too much even to name in this place the centaurs, sirens, cynocephali, satyrs, pigmies[3], giants, hermaphrodites, and other idle creatures of that kind. Still, I consider it necessary to spend a little time upon the men with tails, since they have fallen in with some modern patrons. There is an old story about the islands of the Satyrs in Pliny[4], Ptolemy[5], and Pausanias[6], and often repeated afterwards by Marco Polo, Munster and others, that men exist there with shaggy tails, like the pictures of the satyrs, who are of incredible swiftness, &c. When the passages in these writers have been compared, it seems most likely that these islands of the Satyrs answer to our Borneo, Celebes[7], &c., and that the tailed apes have been taken for men. But a new story about men with tails to be found here and there has made much more to do. For partly, it is said, that men having tails are found about the city of Turkestan[8], in the island of Formosa[9], Borneo[10], Nicobar[11], &c.; partly the very pictures of tailed men of this kind have been exhibited[12]. But upon a full consideration of the matter, there is much which leads to the belief that the whole story is founded upon the fictions I have spoken of. For, as to the accounts about them, many of them manifestly depend upon the narrations of others; and they who say they have themselves seen tailed men of this kind bear no very good reputation.

---

[1] Haller, *de rutis Reprasi, Nov. Comm. Gott.* T. I. p. 43.
[2] See in Guindant, *Variet. de la nat. dans l'espèce hum.* Paris, 1771, 8vo. in Recueil de Par. altered in ed. De Felice, T. XIII. p. 317.
[3] Comp. the book of Tyson on these stories. Apes were generally palmed upon travellers, and this I suspect to have been the case with the Madagascar pigmies of Commerson, in De la Lande. See Rosier, *Obs. Sept. 1775.*
[4] l. VI. VII. c. 2. p. m. 374. [5] L. VI. c. 11. [6] In Attica.
[7] See after Tyson, Jo. Caverhill, *On the knowledge of the ancients in the East Indies. Phil. Trans.* Vol. LVII. p. 172.
[8] Pet. Rytschkov. *Orenburg. Topogr.* T. II. p. 34.
[9] J. Ott. Helbig. *Eph. N. C. Dec. I. ann. IX.* p. 456. Reaum, *Ost. ind. disc.* p. 216.
[10] Will. Harvey, *de Gen.* p. 194. ed. oper. Lond. 1766.
[11] Nils Matthæson Köping, *Res.* ed. 4to. Wasteras, 1759, 8vo, p. 131.
[12] Martini on Buff. *allg. nat. Gesch.* T. VI. p. 44. Tab. II. *der ganzwöchentl. Mensch.*

The figure I have alluded to is of considerable antiquity, and having been altered in the progress of time, first by one and then by another, has by slow degrees become more and more like the human figure. Martini took his figure from the Amœnitates of Linnæus, who took it from Aldrovandus, and he from Gesner, and, finally, this Swiss polyhistor says that he took his from some description of the Holy Land[1]. Although he does not name the author of the description, yet I could easily see that it was Bernhard Von Breydenbach, and I have thought it worth while to have the genuine figure reproduced from the very rare first edition[2] of his work (Tab. II. fig. 5), which has passed with recent authors for a man with a tail. For on the reverse of the geographical chart on which Palestine is set out he has delineated the figures of six animals with the epigraph; "These animals are faithfully represented as we saw them in the Holy Land." The figure which I have repeated is the last of all, as he adds, "of some nameless animal," but I think I should readily conclude it was of some tailed ape, a Callitrichus, for example (silenus, L.). Certainly the wide separation of the great toe from the others, &c. show it to be a true ape. This in progress of time, and through the carelessness of artists, has been at last transmuted into a figure sufficiently like that of a man, with human feet, &c. The very extraordinary instances of a prolonged coccygis, or of an appendage with a tail, in Trimethius[3], Bauhin[4], Blanchard[5], König[6], and Elsholz[7], relate to monstrous productions, and are out of place here. It is well known to anatomists that variation often occurs in the os sacrum[8] and the number of the coccygeal vertebræ[9].

---

[1] *De quadrup.* p. m. 970.
[2] *Reys in das gelobte land.* Meintz. 1486, fol. I do not find these figures in the Latin edition of the same year, nor in that which he brought out in low Dutch in 1488. But they occur in the French translation of 1489; and the library of the University possesses them all.
[3] *Annal. Hirsaugiens.* T. II. p. 179, ad ann. 1335.
[4] *Theatr. Anat.* p. 69.
[5] *Coll. phys. med.* Part II. ann. 1681. p. 290.
[6] *A. N. C.* Dec. II. ann. 9. obs. 129.
[7] *De conceptionis tubariis,* &c. Col. Brand. 1669. p. 7, Tab. II.
[8] Fallopia speaks of four vertebræ. *Expos. de Oss.* p. 579. See Drevverro. *Obs. Anat.* p. 207. Generally there are five. See six in Vesal. and his followers Bauhin

HOTTENTOTS. 143

As to the cutaneous *ventrale* which has been asserted by old travellers to belong to the Hottentot women, the most recent testimonies[1] compel us to class it with the men's tails, and to consider it, like them, a fable.

---

and Paaw. See also Real. Columb. p. 106. Vesling, p. 10. Sal. Albert. *Hist. plerar. part. hum. corp.* Viterb. 1585, p. 117. Albinus, *Annot. Acad.* l. IV. Tab. VII. f. 4, 5, p. 53. See Doeveren. *l. c.* p. 206. B. S. Albini, *Annot. Acad.* l. IV. c. 11. For more comp. P. Tabarrani *A ct. Scares.* T. III. p. 142; and I myself in my private anatomical collection have three genuine specimens of this kind, provided with five pairs of foramina. Paaw says that he has found seven vertebræ, *de Oss.* p. 102.

[2] Bauhin and Vesling show instances with three vertebræ: generally there are four. Four to five, Winslow, *Exp. An.* T. I. p. 136. Five in the coco. of a woman, Maith. Merian. in Tab. ad *Throt.* Bauhin, T. XLI. f. 9, and Sal. Albertus, *l. c.*, who improperly refers to this bone the first vertebra, which, as is often the case, belongs to the last bone of the os sacrum. Altogether however his specimen had more vertebræ, sacr. 6, coco. 5 = 11.

Fallopia calls those who have a large and prolonged os sacrum, *tailed, l. c.*

[3] Hawkesworth, Vol. III. p. 792. The pendulosity of the labia seems to have imposed upon the older travellers.

DE

GENERIS HUMANI VARIETATE NATIVA.

EDITIO TERTIA.

PRÆMISSA EST EPISTOLA

AD VIRUM PERILLUSTREM

JOSEPHUM BANKS, BARONETUM,

REGIÆ SOCIETATIS LONDINI PRÆSIDEM.

AUCTORE

JO. FRID. BLUMENBACH, M.D.

EIUSDEM SOCIETATIS SODALI.

GOTTINGÆ:
APUD VANDENHOEK ET RUPRECHT.
1795.

*Non hic Centauros, non Gorgonas, Harpyasque
Invenies; hominem pagina nostra sapit.*

MARTIAL, Lib. x. *Epigr.* 4.

CONTENTS.

Letter to Sir Joseph Banks.

Index of the anthropological collection of the author, which he used in illustrating this new edition, viz.

  I. Skulls of different races.
  II. Very characteristic features of the middle and the two extreme varieties.
  III. Hair and hairs of different races.
  IV. Anatomical preparations.
  V. Collection of pictures.

Explanation of the plates.

SECTION I.

ON THE DIFFERENCE BETWEEN MAN AND OTHER ANIMALS.

Difficulty of the question; order of discussion; external conformation; erect position; proved natural to man; broad and flat pelvis; relation of the soft parts to the human pelvis; the hymen, nymphæ, and clitoris; man a bimanous animal; apes and kindred animals quadrumanous; properties of the human teeth; other peculiarities of man; internal peculiarities; internal parts which man has not; intermaxillary bone; difference of internal parts; functional peculiarities of man; mental peculiarities, laughter and tears; diseases peculiar to man; recapitulation of differences falsely ascribed to man.

SECTION II.

ON THE CAUSES AND WAYS BY WHICH ANIMALS DEGENERATE UNIVERSALLY.

Object of this undertaking; what is species; application to the question of human species, or varieties; how the primitive species degenerates into varieties; phenomena of degeneration in animals;

colour, hair; stature; proportion; form of the skull; causes of degeneration; formative force; climate; aliment; mode of life; hybridity; diseased hereditary dispositions; mutilations; are they propagated? cautions to be observed in investigating degeneration.

SECTION III.

ON THE CAUSES AND WAYS IN WHICH MANKIND HAVE DEGENERATED IN PARTICULAR.

Order of discussion; seat of colour; varieties of racial colour; causes of this variety; further illustration of causes; creoles; mulattoes; dark skin with white spots; singular mutations of colour; other properties of racial skin; agreement of hair and skin; varieties of racial hair; agreement of the iris with the hair; colours of the eye; racial face; varieties of racial face; causes thereof; racial form of skulls; facial line of Camper; remarks; *norma verticalis;* racial varieties of skulls; causes of the same; racial varieties of teeth, and causes; other racial varieties; ears; breasts; genitals; legs; feet and hands; varieties of stature; Patagonians; Quimos; causes of racial stature; fabulous varieties of mankind; story of tailed nations; diseased variety; epilogue.

SECTION IV.

FIVE PRINCIPAL VARIETIES OF MANKIND, ONE SPECIES.

Varieties of mankind run into one another; five principal varieties; characteristics and limits; Caucasian; Mongolian; Ethiopian; American; Malay; divisions of other authors; remarks on the Caucasian, &c.; conclusion.

INTRODUCTORY LETTER

TO

SIR JOSEPH BANKS.

———————

THERE are many reasons, illustrious Sir, why I ought to offer and dedicate to you this book, whatever it may be worth.

For besides my wish to express some time or other my sense of gratitude for the innumerable favours you have conferred upon me, from the time I came to have a nearer acquaintance with you; this very edition of my book, which now comes out with fresh care bestowed upon it, owes in great part to your liberality the splendid additions and the very remarkable ornaments in which it excels the former ones. For many years past you have spared neither pains nor expense to enrich my collection of the skulls of different nations with those specimens I was so anxious above all to obtain, I mean of Americans, and the inhabitants of the islands of the Southern Ocean. And besides, when I visited London about three years ago, with the same generous liberality with which you extended the use of your nursery to our Gaertner, and other riches of your museum to others, you gave me in my turn the unrestricted use of all the collections of treasures relating to the study of Anthropology, in which your library abounds; I mean the pictures, and the drawings, &c. taken by the best artists from the life itself. So I have been able to get copies of them and to describe whatever I liked, and at last, assisted by so many new and important additions, to proceed to the recasting of my book, and am bold enough to say, now it has been amplified in so many ways, without incurring any suspicion of boasting, that it has been polished and perfected as far as its nature permits.

Accept then graciously this little work, which is so much in fact your own; and I hope that in this way it will not be displeasing to you because it treats of a part of natural history, which though second to no other in importance, still has most surprisingly been above all others the longest neglected and uncultivated.

It is one of the merits of the immortal Linnæus, that more than sixty years ago, in the first edition of his *Systema Naturæ*, he was the first, as far as I know, of writers on natural history, who attempted to arrange mankind in certain varieties according to their external characters; and that with sufficient accuracy, considering that then only four parts of the terraqueous globe and its inhabitants were known.

But after your three-years' voyage round the world, illustrious Sir, when a more accurate knowledge of the nations who are dispersed far and wide over the islands of the Southern Ocean had been obtained by the cultivators of natural history and anthropology, it became very clear that the Linnæan division of mankind could no longer be adhered to; for which reason I, in this little work, ceased like others to follow that illustrious man, and had no hesitation in arranging the varieties of man according to the truth of nature, the knowledge of which we owe principally to your industry and most careful observation.

Indeed though the general method of Linnæus, of arranging the mammalia according to their mode of dentition, was very convenient at the time he founded it, yet now after so many and such important species of this class have been discovered, I think that it will be useful and profitable to the students of zoology, to give it up as very imperfect and liable to vast exceptions, and to substitute for that artificial system one more natural, deduced from the universal characteristics of the mammalia.

I am indeed very much opposed to the opinions of those, who, especially of late, have amused their ingenuity so much with what they call the continuity or gradation of nature; and have sought for a proof of the wisdom of the Creator, and the perfection of the creation in the idea, as they say, that nature takes no leaps, and that the natural productions of the three kingdoms of nature, as far as regards their external conformation, follow one upon another like the steps in a scale, or like points and joinings in a chain. But those who examine the matter without prejudice, and seriously, see clearly that even in the animal kingdom there are whole classes on the one hand, as that of birds, or genera, as that of cuttle-fish, which can only be joined on to the neighbouring divisions in those kinds of plans of the gradation of natural productions but indifferently and by a kind of violence. And on the other hand, that there are genera of animals, as silkworms, in which there is so great a difference in the appearance of either sex, that if you wanted to refer them to a scale of that kind, it would be necessary to separate the males as far as possible from their females, and to place the different sexes of the same species in the most different places possible.

And in this kind of systems, so far from their being filled up, there are large gaps where the natural kingdoms are very plainly separated one from another. There are other things of this kind; and so although after due consideration of these things, I cannot altogether recognize so much weight and importance in this doctrine of the gradation of nature, as is commonly ascribed to it by the physico-theologians, still I will allow this to belong to both these metaphorical and allegorical amusements, that they do not throw any obstacle in facilitating the method of the study of natural history.

For they make as it were the basis of every natural system, the way in which things rank according to their universal condition, and the greatest number of external qualities in which they coincide with each other, whereas the artificial systems, on the contrary, recognize single characters only as the foundation of their arrangement.

And when I found it was beyond all doubt that a natural system of that kind was preferable to an artificial one, because it is of such use in sharpening the judgment and assisting the memory, I applied myself all the more to bring the class of mammalia into the scope of a natural system of that kind, especially as that artificial one of Linnæus, deduced from comparison of the teeth, in consequence of the accession of so many recently detected species in these times, came every day to be encumbered with more troublesome anomalies and exceptions. So that, for example, just to say a few words on this point, we now are acquainted with two species of rhinoceros, in their habit as like as possible to each other, but so different in their dentition, that if we were now obliged to follow the Linnæan system, we should have to refer one species to the *Belluæ*, and the other to the *Glires*. And in like manner it would be necessary to remove the Ethiopian boar, which is destitute of the primary teeth, from the other *Belluæ* and place it among the *Bruta* of Linnæus. I say nothing of that African *Myrmecophaga dentata* which, according to the idea of Linnæus, would have to be separated from the genus *edentata*, or of some of the Lemures (the *indri* and *laniger*) which, on account of the anomalies of their dentition, would have to be separated from the Linnæan genus of Lemures. No one will deny that this confusion threw the greatest possible obstacles in the way of the study of zoology, and I have tried to remedy it by constructing the following ten natural orders of mammalia, a statement of which I may here subjoin, because I shall frequently make mention of them in the present work.

I. Bimanua.
   1. *Homo.*
II. Quadrumana.
   2. *Simia.*
   3. *Papio.*
   4. *Cercopithecus.*
   5. *Lemur.*
III. Bradypoda.
   6. *Bradypus.*
   7. *Myrmecophaga.*
   8. *Manis.*
   9. *Tatu*[1].
IV. Chiroptera.
   10. *Vespertilio.*

---

[1] I am very far indeed from that itch for innovation which afflicts so many of the moderns, who take a wonderful delight in giving new names to the natural productions which have already received names very well known to all; for this kind of playing at onomatopœia has been a great misfortune to the study of natural

NATURAL ORDERS.

- V. Glires.
  - 11. Sciurus.
  - 12. Glis.
  - 13. Mus.
  - 14. Marmota.
  - 15. Cavia.
  - 16. Lepus.
  - 17. Jaculus.
  - 18. Castor.
  - 19. Hystrix.
- VI. Feræ.
  - 20. Erinaceus.
  - 21. Sorex.
  - 22. Talpa.
  - 23. Didelphis.
  - 24. Viverra.
  - 25. Mustela.
  - 26. Lutra.
  - 27. Phoca.
  - 28. Meles.
  - 29. Ursus.
  - 30. Canis.
  - 31. Felis.
- VII. Solidungula.
  - 32. Equus.
- VIII. Pecora.
  - 33. Camelus.
  - 34. Capra.
  - 35. Antilope.
  - 36. Bos.
  - 37. Giraffa.
  - 38. Cervus.
  - 39. Moschus.
- IX. Belluæ.
  - 40. Sus.
  - 41. Tapir.
  - 42. Elephas.
  - 43. Rhinoceros.
  - 44. Hippopotamus.
  - 45. Trichecus.
- X. Cetacea.
  - 46. Monodon.
  - 47. Balæna.
  - 48. Physeter.
  - 49. Delphinus.

---

history. So I have very seldom deserted the terminology of Linnæus in the systematic names of the mammalia, and then most unwillingly, and only when the name adopted by that learned man evidently involved an erroneous and false notion. So, for example, I have restored to the armadilloes the native generic name of Tatu, for the Linnæan Dasypus had nothing to justify it. We all know this name is Greek, and denotes an animal remarkable for its hairy feet, and so was given by the ancients to the hare and the rabbit, because in them above all others the palms and soles are most hairy, whereas it is scarcely necessary to mention how very different in habit the armour-bearing animals in the new world are from the rabbit. And so in the genus of bats, I think the name of vampyre should be restored to that species of South America which Linnæus called spectrum, and gave on the contrary the title of vampyre to that bat of the East Indies and of the islands of the Southern Ocean, which is commonly called the flying dog. But now it is known that the word vampyre means blood-sucker, and therefore is particularly applicable to that American bat, which is on this account very obnoxious to other animals and especially to man; but does not apply at all to the other one I mentioned, namely, the canine, which is entirely frugivorous, and never, as far as I know, sucks the blood of other animals.

These with everything else, where in the work of which this is the preface, I have on many points departed in opinion from others, I submit to your judgment, illustrious Sir, with equal respect and confidence, to you under whose most dignified and worthy presidency the Royal Society of Science rejoices to be, whose golden motto from its infancy has been, 'Nullius in verba.'

Farewell, illustrious Sir, and be gracious to your most devoted servant.

Dated from the University of the Georgia Augusta, April 11, 1795.

INDEX OF THE AUTHOR'S ANTHROPOLOGICAL
MATERIALS, WHICH HE MADE MOST USE
OF IN ILLUSTRATING THIS EDITION.

There are three special reasons why I have thought it worth while to insert here this index.

First, that my learned and candid readers may know the quantity and the quality of the assistance taken from nature itself, with which I have succeeded at last in publishing this book.

Secondly, that a testimony of my gratitude may remain for the noble munificence which my patrons and friends have thus far shown in enriching my materials for the extension of anthropological studies.

Lastly, that what I am still in want of may be known, which those same friends may further enrich me with, if they have a good opportunity and are still so disposed.

SKULLS OF DIFFERENT NATIONS.

Of this collection, which in number and variety is, so far as I know, unique in its kind, since the similar collections of Camper and John Hunter cannot in these respects be compared to it, I have published a selection, which I have described most fully in three decades, and illustrated with the most accurate engravings, and there I have given an account of the time and the way in which each skull came into my possession. And I always keep together with these treasures a collection of autograph letters, by which documentary evidence the genuine history of each is preserved. Those which seem to be in any way doubtful or ambiguous, I put in a separate place.

A. Five very choice examples of the principal varieties of mankind.

(a) The middle, or Caucasian variety.

1. A Georgian woman, Pl. III. Fig. 2, Pl. IV. Fig. 3 (Dec cranior. illustr. III. Tab. XXI.), a gift of de Asch.

Then the two extreme, or (b) Mongolian and (c) Ethiopic varieties.
2. A Reindeer Tungus, Pl. III. Fig. 1, Pl. IV. Fig. 2 (Dec. II. Tab. XVL), a gift of de Asch.
3. A female African of Guinea, Pl. III. Fig. 3, Pl. IV. Fig. 5 (Dec. II. Tab. XIX.), a gift of Steph. Jo. Van Geuns, Professor at Utrecht.

Lastly, the two intermediate varieties.
(d) The American. (e) The Malay.
4. A Carib chief from the Isle of St Vincent, Pl. IV. Fig. 2 (Dec. I. Tab. I.), a gift of Sir Joseph Banks, Bart.
5. An Otaheitan, Pl. IV. Fig. 4 (Dec. III. Tab. XIVL), from the same.

B. Five other specimens selected in the same way.
(a) The Caucasian variety.
6. Natolian of Tocat, gift of de Asch.
(b) Mongolian.
7. Chinese or Daürian Tungus (Dec. III. Tab. XLIII.), from the same.
(c) Ethiopian.
8. Ethiop. (Dec. I. Pl. 8), from Michael, aulic-counsellor of Hesse-Cassel, and Professor of Marburg.
(d) American.
9. Indian of North America (Dec. I. Tab. IX.), from the same.
(e) Malay.
10. New Hollander (Dec. III. Tab. XLVII.), from Banks.

For the demonstration of the *norma verticalis*, s. 61.

Caucasian variety.
11. Tartar of Kazan (Dec. II. Tab. XII.), gift of de Asch.
Mongolian.
12. Yacutan (Dec. II. Tab. XV.), de Asch.
Ethiopian.
13. Ethiopian. Sömmerring, aulic-counsellor, and Prof. Mogunt.

Three other specimens by which, although they are partly deformed on purpose and partly by disease, the *norma verticalis* still is well elucidated.
14. *Caucasian.* Turk, de Asch.
15. *Mongolian.* Calmuck (Dec. II. Tab. XIV.), de Asch.
16. *Ethiopian.* Ethiop. (Dec. II. Tab. XVII.), de Asch.

Three skulls of infants, clearly demonstrating the *norma verticalis*.
17. *Caucasian.* Jewish girl (Dec. III. Tab. XXVIII.).
18. *Mongolian.* Burat girl (Dec. III. Tab. XXIX.), de Asch.
19. *Ethiopian.* New-born Ethiop. (Dec. III. Tab. XXX.), Billmann, Cassel surgeon.

Specimens remarkable for the manifest transitions by which they connect the different varieties of mankind. These hold a middle place between the Caucasian and Mongolian.
20. Skull of a Cossack of the Don (Dec. I. Tab. IV.), de Asch.
21. Kirgis-Cossack (Dec. II. Tab. XIII.), de Asch.
22. Another of the same, de Asch.

These between the Caucasian and Ethiopian.
23. Egyptian mummy (Dec. I. Tab. I.).
24. Genuine Zingari (Dec. II. Tab. II.), Pataki, physician of Claudinopolis.

These between the Mongolian and American.
25, 26. Esquimaux (Dec. III. Tabb. XXIV. XXV.), Jo. Loretz.

Skulls deformed by particular arts in infancy.
27. Macrocephalic, probably Tartar (Dec. I. Tab. III.), de Asch.
28. Carib female (Dec. III. Tab. XX.), Banks.

Remaining cranial collection.
29. German.
30. Female German.
31. Young Jew.
32. Old Jew.
33. Dutch. Wolff, Utrecht physician.
34. Frenchman. Sömmerring.
35. Italian. de Asch.

36. Italian, Venetian. Michaelis, camp-physician of Hanover.
37. Lombard. Ib.
38. Ancient Roman prætorian soldier. Card. Steph. Borgia.
39. Lithuanian of Sarmatia. de Asch.
40. Calvaria of ancient Cimbrian. Bozenhard, imperial consul general in Denmark.
41, 42. Finn. de Asch.
43. Female Finn.
44. Russian Zingari.
45. Russian youth[1].
46. Russian old man.
47, 48, 49, 50, 51. Russians of Muscovy.
52. Female of Muscovy.
53. Russian of Swenigorod.
54. Old Russian youth.
55. Russian of Wenewski.
56. ——— Romanoff.
57. ——— Ribno.
58. ——— Ribnimi.
59. Kostroman.
60. Female of Krasno. de Asch.
61. Russian of Nyschenovogorod.
62. Kurak.
63. Orlov.
64. Tartar of Orenburg.
65. Tartar (probably of Kazan).
66, 67, 68. Tatara.
69. Tschuwasch.
70. Lesghi.
71. Georgian.
72, 73, 74. Female Turk.
75, 76, 77, 78, 79, 80. Calmucks of Orenburg (76, Dec. I. Tab. v.).
81. Creole Ethiopian from New York. Michaelis, Marburg.
82. Ethiopian of Congo (Dec. II. Tab. XVIII.), de Asch.

---

[1] The very remarkable series of Ruthenian skulls from No. 45 to No. 63 shows great diversity, but always more or less approaches the Mongolian, and is doubtless the product of mixed marriages.

II.

FŒTUSES REMARKABLY CHARACTERISTIC OF THE MIDDLE AND THE TWO EXTREME VARIETIES.

Caucasian variety. German twins of either sex, remarkable for their extreme beauty, four months old.

Mongolian. Calmuck of Orenburg, female, third month. From D. Kosegarten.

Ethiopian. Male Ethiopian, fifth month. Meyer, chief physician, Hanover.

III.

HAIR AND HAIRS OF DIFFERENT NATIONS.

Although at first sight these things may seem too minute, still it cannot be denied that a collection of this kind, when very varied, is of considerable use for accurate anthropological studies. I have here specimens of all the five principal varieties of mankind; some of them are sufficiently remarkable, about which I shall speak below; as the piebald hair of the negress, variegated with white spots, whom I saw at London, &c.

IV.

ANATOMICAL PREPARATIONS.

The greater part of these belong to the natural history of the Ethiopians. I have made copious mention of them in various parts of the book.

V.

COLLECTION OF PICTURES OF DIFFERENT NATIONS, CAREFULLY TAKEN FROM THE LIFE BY THE FIRST ARTISTS.

It is clear that a collection of this kind, especially whenever it is invariably compared with such a collection of skulls as I have been giving an account of, is one of the first, principal, and authentic sources of anthropological studies; and so for the last twenty years I have taken an immense deal of trouble to collect a quantity of such drawings, taken from life, and what is very important, by good artists. There is indeed a large quantity of similar drawings in the books of travels and voyages; but when they are critically examined, very few are found which you can trust[1]. When we leave the representations of Corn. de Bruin in his Persian and Indian travels, and the second voyage of the immortal Cook, illustrated by his own descriptions, and plates drawn by Hodges, we shall soon find that in almost all the others the plates, however splendid they may be, when we examine them closely, and compare them with genuine representations, or with nature, are scarcely of any use for the natural history of mankind. It is necessary, therefore, for this object to bring together all the extant representations of foreign races, and the engravings, as well those edited separately as those scattered up and down in books, and also the very drawings made by the artist's own hand. I have collected a considerable quantity of them, amongst which are particularly conspicuous the figures of Wenc. Hollar, a great artist in this line, which are drawn in *aqua fortis*, and also the splendid plates of some modern English engravers; to mention them singly would transgress the limits of an index. I will only give a list of some of the most remarkable of those which are done by the hand.

Caucasian variety.

1. Turkish woman; drawn with red chalk from the life at Berlin, by Dan. Chodowiecki, who gave it me with his autograph.

2. Hindostan woman; drawn by an Indian painter with wonderful refinement and accuracy: given to me at London by Sam. Lysons.

Mongolian variety.

3. Cossim Ali Khan, formerly nawab of Bengal, who afterwards became a Mohammedan faquir at Delhi. Drawn in colours by a Mohammedan painter, a Moor. It was given to me with the following one by Braun, now deceased, formerly British resident at Berne, and once a colonel in India.

4. The wife of the last Mogul Emperor, Shah Allum, who died 1790; also drawn by an artistic hand[2].

5. Portrait of Feodor Irvanowitsch, a Calmuck, by himself; drawn in black chalk by his own hand, with incomparable skill and

---

[1] Comp. a passage to this effect in Volney, *Ruines, ou méditation sur les révolutions des empires*, p. 349.

[2] I have ascribed these to the Mongolian variety, having regard to the origin of the present rulers of India, although from obvious causes they come very near the Hindostanese in appearance.

taste, and a most exact likeness. Done at Rome, where he studied painting with the greatest success. This handsome present was sent me from Rome by Tatter, of the private British embassy.

6. Two Chinese sailors. Painted at Vienna. A gift from Nic. Jos. de Jacquin, councillor of the imperial mint.

7. Ettuiack, an Esquimaux magician; brought to London in 1773 from the coast of Labrador. This, as well as the following picture, according to the autograph of Nathan. Dance in Banks' museum, was most carefully painted by the famous London painter, O. Hunnemann.

8. Esquimaux woman, by name Caubvic (which in the language of those barbarians means a blind bear); she was brought with Ettuiack to London by Cartwright.

Ethiopian.

9. Hottentot female of Amaqui. This, with the following one, comes from the collection of Banks.

10. Boschman, with wife and child.

11. Hottentot female. This portrait and the four succeeding ones were drawn from the life at the Cape of Good Hope, and sent to the Emperor Joseph II. at Vienna. Most careful copies given me by de Jacquin.

12. Karmup, Hottentot female of Namaqui.

13. Kosjo, Hottentot female of Gonaga, on the borders of Caffraria.

14. Koba, Caffir chief.

15. Puseka, his daughter.

American.

16. An inhabitant of Tierra del Fuego, from Magellan's straits.

17. Female of the same tribe.

Malay.

18. Two New Zealanders.

19. New Zealand chief.

20. Two youths of the same nation.

All these, as well as the Fuegians, are taken from the collection made by Sir Joseph Banks in his voyage.

EXPLANATION OF THE PLATES.

Plate III.

A synoptic arrangement to illustrate the *norma verticalis*.

Fig. 1 answers to fig. 1 of Pl. IV.
Fig. 2 .... fig. 3 ....
Fig. 3 .... fig. 5 ....

Plate IV.

Five very select skulls of my collection, to demonstrate the diversity of the five principal human races.

Fig. 1. A Tungus, one of those commonly called the Reindeer Tungus. His name was Tschewin Amureew, of the family of Gilgegirsk. He lived about 350 versts from the city Bargus; and cut his own throat in 1791. Schilling, the head army-surgeon, was sent thence by Werchnelldinski, to make a legal inquiry as to the cause of his death; he brought back the skull with his own hand, and gave it to Baron de Asch.

Fig. 2. The head of a Carib chief, who died at St. Vincent eight years ago, and whose bones, at the request of Banks, were dug up there by Anderson, the head of the royal garden in that island.

Fig. 3. A young Georgian female, made captive in the last Turkish war by the Russians, and brought to Muscovy. There she died suddenly, and an examination was made of the cause of death by Hiltebrandt, the most learned anatomical professor in Russia. He carefully preserved the skull for the extreme elegance of its shape, and sent it to St Petersburg to de Asch.

Fig. 4. The skull of a Tahitian female, brought at the request of Banks by the brave and energetic Captain Bligh, on his return from his famous voyage, during which he transported with the greatest success stocks of the bread-fruit tree from the Society Islands to the East Indies.

Fig. 5. An Ethiopian female of Guinea; the concubine of a Dutchman, who died at Amsterdam in her 28th year. She was dissected by Steph. Jo. Van Geuns, the learned professor at Utrecht.

SECTION I.

OF THE DIFFERENCE OF MAN FROM OTHER ANIMALS.

1. *Difficulty of the subject.* He who means to write about the variety of mankind, and to describe the points in which the races of men differ from each other in bodily constitution, must first of all investigate those differences which separate man himself from the rest of the animals. The same thing occurs here which we often see happen in the study of natural history, and especially of zoology, that it is much easier to distinguish any species from its congeners at the first glance by a sort of divination of the senses, than to give an account of, or express in words those distinctive characters themselves. Thus we find it very easy to distinguish the rat from the domestic mouse, or the rabbit from the hare, but difficult to lay down the characteristic marks on which that diversity, which we all feel, depends. This difficulty of our present subject has been candidly and publicly confessed by the great authorities of the science; so much so that the immortal Linnæus, a man quite created for investigating the characteristics of the works of nature, and arranging them in systematic order, says, in the preface of his *Fauna Suecica*, "that it is a matter for the most arduous investigation to enunciate in what the peculiar and specific difference of man consists;" nay more, he confesses "that up to the present he has been unable to discover any character, by which man can be distinguished from the ape;" and in his *Systema Naturæ*, he gives it as his opinion, "that it is wonderful how little the most foolish ape differs from the wisest

man, so that we have still to seek for that measurer of nature, who is to define their boundaries;* finally, he did not attribute to man any generic or specific character, but, on the contrary, ranked the long-handed ape as his congener.

2. *Order of treatment.* Meanwhile I may be allowed to enumerate the points, in which, if I have any powers of observation, man differs from other animals, and I mean to treat the subject thus:

First, I shall enumerate those things which affect the external conformation of the human body.

Secondly, those which affect the internal conformation.

Thirdly, the functions of the animal economy.

Fourthly, the endowments of the mind.

Fifthly, I mean to add a few words about the disorders peculiar to man.

And sixthly, I shall reckon up those points, in which man is commonly, but *wrongly,* thought to differ from the brutes.

3. *External conformation.* Under this head I place some characters, which, although they are closely connected with the structure of the skeleton, yet are shown by the external habit of body, which depends upon it; and then the subsequent characters, especially if they are looked at collectively, seem to suffice for a definition of mankind:

(A) The erect position;
(B) The broad, flat pelvis;
(C) The two hands;
(D) The regular and close set rows of teeth.

To these heads all the other peculiarities which the human body exhibits, may be easily referred; and now let us examine them one by one.

4. *The erect position.* Here it is necessary for us to prove two points: first, whether the erect position is natural to man; secondly, whether it is peculiar to man (of which below, s. 10).

The former is evident *à priori*, as they say, from the very structure of the human body; and *à posteriori* from the unanimous concurrence of all the nations of all time that we are acquainted with. It is no more necessary to spend any time on this, than on the argument to the contrary, which some are in the habit of bringing from the instances of infants who have been brought up among wild beasts, and found to go on all-fours. Those who look carefully at the matter will easily see that no condition can be conceived more different to that which nature has designed for man, than that of those wretched children alluded to; for we might just as well take some monstrous birth as the normal idea of human conformation, as take advantage of those wild children to demonstrate the natural method of man's gait and life. Indeed, if we look a little more closely into these stories of wild children, it is more likely to turn out in the instances which are the most authentic, and placed beyond all doubt, as that of our famous Peter of Hameln[1] (Peter the wild boy, *Juvenis Hannoveranus* Linn.), of the girl of Champagne[2], the Pyrenæan wild man[3], and of others, that these wretches used to walk upright; but in the stories of the others who are commonly said to go on all-fours, as the *Juvenis ovinus Hibernus* Linn., there are many things which make the story very doubtful, and of but indifferent credit[4]; so that the *Homo sapiens ferus* of Linnæus (*Syst. Nat.* ed. 12, Tom. I. p. 28) seems no more entitled to the epithet of four-footed than that of shaggy.

---

[1] Comp. particularly Voigt, *Magazin für Physik und Naturgesch.* T. IV. Part III. p. 91, and also Monboddo, *Antient Metaphysics,* Vol. III. Lond. 1784, pp. 57, 367. How much importance the Scotch philosopher attaches to Peter of Hameln is proved amongst other passages by the following: "this phænomenon is more extraordinary, I think, than the new planet, or than if we were to discover 30,000 more fixed stars, besides those lately discovered."

[2] (De la Condamine) *Histoire d'une jeune fille sauvage.* Paris, 1761, 12mo.

[3] Comp. Leroy, *Sur l'exploitation de la nature dans les Pyrénées.* Lond. 1776, 4to. p. 8.

[4] [Blumenbach's note here consists of extracts from the account of this *Juvenis Hibernus* by Tulp: but as that author is rare, I give instead the whole account at length. "The most acute sense of hearing would have been deceived by that genuine bleating which was heard by many others as well as myself to proceed from that Irish youth, who was brought up from infancy among sheep, and whom therefore it will be here worth while to describe exactly as he was. There was

5. *Man's structure proves that he was made upright by nature.* It is irksome and tedious to go a long way about to demonstrate a thing so manifest and evident of itself; but that pair of learned men, P. Moscati the Italian, and A. Schrage[1] the Belgian, who have patronized the opposite paradox, prevent my leaving it quite alone. Still it will be enough to touch on a few points out of many.

The length of his legs, in proportion to his trunk and his arms, show, at the first glance, that man was intended to be upright by nature. For, although I cannot agree with Daubenton, who thinks[2] that no animal besides man has such large hind feet, which are equal in length to the breadth of his trunk and head; for this is negatived by the examples of several mammals, as the *Simia lar* and the *Jerboa Capensis;* still it is plain to every one, that man is so made that he can in no wise go on all-fours; for even infants crawl by resting on their knees, although at that tender age the legs are smaller in the proportion we spoke of than in adults.

It is not however the length only, but the remarkable

[1] brought to Amsterdam, and exposed to the eyes of all, a youth of sixteen years, who, being lost perhaps by his parents and brought up from his cradle amongst the wild sheep in Ireland, had acquired a sort of ovine nature. He was rapid in body, nimble of foot, of fierce countenance, firm flesh, scorched skin, rigid limbs, with retreating and depressed forehead, but convex and knotty occiput, rude, rash, ignorant of fear, and destitute of all softness. In other respects sound, and in good health. Being without human voice he bleated like a sheep, and being averse to the food and drink that we are accustomed to, he chewed grass only and hay, and that with the same choice as the most particular sheep. Turning in the same way every mouthful round, and taking account of each blade separately, he made his selection, and tasted now only this, and now only that, as they seemed more grateful, and more agreeable to his sense of smell and taste.

"He had lived on rough mountains and in desert places, himself equally fierce and untamed, delighting in caves and pathless and inaccessible dens. He was accustomed to spend all his time in the open air, and to put up equally with winter and summer. He kept as far as he could away from the lures of hunters, but at last fell into their nets, although he fled over uneven rocks, and precipitous cliffs, and threw himself most boldly into thorny brakes and sharp jungles, in which being at last entangled he fell into the power of the huntsman. His appearance was more that of a wild beast than a man; and though kept in restraint, and compelled to live among men, most unwillingly, and only after a long time did he put off his wild character.

"His throat was large and broad, his tongue as it were fastened to his palate." Tulp. *Obs. Med.* l. iv. c. 10, 4th ed. p. 296. Ludg. Bat. 1716, 12mo. ED.]

[1] See *Verhandeling over de Loopterring* in the journal called *Gracrs Natuuren Huishond-kundige Jaarboeken*, T. III. Part 1. p. 32.

[2] *Mémoires de l'Acad. des Sciences de Paris,* 1764, p. 569.

strength of the legs compared with the more delicate arms, which clearly shows that the former are intended by nature for the sole purpose of supporting the body. This is particularly made manifest by a fact derived from osteogeny, namely, that in the new-born infant the tarsal bones, and especially the heel-bone, ossify much quicker, and become perfect much sooner than the carpal. This is a natural provision, because the little hands have no necessity for exercising any force in the first years of life, whereas the feet have to be ready to support the body, and provide for the erect gait towards the end of the first year. I say nothing of the powerful muscles of the calf of the leg, especially of the gastrocnemii interni, though these are made so strong and so prominent by nature to keep man upright, that, on that account, Aristotle, with the old anthropologists, thought that true calves should be ascribed to man alone.

The whole construction of the chest shows that man cannot in any way walk like the quadrupeds. For in the long-legged beasts the chest adheres to the sides as if squeezed forwards in a keel-like shape, and they have no collar-bone, so that the feet can more easily converge towards one another from each side, and in that way sustain the weight of the body more easily and more firmly. Besides, quadrupeds are provided either with a longer breast-bone, or with a larger number of ribs, descending nearer to the cristæ ilei, in order to sustain the viscera in the horizontal line of the trunk. But all these things are different in man, the biped. His chest is more flattened throughout, his shoulders are widely divaricated by the insertions of the shoulder-blades, his sternum is short, his abdomen more destitute of bony supports than is the case with those animals we were speaking of; and there are things of the same kind which cannot escape any one who compares with the human skeleton even a few of the quadrupeds, especially the long-legged ones. All these considerations show how ill adapted the human frame is to a quadrupedal walk, and that it cannot be anything else to him but unsteady, trembling, and very irksome and fatiguing.

6. *The broad and flat human pelvis.* What has been said gains particularly additional weight from the consideration of the human pelvis, whose clearly peculiar conformation again affords a diagnostic character by which man is made wonderfully to differ from the anthropomorphous apes, and most manifestly and most decidedly from all and singular the other mammals.

Although it may seem an affected paradox, yet the assertion, that a genuine pelvis is only to be found in the human skeleton might be defended. I mean that peculiar conjunction of the os innominatum with the sacrum and coccyx, which gives the appearance of a *pelvis*, or basin; for it is surprising how far the elongated ribs of the rest of the mammals differ from this basin-shaped formation. The termination of the ribs in the *Simia satyrus* and the elephant seem to come a little nearer the shape of the human pelvis than in other mammals whose skeletons I have examined. Still, in front the length is greater than the breadth, and behind they exhibit a very greatly elongated synchondrosis of the groin; and in both that resemblance to a basin which we spoke of is very much wanting, which is so conspicuous in man alone, in the expansion of the bones of the ilium over the linea innominata, and in the delicacy of the synchondrosis, and also in the curvature of the os sacrum from the promontory and in the direction of the vertebræ of the coccyx towards the front.

7. *The relation of the adjoining soft parts to the form of the human pelvis.* The hinder face of the pelvis gives the foundation to the glutæi muscles, of which the outermost or larger exceed in thickness all other muscles of the body, and being concealed by a remarkable stratum of fat, from the buttocks. Their fleshy, useful, and semicircular amplitude, in which the podex is hidden, form, not only in the opinion of the classical authors of natural history, such as Aristotle[1] and Buffon[2],

---

[1] *De partib. animalium,* IV. 10.
[2] *Hist. Nat.* T. II. p. 544. "Buttocks belong to the human species alone."

but also of the best physiologists, as Galen[1] and Haller[2], the principal character in which man especially differs from the apes, who are manifestly destitute of fundament.

Moreover, in consequence of that curvature of the os sacrum and the coccyx we mentioned, depends particularly the never-to-be-forgotten direction of the interior genital members of the female, and of the vagina also, the axis of which declines much more in front than in other female mammals from what is commonly called the axis of the pelvis. This makes, it is true, parturition more difficult, but, on the other hand, admirably guards against many other inconveniences, to which, especially during pregnancy, the woman, from her erect position, would be exposed.

It is in consequence of this same direction of the vagina, that in mankind the weaker sex is not, like the females of brutes, retromingent. And also because in animals (as far as we know at present) the opening of the urethra does not terminate as in woman, between the exact lips of the pudendum, but opens backwards into the vagina itself, as I have observed in these same anthropomorphous animals, the *Papio maimon* and the *Simia cynomolgus*, which I have anatomically dissected.

And, according to this same direction of the female vagina, that question must be settled which has been often discussed from the time of Lucretius, what position is most convenient to man for copulation?

"*How best to prolongate the soft delight!*"

For although man may perform this ceremony in more ways than one, and this variety of worship has been considered by the low Latinists as one of the things in which he differs

---

[1] *De usu partium*, xv. 6. Spigel, *De humani corporis fabrica*, p. 9, has cleverly elaborated the physico-theological theory of this prerogative. "Man alone of all animals can sit conveniently, since he has large and fleshy buttocks, which serve for a seat and cushion, when his stomach is full, in order that he may sit without annoyance, and easily apply his mind to reflection on divine subjects."
[2] *De corp. hum. functionibus*, T. 1. p. 57. "Nor are the apes distinguished from men by any mark easier than by this."

from brutes, still physical causes sometimes interfere to induce him to copulate[1]

"Like beasts or quadrupeds are used to do."

Still the proportion of the virile member to the vagina seems better adapted for the usual mode of venery[2].

6. *Remarks on the hymen, nymphæ, and clitoris.* In order to finish at one and the same time all those delicate matters which belong to the female part of mankind, I must here throw in something about the hymen, which little membrane, so far as I know, has hitherto been found in no other animal. Though I have examined the females of apes and papios with that view, I have never been able to find any vestige of it, or any remains changed into the *carunculæ myrtiformes;* nor was I more successful with the female elephant which was led about Germany many years ago, whose genitals I particularly examined, because I had been told that Trendelnburg, a famous physician of that day at Lubeck, had observed some kind of hymen in that beast. This little appendage to the female body is all the more remarkable, because I cannot imagine that any physical utility attaches to it. At the same time I am not much satisfied with the conjectures the physiologists offer as to the purpose of the hymen; and least of all with what Haller rather weakly suggests, "since it is found in mankind alone, it must be admitted that this sign of virginity was given for moral ends."

---

[1] Comp. Carpi (Berengarius), *Commentaria super anatomia Mundini*, p. 13. "Man of all animals copulates by embraces and caresses in different positions, and is detestable for this, because he is more wicked and voluptuous and diabolical than rational."

[2] Kæmpf. *Enchiridium Medicum*, p. 181.

[3] When I was at London two years ago, I looked over the vast treasury of engravings preserved in the library of the King of Great Britain; and was particularly struck with and most carefully studied that famous volume of drawings relating both to human and comparative anatomy, etched by the great painter Leonardo da Vinci. Amongst them I observed particularly that remarkable and, in its way, unique representation of the copulation of a man with a woman, in which the trunk of each is so exposed to view, that the relation I hinted at, of the genital member when in a state of tension to the direction of the vagina, is made quite plain. I am indebted for a most accurate copy of this very clever print to the kindness of that most amiable man and excellent artist, John Chamberlaine, librarian of that Royal collection.

Linnæus seems to have been in doubt whether the females of other kinds besides women are endowed with the nymphæ and the clitoris. But I have proved myself that neither of those parts is peculiar to mankind. I have, following many other most competent witnesses, clearly observed the clitoris in many sorts of mammals of different orders, and frequently have found it very large as in the *Papio maimon* and the *Lemur tardigradus*; but most prodigious of all, about the size of a fish, in a specimen of the *Balæna boops* about fifty-two feet in length, which I carefully examined when it was thrown on the shore in Dec. 1791, near Sandfurt in Holland. As to the nymphæ, I have found them exactly like human ones in a *Lemur Mongos*, which I kept alive myself for many years.

9. *Man a bimanous animal*. From what has been so far said about the erect stature of man follows that highest prerogative of his external conformation, namely, *the freest use of two most perfect hands*. By this conformation he so much excels the rest of the animals, as to have given rise to that old saying of Anaxagoras, which has been cooked up again in our time by Helvetius, "that he thought man was the wisest animal, because he was furnished with hands." This is rather too paradoxical: the assertion of Aristotle seems nearer the real truth, "that man alone has hands, which are real hands." For in the anthropomorphous apes themselves, the principal feature of the hands, I mean the thumb, is short in proportion, and almost nailless, and to use the expression of the famous Eustachius, quite ridiculous: so that it is true that no other hand, except the human hand, deserves the appellation of the organ of organs, with which the same Stagyrite glorifies it.

10. *Apes and the allied animals are quadrumanous*. Apes and the other animals, which are commonly called anthropomorphous, of the genera of *Papiones*, *Cercopitheci* and *Lemures*, ought not in reality to be called either bipeds or quadrupeds, but *Quadrumana*. For their hind feet are furnished with a second genuine *thumb*, not with the great toe, which is given

to the biped, man, alone[1]; indeed their feet deserve the name of hands more than their anterior extremities, since it is plain that they are adapted for purposes of prehension; and one kind of cercopithecus (*C. paniscus*) is endowed with a thumb, which is wanting in the anterior hands; but it has never been observed of any quadrumanous animal, that it is destitute of the thumb of the hind-hands.

Hence too it will be easy to settle the dispute which has been raised about the *Simia satyrus* and other anthropomorphous apes, namely, whether it is natural for them in their own woods to go as bipeds, or as quadrupeds. Neither one nor the other. For since the hands are not meant for walking upon, but for prehension, it is at once plain, that nature has designed these animals to spend their lives principally in trees. These they climb, on these they seek for their food, and so they want one pair of hands to support them, and the other pair to pluck fruits with, and other things of the kind; and for the same end nature has provided many of the cercopitheci, who are furnished with but imperfect hands, with a prehensile tail, in order that they may have a more secure hold upon trees.

It is scarcely necessary to point out that it is the result of art and discipline if any apes are ever seen to walk erect, and is plain from any drawings of the *Simia satyrus*[2], which have been taken carefully from the life, how inconvenient and unnatural that affected position of theirs is, in which they are made to lean with their fore-hands on a stick, their hind-hands meanwhile being collected in an unmeaning way into a fist[3]. Nor have I ever come across any example of an ape, or any other mammal except man, who can, like him, preserve an equilibrium

---

[1] That extraordinary lover of paradoxes, Robinet (T. v. *De la nature*, Tab. 9), exhibits the drawing of an embryo, which he gives out for that of the *Simia satyrus*: although it is plain at the first glance from the feet alone, which are furnished with a great toe, not a thumb, that it is a human foetus.

[2] See for example the monograph of Vrolik.

[3] Linnæus therefore was mistaken when he said, "that there were apes which walked with body erect on two feet like man, and who reminded one of the human species by the use they made of their feet and hands."

when standing erect on one leg at a time. Hence it is clear that the erect posture, as we find it to be naturally convenient to man, so also is it peculiar to him. Thus

> "Mankind alone can lift the head on high
> And stand with trunk erect."

11. *Properties of the human teeth.* The teeth of man are more regular than those of any other mammals. The lower incisors are more erect, which I reckon amongst the distinctive characters of the human body. The laniarii are neither too prominent, nor set too far back, but joined in the same line with their neighbours. The molars have singularly round obtuse crowns, by which they most clearly differ from the molar teeth of the *Simia satyrus* and the *S. longimana*, and all the other species of this genus whose skulls I have examined. Finally, the mandibles of man are distinguished by three characters: by their excessive *shortness;* the prominence of the chin, which corresponds with the erect incisors; but, above all, by the singular shape, direction, and junction of the condyles with the temporal bones, which certainly differ from the jaws of all other animals I am acquainted with, and which clearly prove that man is destined by nature for all kinds of food, or is an animal truly omnivorous.

12. *Other things which seem peculiar to the exterior of man, as his hairless body, &c.* I shall say nothing about some points of less importance which are frequently classed among the distinctive characters of man, such as the lobe of the ear, the swelling of the lips, especially the under one, and other things of that kind. But I must dispose in a few words of the glassy smoothness of the human body, and inquire how far it can be included among the diagnostic signs by which man differs from other mammals, who are in some way like him. Linnæus indeed asserts, "that there are some regions where there are apes less hairy than man;" but I candidly confess that I have hitherto made fruitless inquiries as to whereabouts these apes may be. On the contrary, it is proved by the unanimous consent of all travellers who are worthy of credit, and by the specimens of those animals which have been seen frequently in

Europe, that those anthropomorphous apes which are usually included under the common Malay name of Orang-utan, and which are indigenous to Angola as well as to Borneo, and also the *S. longimana*, are naturally much more shaggy than man: insomuch that those which are not even adult, and have delicate health, still are more hairy than man. Though this position is beyond all doubt, yet it is the fact that men have been observed everywhere, and especially in some of the islands of the Pacific ocean, remarkable for their shaggy bodies; but accurate descriptions of them are still wanting.

The first mention of them occurs in the nautical expeditions of the famous Spangberg[1], who, on his return to Kamschatka from the coast of Japan, relates that he found a nation of this kind on the most southern of the Kurile islands[2] (lat. 43° 50'). Anomalous individuals of the same kind were observed, but only here and there, among the inhabitants of the islands of Tanna, Mallicollo, and New Caledonia, by J. R. Forster[3]. There is a report of a similar race in Sumatra[4], which is said to inhabit the interior of the island, and is called *Orang-gugu*. As, however, man is in general conspicuous for his smooth and even skin, so, on the other hand, some particular parts of the human body seem to be more hairy than in brute animals, as the groin and the arm-pit, which characteristic has accordingly been ranked among those peculiar to man.

13. *Remarkable properties of the human body as to its internal fabric.* Having mentioned what was necessary about the absolute properties of the external human body, we are now brought to another point of the discussion, that is, his *internal fabric*; about which however our narrow limits compel us to follow Neoptolemus, and philosophize in a very few words. It will be necessary to divide this discussion into two heads; first,

---

[1] Müller's *Sammlung Russischer geschichte*, T. III. p. 174.
[2] Beyond doubt *Nadigado* island, about whose inhabitants, though only by hearsay, the companion of the great Cook, James King, received the same story. *Voyage to the Northern Hemisphere*, T. III. p. 377.
[3] See his *Bemerkungen auf seiner reise um die Welt.* p. 218.
[4] Marsden, the classical author on that island, tells us what he heard about them. *Hist. of Sumatra*, p. 35 s.

by investigating those things which man alone, or only a few other animals with him, has not got; secondly, those things which are peculiar to him.

14. *Internal parts which man is without.* Those parts which are found in mammals, and especially in the domestic ones, were once, when the opportunities of dissecting human corpses were rare or were entirely neglected with the taste for dissection, generally almost all attributed to man. Thus, for example, the *panniculus carnosus* or subcutaneous muscle, which was wrongly ascribed to him by Galen and his followers, and even by the restorer of human anatomy himself, I mean Vesalius, who was an acute critic of the mistakes of Galen, was properly denied to him by Nicolas of Steno, and ascribed to brute animals alone.

The *rete mirabile arteriosum*, which was also reckoned by Galen amongst the parts of the human body, was demonstrated to be wanting in man by Vesalius, following Berengarius of Carpi.

The *musculus oculi suspensorius s. bulbosus s. septimus*, with which the four-footed mammals are furnished, was first shown to be wanting in man according to the plan of nature by Fallopius. It has lately been found out that the human fœtus has no allantoid membrane, which is common to almost every other mammal.

I say nothing of other parts which though found in but few genera of brute animals, nevertheless have been sometimes falsely attributed to man, as the so-called *pancreas aselli*, *ductus hepaticystici*, *corpus Highmorianum*, &c. or those which are bestowed on some orders of mammals alone, but are so manifestly denied to man, that no one would readily attribute them to him; among which I mean the *membrana nictitans* (which for the sake of the order of discussion I thought it better to mention here, although it rather belongs to the external parts) and the *ligamentum suspensorium colli*, and all other things of that kind. Man shares the *foramen incisivum* behind the upper primary teeth with the quadrupeds, but it is smaller in proportion and simple, whereas in most of the other mammals it is double, and in many of vast size.

15. *The intermaxillary bone.* An account of this remarkable bone is given separately for more reasons than one. The bones of the upper jaw which in man are contiguous to each other, and keep all and each of the upper teeth fixed in their place, in brutes are separated from one another by a singular third bone shaped like a wedge inserted between them. This bone is called by Haller the *os incisivum*, because the upper incisors (where there are any) are fitted in it. As however it is also found in those mammals who are destitute of such teeth, as cattle, the elephant, the two-horned African rhinoceros, or those which belong to the Edentata, as the anteaters and the Balaenae, I think it had better be called the *os intermaxillare*[1]. In some this bone is one and indivisible, but in many bipartite, and in all distinguished by its own sutures from the neighbouring bones of the skull; one, the facial, generally extending in both directions along the nose to the extreme sockets of the incisors, the other, the palatine, running in a curved direction from those sockets to the foramina palatina.

When, therefore, Camper brings forward the want of this bone as one of the principal characters by which man differs from other mammals, a double question arises; First, Is man really without it? secondly, Are all the rest of the mammals provided with it? It was about two centuries and a half ago when this question first gave scope to a most bitter dispute between anatomists. Galen indeed has reckoned the sutures of what we have called the intermaxillary bone among the others of the skull, but Vesalius made use of this argument besides many others, to show that Galen had composed his osteological hand-book, which had so long been accepted as law, not from the skeleton of a man, but from that of an ape. It was thought after the vain attempts of Jac. Sylvius to vindicate[2] his Galen by the most wretched excuses, that this whole

---

[1] It is called by the famous anatomists Vitet and Vicq. d'Azyr os *maxillary inferius*; and by Blair, in his osteography of the elephant, os *palati*.
[2] He so twists about in endeavouring to save his divine Galen, that at last he drops down to this excuse, that although men of the present day have no intermaxillary bone, yet at the time of Galen they might have had one: and so this is

question was completely put an end to, when beyond all expectation even in our own time, Vicq d'Azyr has attempted to demonstrate an analogy between the human and animal constitution as far as the *os intermaxillare* goes, as if it were quite a new thing[1]. The only vestige of similitude on which that analogy rests, namely, the semilunar fissure, which may be seen in the maxillary bones of the human fœtus, and of infants, in a transverse direction behind the sockets of the incisors, and which sometimes remains even in adults, has long been very well known[2]. It was, however, well pointed out more than two hundred years ago according to natural truth by the sagacious Fallopius[3], that the fissure in question was ill designated by the term suture. It is not necessary to mention that the facial side of the maxillary bones in the human skull is marked by no fissure, or even suture, of this kind, though it is conspicuously so in apes[4].

As to the other question, whether man is the only mammal who is destitute of the intermaxillary bone, I must equally confess, that I have in vain sought for it in many skulls of the *Quadrumana*. The sutures which would indicate this bone are wanting in the skeleton of the dead female *Cercopithecus* which is preserved in the museum of the University, whose skull in other ways shows the remaining sutures well enough. Nor did I find them either in another skeleton of the same species, belonging to Billmann, the clever surgeon of Cassel, which however was old at the time of death and has many of the sutures obliterated, so that from this single specimen it would have been impossible to come to any conclusion.

---

no reason for attacking the prince of anatomists—"but there are some natural obstructions, which have taken possession of our bodies from intemperance in diet and venery, and from immoderate vice."
[1] *Mémoires de l'Acad. des Sciences de Paris*, 1780.
[2] See the figures of Vesalius and Coiter.
[3] "I do not agree," says he, "with those who give out publicly that they have found out a suture under the palate attached to a transverse direction to either canine, which is plain in boys, but so obliterated in adults, that no vestige of it remains. For I consider this to be rather an indentation than a suture, since it does not separate one bone from another, nor show on the outside."
[4] Eustachius, *Tab. Anat.* 46, fig. 2.

But I am acquainted with a third specimen of the same *Cercopithecus*, for the knowledge of which I am indebted to my friend Schacht, the worthy Professor of Harderovich, and in this too that bone is absent. So that it seems scarcely worth while to inquire about the presence or absence of this bone in any other specimens of this animal. In the ugly skeleton of that truly vast anthropomorphous ape from the island of Borneo, which I have examined carefully over and over again in the collection of Natural History belonging to the Prince of Orange at the Hague, I did not see the smallest vestige of those sutures; but that this ape was full grown is proved not only by the general condition of the skeleton, but also by the coalition of most of the sutures of the skull[1].

Such, however, is not the case with the skull of a younger anthropomorphous animal of the same kind, the remains of whose skeleton I dissected at London in the British Museum. An old label yet attached to it informs us that it belongs to the ape they call *orang-utan*, and was brought from the island of Sumatra, by the captain of the ship 'Aprice.' In this skull not a shadow of the sutures of the intermaxillary bone was to be found, although the remains of all the others are without exception still apparent. Neither did Tyson find them in his Angolese Satyr, nor does the figure in Daubenton of the skull of a similar animal, from the same locality, exhibit them. However then this may be, it is certain, what may also be held a character of man, that in the skulls of the apes I have been speaking of, the jaws are very prominent and projected forward as in the other mammals.

10. *Differences between some internal parts of man and those of other animals.* It must be seen at once that we can only speak here of a few of these differences, and those the most remarkable. To begin with the head, besides some things of less moment, man has, as it seems, the smallest crystalline lens

---

[1] I wonder Camper should be of the opposite opinion, for he says that this is the skeleton of an anthropomorphous ape not yet adult. *Naturgeschichte des Orangutang*, p. 146.

(the cetacea excepted) in proportion, and it is less convex in the adult than in other animals; the large occipital foramen is placed more forward than in quadrupeds[1], and there are other things of the same kind. The mass of the brain is the largest of all, not indeed (according to the opinion which has prevailed from the time of Aristotle) in proportion to the whole body, but, according to the able observation of Sömmerring, when account is taken of the slenderness of the nerves which issue from it[2]. For if the whole nervous system was divided from a physiological point of view into two parts, one, the nervous part properly so called, which embraces the nerves themselves and that portion both of the brain and the spinal marrow which lies close to their commencement; and the other, or sensorial part, which lies nearer the knot where the functions begin to coincide with the faculties of the mind, we should find that man has much the largest share of that nobler sensorial part.

That too is equally remarkable, the knowledge of which we also owe to the sagacity and acuteness of Sömmerring, that the *arenulæ* of the pineal gland so often already observed by others, are so constantly and perpetually found in human brains, from the fourteenth year of age upwards, that they also deserve to be reckoned amongst the peculiarities of man[3]. Once only, in the pineal gland of a stag, did he find similar arenulæ. And if they are ever really absent in the encephalon of an adult man, it certainly must be considered a very rare anomaly. One instance of this absence I owe to the famous physiologist of Padua, L. M. A. Caldani, who writes me word, that out of four human brains which he examined in 1780 with that object, there was only one, and that of an old man, in which no vestige of a pineal arenula was to be found.

The position of the heart is peculiar to man, and is said to be in the chest, because that entrail does not rest as in quadru-

---

[1] Daubenton, *Mémoires de l'Acad. des Sc. de Paris*, 1764.
[2] See his *Diss. de basi Encephali*. Götting. 1778. Ib. *Über die Körperliche Verschiedenheit des Negers vom Europäer*, and Ebel (J. G.), *Observationes neurolog. ex anatome comparata*, Frankf. ad Viad. 1788.
[3] Sömmerring, *De capillis vel prope vel intra glandulam pinealem sitis*, Mogunt. 1785. A figure is given in *Diss. de decussatione nervorum opticorum*, Ib. 1786.

12—2

peds upon the sternum, but in accordance with the erect position, on the diaphragm. Its base too is not as in them at right angles to the head, but to the vertebræ of the chest, like the tip of the left breast, and hence in them the heart lies right and left, whereas in man it rather has a front and back. Scarcely any other mammals beside man have the pericardium adhering to the diaphragm. The alimentary canal is just as perfect as it ought to be in an omnivorous animal. You might say man resembled the carnivores in the structure of the ventricle, and the shortness of the blind intestine; on the other hand, he is different from the herbivores in the length of the thin intestine, and its great diversity from the thick one; in the bulbous colon; in the absence of the sebaceous glands which secrete smell behind the anus. The *muliebria* too are different in man besides what has been already mentioned, in the singular parenchyma of the womb; and the early fœtus is remarkable for the texture of the placentum, the length of the umbilical funnel and the singular umbilical vein. So far as I know, the hitherto enigmatical *resicula umbilicalis* is peculiar to the young human embryo; and I have mentioned elsewhere[1], that it is common and natural to every human fœtus about the fourth month after conception, where I also have said something about the analogy it bears to the yolk-like bag of the chicken during incubation.

17. *Peculiarities of man, in respect of the functions of animal economy.* Here especial mention must be made of the peculiar tenderness and delicate softness of the human *tela mucosa*, or *cellulosa*, as it is commonly called. It is well known that there is a most remarkable difference in the different genera and species of animals as regards the substance of this tissue; that of eels being very tenacious, that of the herring being very tender: and so it was long since observed by our Zinn, a most eagle-eyed anatomist, that man, other things being equal, had beyond all other mammals the most delicate and subtle cellular substance.

---

[1] *Commeat. Soc. Reg. Scient. Gotting.* T. IX. p. 116.

I am either very much mistaken, or the softness of that envelope is to be counted amongst the chief prerogatives by which man excels the rest of the animals. For as this membrane is on the one side diffused over all parts of the body from the corium to its inmost marrow, and is interwoven like a chain with all and every part of the whole machine, and on the other is the seat of that most universal of all vital forces, contractility, next to which the dynamic power called after Stahl seems to come, I am thoroughly persuaded that to the flexible softness of this mucous membrane in man is owing his power of accustoming himself more than every other mammal to every climate, and being able to live in every region under the sun. As then nature has made man omnivorous in the matter of food as we have seen, so in respect of habitation it has intended him to dwell in every country and climate ($\pi\alpha\nu\tau o\delta\alpha\pi\acute{o}\nu$): and so his body has been composed of a most delicate mucous composition, that he may adapt and accommodate himself more easily to the multifarious effects of different climates.

To this aptitude for accommodation admirably answers that other physiological property of man, namely, *his slow growth, long infancy* and *late puberty*. In no other mammal does the skull unite or the teeth appear so late; no other animal is so long learning to stand upon its feet, or in arriving at its full stature, or so late in coming to the exercise of the sexual functions. In another point of view no other animal, considering the moderate size of his body, has allotted him by nature so protracted a term of life[1]. This incidental mention of his stature recalls to my mind that other singular property which, as far as I know, has been observed in no other animal, and which depends upon his erect position, namely, that his height

---

[1] It is scarcely possible to define the natural duration of human life, though we may consider it to be the more common and, as it were, ordinary goal of protracted old age. It is worthy of remark, what I have learnt from a careful comparison of many tables, that a considerable number in proportion of European old men attain the age of 84, whilst few survive it. Account therefore being taken of human longevity, and comparing it with the duration of the lives of other mammals, it is at once seen what a prerogative is bestowed upon man under that name, or at all events that his long infancy is compensated for with interest.

in the morning exceeds by somewhat more than a finger's breadth his height in the evening[1].

There are also some particulars to be mentioned about the sexual functions. Man has everywhere no particular time of year, as the brutes, in which he desires to copulate[2]. To men alone is conceded the prerogative of nocturnal pollutions, which I am inclined to consider as natural excretions of the healthy man, to the intent that he may be thereby freed from the annoyance and stimulus of superfluous semen when it is suitable to him on account of his temperament or constitution. The menstrual flux, on the other hand, is not less peculiar to women, and is more universal and common to all, so that I think Pliny was right in calling woman the only menstruating animal. I am indeed aware that a flux of the same kind has been frequently attributed by authors to other female animals, especially those of the quadrumanous order; thus, for example, the *Simia Diana* is said to menstruate from the tip of its tail, &c. But for twenty years I have had opportunities of seeing female apes and papios, &c. in menageries, or in travelling caravans, and have made inquiries about this subject. I often found that one or other of them sometimes suffered from uterine hæmorrhages, but that they occurred at no regular period. Such was the assertion of the more honest keepers, who looked on it as a kind of diseased affection contrary to nature, and most of them candidly confessed, that they generally gave it out for a menstruous flux, in order to excite the astonishment of the mob. As to the fabulous stories of credulous antiquity about whole nations whose women are destitute of the menstruous flux, I shall briefly speak of them in another place.

18. *Faculties of the mind which are peculiar to man.* All with one voice declare that here is the highest and best pre-

---

[1] This was first observed in 1724 by an English clergyman, Wasse. *Philos. Trans.* T. xxxiii.

[2] Unless you like to believe Augustine Nipho, who in his singular book on love (which he dedicated to Joan of Aragon, famous for her extreme beauty), discusses the reasons which cause "women to be more lustful and amorous in summer, but men on the other hand in winter."

rogative of man, *the use of reason*. But when any one inquires more particularly what these words mean, we must needs wonder how many different reasons about the meaning of reason are entertained by the most reasonable philosophers. Some think it is altogether a quite unique and peculiar faculty of man, others but the elevated and very superior grade of a faculty, of which only slight vestiges are to be found in the soul of brutes. Some look upon it as the union of all and singular the highest faculties of man; others a particular direction of the faculties of the human mind, &c.

'It is not ours to settle such disputes.'

I trust to resolve the question more briefly and safely, à *posteriori* as they say, by considering it as that prerogative of man which makes him lord and master of the rest of the animals[1]. That he has this kind of dominion is obvious. It is also equally plain that the cause of this dominion does not reside in his bodily strength. It must therefore be referred exclusively to the gifts of the mind and their superiority. And these gifts in which man so far surpasses the rest of the animals, of whatever disposition and nature they may be, we will call reason. Nature, as we have seen, has made man so as to be omnivorous and an inhabitant of the whole world. But this unlimited liberty of diet and locality, according to the almost infinite variety of climate, soil and other circumstances, brings with it also multifarious wants which cannot be met or remedied in one way alone. His Creator has therefore fortified him with the power of reason and invention, in order that he may accommodate himself to those conditions. Hence, even from the most ancient times, by the wisest nations, this chief power of man, that is, the genius of invention, has been celebrated with divine honours. Thoth, for example, by the Egyptians, Hermes by the Greeks. Thus, to compress a good deal in a few words,

---

[1] "Whoever thou art who unjustly depreciate the lot of man, think what gifts our parent has bestowed upon us, what much more powerful animals we put under our yoke, what much fleeter animals we capture, and how there is nothing mortal which is not put under our stroke."—Seneca.

man has made tools for himself, and so Franklin has acutely defined him as *a tool-making animal;* thus he has prepared for himself arms and weapons; thus he has found out ways of eliciting fire; and thus, in order that one man may use the advantages and assistance of another, he has invented *language,* which again must be considered as one of the things peculiar to man[1], since it is not like the sounds of animals, conventional, but, as the arbitrary variety of languages proves, has been invented and turned to use by him[2].

19. *Something about laughter and tears.* Besides that other manifestation of the mind I have just spoken of, I mean language, two others must be mentioned, about which there has hitherto been less doubt, whether, like speech, they are the property of man alone, since they have not been invented by, but are as it were congenital to him, and do not so much belong to the use of reason, as to the passions of the mind; I mean, *laughter,* the companion of cheerfulness, and *tears,*

'The better part of all our senses.'

It is well known that many animals secrete tears, besides man. But it is a question whether they weep from sorrow. Competent witnesses assert it of some; as Steller[3] of the *Phoca ursina,* and Pallas[4] of camels. It seems however more doubtful whether brute animals display pleasure by laughter, although many instances are given in authors. Le Cat, for example, asserts that he had seen the *Satyrus Angolensis* both weeping and laughing[5].

---

[1] The subtleties of the old and more recent schoolmen on the language of brutes are infinite. As a specimen it will be enough to cite Albertus called Magnus, who allows language to one anthropomorphous ape, I mean the pygmaeus, besides man, yet not without a memorable restriction. "The pygmy speaks although it is an animal destitute of reason, but cannot discourse, nor make use of abstract terms, but its words are rather directed to the concrete things about which it speaks."

[2] Hobbes long since perceived that man had himself invented language (about which the, in other respects, most accurate Sussmilch still doubts in our days); "the most noble and profitable invention of all other was that of speech, whereby men declare their thoughts one to another for mutual utility and conversation; without which there had been amongst men neither commonwealth, nor society, no more than amongst lions, bears and wolves."—*Leviathan,* p. 12, ed. 1651.

[3] *Nov. Commerc. Acad. Scient. Petropolit.* T. II. p. 355.

[4] *Nachrichten über die Mongolischen Völkerschaften,* T. I. p. 177.

[5] *Traité de l'Existence du fluide des nerfs,* p. 35.

20. *The most note-worthy diseases peculiar to man.* Although these pathological affections seem at first sight to have very little to do with the natural history of man, still I may be allowed to spend a few words in borrowing a summary of the principal diseases, which are also peculiar to man, especially as these phenomena, which are against nature and peculiar to him, depend on the temperament and constitution of his body, and his animal economy; and may with the same justice be noticed here, as the diseases of some animals peculiar to them are recounted in their natural history, as the *Lues bovilla*, the *Coryza maligna* of horses, or the voluntary madness which seems so frequent in dogs, &c. It will be understood that we shall only speak here of the most remarkable disorders, and that even those few, chosen out of many others, are not yet placed beyond all doubt, since the nosology of brutes, if we once leave aside our few domestic animals, is almost entirely uncultivated on account of its grave and partly insuperable difficulties. Still we may enumerate the following diseases as being with great probability some of those peculiar to mankind:—

Very nearly all the eruptive fevers; or at all events particularly among them,

    Variola[1],   Miliaria,
    Morbilli,   Petechiæ,
    Scarlatina,   Pestis.

Amongst the hæmorrhages;
    Epistaxis (?),
    Hæmorrhoides,
    Menorrhagia.

Amongst the nervous affections;
    Hypochondriasis,
    Hysteria.

---

[1] Some years ago I was informed by letter by the famous doctor Jansen of Amsterdam, that an ape there had contracted a local ulcer from some eruptive contagion, but no fever of that kind.

Disorders of the mind, properly so called, as *Melancholia, Nostalgia,* &c. and perhaps *Satyriasis* and *Nymphomania.*

  Cretinismus.

Of the cachectic disorders;
  Rhachitis (?),
  Scrofula (?),
  Lues Venerea,
  Pellagra,
  Lepra and Elephantiasis.

Of the local disorders;
  Amenorrhœa,
  Cancer (?),
  Clavus,
  Hernia congenita (?).

The various sorts of *Prolapsus,* as that of the *vesica urinaria inversa,* of which we owe a very accurate notice to the sagacity of the famous Bonn[1].

  Herpes (?),
  Tinea capitis.

I am doubtful whether I ought to include here the intestinal worms of man and two species of the genus *pedicula,* observed in no other mammal, as far as I know, but him. I say nothing of those disorders which, though not peculiar to man, are far more frequent in him than in other animals; such as tooth-ache, miscarriage, abortions, difficult parturition, &c.

21. *Short list of those things, in which it is commonly, though wrongly thought, that man differs from the brutes.* Most of these points have been referred to above as opportunities occurred. Those which are left shall be briefly recounted. Such, for example, is the proximity of the eyes, whereas, in

---

[1] I think the reason why this remarkable defect in conformation has been so observed in human infants, but not, as far as I know, in the fœtus of any other mammal, is to be sought for in the narrower proportionate synchondrosis of the pubis in man, that singular and, as it were, bipartite fissure, which also has been so accurately investigated by Bonn. See Roose, *Diss. de sativo vesicæ urinariæ inversæ prolapsu.* Gotting. 1793, 4to, with engravings.

the apes, the eyes are much closer together than in man. The lashes in either eye-lid, which have been furnished not only to man, but to many other quadrumanous animals, and even to the elephant. The *Simia rostrata* has a more prominent nose than man[1]. The ears are not immoveable in all men, nor are they moveable in all the rest of the mammals. For example, the *Myrmecophagæ* must be excepted. The organ of touch is common to most of the quadrumana with man; and so is the *uvula*. I am ashamed to mention some things which are too worthless, as cructation, which has been reckoned one of the prerogatives of man[2]; and that man cannot, like brutes, be fattened[3], and other stuff of the same kind.

---

[1] Buffon, *Hist. des quadrupèdes.* Suppl. T. VII. Tab. II. 12.
[2] Æmilianus, *De ruminantibus*, p. 50. "As man alone walks upright, so he alone, out of so many animals, can eruct; for as the breath is light it seeks a higher region, and, by a sort of natural impetus, is carried to the top."
[3] Larry in *Hist. de la Société de Médicine*, a. 1779.

SECTION II.

OF THE CAUSES AND WAYS BY WHICH THE SPECIES OF
ANIMALS DEGENERATE IN GENERAL.

---

22. *Subject proposed.* Hitherto we have investigated those things in which man differs from the rest of the animals. Now we come nearer to the primary object of the whole treatise, for we are to inquire of what kind and how great is the natural diversity which separates the races and the multifarious nations of men; and to consider whether the origin of this diversity can be traced to degeneration, or whether it is not so great as to compel us rather to conclude that there is more than one original species of man. Before this can be done, there are two questions which must be considered: First, what is *species* in zoology? Secondly, how in general a primordial species may degenerate into varieties? and now of each separately.

23. *What is species?* We say that animals belong to one and the same species, if they agree so well in form and constitution, that those things in which they do differ may have arisen from degeneration. We say that those, on the other hand, are of different species, whose essential difference is such as cannot be explained by the known sources of degeneration, if I may be allowed to use such a word. So far well in the abstract, as they say. Now we come to the real difficulty, which is to set forth the characters by which, *in the natural world*, we may distinguish mere varieties from genuine species.

The immortal Ray, in the last century, long before Buffon, thought those animals should be referred to the same species, which copulate together, and have a fertile progeny. But, as in the domestic animals which man has subdued, this character seemed ambiguous and uncertain, on account of the enslaved life they lead; in the beginning of this century, the sagacious Frisch restricted it to wild animals alone, and declared that those were of the same species, who copulate in a natural state[1].

But it must be confessed that, even with this limitation, we make but little progress. For, in the first place, what very little chance is there of bringing so many wild animals, especially the exotic ones, about which it is of the greatest possible interest for us to know whether they are to be considered as mere varieties, or as different species, to that test of copulation? especially if their native countries are widely apart; as is the case with the *Satyrus Angolensis* (Chimpanzee) and that of the island of Borneo (Orang-utan).

Then it is universally the case that the obscurity and doubt is much smaller, and of much less importance, in the case of wild animals on the point in question, than of those very animals which are excluded by this argument, that is, the domestic. Here, in truth, is the great difficulty. Hence the wonderful differences of opinion about, for example, the common dog, whose races you see are by some referred to many primitive species; by others are considered as mere degenerated varieties from that stock which is called the domestic dog (*Chien de berger*); again, there are others who think that all those varieties are derived from the jackal; and, finally, others contend that the latter, together with all the domestic dogs and their varieties, are descended from the wolf, and so forth.

As then the principle sought to be deduced from copulation is not sufficient to define the idea of species and its difference

---

[1] "When beasts by nature copulate with each other, it is an unfailing sign that they are of the same species." Berthout van Berchem fil. has lately adopted the same test of species, "if animals mix when in a natural state." But he makes no mention of Frisch, or even of Ray, nay, he says, "M. de Buffon, who was the first to abandon the little-to-be-depended-upon distinctions of the nomenclators, was also the first to make it understood that copulation was the best criterion for ascertaining species." See *Mém. de la Société des Sciences Physiques de Lausanne*, T. II. p. 49.

from variety, so neither are the other things which are adduced with this object, for example, the constancy of any character. Thus the snowy colour and the red pupils of the white *variety* of rabbit are as constant as any specific character could possibly be. So that I almost despair of being able to deduce any notion of species in the study of zoology, except from *analogy* and resemblance. I see, for example, that the molar teeth of the African elephant differ most wonderfully in their conformation from those of the Asiatic. I do not know whether these elephants, which come from such different parts of the world, have ever copulated together; nor do I know any more how constant this conformation of the teeth may be in each. But since, so far in all the specimens which I have seen, I have observed the same difference; and since I have never known any example of molar teeth so changed by mere *degeneration*, I conjecture from analogy that those elephants are not to be considered as mere varieties, but must be held to be different species.

The ferret, on the contrary, does not seem to me a separate species, but must be considered as a mere variety of the polecat, not so much because I have known them copulate together, as because the former has red pupils, and from all analogy I consider that those mammals in whom the internal eye is destitute of the dark pigment, must be held to be mere varieties which have degenerated from their original stocks.

24. *Application of what has been said to the question whether we should divide mankind into varieties or species.* It is easily manifest whither what we have hitherto said has been tending. We have no other way, but that of analogy, by which we are likely to arrive at a solution of the problem above proposed. But as we enter upon this path, we ought always to have before our eyes the two golden rules which the great Newton has laid down for philosophizing. First, *That the same causes should be assigned to account for natural effects of the same kind.* We must therefore assign the same causes for the bodily diversity of the races of mankind to which we assign a similar diversity of body in the other *domestic* animals which

are widely scattered over the world. Secondly, *That we ought not to admit more causes of natural things than what are sufficient to explain the phenomena.* If therefore it shall appear that the causes of degeneration are sufficient to explain the phenomena of the corporeal diversity of mankind, we ought not to admit anything else deduced from the idea of the plurality of human species.

25. *How does the primitive species degenerate into varieties?* As we are now about to treat of the modes of degeneration, I hope best to consult perspicuity in dealing with the subject if I arrange it again under two heads; of which the first will briefly relate the principal phenomena of the degeneration of brute animals; and the second will inquire into the causes of this degeneration. This being done, it will be easier in the following section to compare the phenomena of variety in mankind as well with those phenomena of degeneration in brute animals as with the causes of them.

26. *Principal phenomena of the degeneration of brute animals.* A few instances, and those taken from the warm-blooded animals alone, and also as far as possible from the mammals which are most like man in their corporeal economy, will be enough to show that there is no native variety in mankind which may not be observed to arise amongst other animals as a more variety and by degeneration. But it is better to go over these things in separate chapters.

27. *Colour.* Thus in the way of colour, the pigs in Normandy are all white; in Savoy, black; in Bavaria[1], chesnut. The *Pecus bubulum* in Hungary generally varies from white to grey; in Franconia they are red, &c. In Corsica the dogs and horses are beautifully spotted. In Normandy, the peacocks are black; ours, on the other hand, are generally white. On the Guinea coast, the birds, especially of the hen tribe[2], and the dogs, are black like the aborigines; and, what is particularly remarkable, the Guinea dog (which Linnæus calls *C. Ægyptius*,

---

[1] Comp. Voigt, *Magazin.* T. vi. P. i. p. 10.
[2] See Dan. Beeckman's *Voyage to and from Borneo*, Lond. 1718, 8vo. p. 14.

I do not know why, is, like the men of that climate, distinguished for the velvety softness of his smooth skin, and the great and nearly specific cutaneous perspiration[1].

28. *Texture of the hair.* As to the texture of hair, what a difference is there not, I ask, in the wool alone of the sheep of different climates, from the tender Tibetan up to the thick and almost stiff Ethiopian! Or in the bristles of the sow, which are so soft in those of Normandy, that they are not fit for scouring-brushes! And what a difference there is, in this respect, between the boar and the domestic sow, especially as to the short wool which grows between the bristles[1]. How remarkable too is the effect of every region of the globe upon the hair of more than one kind of the domestic mammals, as the effect of the climate of Galatia on the bearded cattle of Angora, and on the rabbits and cats, who are so conspicuous for their woolly softness and the extraordinary length and generally snowy whiteness of their coats.

29. *Stature.* As to stature the difference between the Patagonian and the Laplander is much smaller than what is observed everywhere in other domestic animals of different parts of the world. Thus pigs, when transported to Cuba from Europe, grow to double their natural size[1]. So also do cows when transported to Paraguay[1].

30. *Figure and proportion of parts.* As to the proportion of parts, what a great difference there is between the horses of Arabia or Syria and of northern Germany; between the thick-footed cows of the Cape of Good Hope and the thin-footed ones of England! The hinder legs of the sows of Normandy are much higher than the front legs, &c. The cows in some parts of England and Ireland have no horns at all[1]; in Sicily, on the other hand, they have very large ones; but I must not say anything of the vast horns of the Abyssinian oxen, which Sir Joseph Banks showed me, for they, if we are to trust Bruce,

---

[1] Pechlin, *De Habitu et Colore Æthiopum,* Kilon. 1677, 8vo. p. 56.
[2] Voigt, *Magazin. l. c.*
[3] F. Naver. Clavigero, *Storia Antica del Messico,* T. IV. p. 142.
[4] Comp. also Hippocrates, *De aeribus, aquis, et locis,* s. 44.

ought rather to be referred to some morbific disposition. We may however mention here the *Ovis polycerata;* and as to the variety of hoofs, there are whole races of sows with solid and with three-cloven hoofs[1]. As to some other parts, we have sheep with broad tails; the fringes of the crested canary (what our people call *kapp. vögel*) and other things of this kind.

31. *Above all, the shape of the skull.* The shape has been observed to differ everywhere in the varieties of mankind; but all this difference is not a whit greater, if indeed it can be compared to that which may be observed amongst the different races of other domestic animals. The skull of the Ethiopian does not differ more from that of the European than that of the domestic sow from the osseous head of the boar; or than the head of the Neapolitan horse, which is called from its shape ram-headed, from that of the Hungarian horse, which the learned know well is conspicuous for its singular lowness and the size of its inferior jaw. In the urus, the progenitor of our domestic race of bulls, according to the observations of Camper, very large foveæ lacrymales are visible; which, on the contrary, are entirely obsolete in our country cattle. I say nothing of that manifestly monstrous degeneration of skull in the variety of hen they call the Padusan[2].

32. *Causes of degeneration.* Animal life supposes two faculties, depending upon the vital forces as primary conditions and principles of all and singular its functions; the one, namely, of so receiving the force of the stimuli which act upon the body that the parts are affected by it; the other of so reacting from this affection that the living motions of the body are in this way set in action and perfected. So there is no motion in the animal machine without a preliminary stimulus and a consequent reaction. These are the hinges on which all the physiology of the animal economy turns. And these are the fountains from which, just as the business itself of generation, so also the *causes*

---

[1] Voigt, *Magazin*, l. c.
[2] Pallas, *spicileg. zoologic.* fasc. IV. p. 21, and Sandifort, *Musæum Anatom. Acad. Lugd. Batav.* T. I. p. 306.

of degeneration flow; but in order to make this clear to those even who know but little of physiology, it will be as well to premise with a few words from that science.

33. *Formative force.* I have in another place professedly, and in a separate book devoted to this subject, endeavoured to show that the vulgar system of evolution, as it is called (according to which it is taught that no animal or plant is generated, but that all individual organic bodies were at the very earliest dawn of creation already formed in the shape of undeveloped germs and are now being only successively evolved), answers neither to the phenomena themselves of nature, nor to sound philosophic reasoning. But on the contrary, by properly joining together the two principles which explain the nature of organic bodies, that is the physico-mechanical with the teleological, we are conducted both by the phenomena of generation, and by sound reasoning, to lay down this proposition: That the genital liquid is only the shapeless material of organic bodies, composed of the innate matter of the inorganic kingdom, but differing in the force it shows, according to the phenomena; by which its first business is under certain circumstances of maturation, mixture, place, &c. to put on the form destined and determined by them; and afterwards through the perpetual function of nutrition to preserve it, and if by chance it should be mutilated, as far as lies in its power to restore it by reproduction.

Let me be allowed to distinguish this energy, so as to prevent its being confused with the other kinds of vital force, or with the vague and undefined words of the ancients, the plastic force, &c. by the name of the formative force (*nisus formativus*); by which name I wish to designate not so much the cause as some kind of perpetual and invariably consistent effect, deduced *à posteriori*, as they say, from the very constancy and universality of phenomena. Just in the same way as we use the name of attraction or gravity to denote certain forces, the *causes* of which however still remain hid, as they say, in Cimmerian darkness.

As then other vital forces, when they are excited by their

appointed and proper stimuli, become active and ready for reaction, so also the formative force is excited by the stimuli which belong to it, that is, by the kindling of heat in the egg during the process of incubation. But as other vital forces, as contractility, irritability, &c. put themselves out only by the mode of motion, this, on the other hand, of which we are talking, manifests itself by increase, and by giving a determinate form to matter; by which it happens that every plant and every animal propagates its species in its offspring (either immediately, or gradually by the successive access and change of other stimuli, through metamorphosis).

Now the way in which the formative force may sometimes turn aside from its determined direction and plan is principally in three forms. First, by the production of monsters; then by hybrid generation through the mixture of the genital liquid of different species; finally, by degeneration into varieties, properly so called. The production of monsters, by which, whether through some disturbance and as it were mistake of the formative force, or even through accidental or adventitious circumstances, as by external pressure, &c. a structure manifestly faulty and unnaturally deformed is intruded upon organic bodies, has nothing to do with our present purpose. Nor is this the place to consider hybrids sprung from the commingling of the generation of different species, since by a most wise law of nature (by which the infinite confusion of specific forms is guarded against) hybrids of this kind, especially in the animal kingdom, scarcely ever occur except through the interference of man: and then they are almost invariably sterile, so as to be unable to propagate any further their new ambiguous shape sprung from anomalous venery.

Still, meanwhile, this subject we are now discussing may be illustrated by the history of hybrids sprung from different species; partly on account of their analogy with those hybrids which spring from different *varieties*, of which we shall speak by and by; partly, because, like everything else, they go as proofs to refute that theory about the evolution of pre-formed germs, and to display clearly the power and efficacy of the formative force; a consideration, which will escape no one who rightly appreciates those well-known and very remarkable experiments, in which, in the very rare instances of *prolific* hybrids, when their fecundation has been frequently repeated for many generations by the aid of the male seed of the same species, that new appearance of hybrid posterity has so sensibly deflected from the maternal form as more and more to pass into the paternal form of the other species, and so, finally, the former seems to become quite transmuted into the latter, by a sort of arbitrary metamorphosis[1].

But the mixture of specifically different generation, although it cannot overturn, or as it were suffocate, all the excitability of the formative force, still can impart to it a singular and anomalous direction. And so it happens that the continuous action, carried on for several series of generations of some peculiar stimuli in organic bodies, again has great influence in sensibly diverting the formative force from its accustomed path, which deflection is the most bountiful source of degeneration, and the mother of varieties properly so called. So now let us go to work and examine one by one the chief of these stimuli.

34. *Climate.* That the power of climate must be almost infinite, as on all organic bodies, so especially on warm-blooded animals, will quickly appear to any one who considers first, by how intimate and how constant a bond these animals are bound while alive to the action of the atmospheric air in which they dwell. Besides, how wonderfully this air (which was once held to be a simple element of itself) is made up of what they call multifarious elements, such as gasiform constituents, the accessories of light, heat, electricity, &c. Then of what different proportions of these matters does it not consist, and in consequence of this variety how different must be the atmospheric action on those we call animals! Especially when we

---

[1] Kolreuter. Third account of the news of some experiments relating to the sex of plants, &c., p. 51, s. 24, with the title, "An entirely complete change of one kind of plant into another."

throw in the consideration of so many other things, by whose accession climates differ so much, as the position of countries in respect of the zones of the globe, the elevation of the soil, mountains, the vicinity of the sea or lakes and rivers, the customary winds, and innumerable other things of this kind.

This air, then, which those we call animals suck in by breathing from the time of birth, modified so greatly by the variety of climates, is decomposed in their lungs as it were in a living laboratory. Part of what they inhale is distributed with the arterial blood over the whole body; but as a balance to another portion of this point, elements are liberated, which are partly deposited on the peripheral integuments of the body, and partly are carried back by the flow of venous blood to the respiratory organs; hence arise the various modifications of the blood itself, and the remarkable influxes of these humours, especially of fat, bile, &c. into the secretions. Hence finally the action of all these things as so many stimuli on a living solid, and hence the resulting reaction as well of this thus affected solid, as what especially belongs to our discussion, the direction and determination of the formative force. This great and perpetual influence of climate on the animal economy and the habit and conformation of the body, although there has been no time when it has not attracted the attention of good observers, has in our own time above all been illustrated and confirmed by the great advance that has been made in chemistry, and by a deeper study of physiology. Still it is always a difficult and arduous thing, in the discussion of these varieties, to settle what is to be attributed exclusively to climate, what rather to other causes of degeneration, and finally to the joint action of both. Meanwhile I will bring forward one or two instances of degeneration which seem most clearly to be derived from the effects of climate. For example, the white colour of many animals in northern regions, which have other colours in the temperate zones. Instances are, those of wolves, hares, cattle, falcons, crows, blackbirds, thrushes, chaffinches, &c. That this whiteness must be attributed to cold, we learn from the analogy of animals of the same kind who, under the same climate during winter, change their summer colour into white or grey; as weasels and ermines, hares, squirrels, reindeer, the ptarmigan, snow-bunting, and others[1]. So also I am more inclined to attribute to climate that snowy fleece so conspicuous for its silky softness of some of the animals of Angora than to the kind of diet, because that is shared by those who feed on all sorts of different things, by the carnivorous, as the cat for example, equally with the herbivorous ruminants, as goats, &c.

Such too seems to be the explanation of the coally blackness which under some districts of the torrid zone, as on the coasts of Guinea, animals of different orders, mammalia as well as birds, are seen to put on with the colour of the Ethiopians (s. 27). And it is above all worthy of remark that this Ethiopic blackness, just like that Syrian whiteness, although the animals may be transported into regions of a very different climate, is still preserved permanently for many series of generations. Nor is the power and influence of climate on the stature of organic bodies at all inferior; since cold obstructs their increase, which, on the contrary is manifestly augmented and promoted by heat. Thus the horses of Scotland, or cold North Wales, are small; in Scandinavia the horses and the cattle, like the indigenous races, are of tall and stalwart stature; in Smaland they are sensibly smaller, and in the north of East Gothland are in proportion smallest of all.

35. *Diet.* It seems extremely probable, what has been demonstrated principally by the sagacity of G. Fordyce, that the primary elements, as they are called, of every kind of alimentary substance, whether it be taken from the animal or the vegetable kingdom, are the same. Hence the same sort of chyle, and universally the same kind of blood, is elaborated by all the multifarious warm-blooded animals, carnivorous as well as herbivorous, out of the most different kinds of nourishment, if only it has been properly submitted to the organs of diges-

---

[1] Comp. besides others, Linnæus, in *Flora Lapponica*, p. ss, 352, ed. Smith.

tion. Still, however much this may appear to be true, it cannot be denied that the innumerable adventitious qualities of different matters of food, have had great power in changing the natures and properties of animals; to prove which a few instances will be enough.

Singing birds show that there is some specific power in some kinds of food to change the colour of animals; especially some sorts of larks and finches, which it has been proved, if they are fed upon hemp seed alone, sensibly grow black. The African sheep when transported to England is a proof how wonderfully, when the diet is changed, the texture of the hairs will change also; for its wool which is common by nature, and stiff like the hair of a camel, after it has been fed one year upon English pastures becomes of a most magnificent delicacy[1]. The influence food has towards changing the stature and the proportions, is plain from the comparison of domestic animals. Horses which in marshy countries (called in the vernacular *Maschländer*) live upon rich food, as the Frisian especially, grow large; whereas, on the contrary, in rocky and stony countries, such as those of Œland, or on dry heathy soils, they remain stunted. Thus it is surprising how fat and bellied horses become on a fat soil, though their legs become shorter in proportion. But when they are fed upon drier grass, as, for example, the Cape grass, they secrete less fat, but are remarkable for their strong and fleshy legs; to say nothing of the multifarious diversities of the taste and weight of flesh, which again depend upon the variety of diet.

36. *Mode of life.* When I speak of the kind of life as a cause of degeneration, I include under that head all those points besides climate and diet which so far have to do with the natural economy of animals, that when they act long and continuously upon the same condition of body they are at length strong enough to change it to some extent. The principal of these are cultivation and the force of custom, whose power and

---

[1] Comp. Jam. Bates *On the Literal Doctrine of Original Sin*, Lond. 1766, 8vo. p. 224.

influence are again so manifestly conspicuous in our domestic animals.

Consider, for instance, the vast difference which separates the conformation and the proportions of the parts of the generous horse trained in the school, and the wild horse, which they call a wild beast. The latter, when it fights with others bites rather than kicks; the former, on the other hand, when bridled and armed with iron feet, prefers to attack his enemy with them, and almost unlearns to bite. Many kinds of mammals when subdued by man show by the hanging of their tails and the lapping of their ears a spirit tamed and subdued by slavery. In many the very corporeal functions of secretion, generation, &c. are changed in a wonderful way. In the domestic pig, for example, the adipose membrane appears in a vast mass, which is quite wanting in the boar, whose tender and as it were woolly hairs, on the contrary, inserted between the bristles, sensibly disappear in that domestic variety. These domestic animals are much more liable to monstrous births than their wild aborigines; and also to troops of new diseases, and especially to new kinds of worms of which no vestige is to be found in their wild and original variety; the truth of which assertion, though paradoxical, is not to be invalidated, as may be proved by the instance of the *Hydas intercutis*, called, in the vernacular, *Finnen*, Ital. *Lazaroli*[1]. I place under this head also stunted stature from premature and unseasonable venery, and everything of that kind.

37. *Hybrid generation.* So much for the triple sources of degeneration which only by long and daily action, continued through many series of generations, are sufficiently strong, slowly, and by little and little, to change the primeval character of animals and produce varieties. But the case is different, and a new character is imparted to the immediate offspring, when different varieties of this kind, sprung at length from those

---

[1] Malpighii *Opera Posthuma*, p. 84. ed. Lond. 1697. fol.—so J. A. E. Goeze, *Discovery; that the hydatids in swine's flesh are no glander disease, but true bladder-worms.* 8vo. Hal. 1784.

HYBRIDITY. 201

causes, come to copulate together, for thus they give rise to a hybrid offspring, like neither parent altogether, but participating in the form of each, and being as it were a mean between the two. Hybrid is the name commonly given to the offspring of parents of manifestly different species, as mules sprung from the horse and ass, or birds from the union of the crested canary with the linnet. But this is not the place for us to speak of these, for there is no account to be taken of them in varieties of the human race. Not indeed that horrid stories are wanting of the union of men with brutes, when either men have had to do with the females of beasts (whether carried away by unbridled lust[1], or from some mad idea of continence[2], or because they expected some medicinal aid from this sort of crime[3]), or when we are told that women have been made use of by male brutes (whether that has happened through any violent rape[4], or because women have solicited them in the madness of lust[5], or have prostituted themselves from religious superstition[6]), still we have never known any instance related on good authority of any such connexion being fruitful, or that

---

[1] Comp. Th. Warton on Theocriti *Idyll*. 1. 88, p. 19. "I have been told by a certain learned friend, that when he was travelling in Sicily and investigating closely not only the ancient monuments but also the manners of the people, that even their own priests used to ask the shepherds, who spend a military life in the Sicilian mountains, as a matter of course among the articles of confession, whether they had had anything to do with the she-goats."

[2] See Mart. h Baumgarten Equ. Germ. *Travels in Egypt, Arabia, &c.* p. 73. "As we went out of Alkan, in Egypt, we came to a village called Bethen, where we joined a caravan going to Damascus. There we saw a Saracenic saint, sitting on the heaps of sand, as naked as he came out of his mother's womb. We heard this saint whom we saw in that place publicly praised above all things; that he was a holy man, divine and perfect beyond all measure, because he never had any connexion with women or boys, but only with asses and mules."

[3] With this object Pallas says that when the Persians suffer from hip-gout they copulate with the onagra. *Neue Nordische beytrage*, P. II. p. 38.

[4] Baboons. Comp. Ph. Phillips's *Travels in Guinea* in Churchill's *Collection of Voyages*, T. VI. p. 217. "Here are a vast number of overgrown large baboons, some as big as a large mastiff dog, which go in droves of 50 and 100 together, and are very dangerous to be met with, especially by women, who, I have been credibly assured, they have often seized upon, ravished, and in that kind abused one after another, till they have killed them."

[5] Thus Steller says that the women of Kamtschatka formerly copulated with dogs. *Beschreibung von Kamtschatka*, p. 289.

[6] As the women of Mendes with the sacred goat; on which singular custom see a copious dissertation by D'Hancarville, *Recherches sur l'origine des Arts de la Grèce*, T. 1. p. 320.

any hybrid has ever been produced from the horrid union of beast and man. But we have only to do with those hybrids which spring from the intercourse of different varieties of one and the same species, as when, for example, the green canary bird is paired with the white variety, &c., which connexion has a wonderful effect in changing the colour and conformation of the new progeny which results therefrom; so that this is often applied with the greatest advantage in the impregnation of domestic animals for the purpose of improving and ennobling the offspring, especially in the case of horses and sheep.

38. *Hereditary peculiarities of animals from diseased temperament.* An hereditary disposition to disease would seem at first sight rather to belong to the pathology than to the natural history of animals. But when the matter is more carefully looked into, it is plain that in more ways than one it has something to do with those causes of degeneration we are concerned with. For, in the first place, some external qualities of animals, although according to common ideas they are never referred to a truly diseased constitution, still seem to come very nearly to that, since they are for the most part found in conjunction with an unnaturally weak affection. I include among these, for example, that peculiar whiteness of some animals, which the wise Verulam long ago called the colour of defect. We learn by the example of the Hungarian oxen, whose woolly skin only comes after castration, that we may frequently recognize as a cause the vicious constitution and defect of the corporeal economy. On the other hand, it is proved by the instances of the Angora cats and dogs, that morbid symptoms follow extraordinary whiteness of that kind, for it is a common observation that those animals are almost always hard of hearing.

It is also the case that some genuine diseases when the animal nature has been as it were used to them for a long series of generations seem to get sensibly milder and milder and less inconvenient, so that at last they can scarcely be considered more than a diseased affection. An example is afforded by that vicious species of whiteness which, when united to a deficiency of the black pigment which lines the internal eye of hot-blooded animals, is known by the name of leucæthiopia. This when it seizes sporadically one or other of a family (for it is always a congenital affection) exhibits plainly the symptoms of cachexia, which everywhere comes very near to a leprous constitution. But in other cases when it has been established by a sort of hereditary right for many generations, it becomes a second nature, so that in the white variety of rabbits not a vestige remains of the original morbific affection, the existence of which however is determined by the analogy of other animals which have anomalously white pupils and red eyes. The ferret has been considered by some zoologists as a peculiar species of the genus *Mustela*, whereas, unless I am altogether deceived, it is as I have said above (s. 23) a mere variety of the pole-cat, and that of diseased origin through leucæthiopia.

39. *Problem proposed. Can mutilations and other artifices give a commencement to native varieties of animals?* It is disputed whether deformities or mutilations, effected upon animals either by accident or advisedly, especially in those cases where they have been repeated for many series of generations, can at length in progress of time terminate in a sort of second nature, so that what before was done by art now degenerates into a congenital conformation. Some[1] have asserted this, whilst others[2] on the contrary have denied it. Those who are for the affirmative point to the examples of the young of different kinds of animals, dogs and cats for example, which are born without tails or ears after those parts have been cut off from their parents, as is proved by credible witnesses. And of boys among circumcised nations who are frequently born naturally *apellæ*[3]; and of scars which parents bear from wounds, whose marks afterwards are congenital in the infants. Buffon, indeed, went so far as to derive from the same source the peculiar characters of some animals, as the callosities on the breast and

---

[1] Hippocrates and Aristotle. And very recently Klügel, in Tom. I. of the Encyclopedia, p. 541, ed. 2nd.
[2] See Kant, in *Berliner Monatsschrift*, 1785, T. VI. p. 400.
[3] Voigt, *Magazin*, T. VI. P. 1. p. 22, and P. IV. p. 40.

legs of camels, or the bald scurfy forehead of the rook (*Corvus frugilegus*). Those who do not allow these last instances will not unwisely reject this opinion of Buffon, as what is called a *petitio principii*; but the other instances we spoke of they will think should rather be attributed to chance.

I have not at present adopted as my own either the affirmative or the negative of these opinions; I would willingly give my suffrage with those on the negative side, if they could explain why peculiarities of the same sort of conformation, which are first made intentionally or accidentally, cannot in any way be handed down to descendants, when we see that other marks of race which have come into existence from other causes which up to the present time are unknown, especially in the face, as noses, lips, and eye-brows are universally propagated in families for few or many generations with less or greater constancy, just in the same way as *organic*[1] disorders, as deficiencies of speech and pronunciation, and such like; unless perhaps they prefer saying that all these occur also by chance.

40. *Some considerations to be observed in the examination of the causes of degeneration.* Many of the causes of degeneration we have already spoken of are so very clear, and so placed beyond all possibility of doubt, that most phenomena of degeneration above enumerated may by an easy process be undoubtedly referred to them, as effects to their causes. But on the other hand even in that very way there is frequently such a concurrence or such a conflicting opposition of many of them; such a diverse and multifarious proneness of organic bodies to degeneration, or reaction from it; and besides, these causes have such effects upon these bodies according as they act immediately (so to speak) or otherwise; and finally, such is the difference of these effects by which they are preserved unimpaired by a sort of tenacious constancy through long series of generations, or by some power of change withdraw themselves

---

[1] A remarkable instance is related by Harquast in the *Magazin* of Voigt just cited, T. VI. P. IV. p. 34.

again in a short space of time, that in consequence of this diversified and various relation there is need of the greatest caution in the examination of varieties.

Let me then, if only for the benefit of the student, at the end of this discourse, before we pass to the varieties of men themselves, lay down some maxims of caution at least, as corollaries to be carefully borne in mind in the discussion we are entering upon:

1. The more causes of degeneration which act in conjunction, and the longer they act upon the same species of animals, the more palpably that species may fall off from its primeval conformation. Now no animal can be compared to man in this respect, for he is omnivorous, and dwells in every climate, and is far more domesticated and far more advanced from his first beginnings than any other animal; and so on him the united force of climate, diet, and mode of life must have acted for a very long time.

2. On the other hand an otherwise sufficiently powerful cause of degeneration may be changed and debilitated by the accession of other conditions, especially if they are as it were opposed to it. Hence everywhere in various regions of the terraqueous globe, even those which lie in the same geographical latitude, still a very different temperature of the air and an equally different and generally a contrary effect on the condition of animals may be observed, according as they differ in the circumstances of a higher or lower position, proximity to the sea, or marshes, or mountains, or woods, or of a cloudy or serene sky, or some peculiar character of soil, or other circumstances of that kind.

3. Sometimes a remarkable phenomenon of degeneration ought to be referred not so much to the immediate, as to the mediate, more remote, and at the first glance concealed influence of some cause. Hence the darker colour of peoples is not to be derived solely from the direct action of the sun upon the skin, but also from its more remote, as its powerful influence upon the functions of the liver.

4. Mutations which spring from the mediate influence of

causes of this sort seem to strike root all the deeper, and so to be all the more tenaciously propagated to following generations. Hence, if I mistake not, we are to look for the reason why the brown colour of skin contracted in the torrid zone will last longer in another climate than the white colour of northern animals if they are transported towards the south.

5. Finally, the mediate influences of those sort of causes may lie hid and be at such a distance, that it may be impossible even to conjecture what they are, and hence we shall have to refer the enigmatical phenomena of degeneration to them, as to their fountains. Thus, without doubt, we must refer to mediate causes of this kind, which still escape our observation, the racial and constant forms of skulls, the racial colour of eyes, &c.

SECTION III.

ON THE CAUSES AND WAYS BY WHICH MANKIND HAS DEGENE-
RATED, AS A SPECIES.

41. *Order of proceeding.* Now let us come to the matter in hand, and let us apply what we have hitherto been demonstrating about the ways in and the causes by which animals in general degenerate, to the native variety of mankind, so as to enumerate one by one the modes of degenerating, and allot to each the particular cause to which it is to be referred. We must begin with the colour of the skin, which although it sometimes deceives, still is a much more constant character, and more generally transmitted than the others[1], and which most clearly appears in hybrid progeny sprung from the union of varieties of different colour composed of the tint of either parent. Besides, it has a great connection with the colour of the hair and the iris, and a great relation to the temperament of men: and, moreover, it especially strikes everywhere the eyes even of the most ignorant.

42. *Seat of the colour of the skin.* The mucous, commonly called the cellular membrane, about whose most important function in the economy of the human body we have spoken above, affords as it were a foundation to the whole machine. It is interwoven with almost all parts alike, even to the marrow of the bones, and is collected on the outermost surface of the body

---

[1] Kant, in *Berliner Monatschrift*, 1785, T. VI. p. 391, and in *Teutschen Merkur*, 1788, P. I. p. 48.

into a thick white universal integument, called the *corium*. By this the rest of the body is surrounded and included; and above all it is penetrated by a most enormous apparatus of cutaneous nerves, lymphatic veins, and finally with a most close and subtle net of sanguiferous vessels.

The nerves communicate sensation to the corium, so as to make it the organ of touch, and as it were the sentinel of the whole body. The lymphatic veins make this same corium the instrument of absorption and inhalation. But the sanguiferous vessels have most to do with the subject under discussion, as being the constituent parts of the common integuments of the body, and equally with the lungs and the alimentary canal make up the great purifier and chemical laboratory of the human machine; whose surfaces, as will soon be seen, have a good deal to do with giving its colour to the skin. The corium is lined with a very tender mucus, which from the erroneous description of its discoverer, is called the *reticulum Malpighii*: this affords a sort of glutinous bond, by which the most external stratum of the integuments, the epidermis, or cuticle, stretching over and protecting the surface of the body, and which in the born man is exposed immediately to the atmospheric air, adheres to the corium. The reticulum, just like the epidermis, is a most simple structure, entirely destitute of nerves and vessels, differing both of them as much as possible from the nature of the corium. They agree themselves in more than one way, so that it seems most probable that these similar parts are allied, or that the exterior cuticle draws its origin in some way from its substratum, the reticulum. Besides, each of these allied strata of integuments so make up the *seat of colour*, that in clear-complexioned men, where they are stained with no pigment, they permit the natural roseate whiteness of the corium to be seen through: and in brown or coloured men, although the principal cutaneous pigment may adhere to the Malpighian reticulum, although the epidermis may be paler, still it will manifestly partake of its tint. The darker the reticulum the thicker it is, and the more it approaches the appearnnce of a membrane peculiar to itself; the more transparent it is on the contrary the more tender it becomes, and only appears to have the constitution of a diffused mucus.

43. *Racial varieties of colour.* Although the colour of the human skin seems to play in numberless ways between the snowy whiteness of the European girl and the deepest black of the Ethiopian woman of Senegambia[1]; and though not one of these phases is common either to all men of the same nation, or so peculiar to any nation, but what it sometimes occurs in others, though greatly different in other respects; still, in general, all the varieties of national colour seem to be most referable to the five following classes.

1. The white colour holds the first place, such as is that of most European peoples. The redness of the cheeks in this variety is almost peculiar to it: at all events it is but seldom to be seen in the rest.

2. The second is the *yellow, olive-tinge*, a sort of colour half-way between grains of wheat and cooked oranges, or the dry and exsiccated rind of lemons: very usual in the Mongolian nations.

3. The *copper colour* (Fr. *bronzé*) or dark orange, or a sort of iron, not unlike the bruised bark of cinnamon or tanner's bark: peculiar almost to the Americans.

4. *Tawny* (Fr. *basané*), midway between the colour of fresh mahogany and dried pinks or chesnuts: common to the Malay race and the men of the Southern Archipelago.

5. Lastly, the *tawny-black*, up to almost a pitchy blackness (*jet-black*), principally seen in some Ethiopian nations. Though this tawny blackness is by no means peculiar to the Ethiopians, but is to be found added to the principal colour of the skin in others of the most different and the most widely-separated

---

[1] The indefinite and arbitrary sense in which most authors use the names of colours has caused vast difficulty in all the study of natural history: and will certainly be particularly troublesome in this anthropological disquisition. That I may not be accused of the same fault, I must give notice that I am far from considering such words for example as the English *yellow* and *olive tinge*, &c. which I have subjoined to each of the five principal colours which I have distinguished, as genuine synonyms. All I wanted to do was to show that these words had been used by different authors, and those classical ones, in denoting the national colour of one and the same race.

varieties of mankind: as in the Brazilians, the Californians[1], the Indians, and the Islanders of the Southern Ocean, where, for instance, the New Caledonians in this respect make an insensible transition from the tawny colour of the Otaheitans, through the chesnut-coloured inhabitants of the island of Tongataboo, to the tawny-black of the New Hollanders.

44. *Causes of this variety.* The seat of the colour of the skin has now been placed beyond all doubt. The division of the varieties of colour, and their distribution, seem sufficiently plain and perspicuous. But to dig out the causes of this variety is the task and the trouble. Authors have laboured most in endeavouring to explain the colour of the Ethiopians, which above all other national colours from the most remote period has struck the eyes of Europeans, and excited their minds to inquire. Nor is it surprising that with that object all sorts of hypotheses should be elaborated, which, however, I pass by unnoticed, as being sufficiently known[2], and already explained all together by others[3], and shall go into the details of that opinion alone, which, unless I am much mistaken, seems to come nearest the truth. I think, myself, the proximate cause

---

[1] On the Brazilians comp. G. Forster on Wilson's *Nachrichten von den Pelew Inseln,* p. 36. On the Californians, Baegert, *Nachrichten von Californien,* p. 89.

[2] Buffon attributes most to climate, *Hist. Naturelle,* T. III. p. 526. Zimmermann, *Geograph. Geschichte des Menschen,* T. I. p. 77. Abb. Nanton in *Journal de Physique,* T. XVIII. Sept. 1781. P. Barrere to bile. *Diss. sur la cause physique de la Couleur des Negres,* Perpig. 1741, 12mo. To the blood besides others especially Th. Towns in *Philos. Trans.* T. L. p. 398, who also has doubts about the power of the sun to dye the skin of the Ethiopians. To part of the medical question of Paris, an opinion supported on more than one occasion, as by Des Moles in 1742, and by Moumier in 1775. Kant in *Engel, Philos. für die Welt,* P. II. p. 151, to the abundance of iron in the blood of the Ethiopians, precipitated by the transpiration of phosphoric acid on the *rete mucosum.* I say nothing of a sort of mixture of nervous juice and some secret liquid in the nervous and arterial paps of the integuments by which Le Cat, who was a great physiologist as far as dreaming went, imagined that he had explained the blackness of the Ethiopians, in his *Traité de la Couleur de la Peau Humaine,* Amst. 1765, 8vo., or the elongated fibres in the aborigines of Nubia, the dissolution of the red blood, the evaporation of the serum, and the fixed saline particles of the blood, remaining oily and fat in the skin, by all of which Attomonelli, *Elementi di Fisiologia Medica,* Neap. 1787, T. I. p. 140, tries to explain the same thing.

[3] Thus the opinions of the ancients have been collected by B. S. Albinus, *De sede et causa Coloris Æthiopum,* Ludg. Batav. 1737, 4to. Those of the moderns by Haller, *Element. Physiolog.* T. V. p. 10. A heap of authors are cited by Krünitz, *Hamburgisch Magazin,* T. XIX. p. 379.

of the adust or tawny colour of the external integuments of the skin, is to be looked for in the abundance of the carbon in the human body, which, when it is excreted with the hydrogen through the corium, and precipitated by the contact of the atmospheric oxygen, becomes imbedded in the Malpighian mucus. Hence it is well known that the national colour of their skin is not congenital even to the Ethiopians themselves, but is acquired by the access of the external air after birth and after the intercourse with the mother, by which the fœtus was nourished, has been taken away.

Besides this, the action of the sanguineous vessels of the corium seems necessary as well for secreting as for storing up the carbon. For if this is disturbed or comes to a stop, an unnatural and diseased colour is everywhere brought upon the skin in dark men just as much as in Ethiopians. But on the other hand, although in a white skin that action of the corium may be stimulated, ephelides and spots of tawny colour occur, and sometimes it is found that it puts on an Ethiopic blackness.

Generally carbon seems to be in greater quantity in the atrabilious; for the connexion of the manufactory of the bile with the common integuments, and those which belong to them, as the hair, is plain: indeed both organs, that is, the liver and the skin, must be considered as by far the principal and mutually co-operating purifiers of the mass of the blood.

Then there is the vast influence of climate upon the action of the liver, which in tropical countries is wonderfully excited and increased by the solar heat. Hence the various kinds of bilious and endemic disorders in the tropics. Hence also the temperament of most inhabitants of tropical countries is choleric and prone to anger. Hence also, what was first observed by physicians[1], the bilious constitution and habit of Europeans who dwell in India, and especially in the children which are born there. But there is no other climate, in the vehemence and duration of the heat, or in the peculiar chemical constitu-

---

[1] De Haen, *Prælectiones in Boerhavii Institut. Pathologicas*, T. II. p. 155.

ents that make up the atmosphere there, such as particular winds, and rains, which can be compared to that burning and scorching climate which is to be found on the wet and marshy regions both of eastern and western Africa under the torrid zone. Now the aboriginal Ethiopians have been for a long time and for many series of generations exposed to the action of that climate, since they must without doubt be ranked amongst the most ancient nations of the world[1]. So we must not be surprised if they propagate unadulterated, even under another climate to succeeding generations, the same disposition which has spread such deep and perennial roots in their ancestors from the most distant antiquity. But, on the other hand, from this tenacity and constancy of the constitution of the Ethiopians, this comes out all the clearer, that such a power can only be contracted after a long series of generations, and so it must be considered as a miracle, and against all natural law, if it be true, what we find frequently related that the present descendants of some Portuguese colonists who emigrated to Guinea in the 15th century, have in so short an interval of time, only through the influence of the climate[2], been able to contract the Ethiopian habit of body.

45. *Final exposition of the causes of the colour of the skin.* What I have summarily and succinctly already laid down about the causes of the colour of the skin is strongly corroborated, on more accurate inquiry, by all sorts of arguments answering most accurately to each other, and taken from actual observation of human nature.

We have discovered from the antiphlogistic chemistry of the French[3] that carbon belongs to the radical elements of the

---
[1] Those who like may consult three very learned works: Jac. Bryant, *New System of Ancient Mythology*, Vol. I.; Ja. Bruce, *Journey to the Discovery of the Sources of the Nile*, Vol. I., and Sir W. Jones, *Diss.* in *Asiatic Researches*, Vols. II. and III.
[2] We all know that black men have been found at the Gambia descended from the original Portuguese. But it seems most probable that their blackness has been derived principally from the union of men with the indigenous Ethiopian women, for this reason, that European women when taken directly from their own country to Guinea can very seldom preserve life there; for the effect of the climate is such as to produce very copious menstruation, which almost always in a short space of time ends in fatal hæmorrhages of the uterus.
[3] See Girtanner, *Anfangsgründe der Antiphlogistischen Chimie*, p. 102.

animal body, and is also the cause of dark colour, whether it be yellow, tawny, or blackish. In order that the animal economy may not be disturbed and endangered by a redundancy of this substance various emunctories have been provided, in which the liver and the skin occupy by no means the lowest place. Pathology, here as elsewhere so often the instructor of physiology, shows together with the phenomena just mentioned, the co-operation of the functions of the bile with the common integuments. For although I do not wish to insist too much on the analogy of jaundice with national tints of the skin, still there are various peculiar phenomena which deserve attention, common to those suffering under the regius morbus, and the nations of colour (so to speak) to which I refer, the fact of the albuminous part of the eye being tinged with yellow, a thing common to tawny nations and specially to the Indians[1], the Americans[2], and the Ethiopians[3]. Besides it not unfrequently happens with jaundiced persons, according to the varieties of the disease, that the skin, even after the disorder has been removed, remains always tinged with a different shade, very like the skin of coloured nations[4]. Nor are examples wanting of a genuine sooty blackness being sometimes deposited in atrabilious disorders by a sort of true metamorphosis of the skin[5]. And from the affinity of the bile with fat[6] it is clear that this sort of cherry tint has been observed in tawny peoples[7]. Hence, unless I am mistaken, we must look for the reason why nations

---

[1] I myself have often observed this in those on this side the Ganges. On those beyond the Ganges see De la Loubere in *Descript. du Royaume de Siam*, T. r. p. 81. On the Nicobars, Nic. Fontana in *Asiatic Researches*, Vol. III. p. 151.
[2] On the Caribbees see Rochefort, *Histoire Naturelle des Antilles*, p. 383.
[3] Sömmerring, *Ueber die Körperliche verschiedenheit des Negers vom Europäer*, p. 11.
[4] See Murack, *Observrationes de Febribus Intermittentibus*, l. III. c. 2, *de ictero ex Febre Intermittente*. "I have seen," says he, p. 194, "from such a jaundice that an olive coloured skin, just like that of Asiatics, has remained in the children. Another person has become almost as black as an Indian from fever. The whole body of another has preserved a black complexion, as if he had been born from an Indian father and an European mother; but like such he had the soles of his feet and the palms of his hands white," &c.
[5] Larry, *De Melancholia*, T. I. p. 273.
[6] Fourcroy, *Philosophie Chimique*, p. 117.
[7] Observed in the Ethiopians by J. Fr. Merkel, *Histoire de l'Academie des Sciences de Berlin*, 1757, p. 92, and by Sömmerring, l. c. p. 43.

211   COLOUR.

who feed copiously on animal oil not only smell of it, but also contract a dark colour of skin[1]; while the more elegant Otaheitans on the contrary, who try to be of a pale colour, live every year for some months on the bread-fruit alone, to the use of which they attribute great virtue in whitening the skin[2]; although part of that effect must be attributed to the fact that during the same period they remain at home, covered with clothes, and never go out. How great an influence abstinence from the free and open air has in giving whiteness to the skin, our own experience teaches us every year, when in spring very elegant and delicate women show a most brilliant whiteness of skin, contracted by the indoor life of winter. Whilst those who are less careful in this way, after they have exposed themselves freely to the summer sun and air, lose that vernal beauty before the arrival of the next autumn, and become sensibly browner[3].

If then under one and the same climate the mere difference of the annual seasons has such influence in changing the colour of the skin[4], is there anything surprising in the fact that climates, in the sense defined above (s. 34), according to their diversity

---

[1] Cranz, *Historie von Grönland*, T. 1. p. 178, attributes the tawny skin of the Greenlanders to their particularly oily diet. Sloane declares, *Voyage to Jamaica*, Vol. I. Introd. p. 18, and Vol. II. p. 331, that the skin of Europeans in the East Indies becomes yellow from copious meals of dishes prepared from the callipash of turtles.

[2] See the account of the surgeon Anderson in Cook's *Voyage to the Northern Hemisphere*, Vol. II. p. 147.

[3] From the crowd of witnesses who have observed the same well-known effect of the mode of life in other parts of the world, I will quote only one, Poiret, about the Moors in *Voyage en Barbarie*, p. 31. "The Moors are by no means naturally black, spite of the proverb, though many writers think so; they are born white and remain white all their lives, when their business does not expose them to the heat of the sun. In the towns the women are of such a brilliant whiteness that they eclipse most Europeans; but the Mauritanian mountaineers, burnt unceasingly by the sun and always half-naked, become, even from infancy, of a brown colour, which comes very near to that of soot."

[4] A few examples out of many will suffice. We know the Biscayan women are of a brilliant white, those of Granada on the contrary brownish, so that in this southern province the pictures of the Virgin Mary are painted of the same national colour as is observed by Ol. Torus, *Reise nach Surate*, p. 9. We are told expressly about the Malabars, that their black colour approaches nearer to tawny and yellow the further they dwell towards the north, in *Transquebarischen Missions-Berichten*, Contin. XXII. p. 896. The Ethiopians on the north shore of the Senegal are tawny, on the south, black. See with others Barbot in Churchill's *Collection of Voyages*, T. V. p. 34.

should have the greatest and most permanent influence over national colour: everywhere within the limits of a few degrees of geographical latitude, and still more when a multifarious concourse of the causes[1] above-mentioned has occurred even under the same latitude, a manifest difference in the colour of the inhabitants may be observed[2].

46. *Creoles.* The same power of affecting colour, about which we are speaking, is shown very clearly in *Creoles*, under which name (so frequently improperly confounded even by good authors[3] with the word Mulattos) in a narrower sense[4] we understand those men born indeed either in the East or the West Indies, but of *European parents*. In these the face and colour are so constant and impossible to be mistaken, breathing as it were of the south, and particularly besides the hair and the almost burning eyes, that the most brilliant in other respects and most beautiful women may easily be distinguished by those peculiar characters from others, even their relatives, if these are born in Europe[5]. Nor does this appear only in Europeans, but also in

---

[1] Marsden. *History of Sumatra*, p. 43, notices the effect of sea-air upon the skin, and so Wallis in Hawkesworth's *Collection of Voyages*, Vol. I. p. 260. Hartsink, that of woods, *Beschryving van Guinea*, T. I. p. 9. Bouguer of mountains, *Figure de la Terre*, Intr. p. 101, de Pinto of the altitude of the country, in Robertson's *Hist. of America*, Vol. II. p. 403.

[2] On this point Zimmermann has some deep and learned remarks when discussing the problem why we do not find Ethiopians in America also in equatorial regions, *Geograph. geschichte des Menschen*, T. I. p. 116.

[3] As Thomas Hyde in the notes to Abr. Peritsol, *Itinera mundi*, in Ugolini, *Thesaurus Antiquitatum Sacrarum*, T. VII. p. 141.

[4] This word originated with the Ethiopian slaves transported in the sixteenth century to the mines in America, who first of all called their own children who were born there, *Criollos* and *Criollas*: this name was afterwards borrowed from the Spaniards, and imposed upon their children born in the new world. See Garcilasso, *Del Origen de los Incas*, p. m. 255. Now this word has been extended to the East Indies to the domestic animals which are not indigenous in America, but have been transplanted there by Europeans. Oldendorp, *Geschichte der Mission auf den Caraib. Inseln*, T. 1. p. 232.

[5] On these Creoles of the Antilles, see the curious and elaborate works of Girtanner, *über die Französische Revolution*, T. 1. p. 60—74; 2nd ed.

[6] Hawkesworth's *Collection of Voyages*, T. III. p. m. 374. "If two natives of England marry in their own country and afterwards remove to our settlements in the West Indies, the children that are conceived and born there will have the complexion and cast of countenance that distinguish the Creole; if they return, the children conceived and born afterwards will have no such characteristics," &c.

Asiatics who are born in the East Indies from Persian or Mongolian parents who have emigrated there[1].

47. *Mulattos, &c.* Remarkable too is the constancy with which offspring born from parents of different colours present a middle tint made up as it were from that of either parent. For although we read everywhere of single specimens of hybrid infants born from the union (s. 37) of different varieties of this sort, who have been of the colour of one or other parent alone[2]; still, generally speaking, the course of this mixture is so consistently hereditary, that we may suspect the accuracy of James Bruce about the Ethiopians of some countries in the kingdom of Tigre, who keep their black colour unadulterated, although some of the parents were of one colour and some of another; or about the Arabians, who beget white children with the female Ethiopians like the father alone[3]. But as the hybrids of this sort of origin from parents of various colours are distinguished by particular names, it will be worth while to exhibit them here arranged in synoptical order.

A. *The first generation.* The offspring of Europeans and Ethiopians are called *Mulattos*[4]. Of Europeans and Indians, *Mestizos*[5]. Of Europeans and Americans also *Mestizos*[6] or *Mestinde*[7], or *Metifs*[8], or *Mamlucks*[9]. Of Ethiopians and Americans *Zambos*[10]; by those called also *Mulattos*[11], *Lobos*[12], *Curibocas* and *Kabuglos*[13]. All these present an appearance and colour compounded of either parent, and that more or less

---

[1] See Hodges's *Travels in India*, p. 3.
[2] Comp. Jac. Parsons in *Philos. Trans*, Vol. LV. p. 47.
[3] *Journey to the Sources of the Nile*, Vol. III. p. 106, and Vol. IV. p. 470. See the remarks of Tychsen at T. V. p. 357.
[4] See a law-suit which turned upon the habit and characters of mulattos in Klein, *Annales der Gesetzgebung in den Preussischen Staaten*, T. VII. p. 116.
[5] See the figure of the Cingalese Mestizo in de Bruin, *Reizen over Moskovie*, p. m. 358, and of the Ternatese though less remarkable in Valentyn, *Oud en Nieuw Oost-Indien*, T. I. P. 2, p. 18.
[6] Garcilasso, " Por dezir que somos mezcladas de ambas Naciones."
[7] Twiss' *Travels through Portugal and Spain*, p. 332, from pictures seen by him at Malaga.
[8] Labat, *Voyage aux isles de l'Amerique*, T. II. p. 132.
[9] De Hauterive, *Hist. de l'Acad. des Sc. de Paris*, 1724, p. 18.
[10] Gily, *Storia Americana*, T. IV. p. 310.   [11] Garcilasso, l. c.
[12] Twiss, l. c.   [13] Marcgrav, *Tractatus Brasiliae*, p. 12.

brownish or muddy, with scarcely any redness visible in the cheeks. The hair of Mulattos is generally curly, that of the rest straight, of almost all black; the iris of the eye is brown.

B. *The second generation.* Mulattos forming unions with each other produce *Cusquas*[1]; Europeans and Mulattos *Tercerons*[2], which others call *Quarterons*[3], others *Moriscos*[4] and *Mestizos*[5]. The countenance and hair of all is that of Europeans, the skin very lightly stained with a brownish tint, and the cheeks ruddy. The lips of the female mouth and pudenda violet coloured; the scrotum of the male blackish. The Ethiopians with the Mulattos produce *Griffs*[6], called by others *Zambo Mulattos*[7], and by others *Cabros*[8]. The Europeans with the Indian Mestizos, *Castises*[9]. Those born of Europeans and American Mestizos are called *Quarterons*[10] or *Quatralvi*[11], and by the Spaniards also *Castisi*[12]. Those born of the Americans themselves and their Mestizos are called *Tresalvi*[13]. Those of the Americans and the Mulattos are also called *Mestizos*[14]. Those of Europeans and Zambos or Lobos of the first generation are called indifferently *Mulattos*[15]. Those of the Americans and these same Zambos or Lobos *Zambaigi*[16]. The progeny of the Zambos or Lobos themselves are called contemptuously by the Spaniards *Cholos*[17].

C. *The third generation.* Some call those who are born of Europeans and Tercerons *Quaterons*[18], others *Ocharons*[19], or *Octarons*, and the Spaniards *Alrinos*[20]. In these it is asserted

---

[1] De Hauterive, l. c. [2] Long, *History of Jamaica*, T. II. p. 260.
[3] Aublet, *Histoire des Plantes de la Guiane*, T. II. App. p. 113. [4] Twiss.
[5] Moreton's *Manners and Customs in the West India Islands*, p. 133.
[6] De Hauterive, l. c. [7] *Hist. of Jamaica*, l. c.
[8] Bomare, *Dictionnaire d'Histoire Naturelle*, ed. 4, T. IX. Art. *Nègre*.
[9] Transactions of the Missions-Berichte, Contin. XXXIII. p. 919.
[10] Gumilla, *Orinoco Illustrado*, T. I. p. 83.
[11] Garcilasso, l. c., "to show that they are one-fourth Indian, and three-fourths Spanish." [12] Twiss.
[13] Garcilasso, "to show that they are three parts Indian and one part Spanish."
[14] *Hist. of Jamaica.*
[15] Fermin, *Sur l'Écon. Animale*, T. I. p. 179. [16] Twiss.
[17] Garcilasso, "*Cholo* is a word of the Islands of Barlovento, meaning the same as Dog; and the Spaniards use it by way of contempt or reproach."
[18] *History of Jamaica.* The offspring of Quaterons of this kind from Tercerons of the second generation are called *Tente-end-ryrr*.
[19] Gumilla, l. c. p. 66. [20] Twiss.

by the most acute observers that no trace of their Ethiopian origin can be found[1]. Those of Mulattos and Terceroos *Saltatras*[2]. Of Europeans and Castissi, *Postissi*[3]. Of Europeans and American Quarterons of the second generation *Octavons*[4]. Of Quarterons and American Mestizos of the first generation, *Coyotus*[5]. Of Griffs and Zambo Mulattos with Zambos of the first generation *Giveros*[6]. Of Zambaigis and Mulattos *Cambujos*[7]. There are those who extend even into the fourth generation this kind of pedigree, and say that those born from Europeans from Quarterons of the third generation are called Quinterons[8], in Spanish Puchuelas[9], but this name is also applied to those who are born of Europeans and American Octavons[10]. But that the slightest permanent vestige of their mixed origin[11] is to be found in productions like these, after what we have been told by most credible eye-witnesses about the men of the third generation, that as to colour and constitution they are exactly like the aboriginal Europeans, is a thing that seems almost incredible.

48. *Brown skin variegated with white spots.* What I said above (k. 44) about the action of the sanguiferous vessels of the corium in excreting the carbon, which is afterwards precipitated by the addition of oxygen, is singularly confirmed by the instances of dark-coloured men, especially Ethiopians, whose skin, and that too not always from their first tender infancy[12], is distinguished by spots of a snowy whiteness (Fr. *nègres-pies*; Eug. *piebald negroes*).

I saw an Ethiopian of this kind at London, by name John Richardson, a servant of T. Clarke, who exhibited there (in Exeter Change), live exotic animals as shows and also for sale.

---

[1] Aublet. [2] *Hist. of Jamaica.* [3] *Tranquebarische Missions-Berichte,* l. c.
[4] Gumilla, l. c. p. 13. [5] Twiss. [6] *History of Jamaica.*
[7] Twiss. [8] *Hist. of Jamaica.*
[9] Gumilla, p. 86. [10] Id. p. 83.
[11] Thus those born from the Coyotes of the third generation and the Americans are called *Harnizos;* from the Cambujos and Mulattos, *Alboruzaadus;* finally, Twiss, whom I have so often quoted before, calls those born from the last and Mulattos, *Bersimos.*
[12] W. Byrd, in *Philos. Trans* Vol. XIX. p. 781, mentions the instance of an Ethiopian boy in whom the spots did not appear till his fourth year, and in process of time began to increase in size.

The young man was perfectly black except in the umbilical and epigastric region of the abdomen, and in the middle part of either leg, that is the knees, with the adjoining regions of the thigh and the tibia, which were remarkable for a most brilliant and snowy whiteness, and were themselves again distinguished by black scattered spots, like those of a panther. His hair was also parti-coloured. For the middle part of his sinciput descending in an acute angle from the vertex towards the forehead was white, not however like the regions of the skin we have been speaking of, but a little snowy with a tinge of yellow. The rest of the hair was, as is usually the case with Ethiopians, curly; and this curliness still continues unaltered up to this time, in a specimen of each kind of hair which I obtained from the man himself more than two years ago. I had also a picture taken of the man, which on comparison with three others equally of Ethiopians, which I have by me, a boy and two girls, shows that in all, the regions of the abdomen and legs were more or less white, but that the hands and feet, that is, those parts which with the groin are the first to grow black in newborn Ethiopians, were perfectly tawny, and that in all the disposition of the white regions was thoroughly symmetrical. The gums, to go on to that also, in the man I saw, the tongue and all the jaws, were of an equable and beautiful red.

Both the parents of the man I am speaking of, as of all the other spotted Ethiopians[1] of whom I have found descriptions, were perfectly black, so that the conjecture of Buffon seems badly founded when he attributes such offspring to the union of Ethiopians and Leucæthiopian women, when suffering under a diseased affection of the skin and the eyes, about which I shall take an opportunity of speaking more particularly below.

Care must always be taken that the spots we are speaking about, and which can only be distinguished by a snowy white-

---

[1] See a print of a girl of this kind in Buffon, *Suppl.* T. IV. Tab. 2, p. 565. This, unless I am mistaken, is the same which has been described at length by Gumilla, *Orinoco Illustrado*, T. 1. p. 109. Other instances of this kind of Ethiopians are found in La Mothe, *Bibliothèque Impartiale*, Apr. 1751. See D. Morgan in *Transactions of the Philosophical Society at Philadelphia*, Vol. II. p. 391.

ness from the rest of the skin, the epidermis being in other respects unaffected, be not improperly confounded with those by which the whole integument is covered, which are to be recognized not so much by a different colour as by a degradation of the texture of the corium itself, which becomes rough, and as it were scaly or scurvy. Writers have observed this kind of cutaneous disorder particularly amongst the Malabars[1], and the Tschulymik Tartars[2]. But these snowy, equable and smooth spots which only occur in a disordered action of the smallest vessels of the corium, are by no means confined to the Ethiopians, but sometimes occur amongst our own people. I have myself had the opportunity of observing two instances of this kind in German men, one a young man, the other more than sixty years old. The skin of each was brownish, studded here and there with very white spots of different sizes. In neither were these congenital, but had appeared suddenly and spontaneously in one during infancy, in the other in manhood.

49. *Similar remarkable mutations of the colour of the skin.* As these instances I have just been mentioning seem to demonstrate the power of the smaller vessels of the corium in modifying the colour of the skin; so there are other phenomena which often occur, and point in this direction, by which, unless I am much mistaken, those conjectures I made above (s. 44, 45) about the abundance of carbon, and the impressions of the Malpighian mucus being as it were the proximate cause of that colour, are well illustrated.

Above all others I shall consider in this place the singular change of colour so often observed in European women[3], in some

---

[1] *Transyvarische Missions-Berichte*, Cont. XXI. p. 741, compare the disorder to leprosy.
[2] See Strahlenberg, *Nord-ostlich Europa und Asien*, p. 166, who suspects them to be the same Tartar horde which went under the name of *Pieguja* or *Pedraja orda*. J. G. Gmelin attributes it to disease, *Reise durch Sibirien*, pref. T. II. and J. Bell to some scorbutic affection, *Travels from St Petersburg to diverse parts of Asia*, Vol. I. p. 218.
[3] "In many women the under part of the body (the abdomen) and the rings about the breasts (that is the teats) when they are ill, become quite black." Camper, *Klein Schrift*, T. I. P. 1. p. 47. "In our own time a similar metamor-

of whom, and those in other respects particularly white, at the time of pregnancy a larger or smaller number of the parts of the body are darkened with a coaly blackness, which however gradually disappears again after child-birth, when the original clearness is restored to the body. The solution of this puzzling problem is to be found in the application of modern chemistry to the physiology of pregnancy. When the woman is not pregnant the moderate portion of carbon of her own body is easily excreted by superfluous cutaneous perspiration; but in a pregnant woman, besides her own share, another quantity accrues from the fœtus, which immersed in ammonial liquid does not as yet breathe. Thus the blood of the mother becomes too much laden with the carbon arising from two human bodies joined as it were in one, so that all of it cannot as usual be excreted with the perspiration of the mother: so part of it is precipitated in the Malpighian mucus, and there remains, tinging the skin, until the child being delivered, the original equilibrium between the carbon of her own body and the perspiring vessels of the skin is restored; and the epidermis, which with the mucus lying under it is constantly destroyed by degrees and again renewed at last, recovers its natural whiteness.

In different circumstances the same reason seems to hold good in so many instances of Europeans, in whom the different parts of the body are unnaturally affected by a smoky blackness; since here also it may be referred to a congestion of carbon. Thus, for instance, a similar blackness is observable in women who never menstruate[1]. So also in other atrabilious

---

phosis has been renewed annually in the person of a lady of distinction, of a good complexion, and a very white skin. As soon as she was pregnant, she began to get brown, and towards the end of her time she became a true negress. After her deliveries the black colour disappeared little by little, her original whiteness returned, and her progeny had no trace of blackness." Bomare, *l. c.* Art. *Nègre*. *La Cat, l. c.* In many places; for ex. p. 141. "A peasant of the environs of Paris, a nurse by profession, had the belly regularly quite black at every pregnancy, and that colour disappeared after delivery." "Another always had the left leg black on three occasions," &c. So also Larry, *De Melancholia*, T. 1. p. 298, &c.

[1] Comp. Jas. Yonge in *Philosoph. Trans.* Vol. XXVI. p. 425.

men[1], especially of the lowest sort, and those who suffer from cachexia caused by want and dirt. This is often the case too in scurvy[2], &c. On the other hand we know by experience that the blackness of the Ethiopians is not so constant but what it sometimes is rendered paler, or even changed quite into a white colour. It has been recorded that Ethiopians, when they have changed their climate in early infancy, and from that time forward have inhabited a temperate zone, have gone on getting paler by degrees[3]. The same thing happens also somewhat quicker to the same negroes when they suffer under severe disorders[4]. Many instances also are to be found where, apart from any particular state of health, the natural blackness of the Ethiopian skin has sensibly and spontaneously been changed into a whiteness, such as that of Europeans[5].

50. *Some other national properties of skin.* Besides colour, other singular qualities are often attributed to the skin of some nations, about which I must say a few words at all events. Amongst these there is that smoothness and softness of skin which has been compared to silk, and has been noticed

---

[1] I have in my anatomical collection a specimen of the integuments of the abdomen of a beggar who died here some years ago, which does not yield at all in blackness to the skin of the Ethiop. Others too have shown many instances of that kind in Europeans. See for ex. Haller, *Element. Physiol.* T. v. p. 18. Ludwig, *Epistolæ ad Hallerum scriptæ*, T. I. p. 393. De Itärt, *De organo tactus*, p. 13. Albinus, *De sede et causa coloris Æthiopum*, p. 9. Klinkosch, *De cuticula*, p. 46. Sömmerring, *Ueber die körperl. verschiedenheit des Negers vom Europäer*, p. 48. Comp. Loschge in *Naturforscher*, P. xxiii. p. 214. ib. P. xvi. p. 170, for the description of some brown (*Dunkelbraun*) spots of different size, some of the diameter of a span, observed in a man then sixty years old, in whom they appeared when young during a quartan fever.

[2] Comp. besides others, Jo. Narborough's *Voyage to the Straits of Magellan*, p. m. 64. "Their legs and thighs are turned as black as a hat," &c. He also Phillip's *Voyage to Botany Bay*, p. 229.

[3] "There is a cobbler of this nation still living at Venice, whose blackness, after a great many years, (for he came to this country a boy) has so sensibly diminished, that he seems like one suffering from a slight jaundice." Caldan, *Institut. Physiol.* p. 151, ed. 1786. Comp. also Pechlin, *De habitu et colore Æthiopum*, p. 128, and Oldendorp, T. I. p. 406.

[4] "I have seen them of so light a colour that it was difficult to distinguish them from a white man of a bad complexion." Labat, *Relation d'Afrique occidentale*, T. II. p. 160. And Klinkosch, *l. c.* p. 48.

[5] Comp. Jas. Bate in *Philosoph. Trans.* Vol. LI. P. 1. p. 175.

by writers in many nations, as the Caribs¹, the Ethiopians², the Otaheitans³ and even the Turks⁴. It is clear that in all these it depends either upon a more tender epidermis, or a thicker stratum of the Malpighian mucus. The cause of the coldness to the touch which has been observed in the skin of various nations of Africa⁵ and the East Indies⁶ seems different, and must be referred rather to the chemical affinities of the body and the atmospheric elements. Here also is to be considered that insensible perspiration of Sanctorius, which is accompanied in some nations with a peculiar smell, as in the Caribs⁷, Ethiopians⁸, and others; in the same way that in some varieties of domestic animals, as among dogs, the Egyptian, among horses, those of a reddish-white are well known to have a specific and peculiar perspiration⁹.

51. *Consensus of the hair and skin.* As the hair, especially that of the head, is generated and nourished by the common integuments, so it has invariably a great and multifarious agreement with them. Hence, those variegated Ethiopians we spoke of have also hair of different colour. Men whose white skin is marked with ephelitic spots have red hair¹⁰. Besides,

---

¹ "Their flesh is very dark and soft; when you touch their skin, it feels like satin." Biet, *Voyage de la France Equinoxiale*, p. 352.
² Pechlin, *l. c.* p. 54. and Sömmerring, *l. c.* p. 45.
³ "Their skin is most delicately smooth and soft." Hawkes. *Coll.* T. II. p. m. 187.
⁴ "The wife of every labourer or rustic in Asia (Turkey) has a skin so soft that you seem to touch a fine velvet." Belon, *Obs.* p. III. 198.
⁵ Bruce's *Voyage to the Sources of the Nile*, T. II. p. 552, T. IV. p. 471 and 489.
⁶ On the Indians see Kant in Engel, *Philosophie für die Welt*, P. II. p. 154. On the inhabitants of Sumatra, Marsden, p. 41.
⁷ "They all have a strong and disagreeable smell. I know nothing which can give an idea of it. When anything smells like it, they say in the Antilles, 'a smell of Carib,' which shows the difficulty of expressing it." Thibault de Chanvalon, *Voyage à la Martinique*, p. 44.
⁸ Comp. Sebotte *On the synochus atrabilious*, p. 104. *Hist. of Jamaica*, II. pp. 352, 475.
⁹ So Pausanias in his *Phocics* tells us that the Ozolians, an indigenous people, of Locris, smelt disgustingly on account of something in the air. Comp. Lavater, *Physiognom. Fragmente,* T. IV. p. 263. And J. F. Ackermann, *De discrimine sexuum præter genitalia,* p. 10.
¹⁰ Among ourselves the thing is very common. It has been observed also among the most distant nations; as in the island Otaha of the Pacific ocean. See J. R. Forster, *Bemerkungen auf seiner reise um die welt,* p. 205. Many inhabitants of

there is a remarkable correspondence of the hair with the whole constitution and temperament of the body. This, too, we learn from pathological phenomena, such for example as that those who have yellow hair (*blondins*), in consequence of the tenderer and more impressible cellular texture, break out more easily in rashes and similar eruptions; whilst those who have black hair are almost always of a costive and atrabilious temperament, so much so that it has long since been observed that far the greater number of men in mad hospitals and jails have black hair.

52. *Principal national varieties of hair.* In general, the national diversity of hair seems capable of being reduced to four principal varieties:

1. The first of a brownish or nutty colour (*cendré*), shading off on the one side into yellow, on the other into black: soft, long, and undulating. Common in the nations of temperate Europe; formerly particularly famous among the inhabitants of ancient Germany[1].

2. The second, black, stiff, straight, and scanty; such as is common to the Mongolian and American nations.

3. The third, black, soft, in locks, thick and exuberant; such as the inhabitants of most of the islands of the Pacific Ocean exhibit.

4. The fourth, black and curly, which is generally compared to the wool of sheep; common to the Ethiopians.

Thus, a general division of this kind may be made, which is not without its use. That it is no more a purely natural division than other divisions of the national varieties of human races, is not necessary to dwell upon here. This I will show, though it is quite unnecessary, by one or two arguments, namely, that curliness is not peculiar to the Ethiopians, nor blackness to the three varieties I put in the last place. Some

---

Timur are of a copper colour with red hair; see Van Hogendorp in *Verhandelingen van het Bataviaasch Genootschap*, T. 1. p. m. 319. Marcgrav saw an African woman with an undoubted red skin and red hair, *Tractatus Brasiliæ*, p. 12.

[1] Conring, *De Habitu corporum Germanicorum antiqui ac novi cuusu*, p. 85.

races of Ethiopians are found with long hair[1]; other copper-coloured nations again have curly hair[2], like that of the Ethiopians. There are others, the New Hollanders, whose hair, as I see from the specimens I have in hand, holds so perfectly the middle place between the curliness of the Ethiopians and the locks of the inhabitants of the islands in the Pacific Ocean, that a wonderful difference of opinion is to be found in the accounts of expeditions from the first Dutch ones of the last century to the very latest of the English, as to which variety of hair it should be considered to belong. As to the various colour of hairs, occurring amongst those nations also, who generally have black hair, it is sufficient to cite good witnesses, who say that red hair is frequently found in the three other varieties I reckoned besides the first.

53. *The iris of the eye conforms to the colour of the hair.* We have seen that the hair coincides with the common integuments of the body. Aristotle[3] had, however, long ago taught that the colour of the eyes followed that of the skin. Those whose colour was white had grey eyes; black, black eyes. Thus very often amongst ourselves new-born infants have grey eyes and light hair, which afterwards in those who become dark (*brunet*), is slowly and as it were simultaneously darkened also. In old men as the hair grows white the pigment of the internal eye loses much of its usual dark colour. In the Leucœthiopians, about whom I shall speak more particularly below, as the hair passes from a yellowish tinge to white, so the pigment of the eye is clearly nothing, and hence a pale rosy kind of iris.

It is remarkable that in no case at all is there any variation in the eyes of animals, except in those who vary in the colour of their skin and hair, as we know to be the case not only in men and horses, which was the opinion of the ancients, but also

---

[1] Comp. Bruce on the Gallas, *Journey, &c.* Vol. II. p. 214. As to the inhabitants of the kingdom of Bornou, *Proceedings of the Association,* p. m. 201.
[2] The inhabitants of the Duke of York's Island not far from the New Ireland of the Southern Ocean. See J. Hunter's *Historical Journal of the Transactions at Port Jackson, &c.* p. 133: "they are of a light copper colour, the hair is woolly."
[3] *Problemat.* s. 10. p. 416, ed. Casaub.

in other principally domestic animals. Very often also the iris is variegated with more than one colour in those animals whose skin is variegated. This was first observed in parti-coloured dogs[1]. I have noticed something like it in sheep and horses, but in no animal so plainly as in rabbits. Grey rabbits who have kept their natural wild colour have the iris quite black, whereas the parti-coloured ones, whose skin is spotted with black and white, have the iris manifestly spotted in the same way. Those which are quite white, and like Leucæthiopians, have, as is well known, the iris of a pale red.

54. *Principal colours of eyes.* Aristotle, whom I just quoted, divided well the primary colours of the iris of the human eye into three; first, blue; second, dark orange, called goats' eyes (*yeux de chèrres*[2]); third, dark brown. All these three as they occur everywhere in individuals of one and the same nation, so also are they to be noticed as more constant and as it were racial in different families of the same continent within the limits of a few degrees of geographical latitude. Hence Linnæus[3] attributes those among the Swedish population to the Gothic race, who have white hair, with the iris of the eye of a dark-blue colour; to the Finnic, those with yellow hair and dark iris; to the Lapp, finally, those with black hair and blackish iris. Blue eyes equally with yellow hair were formerly considered as natural characteristics of the ancient Germans. But they are found everywhere amongst the most widely separated nations[4]. The very black irides of the Ethiopians are such that, especially in living subjects, they cannot be distinguished, excepting when very close, from the pupil itself[5].

55. *National face.* I now turn naturally enough from the

---

[1] Comp. Molinelli in *Commentar. Instituti Boxon.* T. III. p. 281.
[2] There is a middle colour between grey and orange of a strange greenish tint, and as it were grass green, which is to be seen in men who have fiery hair, and skin much spotted with freckles. Comp. that singular book Portius, *Sim. De coloribus oculorum,* Florentii, 1550, 4to.
[3] *Fauna Suecica,* p. 1.
[4] I have collected the instances in my notes to J. Bruce, *Reise zu den quellen des Nils.* T. v. p. 339.
[5] Thus must be understood the words of J. G. Walter, *De renis orali,* p. 13. "The Ethiopian has no iris," &c.

eyes to the rest of the face, the diversities of which are all over the world so great and so remarkable in individuals that it is little short of a miracle to find even two who cannot be distinguished from each other, and are, as they say, cast in the same mould. Besides it is certain that this difference of faces may be observed not only in Europeans but also among barbarous nations[1]. Yet, however true all this may be, it is not the less undoubtedly a fact that every different variety of mankind (and everywhere, even in the inhabitants of single provinces[*]) all over the world has a racial face peculiar to each of them by which it may be easily distinguished from the remaining varieties.

56. *Racial varieties of the face.* I have made an attempt, after assiduously comparing a quantity of prints of foreigners made for me from the life by skilled artists, and after seeing myself a great number of men in the markets which are principally frequented by foreigners, to reduce these racial varieties of the face into certain classes. And unless I am much mistaken, although open to particular exceptions, still they will come close to natural truth if they are reduced in the following way to five, as models and principal forms of the other diversities of small moment:

1st. Face oval, straight, the parts moderately marked. The forehead smooth. Nose narrow, slightly hooked, or at all events somewhat high. The jugal bones in no way prominent. Mouth small, lips (especially the lower) gently pronounced. Chin full, round. In general that kind of face, which, accord-

---

[1] Thus on the aborigines of the Friendly Islands that most sagacious observer, W. Anderson: "their features are very various, in so much that it is scarcely possible to fix on any general likeness by which to characterize them, unless it be a fulness at the point of the nose, which is very common. But, on the other hand, we met with hundreds of truly European faces, and many genuine Roman noses amongst them." Cook's last voyage, Vol. I. p. 380. Other instances of this kind observed amongst Ethiopians and Americans will be spoken of below. On the other hand the similarity of individual Europeans with the Ethiopians or Mongolians is so common as to have passed into a proverb.

[*] On this point Libavius, an author by no means to be despised, says two hundred years ago: "The aspect of the Thuringians is one thing; that of the Saxons another; and that of the Suevi another, and nearly every village has its own, so that if you chose to study the subject, you could nearly tell a man's country by his appearance."

ing to our opinion of symmetry, we think becoming and beautiful. This same kind of face constitutes, as it were, a medium which may fall off by degeneration into two exactly opposite extremes, of which the one displays a wide and the other an elongated face. Each of these two includes again two different varieties, which can best be distinguished from each other when seen in profile. For then one of these varieties shows the nose and the remaining parts somewhat indistinct, and, as it were, running into one another. In the other they appear deeper, so to say, cut out, and as it were, projecting angularly. Thus we come to form the four remaining varieties besides that first mean type.

A. *One pair with the face developed in width:—*

2nd. Face wide, at the same time flat and depressed; the parts, therefore, indistinct and running into one another. Interspace between the eyes, or glabella, smooth, very wide. Nose flattened. Cheeks usually rounded, projecting outwards. Opening of the eyelids narrow, linear (*yeux bridés*). Chin, somewhat prominent. This is the countenance common to the Mongolian nations (*the Tartar face* from the common figure of speech which we shall touch on below, confounding the Tartars with the Mongolians).

3rd. Face also wide and cheeks prominent, though not flat or depressed, but the parts when seen in profile more worked and, as it were, deeply cut out. Forehead low. Eyes deeply set. Nose somewhat turned up, but prominent. This is the face of most Americans.

B. *Pair of varieties of the face elongated below:—*

4th. Narrow face, prominent below. Forehead short, wrinkled. Eyes very prominent (à *fleur-de-tête*). Nose thick and half confused with the extended cheeks (*le nez épaté*). Lips (especially the upper) full and swelling. Jaws stretched out. Chin falling back. This is *the Guinea face*.

5th. Face less narrow, somewhat prominent below, when seen in profile the parts more projecting and distinct from each other. Nose full, somewhat broad, as it were diffuse, and thick (*bottled*). Mouth large. This is the face of the Malay, especially of the inhabitants of the islands of the Southern Ocean.

57. *Causes of the racial face.* First of all, notice must be taken that I am not going to speak here of the countenance, taken in a physiognomical sense, (*look, expression,*) as an index of the temperament, which is however itself sometimes racial, and peculiar to some nations, and may be derived from a common source. In that way it is probable that to their diet you may attribute the placid countenance of the abstemious Brahmins and Banyans of India, and the atrocious aspect, on the other hand, of the man-eating Botocudos[1] of Brazil; or you may instance religion by the examples of the pious and devoted countenance by which especially the softer sex is distinguished in some countries of southern Europe (in the vernacular *Madonna faces*); or cultivation and luxury, in which the soft and effeminate Otaheitans so much excel the manly and powerful New Zealanders.

But our business is with the causes of the racial face, that is, of the countenance itself and the proportion and direction of its parts, all of which we see to be peculiar and characteristic to the different varieties of mankind. The mere discussion, however, of these causes is overwhelmed with such difficulties that we can only follow probable conjectures. I am persuaded, myself, that climate is the principal cause of the racial face, on three grounds especially; 1st, we see the racial face so universal in some populations under a particular climate, and always exactly the same in men of different classes and modes of life, that it can scarcely be referred to any other cause. There are the Chinese, for example, amongst whom a sort of flattened face is just as characteristic as a symmetrical and particular beauty is common amongst us Europeans to the English and inhabitants of Majorca[2].

2nd. Unless I am mistaken there are instances of peoples who after they have changed their localities and have migrated

---

[1] I owe my account of this most ferocious and anthropophagous race to two Portuguese Brazilians, de Camara and d'Andrada.
[2] *Mémoires du Cardinal de Retz*, T. III. p. 343.

elsewhere, in process of time have changed also their original form of countenance for a new one, peculiar to the new climate. Thus the Yakutes have been referred to a Tartar origin by most authors on northern antiquities. Careful eye-witnesses assert that now their face is Mongolian, and I myself see it plainly in the skull of a Yakute, with which the munificence of Baron von Asch has enriched my anthropological collection[1]. Something of the same kind will be observed below about the Americans of either coldest zone (s. 88). I have already shown that the Creoles sprung from English parents and ancestors in the Antilles, have finally exchanged to some extent the native British countenance for one more like the aborigines of America, and have acquired their deep-set eyes and their more prominent cheeks[2].

Egypt, however, and India this side the Ganges afford us the clearest examples of all. For as this peninsula has been frequently subdued by the most different nations, because the first conquerors becoming effeminated by living in such a soft climate were at last conquered by other and stronger northern nations who came after them, so also their appearance seems as it were to have accommodated itself to the new climate. In fact, we only know the racial aspect of the old possessors of India and their manifest characteristics from the most ancient works of Indian art, I mean those stupendous statues, which are carved out in a wonderful way in the subterranean temples of the islands of Salsette and Elephanta, wonderful copies of which I saw at London, both in the British Museum, as amongst the antiquarian treasures of the polished C. Townley[3]. The more modern conquerors of India, that is, the Mongolians, have lost much of their original features under a new climate, and approached nearer the Indian type, of which I have had ocular experience from the Indian pictures shown me by John Walsh, a most learned man on Indian antiquity.

As to the racial face of the ancient Egyptians, I am much surprised that some famous archæologists, and those most learned

---

[1] *Decas craniorum altera*, p. 11.
[2] *History of Jamaica*, Vol. II. p. 261.
[3] *Archæologia*, Vol. VII. Tab. 25, 26, 17.

in Egyptian art, have been able to attribute one and the same
common countenance to all alike[1]; when a careful contemplation and comparison of these monuments has easily taught me
to distinguish three sorts of face amongst them. The first like
the Ethiopian; the second the Indian; and the third, into which
both of the others have by the progress of time and the effect of
the specific and peculiar climate of Egypt degenerated, spongy
and flaccid in appearance, with short chin, and somewhat prominent eyes[2].

3rd. We see nations which are reputed to be but colonies of
one and the same stock have contracted in different climates
different racial faces. Thus the Hungarians are considered to
be of the same primitive stock as the Lapps[3]. The latter living
in the furthest North have acquired the face so peculiar to the
most northern nations, whereas the former living in the temperate zone, in the neighbourhood of Greece and Turkey, have
gained a more elegant form of face.

Every one knows that much in all these cases must be attributed to the marriages between different nations, and I myself
intend soon to say something about their influence in changing
the racial face. Still it seems most probable that the influence
of climate alone is very great on this point, especially when we
add what was noticed above about the causes and ways in which
brute animals degenerate.

To find out the reason why one climate turns out this and
another that kind of racial face seems extremely difficult; yet
most sagacious men have made the attempt when endeavouring
to explain the face of different nations; as Kant upon the Mongolian[4] and Volney upon the Ethiopian[5]. That accessory

---

[1] Winkelmann, *Description des pierres gravées de Stosch*. p. 10, and elsewhere.
D'Hancarville, *Recherches sur l'origine des arts de la Grèce*, Tom. I. p. 300.
[2] I have said more about this triple character of the ancient art of Egyptian
monuments in *Philosoph. Trans.* 1794, P. II. p. 191.
[3] Comp. Ol. Rudbeck, Jun., *Analogia linguæ Finnonicæ cum Ungaricâ*, at the
end of *Specim. usus linguæ Gothicæ*, Upsal. 1717, 4to, p. 77; and amongst other
recent writers, J. Hager, *Neue Beweise der verwandtschaft der Ungarn mit den
Lappländern*, Wien, 1794, 8vo.
[4] In Engel, *Philosoph. für die Welt*, T. II. p. 146.
[5] *Voyage en Syrie et en Egypte*, T. I. p. 74. "In fact I see that the face of the

causes sometimes endemical to peculiar climates, such as constant clouds of gnats, may do something towards contracting the natural face of the inhabitants, may be gathered from the observation of Dampier about the inhabitants of the south of New Holland[1].

I am not sure whether the opinion of our Leibnitz about the similitude of nations to the indigenous animals of the country is to be interpreted as referring to the influence of climate on the conformation of man and brute animals alike; as it seems that the Lapps recall the face of the bear, the Negroes of the ape, of which also the people of the extreme East likewise partake[2].

Besides the climate we find it stated that the kind of life sometimes contributes to the racial form of face, as in the instance of the Ethiopians, whose thick nose and swelling lips are always attributed to the way in which, whilst in their infancy, they are generally carried on the backs of their mothers, who give them suck whilst they pound millet, or during their hard and heavy tasks[3].

Negroes indicates exactly that state of contraction which seizes our own countenance, when it is struck by the light and a strong reflection of heat. Then the eyebrow frowns; the cheek bones become elevated, the eyelid closes, the mouth is pinched up. Cannot this contraction which is perpetually taking place in the bare and warm country of the Negroes, become the peculiar characteristic of their faces?"

[1] "Their eyelids are always half-closed to prevent the gnats getting into their eyes. Hence it happens, that being incommoded by those insects from their infancy, they never open their eyes like other people." T. II. p. 169.

[2] Feller, *Otium Hanoveranum*, p. 158. I will add here, on account of the resemblance of the argument, a passage from Marsden, *History of Sumatra*, p. 175: "Some writer has remarked that a resemblance is usually found between the disposition and qualities of the beasts proper to any country, and those of the indigenous inhabitants of the human species, where an intercourse with foreigners has not destroyed the genuineness of their character. The Malay may be compared to the buffalo and the tiger. In his domestic state he is indolent, stubborn, and voluptuous as the former, and in his adventurous life, he is insidious, blood-thirsty and rapacious as the latter. Thus the Arab is said to resemble his camel, and the placid Gentoo his cow."

[3] Comp. besides many others, Barbot in Churchill's *Collection of Voyages*, Vol. v. p. 36. "The wives of the better sort of men being put to no such hard labour as the meaner, it has been observed that their children have not generally such flat noses as the others; whence it may be inferred that the noses of these poor infants are flattened by being so long carried about on their mothers' backs, because they must be continually beating on them when the motion of their arms or bodies is

In various barbarous nations also, such as the Ethiopians[1], the Brazilians[2], Caribs[3], the Sumatrans[4], and the inhabitants of the Society Islands in the Southern Ocean[5], it is placed beyond all doubt by the testimony of eye-witnesses most worthy of credit that considerable force is used to depress and, as it were, subdue into shape the noses of the new-born infants; although perhaps it is going too far in what they say about the bones of the nose being broken or dislocated in this way[6].

It is however scarcely necessary to recollect that the natural conformation of the nose can only be exaggerated by this violent and long continued compression of the nose when soft, but can in no wise be made thus originally, since it is well known that the racial face may be recognized even in abortions.

Finally, these kinds of racial face just like the colour of the skin, become mingled, and as it were run together in the offspring from the unions of different varieties of mankind, so that the children present a countenance which is a mean between either parent. Hence the mixed appearance of the Mulattos; hence the progeny of the Cossacks[7] and the Kirghis[8] becomes sensibly deformed by marriages with the Calmucks, whereas the offspring of the Nogay Tartars is rendered more beautiful through unions with the Georgians[9].

The ancient Germans[10] gave formerly instances of the unadulterated countenance of nations unaffected by any union with any other nation, and to-day the genuine Zingari, inhabitants

---

anything violent; especially when they are beating or pounding their millet every morning, which is the constant task of the women of inferior rank."

[1] Besides a format of other evidence see *Report of the Lords of the Committee of Council for the Consideration of the Slave Trade*, 1789, fol. P. 1. fol. O. 1b.
[2] Lery, *Voyage en la terre du Brésil*, p. m. 98, 163.
[3] De la Borde, *Relation des Caraïbes*, in the smaller collection of M. Thevenot, Paris, 1674, 4to, p. 19.
[4] Marsden, *History of Sumatra*, p. 38.
[5] J. R. Forster, *Bemerkungen auf einer reise um die Welt*, pp. 482, 516.
[6] Camp. Kolbe, *Beschreibung des vorgebürges der guten Hofnung*, p. 567.
[7] *Decas craniorum prima*, p. 18.
[8] *Decas craniorum altera*, p. 8.
[9] Peyssonel, *Sur le commerce de la Mer Noire*, T. 1. p. 177.
[10] Tacitus, *De moribus Germanorum*, c. 4.

of Transylvania[1] do the same; and above all the nation of the Jews, who, under every climate, remain the same as far as the fundamental configuration of face goes[2], remarkable for a racial character almost universal, which can be distinguished at the first glance even by those little skilled in physiognomy, although it is difficult to limit and express by words[3].

58. *Racial form of skulls.* That there is an intimate relation between the external face and its osseous substratum is so manifest[4], that even a blind man, if he has any idea of the vast difference by which the Mongolian face differs from the Ethiopian, can undoubtedly, by the mere touch, at once distinguish the skull of the Calmuck from that of the Negro. Nor would you persuade even the most ignorant person to bend over the head of one or other of them as he might over those after whose models the divine works of ancient Greece were sculptured. This, I say, is clear and evident so far as the general habit goes.

But it might have been expected that a more careful anatomical investigation of genuine skulls[5] of different nations would throw a good deal of light upon the study of the variety of mankind; because when stripped of the soft and changeable parts they exhibit the firm and stable foundation of the head, and can be conveniently handled and examined, and considered under different aspects and compared together. It is clear from a comparison of this kind that the forms of skulls take all sorts of

---

[1] *Decas craniorum altera*, p. 3.
[2] Hence it is generally considered as the highest proof of the art of the Dutch engraver, Bernh. Picart, that in his well known work, *Cérémonies et coutumes religieuses*, he has represented an immense number of Jews, as far as the lineaments of the face go, each differing from one another, yet all bearing the racial character, and most clearly distinguished from the men intermingled with them of other nations.
[3] The great artist Benj. West, President of the Royal Academy of Arts, with whom I conversed about the racial face of the Jews, thought that it above all others had something particularly goat-like about it, which he was of opinion lay not so much in the hooked nose as in the transit and conflux of the septum which separates the nostrils from the middle of the upper lip.
[4] Comp. Sir Thos. Brown's *Discourse of the Sepulchral Urns found in Norfolk*, p. m. 13. This sagacious author was the first, as far as I know, who attended to the racial form of the Ethiopian skull: "it is hard to be deceived in the distinction of Negro skulls."
[5] The rules and criteria which I use for this object in forming an opinion upon skulls are laid down in my *Decas prima collectionis craniorum*, p. 5.

license in individuals, just as the colour of skins and other varieties of the same kind, one running as it were into the other by all sorts of shades, gradually and insensibly: but that still, in general, there is in them a constancy of characteristics which cannot be denied, and is indeed remarkable, which has a great deal to do with the racial habit, and which answers most accurately to the nations and their peculiar physiognomy. That constancy has induced some eminent anatomists from the time of Andr. Spigel[1] to set up a certain rule of dimensions to which as to a scale the varieties of skulls might be referred and ranked; amongst which, above all others, the facial line of the ingenious Camper deserves special mention[2].

59. *Facial line of Camper.* He imagined, on placing a skull in profile, two right lines intersecting each other. The first was to be a horizontal line drawn through the external auditory meatus and the bottom of the nostrils. The second was to touch that part of the frontal bone above the nose, and then to be produced to the extreme alveolar limbus of the upper jaw. By the angle which the intersection of these two lines would make, this distinguished man thought that he could determine the difference of skulls as well in brute animals as in the different nations of mankind.

60. *Remarks upon it.* But, if I am correct, this rule contains more than one error. First: what indeed is plain from those varieties of the racial face I was speaking of (s. 56), this universal facial line at the best can only be adapted to those varieties of mankind which differ from each other in the direction of the jaws, but by no means to those who, in exactly the contrary way, are more remarkable for their lateral differences.

Secondly: it very often happens that the skulls of the most different nations, who are separated as they say by the whole heaven from one another, have still one and the same direction of the facial line: and on the other hand many skulls of one and the same race, agreeing entirely with a common disposition, have

---

[1] *De corporis humani fabrica*, p. m. 17.
[2] See *Kleinere schriften*, T. I. P. I. p. 15, and *Naturgeschichte des Orang utan*, pp. 181, 117; and his separate book, *Über den natürlichen unterschied der gesichtszüge*, &c.

a facial line as different as possible. We can form but a poor opinion of skulls when seen in profile alone, unless at the same time account be taken of their breadth. Thus as I now write I have before me a pair of skulls, viz.: an Ethiopian of Congo[1], and a Lithuanian of Sarmatia[1]. Both have almost exactly the same facial line: yet their construction is as different as possible if you compare the narrow and, as it were, keeled head of the Ethiopian with the square head of the Sarmatian. On the other hand, I have two Ethiopian skulls in my possession, differing in the most astonishing manner from each other as to their facial line[2], yet in both, if looked at as in front, the narrow and, as it were, squeezed-up skulls, the compressed forehead, &c. sufficiently testify to their Ethiopian origin.

Thirdly, and finally, Camper himself, in the plates appended to his work, has made such an arbitrary and uncertain use of his two normal lines, has so often varied the points of contact according to which he has drawn them, and upon which all their value and trustworthiness depends, as to make a tacit confession that he himself is uncertain, and hesitates in the application of them.

61. *Vertical scale for defining the racial characters of skulls.* The more my daily experience and, as it were, my familiarity with my collection of skulls of different nations increases, so much the more impossible do I find it to reduce these racial varieties—when such differences occur in the proportion and direction of the parts of the truly many-formed skull, all having more or less to do with the racial character—to the measurements and angles of any single scale. That view of the skull however seems to be preferable for the diagnosis which is our business that presents together at one glance the most and the principal parts best adapted for a comparison of racial characters. With this object I have found after many experiments that position answers best in which skulls are seen from above and from behind, placed in a row on the same plane, with

---

[1] *Decas cran. altera*, Tab. 18.　　[2] *Decas tertia*, Tab. 12.
[3] *Decas prima*, Tabb. 7, 8.

the malar bones directed towards the same horizontal
jointly with the inferior maxillaries. Then all that most conduces to the racial character of skulls, whether it be the direction of the jaws, or the cheekbones, the breadth or narrowness of the skull, the advancing or receding outline of the forehead, &c. strikes the eye so distinctly at one glance, that it is not out of the way to call that view the vertical scale (*norma verticalis*). The meaning and use of this will easily be seen by an examination of Plate III., which represents, by way of specimen, three skulls disposed in the order mentioned. The middle one (fig. 2) is a very symmetrical and beautiful one of a Georgian female; on either side are two skulls differing from it in the most opposite way. The one (fig. 3) elongated in front, and as it were keeled, is that of an Ethiopian female of Guinea; the other (fig. 4) dilated outwardly toward the sides, and as it were flattened, is that of a Reindeer Tungus.

In the first, the margin of the orbits, the beautifully narrowed malar bones, and the mandibles themselves under the bones, are concealed by the periphery of the moderately expanded forehead; in the second, the maxillary bones are compressed laterally, and project; and in the third, the malar bones, placed in nearly the same horizontal plane with the little bones of the nose and the glabella, project enormously, and rise on each side.

62. *Racial varieties of skulls.* All the diversities in the skulls of different nations, just like those of the racial face we enumerated above, seem capable of reduction also to five principal varieties; of which specimens selected out of many are exhibited in Plate IV.

1. That in the middle is beautifully symmetrical, somewhat globular; the forehead moderately expanded, the malar bones somewhat narrow, nowhere projecting, sloping down behind from the malar process of the frontal bone; the alveolar ridge somewhat round; the primary teeth of each jaw perpendicular. As a specimen (Plate IV. fig. 3) I have given a most beautiful skull of a Georgian female. This beautiful form of skull comes between two extremes; of which one has

2. The head almost square, the malar bones projecting outwards; the glabella and the little bones of the flattened nose lying in almost the same horizontal plane with the malar bones: scarcely any supraciliary ridge; narrow nostrils; the fossa malaris only gently curved; the alveolar ridge obtusely arched in front; the chin slightly prominent. This form of skull is peculiar to the Mongolian nations. Pl. IV. fig. 1, gives one of this kind, of a Reindeer Tungus.

The other extreme

3. Has the head narrow; laterally compressed; the forehead knotty and uneven; the malar bones projecting forwards; nostrils ample; the fossa malaris deeply winding behind the infraorbital foramen; the jaws projecting; the alveolar margin narrow, elongated, and very elliptical; the primary upper teeth slanting; the lower jaw large and strong; the head generally thick and heavy, common to the Negro, such as (Plate IV. fig. 5) of an Ethiopian female of Guinea. Finally, the two following varieties are intermediate between the first and those two extremes, for example:

4. That with broader cheeks but more arched and rounded than in the Mongolian variety, not as in this stretched out on each side and angular; the orbits generally deep; the form of the forehead and vertex frequently artificially distorted; the skull usually light. This is the American variety. Pl. IV. fig. 2 is the head of a Carib chief from the island of St Vincent.

5. The calvaria moderately narrowed; forehead slightly swelling; cheek bones by no means prominent; upper jawbone somewhat prominent; the parietal bones extending laterally. Common to the Malay race throughout the Southern Ocean. A specimen in Pl. IV. fig. 4, the skull of an Otaheitan. This racial form of the skull is so universally constant that it may be observed even in the skulls of young infants. Thus I possess the skull of a Burat infant[1] with very manifest Mongolian characters; and another of a newly-born Negro[2] as manifestly Ethiopian.

---

[1] *Decas tertia*, Tab. 29. [2] *Ib.* 30.

63. *Causes of the racial variety of skulls.* The bones of all parts of the human body alike are very solid, and particularly firm, so that they may adhere together as foundations and props to the other solid parts; still it is clear from pathological phenomena and physiological experiments that they are not less liable to perpetual mutations than the soft parts of the body. The elements of the bones, although imperceptibly so, are in a continual sort of flux and reflux; and fresh secretions from the red stream of the blood are deposited in their place, and at last solidify and repair the loss. By this continual permutation of the osseous material, which is perpetually going on from the first formation of the bones, it results that these accommodate themselves to the neighbouring parts, and are to some extent formed and modelled by their action.

This is most particularly evident from the configuration of the skull in advanced age. For then the internal basis of the skull gives, as it were, a sort of cast of the lobes and convolutions of the brain to which it was fitted. The exterior osseous face gives unmistakeable marks as well of the action of the muscles as of the whole countenance, whose general appearance and character may very easily be divined from the skull when stripped of flesh. So, if it is true, and it seems very true indeed, that the influence of climate on the racial face is great, it is at once clear that the same cause must have a great though an indirect share in forming the racial character of the skull, especially as regards the bones of the face itself.

Besides this principal cause, it seems to me very probable that others also are accessory, as the violent and long-continued pressure, in having an effect upon these facial bones. My collection rejoices, owing to the liberality of the illustrious Banks, in the very rare skull of a New Hollander[1] from the neighbourhood of Botany Bay, conspicuous beyond all others for the singular smoothness of the upper jaw, where the upper teeth and the canines are inserted. But it is now known that those barbarians have a paradoxical custom of perforating the septum

---

[1] *Decas tertia*, Tab. 27.

of the nose with a piece of wood inserted crosswise, and of so stopping up their nostrils with a sort of peg that they cannot breathe except through the open mouth. It seems credible, therefore, that this smoothness may have been gradually effected by the perpetual pressure of this transverse insertion. It is, however, much more often the case that the smooth bones of the calvaria suffer through constant pressure a peculiar and everywhere the same sort of change towards the racial conformation, whether it be induced by the common method which obtains in some nations of treating infants in the cradle, or by some more violent manual application, long and carefully continued. Hence Vesalius said, that in his day the Germans were generally remarkable for having the occiput compressed and the head broad, because the children were always placed on their backs in the cradle. But he attributed more oblong heads to the Belgians, because their mothers wrapped up the male infants in swaddling-clothes, and made them sleep as much as possible on their sides and temples.

Hence also the wild Americans from South Carolina as far as New Mexico are remarkable for having depressed calvaria, which the infants contract from their low position in the cradle, in which their head and the weight of their whole body reposes immovably in a small bag filled with sand[1]. As to other artifices, such as the pressure of the hands, and the reduction of the head of newly-born infants by bands or other instruments into some racial form, they, it is well known, have been in use equally amongst the most ancient races as those of to-day, amongst ourselves as in the most remote nations[2].

---

[1] See Adair's *History of the North American Indians*, p. 9: "they fix the tender infant on a kind of cradle, where his feet are tilted, above a foot higher than a horizontal position;—his head bends back into a hole, made on purpose to receive it, where he bears the chief part of his weight on the crown of the head, upon a small bag of sand, without being in the least able to move himself. By this pressure, and their thus flattening the crown of the head, they consequently make their heads thick and their faces broad."

[2] "The way in which the Author of our being has shaped our heads does not suit us; we must have them modelled from without by midwives and from within by philosophers.—The Caribs are more fortunate by half than ourselves." J. J. Rousseau, *Émile*, T. I. p. m. 19.

DEFORMATIONS.   241

Indeed we find it stated that solemn rites of this kind take place even now, or at all events did recently among the inhabitants of some provinces of Germany[1], as well as amongst the Belgians[2], the Gauls[3], some of the Italians[4], the islanders of the Grecian archipelago[5], the Turks[6], the ancient Sigynnes[7], and the Macrocephali on the Euxine sea[8], the Sumatrans[9] of to-day, and the Nicobars[10], but especially amongst different people of America, such as the inhabitants of Nootka Sound[11], the Shactas[12], an indigenous race of Georgia, the Waxsaws of Carolina[13], the Caribs[14], the Peruvians[15], and the free Ethiopians of the Antilles[16]. Strange to say there have been lately some authors who have dared to throw doubts upon the whole of this artificial habit of moulding the heads of infants[17]. Yet it is a thing proved by the unanimous testimony of many eye-witnesses; from which a name has been given to several nations

---

[1] On the Varisci of to-day, see J. C. G. Ackermann in Baldinger, Neues Magazin für Aerzte, T. 11. p. 506. On the Hamburghians of his day, see Laurenberg, Pasicompas, p. 63.
[2] Spigel, De Humani Corporis Fabrica, p. 17.
[3] On the Parisians, see Andry, Orthopédie, T. 1L p. 3.
[4] On the Genoese, see Vesalius, De Corp. Hum. Fabrica, p. m. 23. Spigel, l.c.
[5] My dear old pupil, Philites, M. D. of Epirus, an eye-witness, told me personally about the Chians.
[6] Baron de Asch informed me in a letter dated the 20th July, 1788, that the midwives of Constantinople generally inquire of the mother, after the birth, what form she would like to have given to the head of the newly-born infant? and that the Asiatics prefer that, which is produced by a bandage passed over the forehead and tied tight round the occiput, because they think that in that way the red coverings they use for the head are made to sit better. Comp. Decas Craniorum prima, l. 2.
[7] Strabo, l. 11. p. 358, ed. Casaub.
[8] Hippocrates, De aëribus, aquis, et locis, ed. Charter, T. VI. p. 206.
[9] Marsden, Hist. of Sumatra, p. 38.
[10] Nic. Fontana in Asiatic Researches, Vol. III. p. 151.
[11] Meares' Voyage, p. 249.
[12] Adair, l.c. pp. 8, 384. Comp. Decas Craniorum prima, Pl. 9.
[13] Lawson's History of Carolina, p. 33.
[14] Oviedo, Historia General de las Indias, Sevilla, 1535, fol. p. 156. Raymond Breton, Dictionnaire Caraibe-François, Auxerre, 1665, 8vo, pp. 58, 92, 145, 289. Comp. Decas Craniorum prima, Pl. 10, and the plates appended to this work, Pl. IV. fig. 2. Decas secunda, Pl. 20.
[15] Torquemada, Monarchia Indiana, Sevill. 1615, fol. T. III. p. 613. Iu Ulloa, Relacion del viage para medir algunos grados de meridiano, Madr. 1748, fol. T. II. p. 535.
[16] Thibault de Chanvalon, Voyage à la Martinique, p 39.
[17] See Haller, Camper, Sabatier, &c.

16

both of North[1] and South[2] America. Two hundred years ago we know it was forbidden to the barbarians of the new world by the councils of the Spanish clergy[3]. We have the particular points of each method most accurately described, and the machines and bands[4] by which they impress upon the flexible infant calvaria a form they like through a daily continuous and uniform pressure kept up for many years. And finally, the heads of these very barbarians, which have been brought to Europe and long since represented in prints[5], exactly and in every point answer to all these things. Although however the fact itself is beyond all doubt, still there is some question about what we read has often been asserted from the times of Hippocrates, that peculiar forms of the skull of this sort, though formed first on purpose and by artifice, when they have been kept up and repeated for a long series of generations, become at last in process of time to be a sort of hereditary prerogative and congenital, and finally a second nature. There is to be found in that golden little treatise of Hippocrates *On Air, Water, and Soil*, a celebrated passage about the Macrocephali, a nation living near the Euxine sea, about whom he speaks first and almost chiefly, because no other nation at all was known to have heads like theirs. He says, that in the beginning custom was the reason of their having such long heads, but that

---

[1] "The name of Omaguas in the Peruvian language, like that of Cambevas, which is given them by the Portuguese of Para, in the Brasilian, means Flat-head; in fact, these people have the strange custom of pressing the heads of their children as soon as they are born between two planks, and of causing them to take the strange shape which is the result, to make them more like the full moon, as they say." De la Condamine in *Mém. de l'Acad. des Sciences de Paris*, 1745. p. 427.
[2] Bullet-heads and Flat-heads. Comp. Charlevoix, *Histoire de la Nouvelle France*, T. III. pp. 187, 323.
[3] Jos. Saenz de Aguirre, *Collectio max. concil. omnium Hispaniæ et novi orbis*, ed. 2, Rom. 1755. fol. T. VI. p. 301, where in the history of the synod of the third diocese of Lima, July 17, 1585, is the decree that the Indians are not to shape the heads of their children in moulds. "Being desirous entirely to extirpate the abuse and superstition under which the Indians everywhere impress certain shapes on the heads of their children, which they themselves call *Caito, Oma Opalta*, we order and enjoin," &c. various punishments for the delinquents, as that a woman who has done so "shall attend the instruction for ten successive days, morning and evening, for the first offence; for the second, twenty," &c.
[4] Comp. the careful pictures of the bands of this sort made use of by the Caribs in *Journal de Physique*, Aug. 1791. p. 132.
[5] In *Mém. de l'Acad. des Sc. de Paris*, 1740, Pl. 16, fig. 1.

afterwards nature had acted in concert with custom. It was thought the most honourable thing among the Macrocephali to have the head as long as possible. This was the beginning of the custom; when an infant of theirs was just born, its head being like wax, or wet and soft clay, they pinched it as soon as possible with their hands, and modulated it so as to compel it to increase in length, and besides, confined it with bands, and tied it round with proper contrivances, so as to prevent the head becoming round and make it increase in length. This custom had at length effected the production of heads of this kind, and in process of time they had been produced naturally, so that it was no longer necessary to use this custom for that purpose. The old man of Cos endeavours to explain the cause of this singular phenomenon by his celebrated hypothesis of generation, which is not very different from that of Buffon: his idea was that the genital liquid proceeded and was as it were elaborated from all the members of the body; and so the forms of the parts, of which moulds, so to speak, were thus taken, conduced to the formation of the fœtus. Hence it happened that bald men produced bald children; grey men, grey; and macrocephali, long-headed. Something of the same kind has been lately reported of other nations, the Peruvians[1] and Genoese[2] for example. I leave this matter however in the abstract just as it is, and shall only refer to what I said above (s. 39) on the occasion of other similar phenomena.

64. *Some racial varieties of dentition, and their causes.* Some varieties of teeth generally closely accompany the forms of skulls, as has been observed in some nations. Thus, as long ago as 1779, I observed a singular anomaly of the primary teeth both in the fragment of a mummified Egyptian, as in the entire skull of a mummy[3]; for the coronæ are not shaped for incision, or furnished with a delicate edge, but are thick and like truncated cones, and the coronæ of the canines cannot be dis-

---

[1] On the inhabitants of the province of Porto Vecchio see Cardanus, *De Rerum Varietate*, T. III. p. 163, ed. Sponii.
[2] J. C. Scaliger, *Comment. in Theophr. de Causis Plantarum*, p. 287.
[3] *Decas Craniorum prima*, Pl. I.

tinguished from their neighbours excepting by position. This same singular conformation has been noticed also in other mummies; as in a mummy at Cambridge[1], and Cassel[2]; something of the same kind also at Stuttgard[3]: and I myself, when I was in London two years ago, found exactly the same sort of incisors in a young mummy, which its possessor, J. Symmons, very kindly allowed me to unrol[4]. Although it is scarcely necessary to observe that during such a series of ages as the custom of preserving corpses prevailed in Egypt, and under the vicissitudes of the lords of its soil and its inhabitants, a very great diversity must necessarily be found between mummies and their skulls, and that no sane person could ever expect to find in all mummies the same extraordinary form of teeth I was speaking of. The variety is however remarkable and perhaps may sometimes be of utility as a distinctive character, by which the mummies of one age or race may be distinguished from those of another. It would be difficult to discover the causes of this peculiar conformation: but it seems very likely that it is in great part to be attributed to the kind of diet, which we are expressly told by Diodorus Siculus, was of a rustic sort amongst the ancient Egyptians, and consisted of cabbages and roots. Hence the teeth became much worn; and when teeth are worn or flattened purposely it has been observed that they increase in thickness, in the case both of men[5] and brutes[6]. Considerable weight is added to this conjecture from the observation of Winslow[7], who noticed a similar remarkable thickness of the incisors, and the like similarity to the molars, in the skull of a Greenlander taken from the Island of Dogs[8], and attributed

---

[1] Middleton, *Monumenta Antiquitatis, Opera,* T. IV. p. 170. "All the teeth are still found firmly adhering to the upper jaw; what however is singular, and may be considered almost a prodigy, is that the anterior incisors are not acute, and adapted for cutting, but are broad and flat, just like the molars."

[2] Comp. the account by Brickmann, the head physician of Brunswick, of that mummy. Brunswick. 1782. 4to.

[3] Storr, *Protr. methodi Mummdism,* Tubing. 1780, 4to, p. 24.

[4] *Philosoph. Trans.* 1794. Part II. p. 184.

[5] Birch's *History of the Royal Society,* T. IV. p. 3.

[6] On the ivory tusks of elephants, see *Transzuckerische Missions-Berichte,* Contin. CVI.

[7] *Mém. de l'Acad. des Sc. de Paris,* 1722, p. 323.

[8] *Hond-Eyland.* "This Island, lying in Disko Strait on the coast of south

it to the fact that those barbarians live on raw flesh[1]. This observation is also supported by the thick and wonderfully worn teeth in two Esquimaux skulls which have lately come to me from the colony of Nain in Labrador[2]. It is well known that the Esquimaux and the Greenlanders belong to one and the same stock, and their racial name is commonly derived from their habit of eating raw flesh. What several authors have related about the teeth of the Calmucks[3], that they are very long and separated by large interstices, I find at last has been taken originally, and then not quite accurately, from the account of Yvo, a priest of Narbonne, originally written in 1243, and afterwards garbled by many, nor does it agree with the modern Mongolian skulls which I now have in my collection. Finally, other racial peculiarities of the teeth are due exclusively to artifice, as in some groups of negroes who by filing their teeth sharpen them like saws[4]; or, as in some Malay nations, who remove a great part of the enamel of the teeth[5], or cut furrows

---

Greenland, is as well known, and so clearly laid down in all good geographical maps of that country from the time of Zorgdrager, that I must confess I cannot understand what Camper meant when he went so far as to accuse Winslow of ignorance, and to correct him according to Hübner's geography, in which forsooth the Island of Dogs is relegated to the Pacific Ocean under the tropic of Capricorn. Did he not know that this southern island was described by its discoverer Schouten in 1616, in his well-known journey, as being altogether uninhabited, and, so far as I know, from that time forth never visited again by any European? Whereas that northern land from which Winslow received his skull is frequented by numberless Europeans engaged in the whale-fishery."

[1] "The incisors are short," says Winslow, "large behind and flat, instead of being cutting, and are more like molars than incisors. M. Illocke (the finder of the skull) tells me that the inhabitants of that island eat flesh quite raw. They make many extraordinary movements with the jaw, and many grimaces in chewing and swallowing. It was chiefly the sight of this which induced M. Illocke to look for the corpses of these islanders to see if their jaws and their teeth had any peculiar conformation."

[2] Comp. Buffon, Erxleben, &c.

[3] Van Linschoten, Schipvaert naer Oost, Part I. p. m. 69. Von der Gröben, Guineische Reisebeschreibung, pp. 81, 94. Harlot in Churchill's Collections of Voyages, Vol. v. pp. 139, 143, 383. Schotto in Philosoph. Trans. Vol. LXXIII. Part I. p. 92. Report of the Lords of the Committee of Council for the consideration of the Slave Trade, fols. L and M.

[4] I am surprised that some famous authors, as Römer and Niebuhr, have taken this artificial deformation of the teeth for a natural disposition. See Römer, Efterretning om Kysten Guinea, p. 21. Niebuhr, Diss. in Deutsche Museum, 1787, Part I. p. 415.

[5] On the Philippines of Maginda, see Forrest, Voyage to New Guinea, p. 237. On the Sumatrans, Marsden, p. 46.

in it', &c. I have seen something of the same kind myself in some Chinese from Java, who had carefully and regularly destroyed with a whetstone the same substance from the extremity of the primary teeth.

65. *Some other racial varieties in respect to particular parts of the body.* Thus far we have investigated the chief varieties of different nations, which are observable either in their colour (as that of their skin, hair, or eyes) or in their countenance and form of the skull. Some few things still remain to be observed respecting other parts of the body, which although certainly of less importance can by no means be passed over unnoticed, and so I may say a little of each of them in a few words. And although it would be impossible to explain with equal clearness the causes and reasons of them all, still there is nothing so singular or so enigmatical but what may be rendered more easy of comprehension by comparing with analogous phenomena such observations as we have compiled in the section above on the brute animals.

66. *Ears.* It is known to antiquarians that many of the idols of ancient Egypt, both of bronze and pottery, or those cut out of different kinds of stones or sycamore wood, and finally those painted on the sarcophagi, are remarkable for having the ears too high up. A recent author[2] has summarily been pleased to attribute this to the fault of the artists, unskilled in the art of drawing. But I cannot quite give my adhesion to this view, because of the elaborate art and taste with which I see many of them are executed, and also because I have observed it particularly in those which have an Indian cast of countenance[3]; and a similar collocation is to be found in genuine pictures of Indians, which have been executed with the greatest care. Altogether however this diversity is no greater than what we see everywhere in varieties of domestic animals, especially in horses and pigs, in the position and collocation of the ears, especially inasmuch as, if we take into consideration in these same Egyptians

---

[1] On the Javanese, Hawkesworth, Vol. III. p. 349.
[2] *Recherches Philosophiques sur les Egyptiens,* T. I. p. 113.
[3] *Philosoph. Trans.* 1791, Part II. p. 191, Plate 16, fig. 2.

and Indians the inclination of the aperture of the eyelids, from the root of the nose towards the ears, we shall find that the elevation of the ears depends upon the way in which the head is carried, the occiput being elevated, and the chin depressed. We find also, not only from passages in the ancient authors, but also from ancient representations, that the ears of the aboriginal Batavians were remarkable for their form and position[1]. So also the ears of the Biscayans were remarkable for their size[2].

It is well known that in barbarous nations the ears often stand out a good deal from the head, and are moveable; and in many races, especially of the East Indies and the Pacific Ocean, the lobe of the ear is enlarged and prodigiously elongated by various artifices. This absurd custom has no doubt given rise to the exaggerated stories of ancient writers about the enormous ears of certain races.

67. *Breasts.* There is a cloud of witnesses to prove that the breasts of the females in some nations, especially of Africa[3] and some Islands of the Pacific Ocean[4], are very long and pendulous. Meanwhile I must observe first, that their proportions have been exaggerated beyond the truth; and also that this conformation is not common to all the women of the same race. Even in the Islands of the Southern Ocean[5] many women, and also many Ethiopians[6] every day in the European markets, are to be

---

[1] Smetius has some drawings of them in *Antiquitates Neomagenses*, p. 70, and Cannegieter, *De Brittenburgo, Matribus Brittis, &c.* p. 144.

[2] Mm. Countess d'Aunoy, *Relation du Voyage d'Espagne*, T. 1. p. m. 13. Diese in his notes to Pernetz, *Reise durch Spanien*, T. 11. p. 271, vindicates the authority of this deserving work.

[3] Comp. about the Ethiopians, Fermin, *Sur l'Economie Animale*, T. 1. p. 117. About the Hottentots, Kolbe, p. 474.

[4] See the inhabitants of Horn Island in Schouten in Dalrymple's *Collection*, Vol. 11. p. 58.

[5] See the assertion of Towrson in Hakluyt's *Collection*, T. 11. p. 26, about the negroes of the Isle of St Vincent. "Divers of the women have such exceeding long breasts, that some of them will lay the same upon the ground and lie down by them." And of Bruce, about the breasts of the Shangalla, which in some of them hang down almost to the knees. *Reise nach den Quellen des Nils*, T. 11. p. 546. Nor have I any greater faith in the story of Mentzel about the tobacco-pouches made out of the breasts of Hottentot women, and sold in great quantity at the Cape of Good Hope. *Beschreibung des Vorgebirge der guten Hoffnung*, T. 11. p. 564.

[6] J. R. Forster, *Bemerkungen, &c.* p. 242.

seen, who are remarkable for the extreme beauty of their breasts. Besides, this excessive size is by no means peculiar to barbarous nations alone, but has been observed frequently in Europeans, as amongst the Irish[1], and up to this day amongst the Morlachians[2]. It seems the principal reason is to be looked for in the way the mother gives suck to the infant attached to its back, and partly because lactation is kept up long, sometimes for years. And we read too that the breasts are often artificially elongated amongst nations, who reckon that feature a beauty[3].

Other nations are conspicuous for the size and turgescence of the breasts, like the Egyptians. Juvenal long ago said,

"Or breasts at Meroe big as good-sized babes,"

as if speaking of a thing common and well known to all. And not only the women, but also the men in Egypt, are said to be very large-breasted[4]. Amongst European nations the Portuguese women have very large breasts[5], whilst those of the Spanish on the contrary are thin and small; and in the last century especially they took pains to compress them and obstruct their growth[6]. That by taking pains the circumference of the breasts can be increased is indubitable. How far, moreover, precocious venery may operate in that direction is shown by the remarkable instances amongst the immature and girlish prostitutes who flock to London, especially from the neighbouring suburbs, and offering themselves for hire, wander about the streets by night in great numbers.

---

[1] Lithgow's *Rare Adventures and Painefull Peregrinations*, p. m. 432. "I saw in Ireland's North parts women travayling the way, or toyling at home, carry their infants about their neckes, and laying the duggs over their shoulders, would give sucke to the babes behinde their backes, without taking them in their armes; such kind of breasts, me thinketh, were very fit, to be made money bags for East or West Indian merchants, being more than halfe a yard long, and as well wrought as any tanner, in the like charge, could ever mollifie such leather."

[2] Fortis, *Viaggio in Dalmazia*, T. I. p. 81.

[3] On the inhabitants of the coast of Western Africa, between the white promontory and the river Senegal, see Cadamosto in Ramusio, T. I. p. m. 100. Comp. Lamiral, *L'Afrique et le peuple Africain*, Paris, 1789, 8vo, p. 45. "In Senegal the young girls study to make their breasts depend, in order that they may be thought women, and treated with more respect."

[4] Alpinus, *Historia Naturalis Ægypti*, T. I. p. 14.

[5] I have this from Abildgaard, just returned from a journey in Portugal.

[6] Countess d'Aunoy, l. c. T. II. p. 128.

GENITALS. 249

68. *Genitals.* Linnæus says in the prolegomena of his *Systema Naturæ*, "that a too minute inspection of the genitals is abominable and disagreeable." It is evident however by the terminology of his conchylia that in process of time he came to think otherwise, and above all we find it so from the *Venus Dione*, depicted by him in a sufficiently licentious metaphorical style. The shade therefore of this illustrious man will no doubt pardon me if I enumerate here shortly what seem to me worthy of mention about some racial varieties of the genitals.

It is generally said that the penis in the Negro is very large. And this assertion is so far borne out by the remarkable genitory apparatus of an Æthiopian which I have in my anatomical collection. Whether this prerogative be constant and peculiar to the nation I do not know[1]. It is said that women when eager for venery prefer the embraces of Negroes to those of other men[2]. On the other hand, that Ethiopian[3] and Mulatto[4] women are particularly sought out by Europeans. The cause of this preference may be various, but I do not know what it is. Perhaps they resemble the Mongolian[5] women and those of some American tribes[6], about whom we are told that the muliebria remain small, not only after marriage but even after childbearing. Steller[7] attributes the contrary character to the pudenda of the Kamtschadales. He also says that many of them are remarkable for long and protruding nymphæ; which some say in Hottentot women come to be appendages like fingers[8]. But this *sinus pudoris*, as Linnæus called it, seems rather to

---

[1] The same was said of the northern Scotch, who do not wear trowsers, by Faust, *Wie de Geschlechtstrieb der Menschen in Ordnung zu bringen*, p. 52. I have shown however on the weightiest testimony that this assertion is incorrect, in *Medicinische Bibliothek*, T. III. p. 413.
[2] Naar, *Ostindische Kriegsdienste*, p. m. 45.
[3] Chanvalon, *Voyage à la Martinique*, p. 61. Sparrmann, *Reise nach dem Vorgebirge der guten Hoffnung*, p. 72.
[4] *De Werken van* W. V. Focquenbroch, T. II. p. 421.
[5] Georgi, *Beschreibung aller Nationen des Russischen Reichs*. Part II. p. 120.
[6] Vespucci, *Lettera a Lorenzo de' Medici*, p. 110, ed. Bandini. Illolani Bl. *Anthropographia*, p. m. 306.
[7] *Beschreibung von Kamtschatka*, p. 299.
[8] Comp. W. ten Rhyne, *De Promontorio bonæ Spei*, Sculus. 1686, 8vo, p. 33.

exists in the elongation of the labia themselves[1], which is said to be due to artifice[2]; and has given a handle for that story about the skinny ventrale, which credulous authors have thought hung down from the abdomen[3] and concealed the pudenda of these women[4].

69. *Legs.* Some difference in the proportion and appearance of the legs is known to exist in certain nations. Thus the Indians are remarkable for the length of their legs[5], the Mongolians on the other hand for their shortness[6]. The Irish women are said to have very large thighs[7]. The legs of the New Zealanders are so thick as to appear œdematous[8]. Others tell us that these antipodes of ours have those same legs crooked and deformed, and that such evils are contracted from the position in which they usually sit. Bandy legs however are very common amongst the Calmucks, and are ascribed as well to the kind of cradles their children have, as to the fact that they are accustomed to be on horseback from tender youth[10]. The feet of the Tierra del Fuegians[11], who are called by De Bougainville[12] Pescheras, are described as being remarkably deformed.

That the populations of Africa, however, are those in which deformities of the legs and feet are racial, has been noticed by the ancients, especially in the case of the Egyptians[13], the Ethi-

---

[1] Hawkesworth's *Collection*, T. III. p. m. 388. I owe to the liberality of Sir Jos. Banks several drawings of this *Sinus pudoris* taken from nature at the Cape of Good Hope. In one of them the labia are so elongated that they measure six inches and a half Rhine-land measure.
[2] Le Vaillant, *Voyage dans l'Intérieur de l'Afrique*, pp. 3. 371.
[3] See a print in F. Legnat, *Voyage et Aventures*, T. II. Plate 13.
[4] Voltaire makes use of this fabulous *ventrale*, with other arguments of the same weight, to prove that the Hottentots cannot be referred to the same species of man as Europeans. *Lettres d'Amabed*, Oper. T. XLV. p. m. 214.
[5] De la Boullaye le-Gouz, *Voyages et Observations*, p. 133. Kant in Engel, *Philosoph für die Welt*, T. II. p. 155.
[6] Yvo Nartoncusii in Matthew Paris, *Historia Major*, ed. Wats. p. 530.
[7] Twiss' *Tour in Ireland*, p. 39.
[8] Musseron in de la Borde, *Histoire de la Mer du Sud*, T. II. p. 97.
[9] G. Forster's *Voyage round the World*, Vol. II. p. 480.
[10] Pallas, *Ueber die Mongolischen Völkerschaften*, T. I. p. 98.
[11] J. R. Forster, *Bemerkungen*, p. 535. "The feet bear no proportion to the upper limbs; the shanks are thin, the legs crooked, the knees bent outwards, the toes turned inwards."
[12] *Voyage autour du Monde*, p. 147. "We called them Pecherais, because that was the first word they pronounced on meeting us, and which they repeated without stopping."
[13] Aristotle, *Problemata*, §. 14, p. 431, ed. Casaub.

opians[1], and the negro slaves[2]. In the legs of black slaves of our day three defects are to be seen, attributed to three different causes; bandy legs[3] (fr. *jambes cambrées*); disagreeable thickness[4]; and the chinks and fissures in which they are said frequently to open[5]. The crookedness appears to be due principally from the posture in which the infants whilst sucking are obliged to hold tight by the knees to the mother's back[6]. Some deformities of this kind may also be traced to morbific causes[7]. The thickness of the feet (unless this too is to be referred to pathological causes) is most probably brought about by severe and continuous labour. Finally, there is scarcely any reason to doubt but what the fissures into which the thick epidermis of the Ethiopians is liable to break out, especially in the sole of the foot, are due to their sandy soil[8].

70. *Feet and hands.* Lastly, good observers have remarked that the hands and feet of some nations are of singularly small proportions. This is said of the Indians[9], the Chinese[10], the Kamtschadales[11], the Esquimaux[12], the Peruvians[13], New Hollanders[14] and Hottentots[15]. That artifice has a good deal to do

---

[1] Virgil, *Moretum*, 35. Comp. Heyne's *Notes*, T. IV. Op. Virgil.
[2] Petronii *Satyricon*, c. 102.
[3] Sömmerring, *Ueber die Körperliche Verschiedenheit des Negers*, &c. p. 40. Chanvalon, *Voyage à la Martinique*, p. 38. "That form of the legs is sufficiently common also among the Americans, but sometimes less observable than amongst the negroes."
[4] Alb. Dürer, *Von Menschlicher Proportion*, fol. T. III. ed. 1528. Ramsay, *On the Treatment and Conversion of African Slaves*, p. 217.
[5] I received in Jan. 1789 the fresh right leg, perfectly sound in other respects, of an Ethiopian who had just died at Cassel, part of which I still have in my anatomical collection: the epidermis of the sole of the foot is wonderfully thick, wrinkled, and gaping in many divided flakes.
[6] Chanvalon, *l.c.*
[7] Fr. Allamand in *Nova Acta Academiæ Naturæ Curiosorum*, T. IV. p. 89.
[8] See Hier. Mercurialis, *De decorationibus*, p. m. 102.
[9] "It has been observed of the arms of the Hindoos frequently brought to England, that the gripe of the sabre is too small for most European hands." Hodges, *Travels in India*, p. 3.
[10] Dampier, *Suite de Voyage autour du Monde*, p. 100. De la Barbinais, *Voyage autour du Monde*, T. II. p. 61. Osbeck's *Ostindisk Resa*, p. 171.
[11] Steller, *l. c.*
[12] Ellis, Cranz, &c. and lately the famous astronomer Wales, in *Philosoph. Trans.* Vol. LX. p. 100, and Curtis, *Ib.* Vol. LXIV. p. 383.
[13] De L'Ulloa, *Nachrichten*, &c. T. II. p. 97.
[14] Watkin Tench's *Account of the Settlement at Port Jackson*, p. 179.
[15] Sparrmann, *l. c.* p. 171.

252   STATURE.

with this we know from the ostrich feet of the Chinese women. But it seems very likely that the mode of life¹ and poor sort of diet² may also be to blame.

71. *Racial varieties in respect of stature.* Having now despatched what seems most worthy of remark about the relative proportion and conformation of particular parts, it seems proper to investigate briefly the varieties of the entire stature. This chapter of anthropological discussion has been handed down to us deformed almost entirely by fables, hyperbolical over-layers, and misinterpretation. These have, however, in our day been in a great part so refuted and explained, and reduced to their genuine sources, that it is scarcely necessary to mention them further, much less discuss them over again with fresh attention.

Thus it has been shown that under the Ethiopian pigmies of the ancients nothing else was intended but a symbolical signification of the degrees in the Nilometer. Thus the enormous bones dug up everywhere in our own country, which prejudiced opinion formerly attributed to giants, have been restored to the beasts by a more careful osteological study[3]. On the contrary, all the relics which have survived to our day, and the ancient furniture from which we may estimate the stature of ancient races, as mummies, bones, and especially the human

---

[1] "An (American) Indian man is small in the hand and wrist, for the same reason for which a sailor is large and strong in the arms and shoulders, and a porter in the legs and thighs." Jefferson in Morse's *American Universal Geography*, Vol. 1. p. 87.

[2] Neo Tench, from the observations of the Governor of the Cape: "Colonel Gordon told me that it indicated poverty and inadequacy of living. He instanced to me the Hottentots and Caffres; the former fare poorly, and have small hands and feet; the Caffres, their neighbours, live plenteously, and have very large ones."

[3] It is strange that in late times Buffon could have attributed many fossil bones of this kind, dug up at different times and places, to giants, in the 5th Vol. of the supplement of his classical work; such as those which in 1577 were dug up near Lucerne and preserved up to the present day in the court-house of that city, where I have seen them myself, and recognised them at the first glance to belong to an elephant. That most deserving physician, and even learned anatomist, Felix Plater, at the time when these geognostic monuments were dug up, measured them and examined them most carefully, and declared with the utmost confidence that they belonged to a human giant 17 feet in length, and had made a wonderful colossal picture of a human skeleton of that magnitude, which is still to be seen in the Jesuit's College at Lucerne; a memorable example of the power of prejudice against the very evidence of the senses, when once it has struck root in the mind.

teeth found in urns and sepulchres[1], armour, &c., tend to the conviction that those nations by no means surpassed men of the present day in stature. Amongst these also there is an indisputable racial diversity. Amongst European races the Scandinavians and some of the Swiss, as the Suitens, are tall: the Lapps short. In the new world the Abipones are large in size, the Esquimaux shorter: but neither more than moderately so. Altogether there is no variety in respect of stature so great amongst nations of the present day, but what may be easily explained by the common modes of degeneration, and the analogous phenomena which may be observed in other mammals. There are, however, two varieties of this kind which must be treated separately, of which it is said that even in these present times one differs greatly in excess, and the other by defect, from the common stature of mankind.

72. *Patagonians.* There is at the extremity of the continent of South America, towards the north-east, a nation, which from the time of Magellan's voyage has been known to Europeans, who invented for them the composite name of Patagonians, because they thought them related to their neighbours the *Choni*, and that their feet, which they used to wrap in the skins of the guanaco, were like the shaggy feet of brutes, called in Spanish *patas*. Their proper and indigenous name, however, is Tchueletæ. These people, then, commonly called Patagonians, Anton. Pigafetta, the companion of Magellan in his voyage, was the first in his account to pretend were giants double the size of Europeans[2]. From that time on for two centuries and a half the stories about the expeditions undertaken by the Europeans in that part of the new world are so repugnant to each other, and so contradictory and so wonderfully inconsistent as far as their notices of the Patagonians, that, once for all, they may serve as a warning to us to be

---

[1] I owe to the liberality of Rosenhard, Imperial consul-general in Denmark, the calvaria and other bones of a man of advanced age found not long ago in a very ancient Cimbrian tomb, in proportions and size yielding nothing to the common nature of our countrymen.

[2] See his *Viaggio atorno il mondo*, in Ramusio, T. I. ed. 4. p. 353.

cautious and diffident in trusting the accounts of travellers. I give in a note a decade of authors[1], for the benefit of those who are interested in examining and comparing these different accounts, and the opinions of anthropologists about them. It will be sufficient for us at present to put forth those results which seem most like the truth, after weighing and duly criticising everything.

It is then a race of men by no means of gigantic height, but conspicuous for tall bodies and a very muscular and knotty habit[2]. To define their exact stature amidst such a quantity of ambiguous stories would be impossible. From the evidence of the best witnesses, however, it seems scarcely to exceed six feet and a half of English measure; and this is the less to be thought prodigious, since it has long been known that other indigenous races of America (especially in the South) are very tall. It is very probably the case with them what Tacitus tells us about the ancient Germans, that they never mix with any other nation in marriage, and preserve their race peculiar, unadulterated, and always like itself. They are Nomads, like the people of Tierra del Fuego, and the other wandering nations of South America; and thence it is not surprising if they have not always appeared to be men of the same lofty stature to the Europeans who have approached the same coasts indeed of that country, but at different times.

It is not difficult, on the other hand, to understand how the story of the Patagonian giants arose. First, that old tradition about the giants of the old world preoccupied all minds, and so those travellers in the new world who were on the look out for

---

[1] Buffon, *Histoire Naturelle*, T. III, and *Suppl.* T. v. De Brosses, *Histoire des Navigations aux terres Australes*, T. I. De Pauw, *Recherches sur les Americains*, T. I. Ortega, *Viage del Comand. Byron al rededor del mundo, traduc. del Ingles*. Robertson's *History of America*, Vol. I. Zimmermann, *Geographische Geschichte des Menschen*, T. I. J. R. Forster, *Bemerkungen*. Comp. Carli Rubbi, *Lettere Americane*, T. I. Pennant, *Of the Patagonians*. *Relacion del ultimo viage al Estrecho de Magallanes en 1785*, y 86.

[2] Such they are unanimously described by the most credible eye-witnesses. Such too were those who towards the end of the sixteenth century were brought to Spain; the sole and only Patagonians, as far as I know, whom Europe has ever seen. Van Linschoten, a great and truly classical traveller, saw these very ones at Seville, and says of them: "they were of good stature and with large muscles," &c.

prodigies, reverted to that when they found men who were in reality tall and muscular, and tombs of wonderful length[1], and every where in them bones of a large size[2]. The Spaniards too might also have had the design of deterring the other nations of Europe from navigating the Straits of Magellan by stories of this kind[3]. And in others blind fear, and the desire of boasting, such as even in the present century has induced the author of a Dutch account of the voyage of Roggewein, to give out the inhabitants of Easter Island in the Pacific Ocean as giants of twelve feet high[4].

73. *Quimos.* There was an old story which even in the last century was exposed by the classical writer Stephen Flacourt as a fictitious invention, that there existed in the inner mountains of the Island of Madagascar a nation, pigmy in stature, but of a very warlike spirit, and which afflicted the other inhabitants by its sudden invasions. They were called Quimos or Kimos.

This story has lately found defenders in our time, in the pilot Modave, and the famous botanist Commerson. But if you take away all that is mere hearsay in their accounts, and their discrepancies, which are not few, all that remains will be that the pilot bought a certain small servant maid, who was sold to him

---

[1] Comp. Ed. Brown's *Travels*, p. m. 10. "Mr Wood, who has made very accurate maps of the Straits of Magellan, &c. told me, that he had seen divers graves in the southern parts of America near four yards long, which surprised him the more, because he had never seen any American that was two yards high, and therefore he opened one of these long sepulchres from one end to the other, and found in it a man and a woman, so placed, that the woman's head lay at the man's feet, and so might reasonably require a tomb of near that length."

[2] Of horses in fact, whose skeletons they place near the tombs of their relations. See Falkner, *Beschreibung von Patagonien*, p. m. 149. A most ancient custom everywhere, and which has prevailed amongst the most different nations, of entombing the horses of warriors together with them, gave afterwards a han Ile to the idea that the horses' bones were those of giants. Thus horses' bones are found in the oldest sepulchres of Siberia; see J. Gmelin, *Reisen*, T. III. p. 313. Even in the sarcophagi of Christian knights, buried in churches, during what are called the middle ages, besides their own arms and bones, those of horses also are found. See Dorville, *Sicula*, p. 148.

[3] See John Winter in Hakluyt's *Collection*, Vol. III. p. 751. Sir J. Narborough's *l'oyage to the Straits of Magellan*, p. m. 90.

[4] See Anon, *Tergiaersige Reys rondom de wereld*, Dordr. 1728. 4to. Much more trustworthy and accurate, on the other hand, is Behrens (by profession a confectioner), who was in the same voyage, in *Reise durch die Süd Länder und um die Welt*, Francof. 1737. 8vo, where, p. 87, he calls the inhabitants of Easter Island, then first discovered, only "well-built, with strong limbs."

for á Quimo, pale in colour, with pendulous breasts, and remarkable for the length of her arms, which reached nearly to the knees. Baron de Clugny, moreover, who spent nearly one whole month in the same ship with this identical pigmy, clearly showed that she was only a dwarf of bad conformation and diseased constitution, macrocephalous, stupid, and an utterer of confused sounds; from all which circumstances I am persuaded that her malady should be referred to Cretinism, since these symptoms occur in Cretins; and the length of the arms has been noticed in many of them, and particularly in those of Salzburg, in express words, by observers. On the other hand Sonnerat has ingeniously explained the whole tradition as if it was to be understood about the *Zaphe-Itacquimusi*, that is, the six chiefs of the race who inhabit Manatann, a province of that Island, which chiefs are descended from an ancestor who was very small; a fact expressed by that barbarous word[1].

74. *Causes of Racial Stature.* We must allow then that there is no entire nation of giants or pigmies. But the racial variety of stature which we touched upon above (s. 71) seems to be confined within smaller limits in proportion than those which have been everywhere observed in the case of other domestic animals (s. 29); and this will easily be understood by a consideration of what has been said about the causes of degeneration. That climate has something to do with it, besides many other proofs, is seen from a comparison of the Laplanders with the Hungarians, who are two colonies from one race, but have reached a very different stature under a different climate. Physiology also clearly shows the great influence of diet in augmenting or diminishing the stature. Hence the tall bodies of the nobles of Otaheite is ascribed to the more generous diet they indulge in[2].

---

[1] Pallas seems to have deduced the origin of the Quimos from some hybrid generation. See his *Observations sur la formation des montagnes*, p. 14, where on the origin of the Ethiopians he says: — "We need not have recourse in this case to any improper connection of the human species, which seems to have been the case in the production of the long-armed mountaineers or Quimos of Madagascar."

[2] See J. R. Forster, *Bemerkungen*, p. m. 236.

On the other hand we are told that the stature of some barbarous nations has diminished sensibly for a series of generations after they have accustomed themselves to the abuse of aquavitæ and ardent spirits[1].

Here also mention ought to be made of the period of puberty, which differs in different nations, and has a good deal to do with the racial stature, since those who remain longest before arriving at puberty, by this constancy (as Cæsar long since observed of the ancient Germans) increase their stature: whereas the best authors have with one voice observed that under every sort of climate and place premature venery is injurious to procerity of body[2]. Nations preserve their peculiar stature when they mingle least with the immigrants and strangers of other races: as on the other hand racial stature is altered after a series of generations when they have been mingled in union with other nations of a different size[3]. Lastly, we learn from indisputable instances of families remarkable for height or shortness that the influence of the ancestral constitution is great as to the stature of the offspring.

75. *Fabulous varieties of mankind.* Infinite in number are the stories we have received from the time of Herodotus downwards, from all sorts of sources, principally from Aristeus, Ctesias, and Megasthenes, and which the Cosmographists have told us about nations of monstrous appearance, such as the Arimaspi, with only one eye; the Cynamolgi, with dogs' heads; the Monosceles, with only one leg; the wild men of the Imaus, with their feet fronting the back part of the legs, &c.[4] It is not my business to spend any time upon these things here; though the investigation of these matters brings both pleasure and profit; for that is equally true of anthropology which prevails in

---

[1] On the barbarians of Hudson's Bay see H. Ellis, *Reise nach Hudson's Meerbusen*, p. 201. Umfreville, *Ueber den gegenwärtigen Zustand der Hudsonsbay*, p. 21.
[2] Comp. besides others on the Kamtschadales, Behm in Cook's *Voyage to the Northern Hemisphere*, Vol. III. p. 372. On the Otaheitans, Cook in Hawkesworth's *Collection*, Vol. II. p. m. 187. On the Sumatrans, Marsden, p. 41.
[3] Maupertuis, *Venus Physique*, p. m. 131.
[4] Comp. J. A. Fabricius, *Diss. de hominibus orbis nostri incolis*, &c. Hamb. 1721, 4to.

every other department of natural history, that scarcely any story, however absurd and foolish, has ever been told in it, which does not contain some foundation of truth, but perverted by hyperbolical exaggeration or misinterpretation[1]. I mean to touch here upon only one instance out of this crowd of prodigies, that is, the often repeated story of nations with tails, as being one which we have been told of again and again by all sorts of authors of all sorts of times[2].

76. *Reports of nations with tails.* First Pliny, then Pausanias, make mention of the tailed men of India: then in the middle ages their existence was asserted by the Nubian Geographer, the Venetian Marco Polo, and others; lastly, in more recent times many writers of travels have brought back similar reports about the various tailed islanders of the Indian Archipelago[3]; others about people of the same kind in some province of Russia[4]; and others other stories[5].

Proper consideration however will easily show that very little weight is to be attached to these assertions. Many authors have derived their information entirely from hearsay. Then again it cannot be denied that many of their witnesses who boast of having seen the thing themselves are undoubtedly of very dubious repute[6]. Moreover the stories themselves on this point differ very suspiciously from each other[7]. On the other

---

[1] Thus Heyne has traced the fabulous stories about the hermaphrodites of Florida to their genuine sources in *Comment. Soc. Reg. Scient. Gottingens.* T. I. p. 39.

[2] The most recent patron and asserter of men with tails is Monboddo, in both his works, *The Origin and Progress of Language*, Vol. I. p. 234, and *Ancient Metaphysics*, Vol. III. p. 250.

[3] Besides the authors cited by and by, see Harvey, *De Generatione Animalium*, p. m. 10, about the inhabitants of Borneo.

[4] Rytschkow, *Orenburgische Topographie*, T. II. p. 14. Falk, *Beyträge zur Kenntniss des Russischen Reichs*, T. III. p. 525.

[5] On the island of Tierra del Fuego see the geographical tables in Alons. d'Ovaglie, *Relazione del Regno di Cile*, Rom. 1646, fol.

[6] On the Nicobars see, full of the most foolish stories, *Beschrifning om en Resa genom Asia, Africa, &c.* af. N. Matthes. Köping (Skepps-Lieut.), p. m. 131: which however Linnæus calls a most trustworthy account in his letters to Monboddo, *Of the Origin of Language*, l. c. Dav. Tappe, *15-Jährige ostindische Reisebeschreibung*, p. 49, on the Sumatrans.

[7] Comp. about the tailed Formosans a triad of witnesses who call themselves eye-witnesses: J. Strauss, J. O. Helbig, and El. Ilesso. The first says, *Reisen*, p. m. 32, "A Formosan from the south side of the island with a tail a good foot

LEUCŒTHIOPIA.   259

hand the boldest and most careful explorers of those countries are either silent about that monstrous prodigy; or relying on the authority of the inhabitants plainly declare it a lying fiction[1]. And finally, some expressly tell us what it is that has given rise to this erroneous report; viz.: either a pendulous addition to the clothes of the back[2]; or some tailed anthropomorphous apes[3]. So that not one single instance of a tailed race can be proved by the consent of any number of trustworthy eye-witnesses, nay, not even of a single family remarkable for such a monstrous anomaly; whilst instances of monstrosities in families, in which, for example, six fingers have been hereditary for generations, are very well known. As to individuals, who are here and there to be seen amongst Europeans, remarkable for a monstrous excrescence of the os coccygis, it is at once understood that we do not mean to say anything of them here, any more than of numberless other monstrous productions.

77. *Racial variety from morbific affection.* I have spoken above on the subject of the morbific disorders which so change the appearance and even the colour of animals, that when that is propagated by hereditary causes for a long series of generations it shades sensibly away into a sort of second nature, and in some species of animals gives rise to peculiar and constant varieties. We have cited the well-known examples of the white variety of the domestic mouse and the rabbit, whose snowy fur and rosy pupils are most certainly due to a morbific affection, in fact to leucœthiopia. The same kind of affection is frequently seen in mankind. Still only sporadically, certainly nowhere is it so frequent and so constant as in the brute animals just spoken of; for in them it degenerates into a particular and copious variety. Still, even human leucœthiopia must be spoken of,

---

long, and all covered with rough hair." The second in *Ephem. Naturæ Curiosor.* Dec. I. ann. IX. p. 456, "have tails like those of pigs." The third, *Ostindisch. Reisebeschreibung*, p. m. 216: "Among our other slaves at the mine we had also a female slave who like a brute beast was disfigured behind with a short stump or goat's tail."

[1] Thus about the Philippines, Le Gentil, *Voy. dans les mers de l'Inde.* T. II. p. 52.
[2] Nic. Fontana *On the Nicobar Isles,* in *Asiatic Researches,* Vol. III. p. 151.
[3] [I have omitted here a long note which repeats what was said before (p. 142) about the figure represented in Pl. 2. ED]

though briefly. Briefly, I say, both because in man it can scarcely be said to constitute a particular variety, and also because it would be tedious to repeat those things which I have in another place said about this remarkable disorder[1].

78. *Human leucæthiopia.* The affection must be considered cachectic, which is plain from two pathological and constant symptoms. One of these consists in a singular colour of the skin, a sickly white partly shading into an unnatural redness, very often presenting the appearance of a slight leprosy[2]; and also in an anomalous whiteness of the hair and groin, not silver white as in old men, nor nicely yellowish, verging to cinericial, as may be seen in many of our own countrymen, who are therefore called yellow (fr. *blondins*), but rather straw-coloured, or cream-coloured. The other affects the organs of sight, and deprives them of their dark pigment which in sound eyes lines some of the internal membranes, and is destined for the absorption of the excess of light, a thing of the utmost importance for good and clear vision. Hence the iris of the eye of a leucæthiop is of a pale rose, and half transparent: the pupil is bright and of a more intense red, like a sardonyx or carbuncle of a pale colour.

These two symptoms occur united with a singular constancy, so that, as far as I know, that peculiar redness of the eye is never seen alone, or without that false whiteness of the hair on the head and elsewhere. It is not, however, to be wondered at if the redness of the pupils has not always been noticed by observers, since the other symptoms we have spoken of strike the eye more, and the leucæthiopians not being able to endure the light have a habit of constantly winking the eyelids.

The disease is always congenital; never, so far as I know, being contracted after birth. Always incurable; for there is no single known instance of the black pigment being ever added to the eyes after birth. It is very often hereditary; for

---

[1] *Commentat. Soc. Reg. Scientiar. Gottingens.* T. VII. p. 29, and *Medicin:sche Bibliothek*, T. II. p. 537.
[2] Comp. Hawkesworth's *Collection*, Vol. II. p. m. 188.

it is false what has been said by some that leucœthiopians are sterile or incapable of generating or conceiving. Generally, all the accounts we have of this remarkable disorder are wonderfully deformed with errors of all sorts. Thus some have doubted whether leucœthiopia ought to be considered as a true morbific affection; others have foolishly confounded it with cretinism, others with the history of the *Simia satyrus;* others have rashly asserted that this affection is only to be seen within the tropics. For although it was no doubt first observed amongst the Ethiopians, for the reason that in a black nation this whiteness of the skin and hair would necessarily strike most every one's eye, and hence the name of leucœthiopians (fr. *négres blancs*) was given to those suffering under that malady (who are called in the East Indies contemptuously by the Batavians *Kackerlacken,* after a light-shunning insect, by the Spaniards *Albinos,* the French *Blafards,* &c.); it is so far from being the case that it occurs only amongst the negroes, or even only in the torrid zone, that on the contrary nothing is more certain than that there is no variety of mankind, no part of the world which is unfit for the manifestation of that disease.

Sixteen examples of leucœthiopians have already come under my notice born in different provinces of Germany[1]. Then in the rest of Europe some among the Danes[2], the English[3], the Irish[4], the French[5], the Swiss[6], the Italians[7], the islanders of the Archipelago[8], the Hungarians[9]. Then out of Europe amongst

---

[1] An account of many is given in *Medicinische Bibliothek,* T. III. p. 161.
[2] *Ib.* p. 170.
[3] Benj. Duddell's *Supplement to his Treatise on the Diseases of the Horny-coat,* Lond. 1736, 8vo, p. 19; and Jo. Hunter, *On certain Parts of the Animal Economy,* p. 206.
[4] C. Perceval in *Transactions of the Irish Academy,* Vol. IV. p. 97.
[5] Le Cat, *De la Couleur de la peau Humaine,* p. 103.
[6] *Medicinische Bibliothek,* T. I. p. 545.
[7] About the Savoyards whom I have described myself, see Haussure, *Voyages dans les Alpes,* T. IV. p. m. 303. Bourguet makes mention of a Venetian in *Lettres Philosophiques sur la formation des sels,* p. 163. Buzzi dissected a Milanese, see his *Dissertazione sopra una Varietà Particolare d' Uomini Bianchi Eliofobi,* Mediol. 1784, 4to. Jo. Hawkins informed me that he saw a similar girl at Rome.
[8] From the account of the same John Hawkins, my friend whom I have just quoted, who saw two twin-brothers, leucœthiopians, about twelve years old in his first journey to the Archipelago and the seas in the Island of Cyprus, natives of Larulea.
[9] Mich. Klein, *Natur. seltenheiten von Ungarn.* Presb. 1778, 8vo, p. 15.

the Arabians[1], the Malabars[2], Madagascans[3], Caffres[4], Negroes[5] (as well those born in Africa itself as amongst the Ethiopian creoles of the new world). Then amongst the Americans of the Isthmus of Darien[6], and Brazil[7]. Finally, amongst the barbarous islanders of the Indian and Pacific Oceans; as in Sumatra[8], Bali[9], Amboyna[10], Manilla[11], New Guinea[12], the Friendly[13] and Society Islands[14].

Moreover, this affection of which we are speaking is by no means peculiar to mankind, but has been observed in many other warm-blooded animals of both classes. Of the mammals, besides the common instances of the rabbits, the mice, the weasels and horses (in which four kinds of animals this affection in process of time seems to have become a sort of second nature), instances of apes[15] have been reported to me, squirrels[16], rats[17], hamsters[18], guinea-pigs[19], moles[20], opossums[21], martins[22], weasels[23], and goats[24]. Amongst birds, crows[25], thrushes[26], canary-birds, partridges[27], hens and peacocks. It is remarkable that

---

[1] Ledyard in *Proceedings of the African Association*, p. 45.
[2] *Tranquebarische Missions berichte*, Contin. XLVI. p. 1359.
[3] Coalgny in *Histoire de l'Acad. des Sc. de Paris*, a. 1744, p. 13.
[4] De la Nux, *Ib.* a. 1760, p. 17.
[5] Out of the crowd of eye-witnesses it will be enough to quote three: Oliv. Goldsmith, *History of the Earth*, Vol. II. p. 140. Buffon, *Supplément à l'Histoire Naturelle*, T. IV. p. 519, and Artband in *Journal de Physique*, Oct. 1789.
[6] Wafer's *Description of the Isthmus of America*, ed. 2, p. 107.
[7] De Pinto in Robertson, *History of America*, Vol. II. p. 405.
[8] Van Sperren in *Verhandelingen van het Bataviaasch Genootschap*, T. I. p. 314.
[9] Id. l. c. with a plate.
[10] Valentyn, *Beschryving van Amboina*, T. II. p. 146.
[11] Camelli in *Philosophical Transactions*, Vol. XXV. p. 2268.
[12] Argensola, *Conquista de las islas Malucas*, p. 71.
[13] Cook's *Voyages to the Northern Hemisphere*, Vol. I. p. 381.
[14] Hawkesworth's *Collection*, Vol. II. p. 99 and 188.
[15] Sir R. Clayton in *Memoirs of the Soc. of Manchester*, Vol. III. p. 270.
[16] Wagner, *Histor. Natur. Helvetica*, p. 185. Gunner on Leem, *De Lapponibus Finmarchiæ*, p. 187.
[17] Gesner, *De quadrupedibus*, p. 829.
[18] The author (Sulzer) of the Classical Monograph on the hamster gave me one of this kind.
[19] Boddaert, *Natuurkundige Beschouwing der Dieren*, T. I. p. 110.
[20] *Ib.* [21] *Ib.*
[22] Kramer, *Elench. Animalium Austr.* p. 312. [23] Boddaert, l. c.
[24] Thenel in *Oberrrzgebirgisches Journal*, Freyberg, 1748, 8vo, P. I. p. 47.
[25] From the account of my friend Sulzer.
[26] Jo. Hunter, *On certain Parts of the Animal Economy*, p. 204.
[27] Buffon, *Histoire Naturelle des Oiseaux*, T. II. p. 146.

not a single example, so far as I know, of this affection has been observed in any cold-blooded animal.

79. *Epilogue to this section.* Let so much suffice about the causes and ways in which mankind degenerates into varieties in respect of colour, structure, proportion, and stature. In this enumeration I have left untouched no point that I know of which can in any way help to unravel the famous question about the unity or plurality of the species of man. We shall see in the following section, after this general discussion, how that species is in reality composed according to nature.

SECTION IV.

FIVE PRINCIPAL VARIETIES OF MANKIND, ONE SPECIES.

80. *Innumerable varieties of mankind run into one another by insensible degrees.* We have now completed a universal survey of the genuine varieties of mankind. And as, on the one hand, we have not found a single one which does not (as is shown in the last section but one) even among other warm-blooded animals, especially the domestic ones, very plainly, and in a very remarkable way, take place as it were under our eyes, and deduce its origin from manifest causes of degeneration; so, on the other hand (as is shown in the last section), no variety exists, whether of colour, countenance, or stature, &c., so singular as not to be connected with others of the same kind by such an imperceptible transition, that it is very clear they are all related, or only differ from each other in degree.

81. *Five principal varieties of mankind may be reckoned.* As, however, even among these arbitrary kinds of divisions, one is said to be better and preferable to another; after a long and attentive consideration, all mankind, as far as it is at present known to us, seems to me as if it may best, according to natural truth, be divided into the five following varieties; which may be designated and distinguished from each other by the names *Caucasian, Mongolian, Ethiopian, American,* and *Malay.* I have allotted the first place to the Caucasian, for the reasons given below, which make me esteem it the primeval one. This diverges in both directions into two, most remote and very different from each other; on the one side, namely, into the Ethiopian, and on the other into the Mongolian. The remaining two occupy the intermediate positions between that primeval one and these

two extreme varieties; that is, the American between the Caucasian and Mongolian; the Malay between the same Caucasian and Ethiopian.

82. *Characters and limits of these varieties.* In the following notes and descriptions these five varieties must be generally defined. To this enumeration, however, I must prefix a double warning; first, that on account of the multifarious diversity of the characters, according to their degrees, one or two alone are not sufficient, but we must take several joined together; and then that this union of characters is not so constant but what it is liable to innumerable exceptions in all and singular of these varieties. Still this enumeration is so conceived as to give a sufficiently plain and perspicuous notion of them in general.

Caucasian variety. Colour white, cheeks rosy (s. 43); hair brown or chestnut-coloured (s. 52); head subglobular (s. 62); face oval, straight, its parts moderately defined, forehead smooth, nose narrow, slightly hooked, mouth small (s. 56). The primary teeth placed perpendicularly to each jaw (s. 62); the lips (especially the lower one) moderately open, the chin full and rounded (s. 56). In general, that kind of appearance which, according to our opinion of symmetry, we consider most handsome and becoming. To this first variety belong the inhabitants of Europe (except the Lapps and the remaining descendants of the Finns) and those of Eastern Asia, as far as the river Obi, the Caspian Sea and the Ganges; and lastly, those of Northern Africa.

Mongolian variety. Colour yellow (s. 43); hair black, stiff, straight and scanty (s. 52); head almost square (s. 62); face broad, at the same time flat and depressed, the parts therefore less distinct, as it were running into one another; glabella flat, very broad; nose small, apish; cheeks usually globular, prominent outwardly; the opening of the eyelids narrow, linear; chin slightly prominent (s. 56). This variety comprehends the remaining inhabitants of Asia (except the Malays on the extremity of the trans-Gangetic peninsula) and the Finnish populations of the cold part of Europe, the Lapps, &c. and the race of

Esquimaux, so widely diffused over North America, from Behring's straits to the inhabited extremity of Greenland.

Ethiopian variety. Colour black (s. 43); hair black and curly (s. 52); head narrow, compressed at the sides (s. 62); forehead knotty, uneven; malar bones protruding outwards; eyes very prominent; nose thick, mixed up as it were with the wide jaws (s. 56); alveolar edge narrow, elongated in front; the upper primaries obliquely prominent (s. 62); the lips (especially the upper) very puffy; chin retreating (s. 56). Many are bandy-legged (s. 69). To this variety belong all the Africans, except those of the north.

American variety. Copper-coloured (s. 43); hair black, stiff, straight and scanty (s. 52); forehead short; eyes set very deep; nose somewhat apish, but prominent; the face invariably broad, with cheeks prominent, but not flat or depressed; its parts, if seen in profile, very distinct, and as it were deeply chiselled (s. 56); the shape of the forehead and head in many artificially distorted. This variety comprehends the inhabitants of America except the Esquimaux.

Malay variety. Tawny-coloured (s. 43); hair black, soft, curly, thick and plentiful (s. 52); head moderately narrowed; forehead slightly swelling (s. 62); nose full, rather wide, as it were diffuse, end thick; mouth large (s. 56), upper jaw somewhat prominent with the parts of the face when seen in profile, sufficiently prominent and distinct from each other (s. 56). This last variety, includes the islanders of the Pacific Ocean, together with the inhabitants of the Marianne, the Philippine, the Molucca and the Sunda Islands, and of the Malayan peninsula.

83. *Divisions of the varieties of mankind by other authors.* It seems but fair to give briefly the opinions of other authors also, who have divided mankind into varieties, so that the reader may compare them more easily together, and weigh them, and choose which of them he likes best. The first person, as far as I know, who made an attempt of this kind was a certain anonymous writer who towards the end of the last century divided mankind into four races; that is, first, one

of all Europe, Lapland alone excepted, and Southern Asia, Northern Africa, and the whole of America; secondly, that of the rest of Africa; thirdly, that of the rest of Asia with the islands towards the east; fourthly, the Lapps[1]. Leibnitz divided the men of our continent into four classes. Two extremes, the Laplanders and the Ethiopians; and as many intermediates, one eastern (Mongolian), one western (as the European)[2].

Linnæus, following common geography, divided men into (1) the red American, (2) the white European, (3) the dark Asiatic, and (4) the black Negro[3]. Buffon distinguished six varieties of man: (1) Lapp or polar, (2) Tartar (by which name according to ordinary language he meant the Mongolian), (3) south Asian, (4) European, (5) Ethiopian, (6) American[4].

Amongst those who reckoned three primitive nations of mankind answering to the number of the sons of Noah, Governor Pownall is first entitled to praise, who, as far as I know, was also the first to pay attention to the racial form of skull as connected with this subject. He divided these stocks into white, red and black. In the middle one he comprised both the Mongolians and Americans, as agreeing, besides other characters, in the configuration of their skulls and the appearance of their hair[5]. Abbé de la Croix divides man into white and black. The former again into white, properly so called, brown (bruns), yellow (jaundtres), and olive-coloured[6].

Kant derives four varieties from dark-brown Autochthones: the white one of northern Europe, the copper-coloured American, the black one of Senegambia, the olive-coloured Indian[7]. John Hunter reckons seven varieties: (1) of black men, that is,

---

[1] *Journal des Savans*, a. 1684, p. 133. Comp. Rob. de Vaugondy, *Nouvel Atlas portatif*, Paris, 1778, 4to, Pl. 4.
[2] In Feller in *Otium Hanoveranum*, p. 159.
[3] After the year 1735, in all the editions of his immortal work. Gmelin has added to the last edition, brought out by himself, my division, T. I. p. 23.
[4] These six varieties have been beautifully described, and in fact painted as it were by the glowing brush of Haller, in his classical work, *Idea sur philosophie der geschichte der menschheit*, T. II. p. III. 4—68.
[5] Comp. *A New Collection of Voyages*, &c. Lond. 1767, 8vo, Vol. II. p. 273.
[6] See *Geographie moderne*, T. I. p. 62, ed. 5, and Vaugondy, l. c. Pl. 3.
[7] Both in Engel, *Philosoph. für die Welt*, T. II. and in *Berliner monatschrift*, 1785, T. VI.

Ethiopians, Papuans, &c.; (2) the blackish inhabitants of Mauritania and the Cape of Good Hope; (3) the copper-coloured of eastern India; (4) the red Americans; (5) the tawny, as Tartars, Arabs, Persians, Chinese, &c.; (6) brownish, as the southern Europeans, Spaniards, &c., Turks, Abyssinians, Samoiedes and Lapps; (7) white, as the remaining Europeans, the Georgians, Mingrelians and Kabardinski[1].

Zimmermann is amongst those who place the aborigines of mankind in the elevated Scythico-Asiatic plain, near the sources of the Indus, Ganges and Obi rivers; and thence deduces the varieties of Europe (1), northern Asia, and the great part of North America (2), Arabia, India, and the Indian Archipelago (3), Asia to the north-east, China, Corea, &c. (4). He is of opinion that the Ethiopians deduce their origin from either the first or the third of these varieties[2].

Meiners refers all nations to two stocks: (1) handsome, (2) ugly; the first white, the latter dark. He includes in the handsome stock the Celts, Sarmatians, and oriental nations. The ugly stock embraces all the rest of mankind[3]. Klügel distinguishes four stocks: (1) the primitive, autochthones of that elevated Asiatic plain we were speaking of, from which he derives the inhabitants of all the rest of Asia, the whole of Europe, the extreme north of America, and northern Africa; (2) the Negroes; (3) the Americans, except those of the extreme north; (4) the Islanders of the southern ocean[4]. Metzger makes two principal varieties as extremes: (1) the white man native of Europe, of the northern parts of Asia, America and Africa; (2) the black, or Ethiopian, of the rest of Africa. The transition between the two is made by the rest of the Asiatics, the inhabitants of South America, and the Islanders of the southern ocean[5].

84. *Notes on the five varieties of Mankind.* But we must

---

[1] *Disput. de hominum varietatibus,* Edinb. 1775. p. 9.
[2] In that very copious work *Geographische geschichte des Menschen,* &c. T. 1.
[3] See his *Grundriss der Geschichte der menschheit,* ed. 2. Langov. 1793, 8vo.
[4] See his *Encyclopædie,* T. 1. p. 513, ed. 1.
[5] See his *Physiologie in Aphorismen,* p. 5.

return to our perusal of the varieties of mankind. I have indicated separately all and each of the characters which I attribute to them in the sections above. Now, I will string together, at the end of my little work, as a finish, some scattered notes which belong to each of them in general.

65. *Caucasian variety.* I have taken the name of this variety from Mount Caucasus, both because its neighbourhood, and especially its southern slope, produces the most beautiful race of men, I mean the Georgian[1]; and because all physiological reasons converge to this, that in that region, if anywhere, it seems we ought with the greatest probability to place the autochthones of mankind. For in the first place, that stock displays, as we have seen (s. 62), the most beautiful form of the skull, from which, as from a mean and primeval type, the others diverge by most easy gradations on both sides to the two ultimate extremes (that is, on the one side the Mongolian, on the other the Ethiopian). Besides, it is white in colour, which we may fairly assume to have been the primitive colour of mankind, since, as we have shown above (s. 45), it is very easy for that to degenerate into brown, but very much more difficult for dark to become white, when the secretion and precipitation of this carbonaceous pigment (s. 44) has once deeply struck root.

66. *Mongolian variety.* This is the same as what was formerly called, though in a vague and ambiguous way, the Tartar variety[2]; which denomination has given rise to wonderful mistakes in the study of the varieties of mankind which we are now busy about. So that Buffon and his followers, seduced by that title, have erroneously transferred to the genuine Tartars, who

---

[1] From a cloud of eye witnesses it is enough to quote one classical one, Jo. Chardin, T. I. p. m. 171. "The blood of Georgia is the best of the East, and perhaps in the world. I have not observed a single ugly face in that country, in either sex; but I have seen angelical ones. Nature has there lavished upon the women beauties which are not to be seen elsewhere. I consider it to be impossible to look at them without loving them. It would be impossible to paint more charming visages, or better figures, than those of the Georgians."

[2] On the origin of this erroneous confusion, by which the name of Tartars began to be transferred to the Mongolian nations, compare J. Eberh. Fischer, *Conjecturae de gente et nomine Tatarorum* in his *Quaestiones Petropolitanae*, p. 46, and his *Sibirische Geschichte*, T. I. p. 28, 142.

beyond a doubt belong to our first variety, the racial characters of the Mongols, borrowed from ancient authors[1], who described them under the name of Tartars.

But the Tartars shade away through the Kirghis and the neighbouring races into the Mongols, in the same way as these may be said to pass through the Tibetans[2] to the Indians, through the Esquimaux to the Americans, and also in a sort of way through the Philippine Islanders[3] to the men of the Malay variety.

87. *Ethiopian variety.* This variety, principally because it is so different in colour from our own, has induced many to consider it, with the witty, but badly instructed in physiology, Voltaire, as a peculiar species of mankind. But it is not necessary for me to spend any time here upon refuting this opinion, when it has so clearly been shown above that there is no single character so peculiar and so universal among the Ethiopians, but what it may be observed on the one hand everywhere in other varieties of men[4]; and on the other that many Negroes are seen

---

[1] The original source, from which the description of the Mongols which has been so often repeated, and which has been copied as if that of Tartars by so many authors on natural history, I have found in the letter of a certain Yvo, a churchman of Narbonne, dated at Vienna in 1243, and sent to Giraldus, archbishop of Bordeaux, and inserted by his contemporary Matthew Paris, the English monk of St Albans, in what is called his *Historia Major*, p. 539, ed. Lond. 1686, fol. This letter of Yvo is about the terrible devastations of that inhuman nation called the Tartars, and he speaks of them in the following words: "The Tartars have hard and strong breasts, thin and pale faces, stiff and upright cheekbones, short and twisted noses, chins prominent and sharp, the upper jaw low and deep, the teeth long and few, the eyebrows reaching from the hair of the head to the nose, the eyes black and unsettled, the countenance one-sided and fierce, the extremities bony and nervous, the legs also big, but the calf-bones short, the stature however the same as our own; for what is wanting in the legs, is made up for in the upper part of the body."

[2] Thus, at least, I consider myself entitled to conclude from the pictures of the Tibetans, painted from nature by the great artist Kettle, and shown me by Warren Hastings.

[3] The Indian from the Philippine Islands, whom I saw alive in London at Alex. Dalrymple's, was in appearance exactly this sort of middle man.

[4] There is only one thing I should like to add to what has been more copiously discussed about this point in the section above, that the sort of powder-like soot which can be distinguished in the skin of black men, can by no means, as some authors think, be peculiar to the Malpighian mucus of the Ethiopians, because I have perfectly observed the same thing, although more scattered and less equally distributed, in so many of these Indian sailors who are called Lascars. In one Indian woman, a native of Bombay, who is a servant in my household, I can see

to be without each. And besides there is no character which does not shade away by insensible gradation from this variety of mankind to its neighbours, which is clear to every one who has carefully considered the difference between a few stocks of this variety, such as the Foulahs, the Wolufs, and Mandingos, and how by these shades of difference they pass away into the Moors and Arabs.

The assertion that is made about the Ethiopians, that they come nearer the apes than other men, I willingly allow so far as this, that it is in the same way that the solid-hoofed (s. 30) variety of the domestic sow may be said to come nearer to the horse than other sows. But how little weight is for the most part to be attached to this sort of comparison is clear from this, that there is scarcely any other out of the principal varieties of mankind, of which one nation or other, and that too by careful observers, has not been compared, as far as the face goes, with the apes; as we find said in express words of the Lapps[1], the Esquimaux[2], the Caaiguas of South America[3], and the inhabitants of the Island Mallicollo[4].

88. *American variety.* It is astonishing and humiliating what quantities of fables were formerly spread about the racial characters of this variety. Some have denied beards to the men[5], others menstruation to the women[6]. Some have attributed

---

as time goes on, the same blackness in the face and arms gradually vanish, though in other respects the precipitated carbon remains unaltered, of a chesnut colour, effused under the epidermis.

[1] Thus Regnard concludes his description of the Lapps in these words: "Such is the description of that little man they call the Laplander, and I may say that there is no animal, after the ape, which so nearly approaches the man." *Œuvres,* T. I. p. 71.

[2] When the Esquimaux Attiuloch, whose picture taken from the life I owe to Sir Joseph Banks, saw an ape in London for the first time, he asked his companion Cartwright in astonishment, "Is that an Esquimaux!" and he adds in his account, "I must confess, that both the colour and contour of the countenance had considerable resemblance to the people of their nation."

[3] "As like apes as men," says Nic. del Techo of them, *Relatione de Caaiguarum gente,* p. m. 34.

[4] Of these, J. H. Forster says in his *Bemerkungen,* p. 217, "The inhabitants of the Island Mallicollo appear to have a nearer relationship to the apes than any I have ever seen."

[5] See De Pauw in *Recherches philosophiques sur les Americains,* T. I. p. 37.

[6] See Schurigius, *Parthenologia,* p. 100.

one and the same colour[1] to each and all the Americans; others a perfectly similar countenance to all of them[2]. It has been so clearly demonstrated now by the unanimous consent of accurate and truthful observers, that the Americans are not naturally beardless, that I am almost ashamed of the unnecessary trouble I formerly took to get together a heap of testimony[3], by which it is proved that not only throughout the whole of America, from the Esquimaux downwards to the inhabitants of Tierra del Fuego, are there groups of inhabitants who cherish a beard; but also it is quite undeniable as to the other beardless ones that they eradicate and pluck out their own by artifice and on purpose, in the same way as has been customary among so many other nations, the Mongolians[4] for example, and the Malays[5]. We all know that the beard of the Americans is thin and scanty, as is also the case with so many Mongolian nations. They ought therefore no more to be called beardless, than men with scanty hair to be called bald. Those therefore who thought the Americans were naturally beardless fell into the same error as that which induced the ancients to suppose and persuade others, that the birds of paradise, from whose corpses the feet are often cut off, were naturally destitute of feet.

The fabulous report that the American women have no menstruation, seems to have had its origin in this, that the Europeans when they discovered the new world, although they saw numbers of the female inhabitants almost entirely naked, never seem to have observed in them the stains of that excretion. For this it seems likely that there were two reasons; first, that

---

[1] See Home in *Sketches of the History of Man*, Vol. I. p. 13.
[2] Comp. Robertson's *History of America*, Vol. II. p. m. 404.
[3] I cited a few out of many others some years ago in *Göttingisch. Magazin*, 2d year, P. VI. p. 419.
[4] See besides many others J. G. Gmelin, *Reise durch Sibirien*, T. II. p. 175. "It is very difficult to find amongst the Tongus, or any of these people, a beard. For as soon as one appears, they pull the hair out, and at last bring it to this that there is nothing more spring up."
[5] Comp. on the Numairans, Marsden; on the Magindans, Forrest; on the Pelew Islanders, Wilson; on the Papuans, Carteret; on the inhabitants of the Navigator's group, Bougainville, &c.
[6] Lery, *Voyage faict en la terre du Bresil*, p. m. 270.

COLOUR. 273

amongst those nations of America, the women during menstruation are, by a fortunate prejudice, considered as poisonous, and are prohibited from social intercourse, and for so long enjoy a beneficial repose in the more secluded huts far from the view of men[1]; secondly, because, as has been noticed[2], they are so commendably clean in their bodies, and the commissure of their legs so conduces to modesty, that no vestiges of the catamenia ever strike the eye.

As to the colour of the skin of this variety, on the one hand it has been observed above, that it is by no means so constant as not in many cases to shade away into black (s. 43); and on the other, that it is easily seen, from the nature of the American climate[3], and the laws of degeneration when applied to the extremely probable origin of the Americans from northern Asia[4], why they are not liable to such great diversities of colour, as the other descendants of Asiatic autochthones, who peopled the ancient world. The same reason holds good as to the appearance of the Americans. Careful eye-witnesses long ago laughed at the foolish, or possibly facetious hyperbole of some, who asserted that the inhabitants of the new world were so exactly alike, that when a man had seen one, he could say that he had seen all[5], &c. It is, on the contrary, proved by the finished drawings of Americans by the best artists, and by the testimony of the most trustworthy eye-witnesses, that in this variety of mankind, as in others, countenances of all sorts occur[6]; although

---

[1] Comp. Sagard, *Voyage du pays des Hurons*, p. 78.
[2] Van Berkel's *Reisen nach R. de Berbice und Surinam*, p. 46.
[3] Zimmermann, *Geographische geschichte des menschen*, T. 1. p. 87.
[4] Kant, in *Teutschen Mercur*, a. 1798, T. 1. p. 119.
[5] See Molina, *Sulla storia naturale del Chili*, p. 336. "I laugh in my sleeve when I read in certain modern writers, supposed to be diligent observers, that all the Americans have the same appearance, and that when a man has seen one, he may say that he has seen them all. Such authors allow themselves to be too easily deceived by certain vague appearances of similarity which have to do for the most part with colour, and which vanish as soon as ever the individuals of one nation are confronted with those of another. A Chilian does not differ less in aspect from a Peruvian, than an Italian from a German. I have seen myself Paraguayans, Cujanos, and Magellans, all of whom have their peculiar lineaments which are easily distinguished from those of the others."
[6] Thus, to bring a few examples from South America alone, Nic. del Techo describes the Caaigas with apish nostrils: Mart. Dobrizhoffer says that the neigh-

18

in general that sort of racial conformation may be considered as properly belonging to them which we attributed to them above (s. 56). It was justly observed by the first Europeans[1] who visited the new continent, that the Americans came very near to the Mongolians, which adds fresh weight to the very probable opinion that the Americans came from northern Asia, and derived their origin from the Mongolian nation. It is probable that migrations of that kind took place at different times, after considerable intervals, according as various physical, geological, or political catastrophes gave occasion to them; and hence, if any place is allowed for conjecture in these investigations, the reason may probably be derived, why the Esquimaux have still much more of the Mongolian appearance[2] about them than the rest of the Americans: partly, because the catastrophe which drove them from northern Asia must be much more recent, and so they are a much later arrival[3]; and partly because the climate of the new country, which they now inhabit, is much more homogeneous with that of their original country. In fact, unless I am much mistaken, we must attribute to the same influence I mentioned above (s. 57), which the climate has in preserving or restoring the racial appearance, the fact that the inhabitants of the cold southern extremity of South America, as the barbarous inhabitants of the Straits of Magellan, seem to come nearer, and as it were fall back, to the original Mongolian countenance[4].

---

bouring Abipones, on the contrary, are often remarkable for aquiline noses: Ulloa attributes a narrow and hooked nose to the Peruvians; Molina, one somewhat broad to the Chilians; G. Forster, one very depressed to the islanders of Tierra del Fuego.
[1] *Lettere di Amer. Vespucci*, p. 9, ed. Bandini. "They are not very handsome, because their faces are wide, which makes them like Tartars."
[2] This I see most clearly both in two Esquimaux skulls from Nain, a colony of Labrador, which adorn my collection, and in the pictures of these barbarians taken from the life by good artists, which I owe to the liberality of Sir J. Banks.
[3] The paradox of Robertson, who derived the Esquimaux from the Norwegians, in his *History of America*, Vol. II. p. 40, scarcely deserves a refutation at this time.
[4] Thus that classical Argonaut and capital eye-witness and observer, Linschot, compares the inhabitants of the strait of Magellan whom he saw, in physiognomy, appearance, colour, hair and beard, to the Samoiedes, with whom he was very well acquainted through his famous journey to the strait of Nassovitch, in his notes to *Aroma*, p. 46 b.

MALAY. 275

89. *The Malay variety.* As the Americans in respect of racial appearance hold as it were a place between the medial variety of mankind, which we called the Caucasian, and one of the two extremes, that is the Mongolian; so the Malay variety makes the transition from that medial variety to the other extreme, namely, the Ethiopian. I wish to call it the Malay, because the majority of the men of this variety, especially those who inhabit the Indian islands close to the Malacca peninsula, as well as the Sandwich, the Society, and the Friendly Islanders, and also the Malambi of Madagascar down to the inhabitants of Easter Island, use the Malay idiom[1].

Meanwhile even these differ so much between themselves through various degrees of beauty and other corporeal attributes, that there are some who divide the Otaheitans themselves into two distinct races[2]; the first paler in colour, of lofty stature, with face which can scarcely be distinguished from that of the European; the second, on the other hand, of moderate stature, colour and face little different from that of Mulattos, curly hair, &c.[3] This last race then comes very near those men who inhabit the islands more to the south in the Pacific Ocean, of whom the inhabitants of the New Hebrides in particular come sensibly near the Papuans and New Hollanders, who finally on their part graduate away so insensibly towards the Ethiopian variety, that, if it was thought convenient, they might not unfairly be classed with them, in that distribution of the varieties we were talking about.

90. *Conclusion.* Thus too there is with this that insensible transition by which as we saw the other varieties also run together, and which, compared with what was discussed in the earlier

---

[1] Sir J. Banks first of all showed this in Hawkesworth's *Collection*, Vol. III. p. 373, then after him Bryant in Cook's *Voyage to the Northern Hemisphere*, Vol. III. App. No. 2, p. 518, and Marsden in *Archaeologia*, Vol. VI. p. 154.
[2] See Bougainville in *Voyage autour du Monde*, p. 213.
[3] Thus long ago the immortal De Quiros, who first discovered the Society Islands, accurately distinguished three varieties among the inhabitants of the Islands in the Pacific Ocean, when he called some white, and compared some to the Mulattos, and some to the Ethiopians. See Dalrymple, *Collection of Voyages to the South Pacific Ocean*, Vol. I. p. 164.

sections of the book, about the causes and ways of degeneration, and the analogous phenomena of degeneration in the other domestic animals, brings us to that conclusion, which seems to flow spontaneously from physiological principles applied by the aid of critical zoology to the natural history of mankind; which is, *That no doubt can any longer remain but that we are with great probability right in referring all and singular as many varieties of man as are at present known to one and the same species.*

BEYTRÄGE

zur

NATURGESCHICHTE,

VON

JOH. FR. BLUMENBACH,
PROF. ZU GÖTT. UND KÖNIGL. GROSBRIT. HOFRATH.

ERSTER THEIL, ZWEYTE AUSGABE.

GÖTTINGEN:
BEY HEINRICH DIETERICH. 1806.

CONTENTS.

I. On Mutability in the Creation.
II. A Glance into the Primitive World.
III. A Preadamite Primitive World has already lived out its existence.
IV. Remodelling of the Primitive World.
V. Changes in the present Creation.
VI. Degeneration of Organized Bodies.
VII. Especially in the Domestic Animals.
VIII. Degeneration of the most perfect of all domestic animals—Man.
IX. A very peculiar physiological singularity of the Human Body.
X. Something tranquillizing on a common family concern.
XI. On Anthropological Collections.
XII. Division of Mankind into five principal Races.
XIII. On the Negro in particular.
XIV. On the Kakerlacken.

Appendices.

1. On the Gradation in Nature.
2. On the Succession of different Earth-catastrophes.
3. On the so-called Objects of Design.

CONTRIBUTIONS TO NATURAL HISTORY,

BY

J. F. BLUMENBACH.

PART THE FIRST.

I.

On Mutability in the Creation.

"YES, that's the way of the world," says Voltaire; "we can't get any more purple, for the Murex has long since been exterminated. The poor little shell must have been eaten up by some other larger animals." "God forbid," answer the physico-theologians; "it is impossible that Providence can allow of the extinction of a species[1]." Thus says the noble village pastor of Savoy in *Emilie*, "There is no creature in the universe that may not equally be looked upon as the common centre of all the rest." And, says another in addition, "There is no one, so to say, which is not that for all the rest of the creation, which the head of Phidias was for the shield of his artificial Minerva, which could not be removed without the whole of the great work falling to pieces."

"Rather than that," says Linnæus, "let nature create new sorts. Thus not far from Upsala, on the island Södra-Gnesskiacrot,

---

[1] See Pennant's *History of Quadrupeds*, Vol. 1. p. 161. "Providence maintains and continues every created species; and we have as much assurance, that no race of animals will any more cease while the earth remaineth, than seed-time and harvest, cold and heat, summer and winter, day or night."

a new plant has appeared, the *Peloria*, that is undoubtedly a sort of new creation." "Ah," they answer, "nature is an old hen, which will certainly lay nothing more fresh at this time of day." "Certainly not," decides Haller; "and such errors should be denounced, because they will be eagerly snapped up by the atheists, who will be only too glad to demonstrate the instability of nature as well by the appearance of new species, as by the pretended extermination of old kinds. And this must not be; for if order in the physical world comes to an end, so also will order in the moral world, and at last it is all over with all religion."

If I may presume to put in a word here myself, my opinion is that on all sides too much has been made of the matter. The murex exists up to the present day just as much as in the time of the old Phœnicians and Greeks;—the peloria is a monstrous freak of nature, and no new particular independent species. Nature is made common, but is not exactly an old hen,—and the creation is something more solid than that statue of Minerva, —and it will not go to pieces even if one species of creatures dies out, or another is newly created,—and it is more than merely probable, that both cases have happened before now,—and all this without the slightest danger to order, either in the physical or in the moral world, or for religion in general. For my own part it is exactly in these things that I find the guidance of a higher hand most unmistakeable; so that in spite of this recognized instability of nature, the creation continues going on its quiet way; and on that very account it is my opinion that it is well worth the trouble, after such an immense deal has been written upon the pretended unchangeableness of the creation, just once to recollect on the other hand the proofs of the great alterations in it. To do this I shall be obliged to go some way about.

II.

A Peep into the Primitive World.

Every paving-stone in Göttingen is a proof that species, or rather whole genera, of creatures must have disappeared. Our limestone swarms likewise with numerous kinds of lapidified marine creatures, among which, as far as I know, there is only one single species that so much resembles any one of the present kinds, that it may be considered as the original of it; and this is that particular kind of the Terebratulæ in the Mediterranean and Atlantic waters, which from their appearance have received the name of the cock and hen[1]. For one of the two delicate bellied shells rises behind over the other at the junction, and so when it is seen in profile it has some resemblance to a cock which is treading a hen.

Amongst the quite countless host of other lapidified marine creatures, who have found their grave in our soils, there are no doubt many (as amongst the Mytilites, Chamites, Pectinites, &c.) to which most naturalists attribute as many distinct originals, but I have very often compared, in these instances, the petrifaction[2] with the pretended original, and it is not my fault if I have come to the conclusion that both are unmistakeably specifically distinct from each other[3].

In a very great number of the remaining lapidifications of this country the forms differ so very surprisingly from all creatures now known, that I hope no one will in future really

---

[1] *Anomia Vitrea. Chemnitz's Conchylien-cabinet*, D. VIII. Tab. LXXVIII. fig. 707—709.
[2] [Three words are employed somewhat loosely by Blumenbach; *versteinerung, petrefact, fossil*: I have translated them, *lapidification, petrifaction*, and *fossil* respectively.—ED.]
[3] Nearly the only, but therefore all the more important, use of the knowledge of lapidifications, is the solution which the history of the changes of the earth's surface derives from it; but unfortunately to arrive at this requires the most extreme accuracy of observation, especially when we come to the comparison of petrifactions with their pretended originals. Want of accuracy in this has already produced the most extraordinary cosmogonical errors.

try to reckon them amongst these last¹. I will mention two genera only out of all, the Belemnites² and the Ammonites, of both of which I have before me all sorts of different species from most of the countries of Europe, and even from Asia, and which will also most likely be found in the other parts of the world, the islands of the fifth part excepted³. At present they reckon about 200 different species of the Ammonite genus; and I do not think this is an exaggeration⁴, although I have never considered it worth while to count them up advisedly. No true representative of any one of these 200 species has yet been found in the existing creation. It is plain also from observing well-preserved Ammonites, that notwithstanding some are of quite colossal size, they must have been very slender-shelled, light, and unattached conchylia, and could not have lived, as was at first suggested as an evasion, sunk in the depths of our seas. And as we now, by the great voyages through which the king⁵ has caused the larger portion of the fifth part of the world to be discovered, and the boundaries of our earth to be ascertained, are coming to be better acquainted with the

---

¹ Superintendent Schröter considers it as one of the chief uses which we derive from the study of petrifications, that they help us to fill up the gaps in the gradation of nature. "Without them," says he, in the 3rd Vol. of his *Einleitung in die Geschichte der Steine*, &c., s. 94, "we should find the most wonderful gaps in this gradation and chain of nature, which are fortunately filled up for us by means of the science of lapidifications." If we found this remark in any other writer, we should consider it as something witty upon the asserted gradation of nature with regard to the generation of her creatures; for all this can only mean that what the Creator has not given us in nature, at least He has had cast in effigy for the assistance of the physico-theologians and their allegorical images of chains and links in His creation. On this I will say a little more in the *additions*, at the end of this part.

² Belemnites are even still some of the commonest of lapidifications. The Chevalier D'Hancarville, *Recherches sur l'origine des Arts de la Grèce*, B. 1. s. 1,—an unparalleled book—gives as a reason why we do not find them in still larger numbers—that so many of them were shot away, if we can trust his assertion, in the childhood of mankind. For, says he, "before they had copper or iron to arm the points of their darts with, they used to employ these Belemnites. The Arundel marbles place the epoch of the discovery of iron in the year 87 after the arrival of Cadmus in Greece. Before that epoch the spears of the Greeks were necessarily armed with these Belemnites, the name of which has been handed down to our time, and shows the use."

³ J. R. Forster, *Bemerkungen auf seiner reise um die Welt*, s. 19.

⁴ In the *Breslauer Sammlungen* of 1715, it is stated that the zealous and sagacious collector of petrifactions, Rosinus of Munden, had already collected over 300 sorts of Ammonites.

⁵ George III.

ocean than the firm land of our planet, we must consequently give up the hope that the representatives of these widely scattered animals, like thousands of other fossils, are still living, sunk in our oceans.

III.

An old Preadamite Creation has already lived out its existence.

Putting all these things together, in my opinion it becomes more than merely probable that not only one or more species, but a whole organized preadamite creation has disappeared from the face of our planet. Out of all existing theories of the earth with which I am acquainted, there is no single one by which the instantly apparent peculiarities of the petrifactions in our calcareous strata can be brought into any order. But they will be at once easily explained, as soon as it is understood, as I have said, that our earth has already suffered a complete revolution, and experienced one last day. It is plain that other so-called cosmogonical phenomena, as, for instance, the quantity of fossil bones of the elephant, rhinoceros, and other animals of the present earth, which have been dug up in this country, and more of the same kind, must unfortunately be accurately separated and divided from that complete revolution. This it is, if I mistake not, which has till now always been the rock on which even the most sagacious theories of the earth have foundered, so soon as they have endeavoured to refer all these phenomena, which are so different from one another, to one single common revolution, and to explain all by one and the same catastrophe[1]. A naturalist, who is as sagacious as amiable, has recently attempted to connect the origin of those fossil bones found in

---

[1] In opposition to this view, I have in the *Specimen Archæologiæ Telluris*, &c. Götl. 1803, 4to, endeavoured to explain the old history of our planet, and especially the nature, and also in general the sequences of the totally different catastrophes it has gone through, by which the numerous fossil remains of former organic creations have come into their present positions, principally by a critical comparison of these fossils with the organized bodies of the present creation. Of these also a word below, in the additions, at the end of this part.

this country belonging to foreign land-animals and the actual lapidifications of the marine creatures in our calcareous strata in this way with each other, by supposing that the present position of those land-animals is not their original home, but that after their death they fell into rivers, and so by degrees were huddled together by the currents on the existing floor of the sea. But those localities, at all events where I myself have examined the position of the large exotic bones, are very difficult to reconcile with that hypothesis. Thus, for instance, I have myself examined at Burgtonna, in Gotha, the bed of both the elephants which were dug up there in 1695 and 1799, and found that it was so completely made up of strong layers of marl, which were so full of small, delicate, and for the most part uninjured land and river shells and the like, that I consider it is quite impossible this bed could ever have been the floor of the sea; but that most likely the elephants, rhinoceroses, and tortoises, of all of which I have got together[1] instructive specimens for my collection from the Tonna marl-strata, must have been naturalized at one time in that country, no one knows how long after the supposed general revolution. This general revolution, from which may be dated the countless extinct organized creatures in the calcareous strata, is again quite different from the subsequent later one, which must have occurred when the earth was remodelled[2].

---

[1] Comp. Hofr. Voigt, *Ueber Einige Physicalische merkwurdigkeiten der gegend von Burgtonna im Herzogthum Gotha* in his *Magazin für Physik und Naturgeschichte*, B. III. st. 4.

[2] There was a time when the origin of all petrifactions, and the general revolution of the earth itself, was deduced from the Noachian deluge. But, as one of the most sagacious and also certainly one of the most orthodox theologians, R. Walsh, has assured us, we are far from doing the slightest violence to the authority of Holy Scripture, when we deny the universality of the flood of Noah; and in like manner, I cannot for my own part form any satisfactory idea, after what I gather from the history of animals themselves, about the universality of that deluge. Thus, for instance, the pilgrimage which the sloth (an animal which takes a whole hour in crawling six feet) must in that case have performed from Ararat to South America, is always a little incomprehensible. We are obliged, with St Augustine, to call in the assistance of the angels, who *jussu Dei sive permissu*, as he expresses himself, first of all collected all the animal kingdom in the ark, and then distributed them again *ad locum inde*, in the distant islands and quarters of the globe.

IV.

Remodelling of the Primitive World.

After therefore that organic creation in the Preadamite primitive epoch of our planet had fulfilled its purpose, it was destroyed by a general catastrophe of its surface or shell, which probably lay in ruins some time, until it was put together again, enlivened with a fresh vegetation, and vivified with a new animal creation. In order that it might provide such a harvest, the Creator took care to allow in general powers of nature to bring forth the new organic kingdoms, similar to those which had fulfilled that object in the primitive world. Only the formative force having to deal with materials, which must of course have been much changed by such a general revolution, was compelled to take a direction differing more or less from the old one in the production of new species[1].

So that we naturally find very few creatures in the present creation which are exactly like the lapidifications of the primitive world, as, for instance, the shell-fish of the Atlantic and the Terebratula mentioned above of our calcareous rocks of the present day. On the other hand, there are quantities of such petrifactions which appear like the present organic bodies, and therefore, as I have said already, on a mere hasty comparison are often taken to be identical with them, but which upon closer inspection present most unmistakeable differences in their formation, and may serve as an example how the formative force in these two creations has acted in a similar, but not exactly in the same way. As to the possible objection, that this difference might also have been occasioned solely by *degeneration* acting for a long series of thousands of years, it can be very

---

[1] So that the formative power of nature in these remodellings partly reproduces again creatures of a similar type to those of the old world, which however in by far the greatest number of instances have put on forms more applicable to others in the new order of things, so that in the new creatures the laws of the formative force have been somewhat modified, as Lucretius expresses himself:

'quod potuit, nequeat; possit, quod non tulit ante.'

easily refuted by those examples in which the difference between fossil and recent shells, which are sufficiently like each other in general, is still of that quality that it unfortunately cannot be considered either as a consequence of degeneration, or as an accidental monstrosity, but can hardly be considered as anything else than an altered direction of the formative force. To give one example out of many. In the North Sea there is a shell, whose pretty house is generally known under the name of *Murex despectus;* and at Harwich on the coast of Essex there is found a fossil shell, which in its general habit has so strong a resemblance to that *Murex,* that at the first glance one might be mistaken for the other. But, in the recent species, as usually happens, the twistings are to the right; whereas, on the contrary, in the fossil species the twists are exactly the other way, to the left[1]; and it is just as contrary to experience to find the fossil *Murex* marked to the right as the recent *Murex* to the left. Such a thing is not a consequence of degeneration, but a remodelling through an altered direction of the formative force.

V.

Mutations in the Existing Creation.

According to all probability therefore a whole creation of organized bodies has already become extinct, and has been succeeded by a new one. So much variation is however to be observed, or, as Haller called it, but falsely, instability of nature, even in this new one, that a person might easily, *à priori* as they say, embrace the idea in this too of the extinction of whole species, and the fresh appearance of others, even if both those observations were not made more than merely probable by actual data.

---

[1] See a pair of instances of this singular fossil, *Murex contrarius*, from my collection, in the second part of the *Abbildungen Naturhistorischer Gegenstände*. Gött. 1797, Tab. XI.

PIMPLE-WORM.

Thus there was still to be found in the time of our fathers, on the Isle of France and on some of the small neighbouring islands, but in no other place in the world, so far as is known, a species of large, plump, lazy land-birds, whose flesh is repulsive, the *Dodos*[1]; whose locality was circumscribed, because they could fly no better than the Cassowary. But according to the account of M. Morel, who instituted a search with that view at the very place itself, this bird has ceased now to exist. It has been exterminated out and out. This is no more incomprehensible or improbable than that the last wolf in Scotland, as is known to have been the case, should have been shot in 1680, although a hundred years before great wolf-hunts used to be held. Just in the same way, but somewhat earlier in England, and thirty years later in Ireland, these beasts of prey were destroyed also. Thus plainly neither the *fauna* nor the *flora* (as these lists of indigenous beasts and plants are called) of a country remain always the same. Creatures enough die away in a locality, and fresh ones again become naturalized and spread themselves. It may be by design, as the carp which has now been artificially naturalized in many northern countries; or accidentally, as the rats of the old world have managed to engraft themselves on the new. So there is nothing contradictory in the idea that also once in the universal flora or fauna of the creation (but especially in the latter), as we have said, a species may have become extinct; and on the other hand a fresh one may likewise be sometimes very easily created subsequently.

The pimple-worm[2] in pigs, which Malpighi was the first to discover, is quite as real and perfect an animal in its kind as man and the elephant in theirs. But, as is well known, this animal is only found in tame swine, and never in any way in the wild pig, from which however the former is descended. It would seem therefore that this worm was no more created at the same time

---

[1] *Didus ineptus*. See *Abbildungen Naturhistorischer Gegenstände*. Part IV. Gött. 1799. Tab. XXXV.
[2] *Hydatis finna*. See *Abbildungen Naturhistorischer Gegenstände* a. a. O. Tab. 39.

as the original stock of the hog than, according to probability, the allied species of the bladder worms, which have been lately discovered, just like those hydatids, in the flesh and among the entrails in human bodies, which must needs have been created after the original parents of mankind. *How* indeed this subsequent creation took place, that I can no more say than how in early times the first spermatic animalcule came into being; that however they *were* subsequently created seems to me undeniable, and I lay that to the account of the great mutability in nature, and this great mutability itself to the active and wise determination of the Creator.

How very limited would be even the sphere of man's operations without this capacity for variation in nature through the labour he may himself bestow upon it. Is it not precisely through this attribute that he becomes really the lord and master of the rest of the creation? To see how much may be done in this way let a man only consider the astonishing alterations which since the discovery of the New World have reciprocally been caused and been experienced by it and the Old.

VI.

The degeneration of organized bodies.

The degeneration of animals and plants from their original stocks into varieties also belongs to the astonishing experiences of variability in creation. In the middle of the 16th century the only tulip known in Europe was the common yellow one. Two hundred years later no kind of flower had a more passionate admirer than these, of which the then Margrave of Baden-Durlach collected no less than three thousand specimens of different varieties[1]. It is not much longer since the first wild green canary bird was brought from its home to Europe, yet these creatures have long since branched out into every sort of variety, not only of colour but also of appearance itself.

---

[1] Bl'Toth. Faisounte. T. xxxiv. p. 284.

The origin of this degeneration has been sought principally in the influence of climate, aliment, and mode of life; and certainly many effects of these three things in degeneration appear unmistakeable. Thus, taken altogether, growth is retarded by cold, and the particular climate of this or that part of the world will have certain manifest operations on the organized bodies which are indigenous to it. As in Syria, many kinds of mammals have astonishingly long and silken hair. Of course very often some of the principal effects which are ascribed to degeneration either run into and destroy one another, or one may equally counteract the other and take away its effect; so that no decided opinion can be arrived at on many of the phenomena of degeneration. Enough that the phenomena themselves must be held as unmistakeable consequences of the variability of nature.

VII.

In domestic animals especially.

The effects of degeneration must naturally have operated in the most profound and various way on those domestic animals which man has for so many generations kept in subjection to himself, to such an extent that they propagate in that condition, and with whom it is not, as in the case of elephants, necessary to catch every individual in the wilderness; and which also can inhabit foreign climates, and are not, like the reindeer, confined within a narrow fatherland.

The common domestic hog is the best example of all, and I select it the more readily because the pedigree of this animal is far less dubious than that of many others. The dog degenerates in many ways, even under our very eyes, but it is not completely made out, and would be very difficult completely to make out, whether all dogs are only varieties of one and the same species or not. Many great naturalists have avowedly considered the shepherd's dog as the common original stock of all the others. Others have put the wolf, the jackal, and the dog together. Others, again, think it not improbable that we ought to assume more than one original stock amongst dogs themselves. In my opinion there is a great deal to be said for the last idea. Not only have we a great difference of appearance in dogs in and of themselves; but they must be very much changed during the long thousands of years since man brought up this animal more than any other in closer intimacy with himself, and partly transplanted it along with him into foreign climates, so that perhaps the original wild[1] dog can no more be found. And this seems to me a ground for assuming that there is more than one original race of dogs, because many, as the badger-dog, have a build so marked, and so appropriate for particular purposes, that I should find it very difficult to persuade myself that this astonishing figure was an accidental consequence of degeneration, and must not rather be considered as an original purposed construction to meet a deliberate object of design[2].

In the hog, again, the power of mere degeneration is much more clearly visible. So far as I know, no naturalist has carried his scepticism so far as to doubt that our domestic hog is descended from the wild boar, and besides this is one of the beasts which was utterly unknown in America before the arrival of the Spaniards, and was first transplanted there from Europe. Meanwhile, notwithstanding the short space of time which is incontrovertibly proved by documents, some of these swine which have been transplanted into that part of the world have degenerated in the most astonishing way into the most extraordinary varieties. Those which were brought from Spain in 1509 to the West India island Cubagua, which was then

---

[1] The difference between being wild originally and becoming wild must be most carefully observed during investigations of this kind. Thus in both worlds we have immense numbers of horses which have become wild; but no one is acquainted with the original wild horse. Thus even in the beginning of the past century wild goats and also wild corn were to be found on the little island of Juan Fernandes (the solitary abode for four years of poor Selkirk, whose true history De Foe has worked up in his Robinson Crusoe); but neither of these belonged originally to the country any more than the wild monkeys which have propagated themselves even up to the present time on the rock of Gibraltar.

[2] See the additions at the end of this Part.

famous everywhere for its pearl fisheries, degenerated into an extraordinary race, with toes which were half a span long[1]. Those in Cuba became more than twice as large again as their European progenitors[2].

This was not the way in which in the old world the tame hog degenerated from the wild hog; but rather in its covering, especially with respect to the woolly hair between the bristles; in the strikingly different form of the skull; in the whole growth, &c. How endless again is the difference in the varieties of the domestic hog itself; that of Piedmont being almost without exception black; that of Bavaria reddish brown; that of Normandy white, &c. How different is the breed of the English hog, with its curved back and pendent belly, from that of the north of France, which is easily distinguished from the former by its elevated croup and its down-hanging head, and both again from the German hog. Hogs with undivided hoofs are to be found gregarious both in Hungary and Sweden, and were known long ago to Aristotle, to say nothing of other more remarkable varieties.

VIII.

Degeneration of Man, the most perfect of all domestic Animals.

But what is the reason that the hog degenerates so particularly? why so much more than any other domestic animal? The solution of this problem flows directly from what has been said above. For the very reason that it is just this animal which is more exposed than any other to the causes of degeneration. No other of our commonly called domestic animals has experienced such a manifold influence of climate as the hog; for no other has been so widely scattered as this over the five parts of the world. None has been subjected so much to the operation

---

[1] Herrera, *Hechos de los Castellanos en las Islas de Tierra Firme del Mar Oceano*, Vol. I. p. 739. Madrid, 1601.
[2] Clavigero, *Storia Antica del Messico*, T. IV. p. 145.

of variety of aliment; for no animal is so omnivorous as the hog, &c. There is only one domestic animal besides (domestic in the true sense, if not in the ordinary acceptation of this word[1]) that also surpasses all others in these respects, and that is man. The difference between him and other domestic animals is only this, that they are not so completely born to domestication as he is, having been created by nature immediately a domestic animal. The exact original wild condition of most of the domestic animals is known. But no one knows the exact original wild condition of man[2]. There is none, for nature has limited him in no wise, but has created him for every mode of life, for every climate, and every sort of aliment, and has set before him the whole world as his own and given him both organic kingdoms for his aliment. But the consequence of this is that there is no second animal besides him in the creation upon whose *solidum vivum* so endless a quantity of various *stimuli*[3], and therefore so endless a quantity of concurring causes of degeneration, must needs operate.

IX.

A very peculiar physiological singularity of the human body.

In order to receive those *stimuli* the *solidum vivum* has been prepared by the forces of life which reside within it, whose diverse although still concurring kinds I have in another place endeavoured to set out and distinguish more precisely[4]. Amongst

---

[1] Even however in the common acceptation of the word man has been before now considered a domestic animal. De Luc says that a very profound psychologist of his acquaintance could find so little connection between the limited power of man's comprehension and the circumference and depth of his actual knowledge, that there must have been in the primitive world a class of higher existences on earth, to whom man acted as a sort of domestic animal and have so received great benefit from the then lord of the creation.
[2] More particularly on this in Part II.
[3] I make use of both these words of art which are universally accepted in the physiology of organized bodies and have so universally understood meaning without turning them into German, since they, as well as the words *organized bodies* themselves, would certainly lose in clearness by translation.
[4] *Institut. Physiolog.* s. IV.

these, by far the most common, and which predominates in both kingdoms of organized creatures, is *contractility*, which is very nearly the same thing that Stahl, one of the most profound physiologists, spoke of under the not sufficiently distinct name of *tone*, or, after the Leiden school, *actuosity*.

The locality of this commonest of vital forces is the mucous membrane, (commonly, but improperly called the cellular tissue,) which constitutes the foundation of almost the whole of an organized body. Thus in a human body, except the enamel of the teeth and some of the outermost coverings of the skin, all the remaining parts consist principally of the mucous membrane, saturated, so to say, and incorporated with other substances. Besides, the mucous membrane is the first organic substance which nature forms out of inorganic saps. Thus the plastic lymph which is squeezed out by inflammations of the lungs is first turned into loose mucous membrane, and this again into the so-called pseudo-membranes with true blood-vessels, &c. The greater or smaller compactness of the mucous membrane however itself differs exceedingly in the different periods of life, and also according to the specific diversity of the species of organized bodies. In the eel, for instance, it is infinitely finer than in the trout. It has been observed, and that long ago, by sagacious zootomists, for instance, our own Zinn, that man, in comparison with other creatures, which are most nearly allied to him in respect of bodily economy, namely the rest of the mammals, has, *ceteris paribus*, the finest and most compact mucous membrane. Let it be well understood *ceteris paribus*, for we must not compare an old gipsy with an unborn lamb.

This exceptional compactness of the mucous membrane and the consequent superior quality of the commonest vital force is, as it seems to me, one of the most distinctive and greatest privileges of man. It is exactly this privilege by which he is enabled to arrive at his greatest object, the habitation of the whole earth, just in the same way as the various kinds of corn, through their delicate and compact cellular texture, are better enabled to thrive in the most different climates than the stronger cedars and oaks. In proportion as this exceptionally compact membrane is in man, as I have said, the first and most important factory of the formative force, it will be easily understood from all these things taken together, how in consequence man is exposed in the formation of his body and its parts to all sorts of degeneration into varieties. It is not improbable moreover that this is the reason why the hog exactly like man can live in the most different climates, and also exactly like him degenerates in manifold ways. At all events there are many remarkable singularities in both creatures with respect to their mucous membrane, as appears most strikingly in the peculiar skin (*corium*), which at bottom is nothing else than the mucous membrane of the outer surface of the body indurated and penetrated with nerves and vessels. Perhaps here too may be found the reason of the similarity which has so often been asserted since the time of Galen between the taste of man's and hog's flesh. As to the reason why, on the other hand, both creatures differ so much from one another in a thousand other ways besides their bodily structure, no one will ask, who knows anything from physiology of the strikingly peculiar privileges by which man, especially with respect to the other noble kind of vital powers, the reaction of the sensorium, &c., is elevated above all the rest of the animal creation.

X.

Something tranquillizing on a common family concern.

There have been persons who have most earnestly protested against their own noble selves being placed in a natural system in one common species with Negroes and Hottentots. And again, there have been other people who have had no compunction in declaring themselves and the orang-utan to be creatures of one and the same species. Thus the renowned philosopher and downright caprice-monger Lord Monboddo says in blunt words, "the orang-utans are proved to be of our species by marks of humanity that I think are incontestable."

On the other hand, another, but not quite so straightforward a caprice-monger, the world-renowned fire-philosopher Theophrastus Paracelsus *Bombastus*, cannot comprehend how all men can belong to one and the same original stock, and contrived on paper for the solution of this difficulty his two Adams.

Perhaps, however, it will contribute something to the tranquillization of many upon this common family affair, if I name three philosophers of quite a different kind, who however much they may have differed otherwise in many of their ideas, still were completely of accord with each other on this point; possibly because it is a question which belongs to natural history, and all three were the greatest naturalists whom the world has lately lost—Haller, Linnæus, and Buffon—all these three considered man different by a whole world from the orang-utan, and on the other hand all true men, Europeans, Negroes, &c., as mere varieties of one and the same original species. It will however be very likely of much more service to most of my readers, if instead of these three names I give the three principal rules which I have always followed, as I have reason to think, with the greatest advantage in my investigations on this subject, and through which I have fortunately escaped many an otherwise sufficiently common, but false conclusion.

I. In these investigations we must have principally before our eyes the physiology of organized bodies. We must not remain attentive merely to man, and act as if he was the only organized body in nature; and must expect to find some differences in his species which are strange and puzzling, without forgetting that all these differences are not a whit more surprising or unusual than those by which so many other species of organized bodies, equally degenerate under our eyes.

II. Neither must we take merely one pair of the races of man which stand strikingly in opposition to each other, and put these one against the other, omitting all the intermediate races, which make up the connection between them. We must never forget that there is not a single one of the bodily differences in any one variety of man, which does not run into some of the others by such endless shades of all sorts, that the naturalist or physiologist has yet to be born, who can with any grounds of certainty attempt to lay down any fixed bounds between these shades, and consequently between their two extremes.

III. Inasmuch as no firm steps can be taken in the determination of the varieties in mankind, any more than in the rest of natural history, without actual knowledge, I have laid down for myself as the third principal rule for a considerable number of years, since I busied myself with these investigations, to make use of everything, so as to provide myself always more and more supports in this behalf out of nature itself. For all the accounts on that point which one adopts, even with the most critical judgment possible, from others, are in reality, for the truth-seeking investigator of nature, nothing more and nothing further than a kind of symbolical writing, which he can only so far subscribe to with a good conscience, as they actually coincide with the open book of nature. And in order to pass an opinion upon that, he must make himself as well read and through that gather as much experience as possible in this book; and this is what I have always endeavoured to do to the best of my ability in my studies on the natural history of mankind. The result of this earnest labour has surpassed all my original expectations, so that I now find myself in possession of a collection for the natural history of mankind, which was the first regular and instructive, and complete one, and so far as I know remains still the only one of its kind.

XI.

On Anthropological Collections.

It seems above everything else hard to understand how it is that considering the zeal with which natural history has been cultivated at all times amongst all scientifically civilized nations, the naturalist was so very late in finding out that man also is a natural product, and consequently ought at least as much as any other to be handled from the point of natural history according to the difference of race, bodily and national peculiarities, &c. Already in the last century the great collectors of writings on natural history,—Gesner, Aldrovandus, Jonston, and Ray,—in their numerous, and also voluminous, and always classical works, embraced the history of all the three natural kingdoms; everything in fact, with the single and solitary exception of the natural history of man himself. And, if I am not mistaken, it was no naturalist by profession, but a mathematician in Upsala, Harald Waller, who was the first that finally in the beginning of the last century attempted to fill up this void which had for such a wonderful length of time remained open in a writing[1], which was a large one for those days, and which forms quite an epoch in the history of natural history.

It is not, however, less astonishing that still for many decades of years after this, the natural history collectors, though in other matters their boundless acquisitiveness not only degenerated into luxury, but very often into folly, still, in order to fill their cabinets, preferred making incursions all over the creation, rather than into that department which could assist the natural history of mankind and his varieties[2]. It is of course easily seen that the construction of such a regular and instructive apparatus for this department is implicated with incomparably greater difficulties than in most other departments of natural collections. That, however, these are not insuperable when the collector shows zeal and perseverance, and can obtain the active co-operation of men who have opportunities of helping him in his object, is shown by the most remarkable portion of my anthropological collection, I mean the skulls of foreign nations.

---

[1] *De Varia Hominum Forma Externa*, 1705, 4to. After him came in 1721 the never-to-be-forgotten polyhistor of Hamburg, J. A. Fabricius, with his *Diss. critica de hominibus orbis nostri incolis, specie et ortu arito inter se non differentibus*.

[2] What perverted and extraordinary notions, even till lately, distinguished naturalists had of what ought to be comprised in such a natural-historical or anthropological collection, may be seen from the following passage in Homare's *Diction*. T. vi. p. 633. 1791, where he is saying what a cabinet of natural history ought to possess. "The cupboard which contains the history of man, consists of an entire myology, a separate head preserved, a brain, the parts of generation of either sex, a neurology, an osteology, embryos of every age with their after-birth, monstrous productions, and an Egyptian mummy. There should also be some nice pieces of anatomy represented in wax and wood, and some stony concretions taken from the human body."

DEDUCTIONS.

There are two questions which have often been put to me on the sight of these skulls, namely, what utility can be made of this collection? and then how can any one be certain of the genuineness of the foreign skulls? These questions are so natural and so reasonable, that the answers to them may properly find a place here.

1. This collection has amongst other things been useful to me in determining the principal corporeal characteristics of humanity, which it is my opinion I have found to consist in the prominent chin and the consequently resulting upright position of the under front teeth. In the animals there is scarcely a particular chin which can be considered as comparable to that of man: and in those men who, as is often said, seem to have something apish in their countenance, this generally resides in a deeply-retreating chin. The upper front teeth have indeed in many nations of different races a more or less oblique direction, whereas, on the other hand, the under ones in all that are known to me stand up vertically.

2. Also for the determination of the really most beautiful form of skull, which in my beautiful typical head of a young Georgian female always of itself attracts every eye, however little observant.

3. As a leading argument for the identity of mankind in general, since here also the boundless passages between the two extremes in the physical scale of nations, from the Calmuck to the Negro, join unobservedly into each other.

4. Then also as an evidence of the natural division of the whole species into the five principal races of which I shall speak in the next section.

5. Of the mixture of these races with each other, which is as clearly expressed in the skulls of the Cossacks, Kirghis, &c., as anywhere in the Mulattos.

6. For the refutation of many erroneous conclusions as to the pretended similarity of structure, and consequently of relationship between distant nations, as between the old Egyptians and the Chinese, or between these and the Hottentots, &c.

7. On the other hand, for a nearer conclusion on the pro-

bable parentage of puzzling populations, as of the old Guanches of the Fortunate Islands from the Libyan stock of the old Egyptians.

8. For this is learnt from a comparison of the mummy skulls with the Egyptian works of art, that they distinguish three sorts of national characters, which differ very decidedly from one another, of which one is most like the Abyssinians, another the Hindoos, and the third the Berbers, or ancient Libyans.

9. This collection also helps to explain many physiological and national peculiarities, as the extremely wide passages in the nostrils of the keen-scented Negroes and North American Indians.

10. And also, as an example of what has been lately disputed in some quarters, of the constantly enduring shapelessness which many savage tribes, as, for instance, the Caribs and the Choctaws artificially infix upon the heads of their children by continual pressing and binding. Of the various other interesting ideas which the inspection of this collection of skulls calls up, I can only think of the truly melancholy one—that it contains so many relics of former respectable tribes, who have been from time to time, and now are, almost entirely destroyed by their conquerors, just as the Caribs of the West India Islands, the Guanches of the Canary Islands, &c. who have suffered the same fate as some useful varieties of domestic animals, such as the great Irish hound, and the St Bernard's dog, which seem now to be exterminated from the creation.

As to the other of the two questions mentioned above, it will be most easily answered by this fact, that every skull is numbered, and has its own particular description in a special collection of the incidents belonging thereto, which contains all the certificates of them, and the original letters, notices, and a comparison with copies, like portraits[1], of which I myself have

---

[1] Of the value of such really portrait-like and characteristic representations (with which unfortunately their rarity stands in exact proportion) for comparison with the skulls, I can give one example out of many. Twelve years ago I re-

collected a rare apparatus, and also with the characteristic descriptions of the most exact writers of natural history, and of travellers: in short everything that makes up complete warranties, as they have been used in the *Decades* which have been composed from this collection. Besides this, care has been taken in the mode of arrangement, that where it was possible to obtain more than one skull of any savage nations, these, at all events, should stand side by side together, in order to show at the first glance the persistent resemblance with which the heads of each one of those peoples who have mingled only with each other, so far as concerns their national character, seem to be all cast in one mould. They are in this way so easy and so securely distinguished and recognized, that it is to be hoped no one at the sight of this collection will be in the condition of the Cynic Menippus' after his suicide, who, on his arrival in the nether world, said of the skulls which were collected, that forsooth they all looked exactly alike, and who was too obtuse to pick out even that of the beautiful Helena from the others.

XII.

Division of Mankind into Five principal Races.

To return again to the three rules laid down above, which have given rise to this digression. After many a year's industrious observance of them I have arrived at no new striking

---

ceived from Labrador the skull of an Esquimaux, and afterwards through the kindness of Sir Jos. Banks a masterly likeness of Myonek, a deceased Esquimaux woman, who was known in 1796, through the missionary reports of the evangelical brotherhood. She had been in London in 1796, when Sir Jos. had this speaking likeness of the size of life painted by the famous portrait painter John Russell. The resemblance between the remarkable character of this picture with that skull strikes every observant eye that compares them together. In order to prove it to the unobservant, I have had the circumference of that skull, and also that of the picture drawn by means of a glass plate, and then traced from that on two leaves, and when these two are held exactly upon one another against the light, the two drawings in all their parts cover each other like a pair of equally large and equiangular triangles.

¹ In Lucian's *Dialogues of the Dead.*

FIVE RACES.

discovery, but what must be just as satisfactory a conclusion to me, the conviction of an old truth in natural history, on which doubt has been recently cast in some quarters. I have endeavoured particularly to depend upon sensible experience, and where I could not avail myself of this, on the accounts of active and trustworthy witnesses, and after all that I have thus learnt about the bodily differences in mankind, and all the comparisons thus made with the bodily differences in other species of organized beings, especially in the case of the domestic animals, I have found no single difference in the former which may not also be observed in many of the latter, and that too as an unmistakeable consequence of degeneration. Consequently I do not see the slightest shadow of reason why I, looking at the matter from a physiological and scientific point of view, should have any doubt whatever that all nations, under all known climates, belong to one and exactly the same common species.

Still, in the same way as we classify races and degenerations of horses and poultry, of pinks and tulips, so also, in addition, must we class the varieties of mankind which exist within their common original stock. Only this, that as all the differences in mankind, however surprising they may be at the first glance, seem, upon a nearer inspection, to run into one another by unnoticed passages and intermediate shades; no other very definite boundaries can be drawn between these varieties, especially if, as is but fair, respect is had not only to one or the other, but also to the peculiarities of a natural system, dependent upon all bodily indications alike. Meanwhile, so far as I have made myself acquainted with the nations of the earth, according to my opinion, they may be most naturally divided into these five principal races:

1. *The Caucasian*[1] *race.* The Europeans, with the exception of the Lapps, and the rest of the true Finns, and the western Asiatics this side the Obi, the Caspian Sea, and the Ganges along with the people of North Africa. In one word,

---

[1] [These well-known terms do not occur in the first edition (1790) of this treatise: but were first used in the third ed. of *De generis hum. &c.* in 1795. ED.]

the inhabitants nearly of the world known to the ancient Greeks and Romans. They are more or less white in colour, with red cheeks, and, according to the European conception of beauty in the countenance and shape of the skull, the most handsome of men.

2. *The Mongolian.* The remaining Asiatics, except the Malays, with the Lapps in Europe, and the Esquimaux in the north of America, from Behring's Straits to Labrador and Greenland. They are for the most part of a wheaten yellow, with scanty, straight, black hair, and have flat faces with laterally projecting cheek-bones, and narrowly slit eyelids.

3. *The Ethiopian.* The rest of the Africans, more or less black, generally with curly hair, jaw-bones projecting forwards, puffy lips, and snub noses.

4. *The American.* The rest of the Americans; generally tan-coloured, or like molten copper, with long straight hair, and broad, but not withal flat face, but with strongly distinctive marks.

5. *The Malay.* The South-sea islanders, or the inhabitants of the fifth part of the world, back again to the East Indies, including the Malays, properly so called. They are generally of brownish colour (from clear mahogany to the very deepest chestnut), with thick black ringleted hair, broad nose, and large mouth.

Each of these five principal races contains besides one or more nations which are distinguished by their more or less striking structure from the rest of those of the same division. Thus the Hindoos might be separated as particular sub-varieties from the Caucasian; the Chinese and Japanese from the Mongolian; the Hottentots from the Ethiopian; so also the North American Indians from those in the southern half of the new world; and the black Papuans in New Holland, &c. from the brown Otaheitans and other islanders of the Pacific Ocean.

XIII.

Of the Negro in particular.

"God's image he too," as Fuller says, "although made out of ebony." This has been doubted sometimes, and, on the contrary, it has been asserted that the negroes are specifically different in their bodily structure from other men, and must also be placed considerably in the rear, from the condition of their obtuse mental capacities. Personal observation, combined with the accounts of trustworthy and unprejudiced witnesses, has, however, long since convinced me of the want of foundation in both these assertions. But I need not repeat everything which I have elsewhere publicly expressed in opposition to those views; though there are one or two points I cannot leave quite untouched[1]. I am acquainted with no single distinctive bodily character which is at once peculiar to the negro, and which cannot be found to exist in many other and distant nations; none which is in like way common to the negro, and in which they do not again come into contact with other nations through imperceptible passages, just as every other variety of man runs into the neighbouring populations.

The colour of the skin they share more or less with the inhabitants of Madagascar, New Guinea, and New Holland. And there are imperceptible shades, up from the blackest negroes in North Guinea to the Moors: amongst whom many, especially the women, according to the assurance of Shaw, have the very whitest skin that it is possible to imagine. The curly woolly hair is well known not to be common to all the negroes, for Barbot says, even of those in Nigritia itself, that some have curly and some have straight hair; and Ulloa says just the same of the negroes in Spanish America. Secondly, this so-

---

[1] A quantity of the most instructive remarks on this point, taken from nature itself, is to be found in the praiseworthy Dr Th. Winterbottom's *Classical Account of the Native Africans in the Neighbourhood of Sierra Leone*, where the author of this classical work spent four years as physician to the colony.

called woolly hair is very far from being peculiar to the negroes, for it is found in many people of the fifth race, as in the Ygolotes in the Philippines, in the inhabitants of Charlotte Island and Van Diemen's Land, and also in many of the third variety, who, however, are not reckoned as negroes. Many Abyssinians have it, as the famous Abba Gregorius, whose handsome likeness, which Heiss engraved in 1691, after Von Sand, I have before me[1]. Sparrmann also says of the Hottentots, that their hair is more like wool than that of the negroes themselves; and this I find confirmed by the pictures of Hottentots and Kaffirs, which many years ago were forwarded with some transplanted plants from the Cape to Joseph II., and of which I have obtained exact copies, through the kindness of Counsellor von Jacquin. As to the physiognomy of the negro, the difference no doubt is astonishing if you put an ugly negro (and there are ugly negroes as well as ugly Europeans) exactly opposite the Greek ideal. But this is precisely to offend against one of the rules given above. If, on the contrary, one investigates the transitional forms in this case also, the striking contrast between the two very different extremes vanishes away; and, of course, there must be extremes here as well as in the case of other creatures which degenerate into all sorts of races and varieties.

I can, on the contrary, declare that amongst the negroes and negresses whom I have been able to observe attentively, and I have seen no small number of them, as in the portrait-like drawings and profiles of others, and in the seven skulls of adult negroes which are in my collection, and in the others which have come under my notice, or of which I have drawings and engravings before me, it is with difficulty that *two* can be found who are completely like each other in form; but all are more or less different from one another, and through all sorts of gradations run imperceptibly into the appearance of men of other kinds up to the most pleasing conformation. Of this sort

---

[1] "He had curly hair like other Ethiopians," says his friend Ludolph in the description which he gives of him.

was a female creole, with whom I conversed in Yverdun, at the
house of the Chevalier Treytorrens, who had brought her from
St Domingo, and both whose parents were of Congo. Such
a countenance—even in the nose and the somewhat thick lips—
was so far from being surprising, that if one could have set aside
the disagreeable skin, the same features with a white skin must
have universally pleased, just as Le Maire says in his travels
through Senegal and Gambia, that there are negresses, who,
abstraction being made of the colour, are as well formed as our
European ladies. So also Adanson, that accurate naturalist,
asserts the same of the Senegambia negresses; "they have
beautiful eyes, small mouth and lips, and well-proportioned features: some, too, are found of perfect beauty[1]; they are full of
vivacity, and have especially an easy, free and agreeable presence." Now this was exactly the case with the negress of
Yverdun, and with several other negresses and negroes, whose
closer acquaintance I have since that had the opportunity of
making, and who have equally convinced me of the truth of
what so many unsuspected witnesses have assured me about
the good disposition and faculties of these our black brethren;
namely, that in those respects as well as in natural tenderness of
heart[2], they can scarcely be considered inferior to any other race
of mankind taken altogether[3]. I say quite deliberately, taken
altogether, and *natural* tenderness of heart, which has never
been benumbed or extirpated on board the transport vessels or
on the West India sugar plantations by the brutality of their
white executioners. For these last must be nearly as much
without head as without heart, if after such treatment they still

---

[1] "Of a perfect beauty."
[2] "The mildness of the Negro character," says Lucas, the famous African traveller, in the *Proceedings of the African Association.*
[3] Listen to one guarantee for all, our own incomparable Niebuhr: "The principal characteristic of the negro is, especially when he is reasonably treated, honesty towards his masters and benefactors. Mohammedan merchants in Cairo, Jeddah, Surat, and other cities, are glad to buy boys of this kind; they have them taught writing and arithmetic, carry on their extensive business almost entirely through negro slaves, and send them to establish business places in foreign countries. I asked one of these merchants, How he could trust a slave with whole cargoes of goods? and was told in reply, 'My negro is true to me; but if I were to conduct my business entirely by white men, I should have to take care that they did not run off with my property.'"

expect to find true attachment and love from these poor mismanaged slaves. That excellent observer of nature, Aublet, in his true and masterly description of the natural goodness of the negro's character, rests upon the confessions of the Europeans who have been in captivity amongst the Algerines, and have openly admitted that in that position they felt just as ill disposed and just as hostile to their then masters, as a negro in like case could possibly feel towards his master in the colonies. On the other hand, I have daily for a long time had an honest negress before my eyes, of whom I often said in my mind, what Wieland's Democritus says of his good, soft-hearted, curly-locked black, and what has also been so frequently asserted by other unprejudiced observers of uncorrupted blacks, and amongst others very recently with true and warm gratitude by the stout Mungo Park, that it is not worth while to scrape together here the proofs of these facts[1].

At the same time it will not be at all superfluous to point out here some not so well known though remarkable examples of the perfectibility of the mental faculties and the talents of the negro, which of course will not come unexpectedly upon any one who has perused the accounts of the most credible travellers about the natural disposition of the negro. Thus the classical Barbot, in his great work on Guinea, expresses himself as follows: "The blacks have for the most part head and understanding enough: they comprehend easily and correctly, and their memory is of a tenacity almost incomprehensible; for even when they can neither read nor write, they still remain in their place amidst the greatest bustle of business and traffic, and seldom go wrong."—"Since they have been so often deceived by Europeans, they now stand carefully on their guard in traffic and exchange with them, carefully examine all our wares, piece

---

[1] Many speaking examples of the real gratitude, and above all of the humane character, and also of the excellent capacities of our black brethren, are to be found in the following three works, whose meritorious authors were long in the West Indies, and are amongst the most capable and unprejudiced observers of the Negro: Oldendorp's *Geschichte der Mission der evangelischen Brüder auf. S. Thomas*, &c. 1777; Ramsay's *Essay on the Treatment and Conversion of African Slaves*, 1784; Nisbett's *Capacity of Negroes for Religious and Moral Improvement*, 1789.

by piece, whether they are of the samples bargained for in quality and quantity; whether the cloths and stuffs are lasting, whether they were dyed in Haarlem or Leyden, &c."..."in short, they try everything with as much prudence and cunning as any European man of business whatever can do." Their aptitude for learning all sorts of fine handy-work is well known. It is estimated that nine-tenths of the ordinary craftsmen in the West Indies are negroes[1].

With respect to their talents for music, there is no necessity for me to call attention to the instances in which negroes have earned so much by them in America, that they have been able to purchase their freedom for large sums, since there is no want of examples in Europe itself of blacks, who have shown themselves true virtuosos. The negro Freidig was well known in Vienna as a masterly concertist on the viol and the violin, and also as a capital draughtsman, who had educated himself at the academy there under Schmutzer. As examples of the capacity of the negro for mathematical and physical sciences, I need only mention the Russian colonel of artillery, Hannibal, and the negro Lislet, of the Isle of France, who on account of his superior meteorological observations and trigonometrical measurements, was appointed their correspondent by the Paris Academy of Sciences.

Dr Rush of Philadelphia is at work upon a history of the negro, Fuller, in Maryland, who has lately become so famous through his extraordinary capacity for calculation. In order to test him on this point, he was asked in company how many seconds a man would have lived who was seventy years and so many months, &c. old. In a minute and a half Fuller gave the number. Others then calculated it, but the result was not the same. "Have you not forgotten," said the negro, "to bring into account the days of the leap-years?" These were then

---

[1] On the exceptional skill for art, "of the soft and benevolent" negroes in Houssa or Soudan in the interior of Africa, see our Hornemann's *Tagebuch seiner reise von Cairo bis Murzuk*. This book gives us much important information upon the condition of the soil and population of this remarkable part of the earth, which no European before him had visited.

added, and the two calculations coincided exactly. I possess some annuals of a Philadelphian calendar, which a negro there, Benj. Bannaker, had calculated, who had acquired his astronomical knowledge without oral instruction, entirely through private study of Ferguson's works and our Tob. Mayer's tables[1], &c. Boerhaave, de Haen, and Dr Rush[2] have given the most decided proofs of the uncommon insight which negroes have into practical medicine. Negroes have also been known to make very excellent surgeons. And the beautiful negress of Yverdun, whom I mentioned, is known far and wide in French Switzerland as an excellent midwife, of sound skill, and of a delicate and well-experienced hand. I omit the Wesleyan Methodist preacher, Madox, and also the two negroes who lately died in London, Ignatius Sancho and Gustavus Vasa, of whom the former, a great favourite both of Garrick and Sterne, was known to me by correspondence[3]; and the latter, whom I knew personally, has made himself a name by his interesting autobiography[4]; and also many other negroes and negresses who have distinguished themselves by their talents for poetry. I possess English, Dutch, and Latin poems by several of these latter, amongst which however above all, those of Phillis Wheatley of Boston, who is justly famous for them, deserve mention here[5].

---

[1] J. M'Henry, of Baltimore, has printed biographical accounts of this man, and, as he expresses himself, regards "this negro as a new proof that mental faculties bear no relation to the colour of the skin."

[2] This philosophic physician writes of an excellent negro who to my knowledge is still living, to Dr Derham in New Orleans: "I have conversed with him upon most of the acute and epidemic diseases of the country where he lives, and was pleased to find him perfectly acquainted with the modern simple mode of practice in those diseases. I expected to have suggested some new medicines to him, but he suggested many more to me. He is very modest and engaging in his manners, and does business to the amount of 3000 dollars a year."

[3] *Letters of the late Ignatius Sancho, an African*, third ed. London, 1784, 8vo, with the beautifully engraved likeness by Bartolozzi, after Gainsborough's picture.

[4] *The Interesting Narrative of the Life of Olaudah Equiano, or Gustavus Vasa*, written by himself, third ed. London, 1791, 8vo; in German, Göttingen, 1792, 8vo.

[5] *Poems on Various Subjects, Religious and Moral*, by Phillis Wheatley, *Negro Servant to Mr John Wheatley of Boston*, 1773, 8vo. A collection which scarcely any one who has any taste for poetry could read without pleasure. Some particularly beautiful selections from them are to be found in the famous prize essay of the worthy Clarkson, *On the Slavery and Commerce of the Human Species*.

There are still two negroes who have got some reputation as authors, and whose works I possess, whom I may mention. Our Hollmann, when he was still professor at Wittenberg, created in 1734 the negro, Ant. Wilh. Amo, Doctor of Philosophy. He had shown great merit both in writing and teaching; and I have two treatises by him, of which one especially shows a most unexpected and well-digested course of reading in the best physiological works of that day[1]. In an account of Amo's life, which on that occasion was printed in the name of the University Senate, great praise is allotted to his exceptional uprightness, his capacity, his industry, and his learning. It says of his philosophical lectures: "he studied the opinions both of the ancients and moderns; he selected the best, and explained his selections clearly and at full length." It was in his fortieth year that the negro Jac. Elisa Joh. Capitein studied theology at Leyden; he had been kidnapped when a boy of eight years old, and was bought by a slave-dealer at St Andrew's river, and got to Holland in this way at third-hand. I have several sermons[2] and poems by him, which I will leave to their own merits; but more interesting and more famous is his *Dissertatio politico-theologica de servitute libertati Christianae non contraria*, which he read publicly on the 10th March, 1742, in Leyden, and of which I have a translation in Dutch[3], of which again four editions were struck off, one immediately after the other. Upon this he was ordained preacher at Amsterdam in the church d'Elmina, whither he soon afterwards departed. Professor Brugmans of Leyden, who procured for me the writings of this

---

[1] The title of the first is, *Diss. inaug. Philosophica de humanae mentis draσίας mu sensionis ac facultatis sentiendi in mente humana absentia, et corum in corpore nostro organico ac vivo praesentia. auctore Ant. {iuH. Amo, Guinea-Afro.* The other is entitled, *Disp. philosophica continens ideam distinctam eorum quae competunt vel menti vel corpori nostro vivo et organico*.

[2] *l'itgerrogte Predikatien ins Gravenhage en t'Oudtrkerk aen den Amstel gedaan door Jac. Elisa Jo. Capitein, Africaansche Moor, beroepen predikant op D'Elmina aan het Kasteel St George*, Amst. 1742, 4to.

[3] *Staatkundig-Godgeleerd Onderzoekschrift over de Slaverny, als niet strydig tegen de Chrystelyke Vryheid*, Leiden, 1742, 4to. with the beautifully engraved likeness of the author by P. von Ileyswyck. Another portrait of him, after P. van Dyck, has been given by me in the first part of the *Abbildungen Naturhistorischer Gegenstände*, Tab. 5.

ordained negro, sends me word also that according to the circumstances there are two stories about his fate there; either namely that he was murdered, or that he went back to his own savage countrymen, and exchanged their superstitions and mode of life for what he had learnt in Europe. In this last case, his history forms a pendent to that of the Hottentot who was brought up in Europe and civilized, whose similar and thorough patriotism has been immortalized by Rousseau[1]. Nor is this irresistible attraction to the ancestral penates at all events a bit more strange than the fact, that, as is known, Europeans enough, who have been made prisoners of war by the North American Indians, or even by the Caribs of the West Indies, when these still constituted a respectable and warlike nation, and have lived a long time with them and become used to them, have found such a great delight in this wild state of nature as to lose all desire of changing it, and coming back to their own countrymen; nor are there wanting instances, especially among the French Canadians, who of their own free-will have gone over to the savages there, and taken up the same kind of life as they[2].

Finally, I am of opinion that after all these numerous instances I have brought together of negroes of capacity, it would not be difficult to mention entire well-known provinces of Europe, from out of which you would not easily expect to obtain off-hand such good authors, poets, philosophers, and correspondents of the Paris Academy; and on the other hand, there is no so-called savage nation known under the sun which has so much distinguished itself by such examples of perfectibility and original capacity for scientific culture, and thereby attached itself so closely to the most civilized nations of the earth, *as the Negro.*

---

[1] See the vignette to his *Discours sur l'inégalité parmi les hommes.*
[2] Lieut. Paterson speaks of a German at the Cape, who had completely come over in this way to the Hottentots, and had then already lived twenty years in the midst of them, and was entirely naturalised and considered as one of them.

XIV.

The Kakerlacken.

These poor sufferers have come off in the history of man not a bit better than the honest negroes. There have been sceptics who were as unwilling to recognize the Kakerlacken for men of the same species with ourselves as the Moors. The latter were too black for them, and the former too white. In reality the examination of the Kakerlacken has nothing whatever to attach it to the domain of natural history, for it belongs to pathology. Meanwhile, as it has once been dragged into the former, and so has given handle to many wonderful mistakes, I think I may go so far as to say a few words about them; and they join on all the more easily to the former section, because their history was originally confounded with that of the negroes.

For at the very first of all a sort of men was remarked amongst these last, who were distinguished by an unusual whiteness or even redness of skin, and by hair of a yellowish white and pale red eyes; and of course these singularities would strike people more in negroes than in white men; and for that reason the Kakerlacken were first of all known by the name of Leucœthiopians. But just about the end of the last century they were found amongst the Americans also, and very shortly afterwards, besides these, amongst the East Indian populations. Still later Cook saw some on Otaheite and the Friendly Islands; and now at last it is clear that they are also to be found in Europe itself, and that too in greater numbers than we can altogether desire. Since I laid before the Royal Society of Sciences my observations on those two well-known Savoyards, whom I had the opportunity of examining in 1783, on an excursion which I made in company with the younger De Luc, from Geneva to Faucigny, and who afterwards went for some years to London, where they were described by the directors of the circus, I have received accounts of a round dozen of other Kakerlacken who have been found up and down in Germany alone, and have from most of them specimens of their own quite peculiar hair. It seems to have been the case with the Kakerlacken as with many other wonders of nature, that they have been for a long time overlooked in many countries, because they were considered too great rarities to be expected. In one word, the Kakerlacken occur in all the five races of mankind.

Besides, this singularity is not peculiar to mankind alone, but shows itself also just as much in other warm-blooded animals, as in mammals and in birds. Amongst the former, we have notoriously the white rabbits and the white mice, and amongst the latter the white canary birds. On the other hand, in spite of all the researches I have made in that direction, I have not been able to find any single example of Kakerlacken among the animals with red cold blood, either amongst the amphibia or fish. That above all I consider the Kakerlacken as diseased, and consequently white canaries, &c. the same, will be strange to no one who is acquainted with their constitution. Their chief symptom consists in the singular colour of their eyes, the iris of which is a pale pink colour, and the pupils of the colour of a dark carnation, or very much like blackberry juice, whereas in a sound eye these last, whatever the colour of the iris may be, whether blue or brown, must always be entirely black. The reason of that redness lies in a total want of that part which is indispensable to clear sight, namely, the dark brown mucus which is spread over a great part of the inner apple of the eye, in order to absorb the superfluous rays of light. Consequently, the Kakerlacken through this deficiency are generally more or less shy of light. But this deficiency of the black pigment seems always to be only a symptom of an universal cachexia, which in human Kakerlacken finds its particular expression through the peculiar aspect of the skin and the yellowish white colour of the hair; at least so far as I know, no one has ever observed that disease of the eyes without this quality of skin and hair.

The disorder is invariably congenital, and frequently hereditary in families. It seems to be incurable; at least I know of no case in which the symptoms related have ever been got rid of by any single Kakerlack. On the causes of this remarkable disease I do not know how at this moment to say anything satisfactory; for as to the remark that an otherwise quick-seeing traveller, Foucher d'Obsonville, has made, that Leucœthiopians are begotten when the parents are taking mercury or cinnabar at the time, it is impossible to imagine it correct in many of the cases of the nations mentioned, and in many of the animals among whom Kakerlacken are found, even if the whole idea were not to the last extent extremely improbable. So also the old assertion, that no Leucœthiopian of either sex was capable of procreation, is completely untrue. De Bruc has already found an instance in which a Leucœthiopian became pregnant by a negro, and a perfect young negro was born, and the well-known negro Vasa, in his above-mentioned interesting work, has given a remarkable account of a Leucœthiopian female, who was lately married in England to an European, and has borne him three genuine Mulattos with light hair.

APPENDIX I. To p. 284 n.

On the gradation in nature.

Two scientific societies, the one at Rouen and the other at Haarlem, have lately given out as the subject for a prize, *Whether the asserted gradation in nature has any real foundation or not?* I am acquainted with only one essay in answer to this question which was sent in to the last-mentioned learned society, whose renowned author, our worthy Professor De Luc, has handled the whole subject only from a metaphysical à priori point of view, and even in this way comes to the conclusion that there is neither continuity nor imperceptible gradation in the creation, and that the harmony of the creation is rather supported by marked differences, having sharply defined boundaries between them. On the other hand, I long ago[1] pointed out considerations against the reality of the structural conceptions of the gradation of creatures according to their more exterior

---

[1] *Handbuch der Naturgesch.* p. 6, 7th ed.

form, and against the very well-meant, but at the bottom very presumptuous tendency towards this idea, which is found in many physico-theologians; and these are entirely empirical, taken from natural history itself, and from the visible constraint which, in all the various essays on such gradations, is done to nature. Who does not feel how constrained he is when Bradley carries up his scale from the simplest fossils through the vegetable and animal kingdom up to man, but has to put off what he cannot readily make fit into this scale into a second, by which he descends on the other side again from that elevation? or, when in order to stand fast by particular passages and connecting links, Vallisneri brings forward the analogy of grasshoppers with birds, Oehme the analogy of birds with house-flies and other *Dipteræ*, and when Bonnet chooses the shield-lice as creatures of the transition from other insects to the tape-worm, &c. We should find it much easier to excuse the older describers of nature, when, deceived by the great resemblance of the exterior, they located the armadilloes of the genus *Manis* with the lizards, or the sertularia, and above all the corals, with the cryptogamic plants; since with certainly quite as much reason, in consequence of an extremely superficial view of an outward structure very nearly resembling them, many even phanogeramic species of plants out of the genera *Saxifraga, Andromedæ, Aretiæ*, &c. in spite of all their remaining heterogeneity, have had a place found for them on the ladder close to the large-leaved moss.

When that extraordinary wonder-animal of the fifth part of the world, the *Ornithorhynchus paradoxus*, was discovered, many partisans of gradation looked upon it as a fresh support of that theory, whereas, it seems to me much rather to be a new evidence against its reality. It seems to me so very isolated a creature of its sort, that it can be no more brought into the natural arrangement of the animal kingdom without visible constraint, than the tortoises, cuttle-fish, &c., or than many genera of plants, as the *Vitis, Cissus*, &c. in that of the vegetable kingdom. Besides this, in the scale of Bonnet, and simple ones of that kind, the transition department from the birds to the quadrupeds has been long since filled up by the bat; and yet it would be difficult to imagine two forms of mammals, which differ more surprisingly from each other, and which must therefore in any gradation stand further apart from each other, than those of the bat and the ornithorhynchus.

It must be understood that all that has been said here, as well as what was suggested above (p. 283), by the expressions quoted from an otherwise meritorious writer on the use of petrifactions, is only to be regarded as a warning against the misuse of the common conception of gradation, according to the outward form of creatures under the favourite images of ladders and links: since, on the other hand, the very greatest use may be made of this very metaphorical image not only towards the exercise of observation, but also with the greatest advantage towards the regular use of a natural system in the description of nature, and also for the most advantageous arrangement of natural collections. Only instead of the partisans of this gradation acknowledging its value in dividing the productions of nature into kingdoms, classes, &c., and as a means of methodizing study and an assistance to the memory, but allowing that it has no real existence in nature itself; exactly the opposite seems to have come of those structural conceptions, whose unmistakeable value for the science of method cannot be denied, but which are so very far from having any real ground in nature itself, that it has often happened to well-meaning physico-theologians that "they have attributed it to the Creator in the plan of His creation, and have made its completeness and connexion to be sought for in the fact that nature, as the expression goes, *makes no leap, because* creatures with respect to their outward habit can be arranged so closely in gradation one with another."

APPENDIX II. To p. 285.

On the Succession of the different Earth-catastrophes.

If petrifactions can be made of regular use for the archæology and the physical geography of the earth, as the surest documents in the archives of nature for the fruitful history of the catastrophes which have been connected with our planet since its creation, the study of them, and its tendency, demands as well a thorough critical comparison of them with the organized bodies of the present creation, as also an accurate investigation of their different localities, and their geognostical relations. The first important and instructive result which is immediately derived from this two-fold consideration is, that the lapidifications are of extremely unequal antiquity; many, as the still fresh *Salmo arcticus* of the west coast of Greenland, which is, so to speak, merely mummified in the thin clayish-marl beds, is only of yesterday or the day before, in comparison with the thoroughly strange and puzzling impressions of unknown plants which are found in the grau-wacke strata of the Harz on the borders of the Gangberg in the depths of the earth, and which belong to the very oldest evidences of an organized creation on our planet. A wider examination of these differently made fossils, and of their equally various sort of condition, brings us to a closer conclusion as to the oldest history of the body of this earth, and upon the sort and consequences of the numerous catastrophes it has gone through, and through which its crust has acquired its present appearance, which has been built out of such great convulsions. It is therefore my opinion, that the petrifactions may be arranged off-hand, according to their different antiquity, most easily in three principal divisions. First, those whose complete similarity with still existing representatives, as well as the positions they are found in, prove that they must be comparatively the most recent; secondly, those far older, which have not indeed similar but still more or less allied analogues to them in the present creation, although in climates very distant from those which contain such fossil remains; finally, in the third place, the very oldest of all, consisting for the most part of creatures completely unknown, the records of a perfectly strange creation which has been completely destroyed. These three divisions may to a certain extent be compared to the three epochs in the oldest profane writings of an historical, heroic, and mythical period.

The first of these divisions comprises, therefore, the relatively most modern lapidifications, those namely which seem to have been occasioned by partial local revolutions since the last general catastrophe which our planet suffered; and consequently, nothing but those whose representatives are still in existence, and which are closely allied to the fossil remains in the same country. Amongst them I reckon the uncommonly clear casts and remains from all six classes of the animal kingdom, and the numerous kinds of plants which are to be found in, and have made famous, the stinking slate-quarries at Oeningen on the Bodensee. When I travelled in that country I made a collection of them, and I have seen still more in other collections; but amongst all, which I have myself been able to examine accurately, I have unfortunately found nothing exotic, nothing which might not be referred either unmistakeably, or at all events with the greatest probability, to the fauna and flora of that present country and its waters.

To the second of these principal divisions belong fossils of quite another sort and far higher origin; namely, the now innumerable elephants, rhinoceroses, and other now tropical creatures found in this country, which most probably must have been once naturalized here, as is particularly demonstrated by the enormously large dens of huge species of bears in the famous summits of the Harz, the Fichtelberg, in the Thuringian forest and on the Carpathians. Everything goes to show that those bears came alive into those caves, and found their graves there. But there are also found in these caves with them bones and teeth of beasts of prey, like the lions and hyænas of the present earth, of which I have specimens, from most of the dens mentioned, in my collection. Consequently, according to all probability that species of bears was also a tropical one, just as bears still live in many of the tropical zones of the old world; and as those bears and lions are found in positions where it would be difficult for them to have been floated in by any current after death, so this seems very unlikely to have happened either to the elephants or rhinoceroses. Especially when it is considered that quite little flocks of many of these have been found together, as the five individual hippopotami on the Lither Harz, whose fossil remains have been determined and described with a master's hand by our meritorious Hollmann; and that of others, as of the two elephants from Tonna, mentioned above, the complete skeletons have been dug out, &c. And finally, all this derives a new importance from another geological phenomenon, which according to my conviction belongs to a similar division, and must be joined in close connection with it; I mean the remains of tropical animals in certain limestones. Thus in the calcareous strata of Pappenheim there have been found amongst so many other tropical creatures a kind of Molluscan[1] water-flea, and the still articulated arm bones of a species of bat, very much like the flying-dog, and all these so well preserved, even up to the most delicate Indian star-fishes, so clear and in such perfection, that no notion can remain of any transport of them through a general flood from the southern hemisphere here. On the contrary, it is quite clear that those elephants, rhinoceroses, and hyæna-like animals must once have been just as these water-fleas, star-fishes, &c., domesticated in our latitudes, until through some cause which we cannot now determine with any certainty, a total alteration of the climate took place, which occasioned the destruction of the then living generation of those tropical creatures, as of many other genera and species of organized bodies which existed along with them, of which in the present creation no exactly similar, to say nothing of specifically like, representatives are to be found: as the unknown of Ohio among great land-animals, and amongst the marine-animals in the Pappenheim slate-quarries, so many altogether strange species of crabs, the singular hard-armed medusa head, and many others.

This revolution, which seems to have been merely climatic, must be distinguished from those earlier and much more forcible ones, from which we must date the petrifactions of the *third*

---

[1] (The *Pterodactylus*, a reptile; and since the time of Blumenbach, the *Archæopteryx macrurus*, a long-tailed bird. ED.)

division, the oldest of all. In those the firm crust of the earth itself suffered such powerful shocks, that the floors of the previous seas of the primeval world began to cover high mountains with their still uninjured shells; and on the other hand, the previous vegetation of the land was buried deep under the present surface of the sea. It is at once observed that these destructive catastrophes themselves were again of more than one sort, and were very far from happening all at the same time; although it is scarcely possible at present to determine with any certainty the chronological arrangement of the successive periods in which they happened, to say nothing of the causes of them.

APPENDIX III. To p. 292.

On the so-called Objects of Design.

Few scientific theories have been supported and opposed with such incredible prejudices on the one side and on the other, as those about the objects of design of the Creator. With many indeed, who contested this point, it was merely a question of words, whether one ought to speak of design or utility. Others considered the whole question of final causes as entirely useless; and Bacon's *bon-mot* is well known, who compared it to a prudent virgin, who weds heaven, and consequently produces nothing for the world. The great thinker would however have come to a different conclusion if he had been reminded out of the literature of physiology and natural history, what completeness in these important sciences and what useful results to mankind the search into the final purposes of nature has produced. But certainly the teleologists have laid themselves wonderfully open by anxiously catching at those things, and have also used great force to them, because they have thought themselves obliged to demonstrate clearly the aim and object of every disposition of nature, especially in the organic creation. Thus the otherwise praiseworthy anatomist Spigel declares that the reason why in man that part on which he sits has been so visibly more developed than in any other animal is, that people may have a more convenient position in which to apply themselves to higher thoughts[1]. So the physico-theologians thought they had found a perforated disk in a bee-like insect on the front feet of the males, and were not behindhand in demonstrating the use and object of this structure. Wise nature had done this, they said, in order that the pollen of the flower might percolate through the creature, and in that way the fructification of plants be provided for; and from that hour it was immediately called the sieve-bee (*Sphex cribraria*). It is very creditable to a clergyman, Göze of Quedlinburg, who has in every way won great renown in natural history, that he has refuted this mistake out of nature herself, and has shown that the disks on the feet of these insects are not penetrated; and consequently this wise object which was with good intentions attributed to the Creator will not stand.

Others, sometimes, on the contrary, have doubted the reality of any arrangement in nature for the very reason that they cannot find in it any design of the Creator. When I pointed out to my never-to-be-forgotten friend Camper, that, in nature, contrary to every common opinion, the tadpoles of the pipa of Surinam were regularly tailed, he was disposed at first to consider[2] the instance I showed him as an unnatural monstrosity, because he could not understand of what use this fin-tail could be to these little creatures who sit nestled on the back of their mothers. Others, again, have swept the whole road quite clean, and completely denied all design in the creation. Not many years ago a distinguished member of the then Academy of Sciences of Paris

---

[1] "Man alone of all animals sits comfortably, because he has larger fleshy buttocks, and these were given him as a support and a cushion, so that when his stomach was full, he could sit without inconvenience, and apply his mind more readily to reflection upon divine matters."—"There was however a respectable English clergyman of another opinion, who amongst other suggestions as to the delicate and particular propriety of conduct which should be observed in church, used to urge very zealously that the psalms should be sung standing, because it was impossible they could come right from the heart in a sitting posture:" see *Remarks on the Public Service of the Church, with some Directions for our Behaviour there, highly proper to be understood by People of all Ranks and Ages*, Lond. 1768, 8vo.

[2] *Comment. Soc. Reg. Scient. Götting.*, T. 12. p. 119.

declared that it was as ridiculous to suppose that the eye was made to see with[1], as to assert that stones were appointed for the purpose of breaking a man's head. This however, please God, will scarcely be satisfactory to any one who has ever had the opportunity of comparing the interior structure of any animal which is remarkable for striking singularities in its mode of life and functions, and can in this way persuade himself from nature itself most incontrovertibly of this pre-established harmony, as it may easily be called, between the purposed structure of creatures and their mode of life. It would be difficult for anyone who is well acquainted with the natural history of the mole or the seal, and will consider with some little reflection the skeleton and muscular system of the former, and the peculiarities of the circulation and the organs of sense of the latter, to allow himself seriously to utter such an expression as the one mentioned above. The hundredfold proofs which may be deduced from comparative anatomy deprive the weak superficialities of some ancient sophists, who supposed that the animal structure was not ordained for its functions, but that the occupations of animals were only the mere consequence of their organization, of the last shadow of speciousness. Thus the production of so many mere temporary organs which only exist in the animal economy for transitory and extremely limited purposes, and which all the same are as good as those which are most durable in all the rest of the structure of those animals in which they are found, are wonderfully adapted to their mode of life. Thus, to produce only one instance of the kind, in the hedgehog, which rolls itself up in defence with such great muscular power, even the unborn fœtuses are completely furnished with one of these powerful springs, most accurately arranged, but which is afterwards in its way an after-birth[2] quite anomalously deformed, thick, and solid, under which the tender immature creature rests

---

[1] Thus said Lucretius long ago:
"Lumina ne facias oculorum clara creata
Prospicere ut possimus," &c.

[2] I have given representations of this highly remarkable part in my *Handbuch der vergleichenden Anatomie*, Tab. 8.

as under a shield, in order to be as completely as possible protected, on any powerful constriction of the pregnant mother, against the dangerous consequences of that strong grasp from which its abdomen and entrails might thereby suffer.

BEYTRÄGE

ZUR

NATURGESCHICHTE,

VON

JOH. FR. BLUMENBACH,
PROF. ZU GÖTTINGEN.

ZWEYTER THEIL.

GÖTTINGEN:
BEY HEINRICH DIETERICH, 1811.

CONTENTS.

I.

On the Homo Sapiens Ferus Linn.: and particularly of Wild Peter of Hameln.

How Wild Peter was found and brought prisoner to Hameln; what happened to Wild Peter in Hameln; Peter arrives in England, and now becomes famous; Peter's origin; Peter's life and conduct in England; mistaken accounts by the biographers of Peter; genuine sources for Peter's history; Peter compared with other so-called wild children; neither Peter, nor any other *Homo sapiens ferus* of Linnæus, can serve as a specimen of the original man of nature: no originally wild condition of nature is to be attributed to Man, who is born a domestic animal.

II.

On Egyptian Mummies.

[Inedited, see Pref.]

CONTRIBUTIONS TO NATURAL HISTORY

BY

J. F. BLUMENBACH.

PART THE SECOND.

I.

How Wild Peter was found and brought prisoner to Hameln.

ON Friday, July 27th, 1724, at the time of hay-harvest, Jürgen Meyer, a townsman of Hameln, met, by a stile in his field, not far from Helpensen, with a naked, brownish, black-haired creature, who was running up and down, and was about the size of a boy of twelve years old. It uttered no human sound, but was happily enticed, by its astonished discoverer showing it two apples in his hand, into the town, and entrapped within the Bridge-gate. There it was at first received by a mob of street boys, but was very soon afterwards placed for safe custody in the Hospital of the Holy Ghost, by order of the Burgomaster Severin.

II.

What happened to Wild Peter in Hameln.

Peter—that was the name given him on his first appearance in Hameln by the street-boys, and he retained it up to quite old age—Peter showed himself rather brutish in the first weeks of his captivity; seeking to get out at doors and windows, resting now and then upon his knees and elbows, and rolling himself from side to side on his straw bed until he fell asleep. He did not like bread at first, but he eagerly peeled green sticks, and chewed the peel for the juice, as he also did vegetables, grass, and bean-shells. By degrees he grew tamer and cleaner, so he was allowed to go about the town and pay visits. When anything was offered him to eat, he first smelt it, and then either put it in his mouth, or laid it aside with a shake of the head. In the same way he would smell people's hands, and then strike his breast if pleased, or if otherwise shake his head. When he particularly liked anything, as green beans, peas, turnips, mulberries, fruit, and particularly onions and hazel-nuts, he indicated his satisfaction by striking repeatedly on his chest. Just when he was found by Jürgen Meyer he had caught some birds, and eagerly dismembered them.

When his first shoes were put on him he was unable to walk in them, but appeared glad when he could go about again bare-footed. He was just as little pleased with any covering on his head, and extremely enjoyed throwing his hat or cap into the water and seeing it swim. He first of all became used to go with clothes on, after they had tried him with a linen kilt. In other respects he appeared of quite a sanguine temperament, and liked hearing music; and his hearing and smell were particularly acute. Whenever he wanted to get anything he kissed his hands, or even the ground.

After some time Peter was put out to board with a clothmaker. He adhered to this man with true attachment, and was accompanied by him when he went from thence, in Oct. 1725, to Zell, into the hospital there, situated by the House of Correction; but about Advent in the same year King George I. sent for him to Hanover.

III.

Peter arrives in England, and now becomes famous.

In Feb. 1726, Peter, under the safeguard of a royal servant, by name Rautenberg, was brought from Hanover to London; and with his arrival there began his since so widely-spread celebrity. This was the very time when the controversy about the existence of innate ideas was being carried on with the greatest vivacity and warmth on both sides. Peter seemed the much-wished-for subject for determining the question. A genial fellow, Count Zinzendorf, who afterwards became so famous as the restorer and Ordinary of the Evangelical Brotherhood, as early as the beginning of 1726, made an application in London, to the Countess of Schaumburg-Lippe, for her interest, that Peter might be entrusted to his charge, in order that he might watch the developement of his innate ideas; but he received for answer that the king had made a present of him to the then Princess of Wales, afterwards Queen Caroline, well known as one of the most enlightened princesses of any age; and that she had confided him in trust to Dr Arbuthnot, the intimate friend of Pope and Swift, and the famous collaborator of *Gulliver's Travels*, still for the purpose of investigating the *innate ideas* of Wild Peter.

Swift himself has immortalized him, in his humorous production, *It cannot rain, but it pours*[1]. Linnæus gave him a niche in the *Systema Naturæ*, under the title of *Juvenis Hannoveranus:* and Buffon, de Pauw, and J. J. Rousseau, have extolled him as a specimen of the true natural man. Still more recently he has found an enthusiastic biographer in the famous Monboddo, who declares his appearance to be more remarkable than the discovery of Uranus, or than if astronomers, to the catalogue of stars already known, had added thirty thousand new ones[2].

---

[1] [Or, *London strewed with Rarities*, Ed.]
[2] "I consider his history as a brief chronicle or abstract of the history of the progress of human nature, from the mere animal to the first stage of civilised life." *Ancient Metaphysics*, Vol. III. p. 57.

IV.

Peter's Origin.

It is a pity, after all the importance which the great people attached to Wild Peter, that two little circumstances in the history of his discovery should be left out of sight, or neglected; which I will here repeat, as far as possible, from the earliest original documents, which I have before me. First, when Peter was, as I said, met with by the townsman of Hameln, the small fragment of a torn shirt was still fastened with string about his neck. Secondly, the singularly superior whiteness of his thighs compared to his legs, at his first entry into the town, occasioned and confirmed the remark of a townswoman, that the child must have worn breeches, but no stockings. Thirdly, upon closer examination, the tongue was found unusually thick, and little capable of motion, so that an army surgeon at Hameln thought of attempting an operation to set it free, but did not perform it. Fourthly, some boatmen related, that as they were descending in their boat from Poll, in the summer, they had seen at different times a poor naked child on the banks of the Weser, and had given him a piece of bread. Fifthly, it was soon ascertained, that Krüger, a widower of Lüchtringen, between Holzminden and Höxter, in Paderborn, had had a dumb child which had run away into the woods, in 1723, and had been found again in the following year, quite in a different place; but meanwhile his father had married a second time, and so he was shortly afterwards thrust out again by his new step-mother.

V.

Peter's Life and Conduct in London.

Dr Arbuthnot soon found out that no instructive discoveries in psychology or anthropology were to be expected from this imbecile boy; and so, after two months, at the request of the philosophic physician, a sufficient pension was settled upon him, and he was placed first with a chamber-woman of the Queen, and then with a farmer in Hertfordshire, where at last he ended his vegetatory existence as a kind of very old child, in Feb. 1785.

Peter was of middle size, but when grown up of fresh robust appearance, and strong muscular developement; his physiognomy was by no means so stupid; he had a respectable beard, and soon accustomed himself to a mixed diet of flesh, &c., but retained all his life his early love for onions. As he grew older he became more moderate in his eating, since in the first year of his captivity he took enough for two men. He relished a glass of brandy, he liked the fire, but he showed all his life the most perfect indifference for money, and what proves, above all, the more than brutish and invincible stupidity of Peter, just as complete an indifference for the other sex.

Whenever bad weather came on, he was always ill-tempered and sad. He was never able to speak properly. *Peter, ki scho,* and *qui ca* (by the two last words meaning to express the names of his two benefactors, *King George* and *Queen Caroline*), were the plainest of the few articulate sounds he was ever known to produce. He seemed to have a taste for music, and would hum over with satisfaction tunes of all kinds which he had often heard: and when an instrument was played, he would hop about with great delight until he was quite tired. No one, however, ever saw him laugh—that cheerful prerogative of mankind. In other respects he conducted himself as a good-natured, harmless, and obedient creature, so that he could be employed in all sorts of little domestic offices in the kitchen, or in the field. But they could not leave him alone to his own devices in these matters; for once when he was left alone by a cart of dung, which he had just been helping to load, he immediately on the same spot began diligently to unload it again.

He probably lost himself several times in the neighbourhood during the first ten years of his residence in England; but at all events one day, in 1746, he unwittingly strayed a long way, and at last got as far as Norfolk, where he was brought before a justice of the peace as the suspicious Unknown —this was at the time when there was a look-out for the supposed emissaries of the Pretender. As he did not speak, he was committed for the moment to the great prison-house in Norwich for safe custody. A great fire broke out there on that very night, so that the prison was opened as soon as possible, and the detained were let out. When after the first fright the prisoners were counted up, the most important of them all was missing, the dumb Unknown. A warder rushed through the flames of the wide prison, and found Peter sitting quietly at the back in his corner; he was enjoying the illumination and the agreeable warmth, and it was not without difficulty that he could be dragged forth: and soon afterwards, from the advertisements for lost things, he was recognized as the innocent Peter, and forwarded to his farmer again. Briefly, as an end to the tale, this pretended ideal of pure human nature, to which later sophists have elevated the wild Peter, was altogether nothing more than a dumb imbecile idiot.

VI.

Mistaken accounts by the biographers of Peter.

Meanwhile the history of this idiot is always remarkable, as a striking example of the uncertainty of human testimony and historical credibility. For it is surprising how divergent and partly contradictory are even the first contemporary accounts of the circumstances of his appearance in Hameln. No two stories agree in the year, season, or place where and when he was found by the townsman of Hameln, and brought into the city. The later printed stories are utterly wrong; how he was found by King George I. when hunting at Herrenhausen, or, according to others, on the Harz; how it was necessary to cut down the tree, on the top of which he had taken refuge, in order to get at him; how his body was covered with hair, and that he ran upon all-fours; how he jumped about trees like a squirrel;

how he was very clever in getting the baits out of wolves' traps; how he was carried over to England in an iron cage; how he learnt to speak in nine months at the Queen's court; how he was baptized by Dr Arbuthnot, and soon after died, &c.

VII.

Genuine sources for Peter's history.

I have critically examined everything that there is in print[1] about Wild Peter, and collected besides other accounts of the history of his discovery. The chief of these is a particular manuscript account by Severin, the Burgomaster of Hameln already mentioned, which he despatched in Feb. 1726 to the minister at Hanover, and for which I am indebted to the kindness of the most worthy master of the head school in Hameln, Avenarius. There are, besides, numerous national chronicles, and the unprinted collections of the chamberlain Redeker in the town-house of Hanover. With respect to his later mode of life in England, besides what I found out there myself, many of my friends there, such as the ambassadors of Hanover, Dr Dornford and M. Craufurd, have communicated to me accurate accounts, which they themselves got together in Hertfordshire itself, and which I have made use of.

As to the likenesses of Peter which are in existence, I possess two masterly engravings, which, I am assured, bear a close resemblance to him. The one is a great sheet, in a dark style,

---

[1] *Leipziger Zeitungen von gel. Sachen,* 1725, No. 104, 1726, Nos. 17, 61, 88. *Breslauer Sammlungen,* Vol. XXXIV. Dec. 1725, p. 659, Vol. XXXVI. Ap. 1726, p. 506.
Zuverlässige nachricht von dem bei Hameln gefundenen wildern knaben. Nebst dessen seltsame figur in Kupfer gestochen beifindlich, 1726. 4to.
Spangenberg's *Lehre des Gr. Zinzendorf,* II. B. p. 380.
Swift's *Works,* Vol. III. P. I, p. 132, ed. 1755, 4to.
Ein brief des Hamelschen Burgmeisters Palm, v. 1741, to C. F. Fein's *Entlarvter Fabel vom Ausgange der Hameleschen Kinder,* Hanov. 1749, 4to, p. 36.
Gentleman's Mag. Vol. XXI. 1751, p. 522, Vol. LV. 1785, P. I. pp. 113, 236, P. II. p. 851.
Monboddo, *Ancient Metaphysics,* Vol. III. Lond. 1784, 4to, pp. 57, 367.
[Comp. *Peter the Wild Boy. An enquiry how the Wild Youth lately taken in the woods near Hanover,* &c. &c. 12mo. Lond.—A copy in the Brit. Mus. Ed.]

by Val. Green, from the picture by P. Falconet; it represents him as sitting, a full-length figure, in about his fiftieth year, and was painted at London in 1767, when he was presented to the king. The other is by Bartolozzi, after the three-quarter figure painted by J. Alefounder three years before Peter's death, quite a well-looking old man, whom any one who knew no better, might suppose to be more cunning than he looked.

VIII.

Peter compared with other so-called wild children.

It seems, perhaps, well worth the pains once for all to examine and settle critically the accounts of poor Peter, who has been considered of so much importance by so many of our greatest naturalists, sophists, &c.; principally, because this is the first story which can be set forth according to the real facts: for all the other instances of so-called wild children, almost without exception, are mixed up with so many beyond measure extraordinary and astonishing untruths or contradictions, that their credibility has become in consequence highly problematical altogether.

Taking those instances only, which Linnæus has set out in his rubric on the *Homo sapiens* Ferus, and with which he has introduced his *Systema Naturæ*; his *Juvenis ovinus Hibernus*, who when sixteen years old was carried about as a show in Holland, where he was described by the elder Tulp[1], even entirely according to that account was an imbecile, dumb, and also outwardly deformed creature, but which could hardly have grown up from the cradle among wild sheep in Ireland, because they exist no more there than anywhere else. That he eat grass and hay at Amsterdam in the presence of astonished beholders, is, I think, just as credible, as that the pretended South-sea Islander from Tanna, who some years ago was carried round at harvest-

---

[1] *Obs. Med.* lib. IV. c. X. p. 196, fifth ed. L.B. 1716.

time and fairs, used to munch stones. Besides the extraordinary description, which that otherwise so worthy Burgomaster of Amsterdam gives us of this boy, and also the fact, that so far as I know, no contemporary or even more recent author upon the natural history of Ireland, alludes to him even by a single word, makes me extremely suspicious on the matter; and at all events, I do not think it worth the attention which has been bestowed upon it by our own Schlözer and Herder.

As to the *Juvenis bovinus Bambergensis* of Linnæus, so far as I know, we have no other testimony, except what we are told by the worthy Ph. Camerarius, who says[1], that this Bamberg savage, who at that time had entered into the condition of holy matrimony, informed him that he had been brought up on the neighbouring hills by the cows.

More precise, but still more suspicious, is the account of the eight years old *Juvenis lupinus Hessensis* of 1344 (not 1554, as Linnæus[2] and all his copyists give out), who celebrated the good reception which he had met with from the wolves when they had carried him off about five years before. They had made him a soft nest of leaves, laid all round him, and kept him warm, brought him a share of their spoil[3], &c.

Much also must, at all events, be subtracted from the *Juvenis ursinus Lithuanus;* as, for instance, what we are assured by the authority, the imaginative Connor, in his *Medicina Mystica seu de Miraculis*[4], that it is nothing uncommon in Poland for a bear giving suck, if it happens to find a child, to take it to its lair, and bring it up from its own breast. Many instances indeed are given by the elder Joh. Dan. Geyer, in his monograph *On the Lithuanian Bear-men;* one Poluck bear-man in particular of about eight or nine years old, whom

---

[1] *Oper. horar. subsecivar. Cent.* I. p. 343, ed. 1602.
[2] [In the tenth ed. Linnæus wrote, 1344: the 5 in the twelfth ed. is probably therefore a misprint. Blumenbach seems to me always inclined to bear hard upon Linnæus. ED.]
[3] *Additiones ad Lamberti Schafnaburg. Appendix ab Erphesfordensi monacho anon.* in Pistorii *scrip. rer. a Germ. gestar.* Frf. 1613, fol. p. 264.
[4] p. 133, ed. 1699. Comp. the *History of Poland*, Lond. 1698, 8vo. Vol. I. p. 342; where a little Polack is represented in a respectable copperplate, as to sucked the old bear-mother between two young bears.

King John III. met with, and had baptized; and who was made fife-player to the militia, notwithstanding that he preferred going on four feet instead of two[1].

It is said of the *Puella Transisilana*[2] that she was about eighteen years old, when, in the winter of 1717, she was caught in a net on a search-hunt organized for that purpose by one thousand Krauenburg peasants. She was quite naked except for a scanty straw apron, her skin had become hard and black, but in a little time after her capture it fell off, and upon that a beautiful fresh skin came to light, &c. (I have kept quite close to the account of the witnesses.)

In other respects this wild girl was very friendly, and of good cheerful temper, and was stolen from her parents when a little child in May, 1700.

The *Puella Campanica*, as she was called by Linnæus, or Mad^{lle} le Blanc, according to her French biographers[3], who considered her as an Esquimaux girl sent to France, was first of all observed in the water, where two girls about the size of children of ten years old, and armed with clubs, swam about and ducked in and out like water-hens. They soon quarrelled about a chaplet of roses, which they found; one of them was struck on the head by the other, but she immediately bound up the wound with a plaster made out of a frog's skin tied with a strip of bark. Since then, however, she was seen no more, but Mad^{lle} le Blanc, the victress, covered only with rags and skins, and with a gourd-bottle instead of a bonnet on her head, was entrapped into a neighbouring &c.

Johannes Leodicensis was, according to the account of the credulous Digby[4] a peasant youth of Liege, who ran away for

---

[1] ["A man of credit assured me, that there was found in *Denmark*, a young man of about fourteen or fifteen years old, who lived in the woods with the bears, and who could not be distinguished from them but by his shape. They took him, and learned him to speak; he said then, he could remember nothing but only since the time they took him from amongst the bears." *Life of Vanini*, Anon. 1714. ED.]

[2] *Breal. Samml.* xxii. a. 437.

[3] *Hist. d'une jeune fille sauvage*, Par. 1755. 8vo.

[4] In *Two Treatises, in the one of which the nature of Bodies in the other the nature of Mans sou's is looked into.* Paris, 1644. fol. p. 247.

fear when the soldiers plundered his village into the forest of Ardennes, and lodged there for many years, and lived upon roots, wild pears, and acorns.

There still remain, what are called by Linnæus, *Pueri Pyrenaici* of 1719, on whose traces however I have not yet been able to come again[1]. Meanwhile, what I have here set down about the others will, I hope, tend to give the proper value to those wonderful and various stories about these pretended men of nature in a philosophic natural history of mankind.

IX.

Neither Peter nor any other Homo sapiens ferus of Linnæus can serve as a Specimen of the original Man of Nature.

If we make a fair deduction from the really too tasteless fictions in those stories, and let the rest pass muster ever so indulgently, still it will be at once seen, that these were altogether unnatural deformed creatures, and yet, what also goes very much to show how abnormal they were, no two of them were at all like each other, according to any critical comparison of the accounts we have of them. Taken altogether, they were very unmanlike, but each in his own way, according to the standard of his own individual wants, imperfections, and unnatural properties. Only in this were they like each other, that contrary to the instinct of nature, they lived alone, separated from the society of men, wandering about here and there; a condition, whose opposition to what is natural has been already compared by Voltaire to that of a lost solitary bee[2].

---

[1] [But see *Antient Metaphysics*, Vol. IV. pp. 37, 38, and the Spanish work, *Sommario Erudito*, of 1788, there referred to. ED.]

[2] "If one meets with a wandering bee, ought one to conclude that the bee is in a state of pure nature, and that those who work in company in the hive have degenerated?" Comp. also Filangieri, *Scienza della legislazione*, T. I. p. 64, second ed.

X.

Above all no originally Wild Condition of Nature is to be attributed to Man, who is born a domestic animal.

Man is a domestic animal[1]. But in order that other animals might be made domestic about him, individuals of their species were first of all torn from their wild condition, and made to live under cover, and become tame; whereas he on the contrary was born and appointed by nature the most completely domesticated animal. Other domestic animals were first brought to that state of perfection *through him*. He is the only one who brought *himself* to perfection.

But whilst so many other domestic animals, as cats, goats, &c. when they by accident return to the wilderness, very soon degenerate into the natural condition of the wild species; so on the other hand, as I have said, all those so-called wild children in their other behaviour, and nature, &c., strikingly differed one from another, for the very reason that they had no originally wild species to degenerate into, for such a race of mankind, which is the most perfect of all sorts of domestic animals that have been created, no where exists, nor is there any position, any mode of life, or even climate which would be suitable for it.

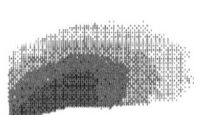

---

[1] Comp. Part I. s. VIII.

GÖTTINGISCHE

GELEHRTE ANZEIGEN.

177 STÜCK.

DEN 4 NOVEMBER, 1853.

GÖTTINGEN.

REMARKS
ON AN
HIPPOCRATIC MACROCEPHALUS,
BY
J. F. BLUMENBACH[1].

The lecture delivered by the Chief Physician-Royal, Blumenbach, in the sitting of the Royal Society, of the 3rd August, consisted of a *Spicilegium observationum de generis humani varietate nativa*, a subject, that since his inaugural dissertation which appeared under this title nearly sixty years ago, the author has always taken pleasure in working at. It was only something on the national characteristics of the three chief races among the five, into which he had thought it most according to nature to divide mankind. Therefore, first of the Caucasian stem, or middle race; and of its two extremes, which are secondly, the Ethiopian, and thirdly, the Mongolian.

Of the first race we have but one skull, but that of the very greatest interest. An old Hippocratic macrocephalus from the Black Sea, exactly answering to the description given by the father of medicine in his golden treatise *On air, water, and soil.* Blumenbach owed this present for his rich collection of national skulls to the kindness of the excellent and much travelled physician of Augsburg, Dr Stephan, who, at the very time when the Russian Government had the ancient funeral mounds of the kings of the Bosphorus opened, which exist on the water-shed of the steppe hills in the vicinity of Kertch (the Panticapæum of the ancients) happened to be there, and obtained the skull in

---

[1] *Götting. gelehrte Anzeig.* 177 st. B. II. s. 1761.

question. This exactly resembles in shape the others which were found there with it. On account of the great age of the burial place it was very rotten and fragile. This was also the case with the other skulls, which were laid by him previously before the Royal Society, of old Greeks, Germans, Cimbrians, Tschudis, &c. which have been described in their *Transactions*. The striking characteristic of the Tauric Macrocephalus, of which we are now speaking, displays itself in a high, but not much vaulted forehead: the parietal bones on the other hand being exceedingly high, quite macrocephalic. The sagittal suture, as well as the other two principal sutures of the occiput were quite obliterated.

Secondly, of the Ethiopian race, which indeed at the first glance contrasts so forcibly with the others that one can easily understand the exclamation of the naturalist Pliny: "Who would have believed in an Ethiopian before he had seen him?" Almost exactly at the same time as that ancient long-headed skull Blumenbach received from his old friend and pupil, Kaufmann, the court physician of Hanover, something of just as great importance to him for his collection, although of quite another kind. It was the fresh clean head of a negro boy from Congo, who had died unfortunately in his fifteenth year, and who might be considered as the most perfect ideal of this race of man. This gave the author of the lecture an opportunity of passing a critical review upon many of the to a great extent groundless assertions on the bodily peculiarities of the negro, which he refuted by the exhibition of preparations. Amongst these were some embryos, and this gave him an opportunity of saying something also on the third principal race,

The Mongolian: not, indeed, upon the character of their skulls, of which Blumenbach, through the kindness of the never-to-be-forgotten Baron von Asch, possesses a most instructive series; but only to contrast with those unborn negroes the fœtus of a female Calmuck three months old, already possessed of the expressive national physiognomy, displaying, namely, that striking oblique direction of the bifurcation of the eyelids towards the root of the nose. . BL.

NACHRICHTEN

VON DER G. A. UNIVERSITÄT UND DER KÖNIGL.
GESELLSCHAFT DER WISSENSCHAFTEN
ZU GÖTTINGEN.

OCTOBER 6.   NO. 11.   1858.

UNIVERSITÄT.

DIE ANTHROPOLOGISCHE SAMMLUNG DES
PHYSIOLOGISCHEN INSTITUTS.

GÖTTINGEN.

ON

THE ANTHROPOLOGICAL COLLECTION OF THE PHYSIOLOGICAL INSTITUTE OF GÖTTINGEN,

BY

PROFESSOR RUDOLPH WAGNER.

WHEN after the death of the respected Blumenbach (Jan. 22, 1840) the undersigned received his summons to this University, and entered upon his present post in the autumn of 1840, the collection of the venerable naturalist had previously by the care of the Curatorium been purchased from the heirs, and the greater part of it had already been incorporated in the Academical Institute. The most valuable part of it was undeniably the collection of skulls, which Blumenbach, supported by pupils of his scattered over all parts of the world, and other numerous donors, had been collecting zealously for his whole life, and which it is well known had served him as the principal foundation for his investigations on the natural history of mankind. Together with the Craniological Collection there was ranked a more extensive body of materials for completing the knowledge of the different accompanying conditions of form and structure in respect of Ethnology, and for illustrating the Lectures on the General Natural History of Mankind.

Already, in 1795, Blumenbach had given a sketch of this, as well of the Craniological Collection, which he incorporated with the third edition of his famous treatise *De generis humani varietate nativa*, under the title *Index suppellectilis anthropologicæ auctoris, qua in adornanda nova hacce editione maxime usus est.* He divided the apparatus into five parts. The first division comprised the eighty-two race-skulls then existing in his Collection, separately detailed, and of which he had already represented thirty in the three first Decades of his *Decades craniorum*. Blumenbach here remarked that his craniological collection was unique of its kind, and that the richest museums of that sort then in Europe, namely, the anatomical collections of John Hunter and Peter Camper could not be compared with it. The other divisions of the so-called anthropological collection consisted of anatomical preparations, specimens of the skin and hair of different nations, and some embryos; then, very good drawings, especially some by the hand, paintings, also engravings, and besides excellent portraits of distinguished individuals of different nations of our planet, executed in water-colours, oil, and crayons.

All this material was handed over by the heirs to the University, and likewise most of the original manuscripts of Blumenbach's works on general natural history, and upon the races of man: they were first of all deposited in the rooms of the academical museum allotted to me, until the erection of the physiological institute in which the whole collection was arranged in the year 1842; where it remains in its entirety under the name of the Blumenbachian Anthropological Museum, in lasting remembrance of that highly deserving man. At present it fills two rooms. In the first room are the skulls, arranged in cabinets on the walls; outside which in like manner stand a collection of plaster casts; and in the middle are some mummies: whilst the other room contains the remaining objects, especially the portraits. From what Blumenbach himself left we have 245 whole skulls and fragments, and an Egyptian and Guanche mummy.

So far as my means and the great difficulty of making acquisitions in an inland country, have permitted, I have endeavoured to make the Collection still more complete. But up to the present time I have been only moderately successful. By purchase we have obtained some interesting mummies and skulls from Peru, which Dr von Tschudi had collected; and I have lately received as a legacy from Professor de Fremery in Utrecht some skulls and the skeleton of a negro. H. M. King Louis of Bavaria, liberal as he had already shown himself in donations to Blumenbach, sent us some years ago seven in part very well preserved skulls from an old cemetery at Nordendorf on the Lech (probably of the second and third century), which were found on the occasion of making the railroad. His Highness the Graf von Görtz Schlitz, who as a pupil of our high school had always kept up a friendly recollection of it, sent us five old Peruvian skulls, which he had dug up himself on the spot, and in the place, on his voyage round the world. Professor Carl Schmidt of Dorpat, likewise a pupil of the Georgia Augusta, presented us with two Lett skulls; Professor Bidder, of Dorpat, added to them an Esthonian skull. To my brother, Dr Moritz Wagner, we owe two skulls from the Crimea and a Greek skull. In this way, and by some recently prepared skulls, some of them murderers for example, the number of skulls and fragments of skulls has reached 310.

The want of skeletons has always been very great; the few left behind by Blumenbach were very defective and useless. Now the Collection possesses several Europeans of different ages, and a well-prepared negro skeleton.

Besides the Egyptian and Guanche mummies we have three Peruvian mummies. Some mummified heads, for example one of a New Zealander, some negro heads in spirits of wine, &c.

As for the Craniological Collection, it can no longer pass for the richest existing. That of Morton, which is now in Philadelphia, is already much richer. Still it has much that is interesting, as will be seen from the following summary, in which, for the most part, I follow the old arrangement of Blumenbach.

A. PEOPLES OF THE OLD WORLD.

I. Caucasian Races (Indo-Atlantic peoples).

- 2 Indian.
- 1 Persian.
- 3 Georgian.
- 1 Lesghi.
- 1 Armenian.
- 4 Gipsy.
- 5 Greek.
- 6 Turk.
- 7 Italian.
- 1 Old Etruscan.
- 5 Old Roman.
- 6 French.
- 1 Lotharingian.
- 1 Burgundian.
- 1 Spaniard.
- 3 English.
- 1 Irish.
- 5 Scot.
- 1 Hebridean.
- 1 Dane.

- 1 Icelander.
- 1 Norwegian.
- 8 Hollander.
- 1 Wend.
- 1 Bohemian.
- 3 Hungarian.
- 1 Pole.
- 4 Lithuanian.
- 1 Esthonian.
- 2 Slavonian.
- 2 Galician.
- 22 Russian.
- 5 Cossack.
- 3 Finns.
- 4 Lapps.
- 2 Old Tschudi.
- 1 Bulgarian.
- 4 Jew.
- 4 Egyptian mummy skulls.
- The remainder German.

II. Mongolian Races (Asiatic nations).

- 10 Tartar.
- 7 Calmuck.
- 2 Baschkir.
- 1 Samoiede.
- 1 Kamtschatdale.
- 1 Tschuvasch.

- 1 Korak.
- 2 Tungus.
- 1 Yakute.
- 1 Burat.
- 2 Burman.
- 9 Chinese.

III. Woolly-haired African Nations (Ethiopian race).

16 Negro skulls.
1 Mulatto.
1 Kafir.
1 Hottentot.
1 Bushman.

B. Peoples of the New World.

IV. Americana.

3 Esquimaux.
4 Greenlanders.
1 Kornäger from Kadjük.
1 Illinois.
4 From Missouri.
2 From Columbia River (artificially flattened).
2 Carib (one artificially flattened).
1 Huanca (Peru, artif. deformed).

1 Mexican.
3 Schitgaganen.
2 Algonquin.
1 Iroquois.
1 Modern Peruvian.
8 Chincha-Peruvian (some artif. deformed).
1 Atura.
1 Botocudo.
6 Brazilian.
1 From Guiana.

V. Malays and South-Sea Islanders.

6 Javanese.
3 From Bali.
2 From Celebes.
1 Mestizo from Celebes.
2 From Madeira.

1 From Otaheite.
2 Nukuhiva.
2 From New Holland.
1 Papuan.

The remaining skulls have reference to congenital departures from the ordinary form, or pathological alterations, as microcephaly, hydrocephalus, &c.

In the original collection the plastic representation of the outward forms of races was limited to one bust of a negro and one of a Botocudo, both moreover of indifferent workmanship.

Much credit is due to Professor von Launitz of Frankfort for his exertions in promoting this above all important, but very much neglected means of forwarding the knowledge of the natural history of mankind by the aid of plaster-casts. He has executed a new though even now unfortunately small series of race-busts with great fidelity to nature and artistic handling, from individuals who came in his way at Frankfort.

I have obtained some beautiful casts for our collection of busts executed by Herr von Launitz. They are as follows:

Benjamin Gattegna, Constantinopolitan Jew.
Grassman, Jew.
Muhamed, Bedouin.
Hassan, Nubian.
Abdallah, Negro.
Zeno Orego, bearded negro from Guadaloupe.
Native North-American.
Chinese.
Cast from the head of a Chinese.
A Gipsy Girl.
Model of the face of an Hungarian, by Fr. Küsthardt, done by a young sculptor of Göttingen.

A Phrenological Collection, based upon genuine busts after the life, is now for the first time in process of being made. The above-named young artist, Fr. Küsthardt, has already got some materials together for it. There is no department so much in want of critically selected materials as this, which has been so seldom treated scientifically.

Another kind of collection, which is now equally for the first time projected, would be that of the form of the foreheads in different individuals. A number of foreheads with the form preserved as much as possible is ready collected, and it seems that a careful comparison of the foreheads of different individuals might really lead to very interesting results, on which perhaps I may say more at another opportunity. Unfortunately no one in Europe appears as yet to have thought of making a collection of race-foreheads of any size, though this must be an important business for the future.

I have also endeavoured to promote the collection of representations of different nations and tried to complete it, and consequently have had the necessity of instruction or education especially before my eyes.

With the interest, which very lately the natural history of Ethnography has excited, in consequence of the notorious disputes about the origin of mankind, I became particularly alive to the necessity of anthropological collections of that sort. Much lies scattered in private collections in Holland and England, and a fresh youthful vigour which would give itself up with zeal and a spirit of investigation to this task, and study the museums in Europe and North America with this object, might bring interesting results to light. I had in earlier years proposed to myself the task at some time or other of editing an anatomy of the races and nations of man, and looked upon my natural history of mankind, published twenty-six years ago, as a juvenile prelude. But the difficulties, first of getting together sufficient materials and then of inspecting with that object all the public and private collections in Europe were so great, that I have long since been obliged to give up this plan, especially since my health has for some years past begun to fail me. The preservation and enlarging of the Blumenbachian Museum, and the utilization of the same partly for the purposes of instruction and partly for foreign inquirers, I have considered incumbent on me as a positive duty. In general, however, the furtherance of anatomical, physiological and zoological investigation in the last ten years has been turned so much in other directions, that the Collection has been used less than I could have wished both by native and foreign students, and in fact has only been honoured with an ordinary inspection. I have, however, pleasure in mentioning these gentlemen: Henle, Huschke, Van der Hoeven, Retzius, Tourtual, Von Tschudi, and Andr. Wagner, who, sometimes in my company, and sometimes alone, have gone through our Collection, and in part have made public use of it for their own inquiries.

The notice given of it now is perhaps sufficient to attract anew the attention of foreign inquirers to our little museum. It seems scarcely necessary to remark that our material is much too scanty for any extended questions upon the individuality and affinity of the nations of our planet. We must have not single, but hundreds of skulls of one and the same nation, to settle certain questions. Blumenbach, with the eye of genius, though from very slender materials, early drew the ground lines, and accurately recognized the typical differences. We have only got beyond Blumenbach's investigations and results in some particulars, and on the whole not much and not essentially. The longer we busy ourselves about the subject, the more again and again we shall have to come back to the ground-plan and the divisions of Blumenbach. Still here I must mention above all as to the present time the works of the famous Retzius[1] in Stockholm, who has himself got together a great apparatus, and must be considered at present as by far the greatest proficient in scientific ethnology.

With respect to our Collection I may remark, that its greatest wealth and value consists in the skulls of Asiatic (Mongolian) nations, which—perhaps with the exception of that of St Petersburgh—are still probably very uncommon in all collections. Nearly all these skulls came from a grateful pupil of Blumenbach, whom he often mentions, the imperial physician, Dr von Asch, in St Petersburgh. Notwithstanding my narrow means and small opportunity for acquisition, I have especially laboured to enlarge the series of particular nations. From this point of view the Negro, the Peruvian, and the Chinese skulls present a particular interest. With a special view to that object, viz. the bringing together large numbers of skulls of one and the same people, I am anxious for assistance

---

[1] [The anthropological works of Retzius (now deceased), have been collected, and are in process of translation for the Society by A. Higgins, Esq. ED.]

from foreign inquirers as well as from naturalists, and grateful should I be in this respect for such support as has lately been given me by Herr Professor Schröder van der Kolk, of Utrecht. Especially, however, should I be thankful for the acquisition of information about well-formed foreheads of known individuals amongst the nations of Europe, or the foreign races of man.

R. WAGNER.

Göttingen,
Sept. 16, 1856.

DISPUTATIO INAUGURALIS

QUÆDAM DE HOMINUM VARIETATIBUS,
ET HARUM CAUSIS EXPONENS,

QUAM ANNUENTE SUMMO NUMINE EX AUCTORITATE
REVERENDI ADMODUM VIRI

GULIELMI ROBERTSON, S.S.T.P.
ACADEMIÆ EDINBURGENÆ PRÆFECTI;

NECNON AMPLISSIMI SENATUS ACADEMICI CONSENSU ET
NOBILISSIMÆ FACULTATIS MEDICÆ DECRETO
PRO GRADU DOCTORIS,
SUMMISQUE IN MEDICINA HONORIBUS ET PRIVILEGIIS
RITE ET LEGITIME CONSEQUENDIS; ERUDITORUM
EXAMINI SUBJICIT

JOANNES HUNTER,
SCOTO-BRITANNUS, SOCIET. MED. SOC. HON.

"The spacious West,
And all the teeming regions of the South,
Hold not a quarry, to the curious flight
Of knowledge, half so tempting or so fair
As man to man."
Akenside.

PRID. ID. JUNII, HORA LOCOQUE SOLITIS.

EDINBURGI:
APUD BALFOUR ET SMELLIE,
ACADEMIÆ TYPOGRAPHOS.
M.DCC.LXXV.
1785

AN INAUGURAL DISSERTATION,

BY

JOHN HUNTER, M.D. F.R.S.[1]

It is not necessary for me when going to write about the varieties of man, and the causes of them, to try and prove the importance of the subject. Much has been written by many about animated beings, nature, and the gods; and there are and have been those, who have attempted to gauge the strength and faculties of the human mind. But nothing has yet been written clearly by any writer upon the matters which regard the

---

[1] Many persons, amongst others, J. A. Meigs of Philadelphia, have been under the idea (see Nott and Gliddon, *Indigenous Races of Man*, p. 216), deceived by the similarity of name, that this treatise is the production of the celebrated surgeon John Hunter. A consideration of the date 1775, would have been quite enough to prove the contrary, nor does *the* Hunter appear at any time to have taken the degree of M.D. Not much is known about the author. He was a physician to the army, and wrote some papers on the health of the service, which are to be found in the medical journals. The principal interest attaching to this treatise arises from the fact that it appeared in the very same year, and a month or two before the more famous work of Blumenbach on the same subject. It is very inferior in its mode of treating the subject to the effort of the German naturalist; nor does the author seem to have prosecuted his researches further in this direction. Still anthropology has progressed so very little, that some parts of it are quite on a level with the science of the present day, and it may still be read with interest. The original has become very rare, though four copies are to be found in the British Museum; but it has been thought that a translation would be acceptable to many who might not care to wade through the Latin of a modern physician.

external appearance of man, his countenance, his colour, the dimensions of his body, and other similar topics. Yet it cannot be denied for a moment that many diversities and anomalies do exist among men. Do not those who spring from the same race, and are born of the same parents, differ from each other in temperament, health, strength, stature, colour, form, and above all, in disposition and power of mind? And a greater difference is found between those who live in different climates, and inhabit widely-separated regions of the earth, very diverse from each other. Others differ also by being of a white or black colour, of a handsome or ugly body, by softness of disposition or the reverse, and by polished or rude manners. Such important discrepancies, so well known to all, supply a mass of materials quite sufficient for philosophers, and those who investigate nature, to employ themselves upon. Many[1] who have considered these questions, and endeavoured to ascertain their causes, have thought them too great to be ascribed to natural causes, but that they should be referred to the will of the Governor of all things, the supreme Law of nature, as if He had in the beginning marked out men by so many diverse distinctions. Now if we take up this mode of philosophizing, and attribute everything for which we can give no reason to the Divine interference, we shut the door and stop up all the sources from which all those things spring which adorn life, promote the arts, and finally increase the force and the faculties of the human mind. And therefore it is worth while first of all to inquire what amount of proof there may be for the opinion of those who impute all diversities to the Deity, and therefore imagine man to consist of different species.

Those who believe in the diversity of species contend that the diversities are such that they cannot be explained in any other way, whether by climate or other external causes. What, they ask, is the cause of the copper colour and the beardless chin of the Americans? or of the black teats of the Samoide

---

[1] *Sketches of the History of Man*, Vol. 1. Bk. 1.

women? of the black colour and thick lips of the Africans? of the swelling pudenda of the female inhabitants of the Cape of Good Hope? What man has ever explained these and similar things? So they affirm these things cannot be explained, but must be attributed to God[1].

How much this superstition, which refers everything that seems to us inexplicable, to the Divine hand and the will of God, stands in the way of science, has been said above.

Besides these diversities which it is true we cannot explain, there occur others equally inexplicable, where the notion of a diversity of species cannot be entertained. Who has ever explained the high cheek-bones of the Scotch? No one; but is that a reason for considering them a different species? Nor has any explanation ever yet been given for the blue eyes of the Goths[2]. And are they then of a different species? By this mode of reasoning, it would follow that there are different species in the same family.

In order to prove diversity of species, writers have had recourse even to the mental faculties[3]. This one is brave; that man timid. How then can they be of the same species? This man receives strangers with pleasure; that one keeps them off as much as ever he can. Are they therefore of the same species?

If this were so, and discrepancies of this kind were accepted for signs and certain proofs of diversities of species, would not different species be produced in almost every single family? Could it not be said of the same man at different times that he is in like way was of a different species from himself?

Those who defend this opinion of the diversity of species, not content with these arguments, seek out others from the Final Cause. For inasmuch as the regions inhabited by man are excessively different in climate, soil, heat, and innumerable other points, therefore they believe that different species of

---

[1] *Sketches of the History of Man*, Vol. I. p. 12.
[2] Linn. *Fauna Suecica*, p. 1. [3] *Sk. of the Hist. of Man*, Vol. I. p. 15.

men were necessarily accommodated to different regions¹. But who can say that it is not more agreeable to perfect wisdom to have given to different animals that kind of nature, by which they could easily accommodate themselves to whatever might happen, than to have created a fresh species adapted to each change of external circumstances?

This question has with justice been most fiercely agitated, for it is by no means one of mere curiosity. For if it be allowed that men are of different species, then they must be so considered in medical, natural, civil, and theological disquisitions, and lastly, in all works which treat of man; and whatever might be said of one species, might possibly be most erroneously predicated of another.

For if it were so, it would be incredible that the Wisdom which framed the universe should have created different species, distinguished only by colour, or thick lips, or a depressed nose, and not of a different nature, and intended for some particular end. So, whatever learned men have written about one species, which has been applied to another, falls to the ground; and the sources of reasoning, from which it has often been thought that truth is derived, that is the comparisons made between various nations, are altogether sealed up. But what are we to think of those, who, although they consider men to vary in species, nevertheless persist in discoursing of man, as if he were always in all regions and in every place the same?

There is another error which must be noticed here. Whilst authors dispute in this way with each other about *species*, they do not explain what sense they attach to that word. The definition given by Ray, and adopted by Buffon, they reject as refuted, but they give no other in its place. And yet, without in any way defining species, they go on to pronounce the species of men to be different. But this is surely quite unjustifiable, unless the meaning of the word *species* is first of all explained.

As this is the case, in order that others may not make the

---

¹ *Sketches of the History of Man*, Vol. I. p. 10.

same objection to us, pray accept our definition of the word *species*, and our idea of the way in which these notions are conceived in the mind.

As all our ideas of everything arise from nature, and its contemplation, so from the same source, and not from the dogmas of the schools, or the disquisitions of logic, is the meaning of the word *species* to be deduced. Whoever looks round the earth, will find it full of animals, everywhere offering themselves to his eyes, and will find amongst some of them an almost perfect resemblance, and a very strong affinity, but amongst more, the greatest possible difference. He who examines this diversity or congruity, will quickly come to distribute animals into various classes, according to their various likenesses or unlikenesses. And since nature, as they say, makes no leaps, it frequently happens, that animals are at the same time so like and so unlike each other, that it is sometimes doubtful to which class any particular one should be referred.

What is to be the rule, or criterion for deciding this? If any two animals, whose likeness to each other is not quite perfect enough to compel one to assign them to the same species, produce an offspring which is either at once like, or afterwards becomes like either parent; then however they may differ from each other in many points, yet they must be considered to be of the same species. And with these preliminary observations, this is the way in which I think species should be defined.

A class of animals, of which the members procreate with each other, and the offspring of which also procreate other animals, which are either like their class, or afterwards become so.

This definition of species may be conveniently illustrated by taking an instance from man, about whom our business now is. Take, of all who bear the name of man, a man and a woman most widely different from each other; let the one be a most beautiful Circassian woman and the other an African born in Guinea, as black and ugly as possible. Take, moreover, as you certainly may, the males and females sprung from this pair, and join the children of the latter in marriage with their maternal race, and the children of the former with the paternal, and then, if after several generations the offspring of the female becomes in all things to resemble the mother, and the offspring of the male the father, we may come to the definite conclusion that the parents were of the same species. That this is a fact, is proved every day by the unions of the black and the white. And if any one denies the truth of this definition, what order, what certainty does he leave in the animal kingdom? One species may change into another. The ox may become a horse, the ape a man. And if reason and common sense did not revolt from such absurd and monstrous positions, some would eagerly declare that such things might take place. Let a man look round the world, and contemplate nature. What does he find? Does the varied appearance of things supply any proofs by which such a notion can be confirmed? Have not the classes of animals always remained distinct up to this time? and why should they not remain so for ever? A lawless and blind wish has often desired the existence of such mutations, and even of new genera, if it were possible. And many have tried very hard to bring about something of the kind, but no one has yet succeeded in making a new species, or turning one into another. From all which we may conclude that each and every species of animals has been circumscribed within fixed boundaries from the beginning by Divine Wisdom; and no desire, like those which are contrary to the laws of nature, is strong enough to cause nature's divisions, that is, her animals to be commingled, or disordered. And in truth, about most animals there is no doubt, because they are distinguished at the first glance, by external appearance, and manifest tokens; and the sole contention is about man, and a few other species, principally of the domestic animals. As to these there are two reasons, why writers have had doubts about them. First, because every variety and aberration from the general order takes place before our eyes, and is most easily observed. The second and more powerful reason is, because animals, placed under our care, entirely contrary to their instincts, and subjected to duties and modes of life which do not at all suit them, for this reason especially, and all the more, the more care we take of them, become altered[1].

The varieties of dogs seem almost infinite; for they pass their lives with men, suffer like them, and share their sports and their hearths. If any one should say that the varieties of dogs indicate a diversity of species, would it not be the same thing as to affirm that the dog can carry different species at the same time in its womb? For it is common enough for a bitch to bring forth in the same litter varieties of whelps, which varieties such persons would call species. And to those who think what they call the different and permanent orders of dogs are of great weight in proving them to be of different species, we may answer that no such orders are permanent and constant without the careful interference of man. Who does not know how difficult it is to produce the *Canis Gallicus* (*Graius* Linn.) or the *Canis Odorus* (*Sagax* Linn[1])?

For these reasons, my opinion is that men must be held to be of the same species. And as in the vegetable kingdom, the same species sometimes comprehends many varieties, which all depend upon the climate, the soil, and cultivation, so to use the language of botanists, the diversities of men are to be considered as varieties of the same species, and, in the same way, to be deduced from natural causes.

No one can be ignorant how much influence events have in affecting and changing men. On these depend almost all disorders, and the numerous changes in the human body. To explain properly their effects and the varieties of the human species, and to show clearly how they take place, not only is an intimate knowledge of human nature required, as far as regards its motions and mutations, and its increase and decrease, but also a deep knowledge is necessary of all things which can affect man, so far as regards their qualities, and mode of action. For to give an explanation of how two bodies act upon each other, the nature of each must be understood. Who possesses this science? Who has explained the nature of the human body?

---

[1] Buffon, Vol. XII. p. 193; Paris, 1770, 12mo.

Who has investigated the powers of nature? No one. Many things are obscure, which can only be brought to light by great labour, and the united powers of many men in a long space of time. Thus it will easily be understood how difficult is the task I have imposed upon myself. I approach it, however, not from any love of writing, but from a sort of necessity. And so far from being sorry, I shall be glad, if, as I may hope, these my endeavours will call away able men, especially at this time, when natural history is so flourishing, from shells and butterflies, to studies worthy of man.

In order that I may conduct my work on some plan, I have thought it best to divide it into four parts; in the first of which I shall treat of the colour of men; in the second, of stature and form; in the third, of the excess or defect of parts, or other differences; and in the fourth, of the mental faculties. These chapters will comprise almost everything which all the curious investigators of this planet have seen and told.

Chapter I.

Of Colour.

THE varieties of colour are wonderful. Thus in men we meet with white, black, brown, copper-colour; lastly, all shades between white and black, some having one, and others another. And in order to show this more clearly, I have subjoined a table of the colours of man, as they differ according to race, which I put forward, not as an absolutely correct history of colours, but only as an example and specimen of varieties.

Table of Colours.

Black.	Africans under the direct rays of the Sun. Inhabitants of New Guinea, and of New Batavia.

TABLE OF COLOURS. 367

Sub-black.	The Moors of Northern Africa.
	The Hottentots, dwelling towards the south of the Continent.
Copper-coloured.	The East-Indians[1].
Red.	Americans[2].
Brown.	Tartars.
	Persians.
	Arabs.
	Africans dwelling on the Mediterranean Sea.
	Chinese[3].
Light brown.	Southern Europeans.
	Sicilians.
	Abyssinians.
	Spanish.
	Turks and others.
	Samoeides and Laplanders.
White.	Almost all the remaining Europeans, as
	Swedes.
	Danes.
	English.
	Germans.
	Poles and others.
	Kabardinski[4].
	Georgians.
	Mingrelians[5].

What is the cause of such different colours? To this the answer is difficult. Yet many philosophers have attempted to discover it. Those who borrow their philosophy from Scripture,

---

[1] These although they vary in colour, as being a little darker or lighter, all more or less approach a copper colour.
[2] This colour scarcely differs from copper. Those who inhabit the Northern part of America are so much whiter, that they nearly lose the red colour altogether.
[3] The Chinese are of all colours between brown and white; in the south, brown; towards the north, white.
[4] Buffon, Tom. v. p. 10.
[5] Perhaps we ought to put here the inhabitants of some of the islands in the great Pacific Ocean.

and explain by it all the works of nature, consider Cain as the father of the blacks, and deduce all the middle grades of colour from the various mixtures of white and black with each other[1]. And yet about this point some stand out very stoutly for Ham[2], while even Ishmael[3] has his supporters. Some take refuge in other causes, as the heat of the sun, thick vapours[4], and the vicinity of scorching sands. It is not my intention either to support or refute these opinions, but rather to deduce my conclusion from matters of fact.

The seat of colour is without controversy in the skin, though it is not diffused throughout that organ, but only occupies[5] that part which is called the cuticle, which is made up of the epidermis and the reticulum; and of these two, resides principally in the latter. In the blacks the cuticle is thicker and harder than in the whites to this extent, that in the latter the reticulum is a sort of thin mucus, and in the latter a thick membrane[6]. The transparent epidermis of the whites has the appearance of a very thin slice of horn: their reticulum is not very different from coagulated mucus, and the epidermis seems to consist of the same, hardened. And some teach[7] that this is its real form and material. But although anatomists are by no means agreed on this point, and it is not for me to settle the matter, I am obliged, from the nature of my subject, to say a few words about it.

In the whites, the parts under the skin, or rather the cuticle, which change colour, cause the colour of the body to be changed, on account of the transparency of the cuticle. In jaundice the skin becomes yellow, because the blood is tinged with bile; and the rush of more blood than usual into the vessels of the face causes blushing. And a kind of typhus, nearly peculiar to the West Indies, is called the yellow fever, because from the congestion of yellow serum in the vessels of the skin

---
[1] *Essai sur la Populat. de l'Amérique*, Tom. IV. liv. 7. c. 19.
[2] Id. cap. 13.   [3] *Spectacle de la Nature*.
[4] *La Bibliothèque impartiale*, Tom. V. Mars et Avril, p. 227.
[5] Albinus, *de Colore Æthiopum*, p. 6.   [6] Haller, *Physiolog.* T. v. p. 7.
[7] Ib. p. 19.

this becomes yellow. Moreover, if pigments are applied inside the epidermis, they stamp on it so permanent a colour, that it remains to the end of life. If gunpowder is burnt into the skin, who does not know how long it remains there? And in some such fashion many barbarous nations[1], like our ancestors[2], used to paint and mark their skin with various figures, for the sake of ornament.

Hence we may draw these conclusions. First, the cuticle must have no vessels, or at all events extremely few. For, if it were furnished with only a few more vessels, it would admit bile mixed with blood to its innermost parts and furthest recesses, and then what would stand in the way of yellowness remaining in it a long time, like any other colour caused by pigments? Moreover, the fact of the condition of the pigment when coloured being fixed, shows that it consists of parts which are very permanent, and therefore are furnished with very few, if any, vessels. Writers do not attribute bones to those parts of the body which abound in vessels; yet these parts, when stained with any colour, do not cease to change all their particles, until they have recovered their original tint. Hence we may conclude for certain that the cuticle is furnished with very few, if any, vessels, and that its component parts scarcely ever change.

So much being premised about colour, and the structure of its seat, we must investigate the causes of it, and, first of all, of blackness. And perhaps it will be worth while to begin by inquiring into the causes of the change of colour in the regions of the epidermis and the reticulum; and this all the more, because nature, in its simplicity, generally uses the same means to effect the same ends.

Air, dirt, and the heat of the sun, the transparency of the cuticle being destroyed, give it a brown colour, and at the same time make it harder.

He who wishes to have his hands shining and white will not find it enough to protect them from the sun and the heat,

---

[1] Hawkesworth's *Voyages*, Vol. II. p. 191.   [2] Cæsar, *Comment.* Lib. v. cap. x.

but must also keep them from the air, as is well known to women, who use gloves at all times. Besides, the colour of the face is never so fair as in other parts of the body which are always covered, although it be never exposed to the sun.

Those who have to work hard at manual labour, never have white hands. Gunpowder, as has been said, when introduced below the epidermis, makes the colour black. Dirt and pigments can do the same thing, though in a minor degree. And this seems to be confirmed by the use of washes, with which the blacks besmear themselves, so as to make themselves blacker.

The heat of the sun is the most powerful cause. Its force is shown if you expose to it the whitest possible face, for it will lose all its whiteness in one day, and come out brown or red. It is particularly efficacious in the summer on red-haired persons with light skin; and can affect the whole skin with brown spots, but especially the hands and face, because they are most exposed to it, which Linnæus[1] makes a disorder, and calls *Ephelides*. Nor is there any doubt, that if the heat were kept up long enough, the whole skin would become of the same brown colour.

If then these causes, the air, namely, and the heat of the sun, can cause such changes in these regions where, by means of houses and clothes, we are so much protected from them, at all events we need not be surprised that greater blackness is thereby effected in much hotter regions where men are exposed naked to a burning sun at almost all times.

But besides the heat of the sun, and the effects of the air, where any one is exposed to it, other causes bring on greater blackness like that of the Africans.

The parts of the cuticle are very rarely changed, as was said before, and all the more rarely the thicker it is. And, therefore, when the same particles are exposed for a long time to great heat, the effect is great, that is, much blackness is necessarily sub-introduced. And, moreover, it is certain that pig-

---

[1] *Amœnit. Acadm.* Vol. VI. p. 485.

ments can do much to increase this, by which, as has been said, their bodies are rendered blacker, or, as they think, more beautiful.

The cuticle of the blacks is said to be thicker and less transparent than that of the whites, and therefore, when the causes of blackness are induced, will also be blacker; if indeed that want of transparency has the effect of putting more particles in the way of the influences which produce blackness. For all, who are skilled in optics, know well, that transparent and coloured plates make colour more vivid and more intense, the more of them there are which are put one above the other: because the rays of light transmitted by the one are reflected by the other, and the brightness of colour is always in proportion to the number of reflected rays. But when the colour of the plates is that of blackness, which consists of the absence of light, the rays which are not suffocated by one are effaced by the other, and so, the light being neither transmitted nor reflected, black colour is produced. If, indeed, it be asked how it is that the cuticle of the blacks is less transparent than that of the whites, although I cannot perfectly explain it, I will try and illustrate it in a few words.

The action of the sun and the air is a sort of stimulus to our bodies, and therefore acts according to those laws which regulate stimulants. The effect of this stimulant, burning and irritating the skin, is to render it harder and thicker, as is the case with the hands of labourers, and with the use of all parts of the body which are affected by stimulants. In the same way the air and the rays of the sun, by their stimulating action, render the skin less transparent. The efficient cause, why the skin becomes thicker, is clear, and the way in which it is made thick, whether by the sun or by other irritating subjects, is pretty much the same. The irritation of the parts brings with it a larger influx of humours, and increases the action of the vessels, which are used in their increment or reparation. And as the continuous action of the sun, and other influences which stimulate the skin, display a great resemblance of action, so the progress of the acting power is the same in either case.

Stimulants and irritants, when first applied to a yet tender skin, cause the appearance of many pimples; but after a certain lapse of time, it becomes harder, thicker, and at last callous, and can never afterwards be inflated into pimples by the same causes. And in like manner, although the rays of a southern sun burn our bodies, and cause many pimples to rise on the skin, still bodies accustomed to those regions, or those who have always been in the way of it, are not affected in the same manner.

The fact therefore of the skin being made thicker by the intemperance of the climate and the heat of the sun, and blacker by the direct rays of the sun and by pigments, proves our whole theory of colour.

We must next inquire how far the explanation we have given is supported by facts, and how far it goes towards explaining facts.

Since all blacks are born white[1], and remain so for some little time, it is clear from this that the sun and the air are necessary agents in turning the skin to a black colour. And this is proved besides by the fact, that when blisterings and burnings are applied to the bodies of the blacks, they change such parts so into white, that the black colour is not brought back to the body for some days[2]. Those parts of the body too which are most protected, and defended from the sun and the air, do not lose their original white colour, as is observed in those blacks who have the gland covered with the prepuce[3]. All the nations which dwell within the torrid zone have their colour more and more verging towards black. This almost universal fact doubtless tends to support the opinion given above. But that such is not the fact is objected by some, because there are no small number of white people in the torrid zone[4]. And although I cannot deny this, still it is quite plain that the inhabitants of the torrid zone are blacker than

---

[1] *Hist. Générale des Voyages*, par M. l'Abbé Prevost, Tom. IV. p. 590.
Ib. Tom. III. p. 1163.
[2] *Hist. de l'Académie des Sciences*, An. 1702, p. 32.
[3] *Essai sur la Population de l'Amerique*, Tom. IV. liv. 7, c. 14.

any others, and that almost all are of a dark colour approaching to black.

However, since the cause of blackness, as we give it, is by no means simple, and does not entirely depend upon a nearer or greater distance from the Equator, and since when one or other of the efficient causes is absent, the whole effect ceases, it will not be foreign to our purpose, if we inquire whether the fact of the whiter populations of the torrid zone goes to refute or confirm what we have advanced.

To render our labours lighter, some general observations may be premised.

The heat is not always found less or greater in exact proportion to the distance of the respective regions from the Equator.

Islands are not so hot as continents, on account of the vapours which rise from the sea, and of the winds which are constantly blowing from it, both of which tend to refrigerate the soil.

Mountainous countries, or countries in the neighbourhood of mountains, greatly temper the heat. The reason of this will be given immediately.

Besides, the wind, sometimes by increasing, sometimes by diminishing them, variously affects heat and cold: coming from hot countries burnt up by the sun it brings heat; blowing from snowy and cold mountains, cold.

Finally, in places where the heat is the same, the same colour is not always the result; for the different mode of life has a great influence in changing it.

I will illustrate these observations by a few examples. As to the first point; many islands enjoy a very temperate climate, and particularly those which are situate furthest from continents[1]. How far their inhabitants preserve their whiteness may be learnt from the instance of those who inhabit the islands of the Southern, or great Pacific ocean[2]. Almost all the East Indies, as they verge towards the south, split up into

---

[1] Hawkesworth's *Voyages*, Vol. II. p. 246.   [2] Ib. Vol. II. p. 187.

islands or peninsulas; which partly explains why the colour found there is copper or brown, and not black.

As to the other observation: the Abyssinians, although placed under the Equator, still are white. In that country the mercury never stands above twenty finger-breadths high in the barometer; whence it appears that Abyssinia is perhaps the highest part of the world inhabited by man, at least two miles above the level of the sea. No one, who has ever been up a mountain, is unaware how much such an altitude will lessen the heat. Thus some mountains of America, though placed exactly under the Equator, are covered the whole year with deep snow and ice. Even the highest point of Etna is covered with perpetual snow[1]. That altitude therefore moderates heat is a fact, and is proved by these examples, nor is the explanation difficult. And although I cannot go into the matter at full length, yet I will say a few words about it.

Heat is caused by the rays of the sun, when they fall either directly or by refraction upon anything. But it is not found to be the same in every substance, on which the rays happen to fall: as when they fall on a transparent body, they do not cause the same heat as when they fall on an opaque one. This is most clearly shown by the fact, that when the focus of a concave metal mirror, opposed to the sun's rays, is thrown upon water, it does not boil, or show any sense of heat; although if copper, or any other metal, is opposed to the mirror, it liquefies, or evaporates, in a moment. And since in the passage of light through a transparent body, a smaller quantity of heat is thrown out, in proportion to the thinness or transparency of the body, but the air is more rarefied as it is higher above the earth; so it on that account transmits light more easily, and almost without any obstacle. For light seems to cause the more heat in proportion to the obstacles to its progress. But enough has been said on this point.

How much influence the wind has in altering heat, may be seen from the instance of America, where, when the north wind

---

[1] Bryden's *Letters*, Vol. I. Lett. 10.

blows, the cold becomes so great that in one night the rivers become frozen and unnavigable. The same thing is shown in Africa, where the winds, sweeping over and rolling about burning sands for many miles, stir up an almost intolerable heat.

I will now point out the effects of the mode of life. Those who are always clothed, and generally live in-doors, are seldom exposed to the causes which produce a change of colour, and so retain their whiteness. This happens to Europeans who inhabit hot countries, who retain their original mode of life, and continue to wear their clothes; whereas the aborigines[1] are always naked, and exposed to the force of the sun and the winds. But if any of them never do expose themselves to the air and the sun, as often happens to the women[2], they come off better in the way of colour than the rest.

As to the objection, that white men are to be found in hot regions, where the observations above collected do not explain their whiteness in any way, and that it is a fact, that in Abyssinia, and in the islands of Java and Madagascar[3], white and black men are found together, that must be explained otherwise. For it must be observed that these black and white men are of different origin, and differ not only in colour but in mode of living, and in many other external circumstances. For it is certain, and has been discovered, that those differences have not crept in among those who have always inhabited those countries from the beginning, but have come from elsewhere out of countries whose temperature was more favourable to whiteness or blackness, with the original inhabitants of such regions. And let no one suppose this can be contradicted. For so far their similarity is of importance, because you can easily in consequence of it trace the origin of individuals to some neighbouring nation; and thus you may gather that the black inhabitants of Abyssinia came thither from other neighbouring parts of Africa. And in the same way

---

[1] Hist. Gén. des Voyages, par M. l'Abbé Prevost, Tom. IV. p. 411.
[2] Buffon, Hist. Naturelle, Tom. V. pp. 18, 19, 70, 81, 90, &c.
[3] Ib. pp. 47, 160.

people as black as the Africans and as white as the Europeans inhabit the islands of the great Pacific ocean[1]: of whom the former have without doubt emigrated from the countries called New Guinea; and the latter, as is likely, from those tracts of Asia which trend more towards the north.

It may still be objected to my view, that two nations, differing at the outset, when they come to inhabit the same regions, although they are exposed to the same external causes, still remain different. But on this point two things are to be considered, namely, that different nations by no means live in the same, but, on the contrary, in very different ways. And it is by no means necessary to have causes so strong, or influences so energetic, to preserve an effect when it is once done, as to produce the same originally. In this way, although in the islands of the Pacific ocean above mentioned, the heat of the sun cannot change the colour from white to black; yet when that is once done, it can keep it so.

Brown colour, diverging from white, is by no means confined to the torrid zone; for the men of northern Europe and Asia, where cold and frost and snow reign in perpetual junction, are of a brown colour[2]. They lead a most wretched life; their food consists of fish and wild beasts. For bread, they dig up roots out of the earth. In winter they hide in hovels, except when compelled to go out by hunger. They construct their hovels under the earth, which is necessary, on account of the intolerable cold. This mode of life is no doubt very unfavourable towards causing or preserving whiteness. And whilst they are catching fish, or hunting wild beasts, they must needs be a great deal exposed to the intemperance of the air. And this inclemency of the air and constant fish-diet have the greatest possible influence in making the skin harder and thicker; and living in dwellings always filled with smoke is certainly no remedy. This is an example of how far the severity of a climate may of itself go to change the colour.

---

[1] Hawkes. Voyages, Vol. I. p. 568, Vol. II. p. 178.
[2] Hist. Gén. des Voy. par M. l'Abbé Prevost, Vol. XIX. p. 6.

So much then I have to say about colour, in general terms, it is true, because the limits of this little treatise did not permit me to speak more fully or copiously: still, I hope there is enough to tend somewhat towards the explanation of colour in all instances.

Chap. II.

Of Stature and Form.

THE differences of human stature are far from being small. The inhabitants of some part of South America grow to a height of seven feet[1]; whilst the inhabitants of the frigid zone scarcely attain the height of four or five feet[2]. The islands called *Huaheine* and *Marianne* produce men of six or even seven feet high[3]; on the other hand, the inhabitants of the promontory of South America, called Cape Horn, are of small stature[4]. But why should I say more, when one sees almost always one and the same country producing men of all kinds of heights? What is the reason of this?

The way in which aliment is taken up into our bodies has scarcely yet been thoroughly investigated, nor are the laws found out by which they grow. But although such is the case, still, until some greater light is thrown on the matter, I may be allowed to say what I think is true, or at least probable.

Growth seems to be due to the action of the heart, by whose renewed pulsations our fibres are rendered longer, and are amplified, and directed to all parts. This is illustrated by the unfolding of the whole human body, and especially of the womb. But the action of the heart is not a cause of itself; nor do men and plants share the same nature. The latter have no power of locomotion, and merely increase and grow to a certain height;

---

[1] Hawkesworth's Voy. Vol. I. p. 31.
[2] *Hist. Gén. des Voy.* par l'Abbé Prevost, Tom. XIX. p. 63.
[3] Hawkesworth, Vol. II. p. 254. Buffon, Tom. V. p. 52.
[4] Hawkes. Vol. I. p. 391.

but it is different with man, who can scarcely come to perfection without movement and action. The action and movement of the body must therefore be conjoined with the reiterated pulsations of the heart, which increase, by a sort of distention, all our parts, both in length and size. How extremely important this cause is will be clear to every one, who has observed the singular increase of every part when much exercised, the very unnatural size which comes, as in many tumours, from distracting causes, and that well-known increase of the ears, which is caused by earrings of great weight[1]; increase, therefore, will be in proportion to the actions of the heart and the motions of the body. But though these may be perpetually continued, the body does not go on for ever increasing, because the great rigidity which is the effect of the action of the muscular fibres puts an end sometimes not only to increase, but to life itself. That this rigidity depends upon the amount of action is proved by this, that if any one, when young, uses immoderate exercise, he scarcely ever attains the full size of a man; and those who are obliged always to labour, and to lead a hard life, do not arrive at old age, or even the confines of it, but perish before their time; and though early in years, still with the appearance and constitution of old men. In this way the causes of growth come at last to neutralize themselves.

This, then, being the immediate cause of man's growth, that is to say, the action of the heart and the movement of the body, and the rigidity of the parts the cause of the stoppage of that effect, we must now find out what are the remote external causes which affect the proximate one, and explain the varieties of human stature.

Of these the principal are climate, food, exercise, and labour. Climate acts either by heat or cold.

Heat, which is almost the origin of many animals, is necessary to all growing bodies; and in ourselves, if it is not the cause of motion and sense, at all events these faculties to some extent, and our other actions, cannot be deprived of it for a

---

[1] Buffon, Tom. VI. p. 34. Dampier, Vol. I. p. 32. Hawkesworth, Vol. I. p. 311.

moment without injury. By stimulating the heart, it greatly increases the sharpness of all our senses, and the mobility of the human body. Hence the inhabitants of warm regions very soon reach their full size, and those who are unrestrained in every way arrive at maturity much later than those who live in warm regions. In the eighth, ninth, or tenth year, women become menstruous, in the twelfth the men are fit for venery[1]; whereas in cold regions, the menses do not appear before the fourteenth, sixteenth, and sometimes the twentieth year: nor are they fit for marriage before the eighteenth or sometimes the twentieth year. Heat too does not seem able to increase the human body, or diminish it much; for both in hot and in temperate countries, small and large men are equally produced. And if it has anything to do with growth, it would seem as if it would be more likely to diminish it, because that violent action of the heart, and great movement of the body, on one side make the increase rapid, and on the other, at the same time, accelerate the rigidity, or rather the firmness of the fibres. And in fact, the inhabitants of hot countries generally yield in stature to those of the temperate zone.

Cold, the exact opposite of heat, or to speak more accurately, the absence of heat[2], the force in which it consists abating, by diminishing all motions and all irritability, and blunting every stimulus, tends to lessen the size of the body. In all very cold regions, torpor is induced; the action of the body, especially in infants, is small: and therefore little adapted to extend or increase it. So that almost all the increase of the body is carried on by the action of the heart. For which reason, since the effect of action and exercise is to make the body beautiful and elegant, it is not to be wondered at, if the men in very cold countries are neither tall nor elegant. And this is confirmed by the observations of writers about the inhabitants of Greenland, and other parts of Northern Europe and Asia[3]. Cold, as it confines all other things in nature, so it does our

---

[1] Buffon, Tom. v. p. 60.
[2] Buffon, Tom. v. p. 3.
[3] Prælect. Dr. Black, Prof. Chem.

bodies, but not in the same way, that is, not by taking away the heat. For its principal action is on the fibres which serve for sense and motion, which are in consequence compelled to contract themselves more; for the heat of the human body is almost exactly the same in all countries, however different the climate may be: that constriction, therefore, will stand in the way of every force which tends to increase the parts of our bodies in length or breadth. The contrary relaxation, which comes from heat, and about which I meant to speak, when I was speaking about heat as a cause of rapid growth, produces also this effect, by acting on the fibres of motion.

Exercise and labour must both be treated of under the title of corporeal motion; for they both consist in the action of the body, and only differ in this, that volition can command the former, but the latter demands the use of reason.

Bodily motion may be violent, moderate, or slight.

Violent action, by the stiffness which follows too frequent exertion, and the exhaustion of the vital force, retards and impedes the growth. Slight motion, or rest, does not impart sufficient strength to the organs to enable them to fulfil their functions; nor can it endow the body with that firmness, or the limbs with that solidity, which action alone can produce. But it is worthy of remark, that those results of motion and rest take place most in tender years before use and custom have formed the body, which is then still unchanged by the powers of nature. For labour is a good thing for adult bodies, or rarely does them harm, and in them rest may create or increase plethora.

The condition of artisans as far as their stature is concerned, confirms, unless I am mistaken, what I have just said. They being obliged to exercise their respective occupations from infancy, pass their lives in work-shops. Bowed down to the ground, and crushed with toil, they turn out deformed, almost dwarfs, hunchbacked, and never arrive at the full stature or size of a man; so that those lines of Martial may well be applied to them:

> Judged by his head, the man a Hector is,
> But an Astyanax judged by his phiz;—

DIET.

and in fact they generally have large heads. Those who inhabit countries very much to the north or to the south[1], are like them, and partly from the same cause, because, in tender years, both have too much repose.

Between these extremes a mean, or moderate exercise, which is the principal means of increasing the body, should without doubt be chosen. But what is moderate, is difficult to define: its latitude, to use the words of those who lay down rules of health, may be so great.

I now pass on to that cause which has the greatest influence in augmenting or diminishing the stature and magnitude of man, I mean diet. Food, although the first necessary for human life, still varies much in the quantity which is convenient for sound health, being one amount for one, another for another. When it is scanty, it is clear small stature will be the result; for the body cannot grow and be enlarged, if part of the material necessary for supporting it be taken away. On the other hand, the first effect of frequent and ample diet is to increase the body. Every herdsman knows of how much importance food is towards improving cattle and other beasts. Oxen brought forth on the barren mountains and plains of Scotland, and afterwards brought up in the more fertile fields of England, grow to double the size.

But there are diversities not only in the quantity, but the quality of food. Thus flesh and vegetables are by no means of the same importance in nourishing the human body. Sometimes when spices are added to some aliments, as flesh, wine, fish, there is more stimulus in them. This makes the increase more rapid, but, in such a way, that the body much sooner decays, worn out as it were by continual stimulus. Food prepared partly from flesh, partly from farinaceous matters, as it can be digested more easily than any other, so does it accelerate the growth more than any other.

So much for the causes of growth treated separately; now it would seem that I ought to speak about them in conjunction,

---

[1] Buffon, Tom. v. p. 3. Hawkesworth, *Voyages*, Vol. 1. pp. 391-2.

and that all the more, because in almost every case they act in conjunction. But since the limits of my paper forbid me to speak of that subject, and to apply the conclusions to the various nations of men, therefore I omit them, and go on to the next point.

I must now speak of the varieties of form. They are in fact as numerous as men. For who has not a face, form, and aspect of countenance peculiar to himself, and which can be distinguished from all others? And besides these which every one has of his own, signs and marks peculiar to each race and nation are not wanting; thus a depressed nose, thick lips, small or large eyes, and other marks common to thousands of individuals, distinguish one race from another. What are the causes of this? That these diversities have nothing to do with diversity of species is clear from this, that this same depression of the nose, or thickness of the lips is frequently to be seen amongst ourselves. Many[1] attribute the depressed nose of the Negroes not to nature, but to art; and, allow it to be the work of art, difficulties, not easy to be overcome, still remain. At least, as far as I am concerned, I confess that I cannot understand how the forms of men and the lineaments of the face come to be so diverse from each other as they are. But when such effects have once been produced, I shall have an occasion of showing, when I come to treat of generation, how they may be retained.

Chap. III.

On the defect or excess of parts of the Human Body.

If any one is ready to trust the reports of writers, he would find ample material on this subject to deal with. Thus we read

---

[1] Buffon, Tom. v. p. 132. *Hist. Gén. des Voy.* par M. l'Abbé Prévost, Tom. III. p. 157.

FABULOUS STORIES.   383

of the Arimaspi, who are remarkable for having but one eye, and that in the forehead; of the Androgyni, who are male and female joined in one; of men with dogs' heads, and men who have no neck and carry their heads on their shoulders[1]. The stature of the Patagonians, which a few years ago, as we used to hear, was scarcely set so low as twelve feet, has now been reduced to seven. But everybody will easily see that all these things are beyond all belief.

And even those who tell more probable stories differ in their testimony so from one another, one denying that which another says he has seen, ever was or could be seen, that it becomes quite uncertain which we ought to believe most, and which not at all. And since I found it at first so very difficult to decide which were true or the contrary, I selected some of the more reliable and better examined varieties to deal with for my present purpose. I am not therefore going to inquire whether there are any men furnished with legs much thicker than others, or with one leg much thicker than the other[2], or tails as some still believe[3]; because these stories are not confirmed by any facts or observations worthy of credit, by which we might find a way to explain, or propose some theory about them.

So the defects or excesses about which our business is, are of this kind; namely, the beardless chin, hanging breasts, or prominent pudenda.

The beard among ourselves, though sometimes more scanty and sometimes thicker, is scarcely ever wanting altogether. So, as to those nations, to whom almost all the writers had declared that no beard was given by nature, in most cases more recent testimonies show that the beard had not been denied by nature, but was plucked out by the people themselves[4]. This

---

[1] C. Plin. *Nat. Hist.* Lib. VII. cap. 2.
[2] Buffon, Vol. V. p. 64.
[3] *Origin and Progress of Language*, Vol. IV. p. 259, 2nd ed. Edin. 1774.
[4] Dampier, Vol. I. p. 407. *Hist. Gén. des Voy.* par M. l'Abbé Prevost, Tom. XVIII. p. 503. Hawkesworth's *Voyages*, Vol. I. p. 608. Buffon, Tom. V. p. 104. Charlevoix, III. p. 179.

therefore is no more a defect, than the long beard of other nations is an excess, and each is only a matter of custom.

Nor have I any doubt as to the mammæ, but what their length and pendulosity[1] among some nations is due to the peculiar way in which the women offer milk to their infants. For if a part becomes bigger than all others by distension or distraction, as has been observed above, is it wonderful that the mammæ, which we are now talking about, when flung over the shoulders, and very eagerly drawn away by infants desirous of milk should become longer?

There has been much angry discussion about the pudenda of the women of the extreme south of Africa; some declare that they are furnished with a ligament stretched under the naturalia, whilst others contend that they have nothing beyond the ordinary nature of women. These miracles, or rather monstrosities, if they exist at all, seem by the most recent testimonies to be reduced to this, that in that country the nymphæ are a little more turgid and prominent, a defect the less to be astonished at in that country, because it is certain that it sometimes occurs in this[2].

Differences of the hair. Hair differs, especially in colour: between which two and the skin there seems to be some connexion. In all countries black hair always accompanies a dark colour of skin, or one which diverges from white. And, on the other hand, red or white hair is joined with white skin. And the colour of both, that is of the skin and the hair, seems to depend upon the same causes, that is, the exposure to air and heat. A proof of which is that the more or less hair is exposed to these causes, the more or less black its colour is. Thus the hair which is not exposed is always less dark than what is.

As to the texture of hair, there seems to be a great difference, for that of some is soft and curly like wool, and that of others harsh and dense. What the cause of this may be, since physiologists are as yet by no means agreed as to the nature

---

[1] Buffon, Tom. v. pp. 4, 55.   [2] Hawk. Voy. Vol. III. p. 792.

of hair, I dare not give any decided opinion, and must be content with one or two conjectures.

Since the hairs are situated on the surface of the body, therefore whatever affects the body, affects them; besides perhaps other influences, so especially does the conflux thither of humours; and in this way, in proportion as the conflux is greater or smaller, so is their increase greater or less. Hence, as is known to all hair-cutters, the hairs grow more in summer than in winter. And this may be observed more frequently in the case of the beard. Therefore the hair grows more luxuriously in hot countries than in cold, and on that account will be thicker and stronger; which, in fact, happens in almost all countries, as in the West and East Indies.

Still, exceptions to this are not wanting. Thus in Africa, the hottest of all countries, and where therefore the hair ought to be thickest, on the contrary, it is scanty, and something like wool. This, although I cannot explain, still I may illustrate by a comparison. In many cutaneous disorders, little ulcers throw out a great deal of matter, which shows that there is a rush of humours to some of the vessels of the skin. And these sorts of disorders are often cured by remedies which cause perspiration. How is this? When a quantity of humour is excreted in the shape of sweat through healthy vessels, thus the excess is averted from the diseased vessels. And thus the little ulcers, which before were moist, become dried up, and crusts are formed, which afterwards fall off, and then show the sound skin underneath. In this way, a rush towards the skin being made in the first instance, the hairs increase in growth; and when this becomes greater and greater, and the humours are more easily eliminated through the vessels of perspiration from the body, the quantity which serves to make the hair increase is diminished, and the attenuated hairs come out like wool. What seems to confirm this opinion is, that in the negroes, whose hair is like wool, the bulbs or roots of the hair are attenuated and small[1], as if through deficiency of nourishment:

---

[1] Haller, El. Physiolog. Tom. v. p. 33.

and it is only in the case of those who inhabit the hottest regions, or who are born elsewhere from the natives of such, that the hair becomes almost a kind of wool.

Chap. IV.

On Generation.

Thus the causes are explained which change the colour, induce a large or small stature, and affect the hair and other parts. It may be objected that they are in no respect efficient causes, and that men are to be distinguished by the marks and varieties just mentioned, as soon as they are born, or at all events that such appear, long before they can be attributed to external causes. And this also, no doubt, is true. And how then is it to be explained? For either our explanations are idle and futile, or many properties which have been acquired by the parent are transferred to the offspring. Are they then so transferred? It would certainly seem so. Thus the father begets a son like himself in every way in form of body, expression of countenance, colour of hair, and sound of voice. The temperament too descends from the father to the son. So also peculiar marks long continue to distinguish the same family of men. But this is particularly shown by the history of disorders; of which there are instances known to all in the cases of gout, scrofula, and madness. Again, diarrhœa and unnatural dilatations of the arch of the aorta long infest the same family. These diseased conditions must be looked on in the same light as other mutations of the corporeal condition. And to speak of both from the same point of view, surely that change which is the origin of the production of black skin may just as easily be communicated by the parent to its offspring, and is no more difficult to explain, than that by which gout is handed down in the same way. Nor is it at all more difficult to understand, why the skin begins to grow black a certain time after birth, than why some years afterwards the offspring of scrofulous parents is infested with ulcers.

Still all the same it is a fact which we cannot explain; and yet there is no manner of doubt that peculiarities acquired by men do descend to their posterity.

Thus the fact being once established, it will be no longer obscure why men undergo, from the causes induced, such great changes of colour, stature, and the other matters we have mentioned. The black colour of the parent may become blacker in the son, if he is exposed to the same external influences, and so in the course of ages may approach more and more to actual blackness; and in that way at last great effects may flow from causes so small as to escape our notice, if each generation contributes something to increase them.

Why one form of appearance and countenance becomes permanent in one nation, and one in another, is explained by this, that parents always produce offspring like themselves.

It would however be difficult to say, how many centuries it takes to change the skin from white to black, or in any other way. But if we may conjecture at all from the sudden effect of the sun and the air in changing the skin, a long time is not necessary. But that Europeans who inhabit hot regions do not acquire even after a very long time a brown or black colour, and that negroes after being a long time in Europe do not grow white, may be for this reason; that the former never try those modes and ways of life, and other external circumstances, which we have said are so powerful in effecting change; and if they do suffer from necessity or adverse fortune, then they do change colour[1]; and that the latter wretched mortals never are able to enjoy that easy kind of life, by which whiteness is so greatly brought about.

Moreover, the way in which the remote causes of whiteness and blackness act is somewhat different; and dark colour is much more easily impressed, and much longer retained, than

---

[1] Hawks. Vol. III. p. 751.

clear colour. Thus the fierceness of one day of sun will inflict a greater amount of brownness than can be effaced by fit precautions taken for a long time to get rid of its effects. And this observation, in the way that those who after having acquired peculiar marks in any region retain them, when removed to another, may be applied so as to make it easy to understand how blackness may still remain in permanence even when its causes are taken away.

Thus then the question, how those marks which distinguish individuals may be transferred by parents to their children, is answered. And now recurs the other, how those marks differ from the ones which are not so transferred, and what is the reason why some marks peculiar to the parent are transferred, and others are not. I must confess this is one I cannot answer. For the Creator has hidden the business of generation in the deepest recesses of nature, and has kept all its processes sunk and overwhelmed in the deepest darkness, never perhaps to be brought to light. And therefore to explain things depending upon such a cause would be a vain and idle undertaking.

But, although this may be so, still I cannot help making mention of some things relating to generation, which, though wonderful, are nevertheless true.

White men are sometimes born amongst the negroes[1], and I have no doubt that other whites are propagated from them.

We only know of one instance of a black being born amongst the whites[2]; and according to the account of James Lind, a clever man, a physician, and an investigator of facts, who says he saw it with his own eyes, this man begot a son like himself.

I indeed am unwilling to appear to compel all nature to my opinion; but those observations, as they show that diversity of species is not necessary for causing blackness of colour,

---

[1] *Hist. Gen. de Voy.* par M. l'Abbé Prevost, Tom. IV. p. 590. Hawks. Vol. II. p. 188. Maupertuis, Tom. II. p. 116.
[2] *Phil. Trans.* No. 414.

and that this property, like others, may be acquired through external circumstances, and so descend from father to son, so also do they in some way confirm the doctrine about colour I have laid down.

The skin of those white men amongst the negroes is, as it were, scurfy[1]; that is, the cuticle peels off in scales, and does not remain long enough to become quite black. The skin of the black man among the whites, as also that of his son, was thick and hard[2], which fact shows that thickness has a great deal to do with causing colour, and is in favour of my opinion.

Chap. V.

On the Varieties of Mind.

The mental varieties seem equal to and sometimes greater than the bodily varieties of man. And on this point I meant to say little, as it seems to be part of our subject.

This chapter seems as if it ought properly to be divided into two parts: in one of which reason and prudence, and in the other manners, should be dealt with. And, in order that my notion may be more easily understood, I will illustrate both by an example before I begin to deal with either. If one man is sharp, and of an acute and docile genius, and another heavy, stupid, and averse to all discipline, that must be referred to the difference of reason and prudence. But if one is sanguine, vivacious, alert and happy, and his opposite is sad, sorrowful and wretched, we call that an affair of manners.

In the former division, the question instantly occurs to the mind, What is the cause of difference? Is it to be referred to God? and is it credible that a Deity who is just and equi-

---

[1] Hauk. Vol. II. p. 188.　　[2] Phil. Trans. No. 414.

table to all should have formed men so different in mind, as
to create one foolish, another wise; one brave, another cowardly? Certainly not, in my opinion; and it is more true and
more equitable to attribute to natural causes the differences
of mind which we see.

To investigate the matter briefly: men's minds do not
seem to me to differ so much by the fortune of birth as by
the use and exercise of reason, and the faculties of the mind
come out smaller or greater by use, almost in the same way
as those of the body. And as there are several reasons for
this exercise, I will consider them under three heads; position,
education, and affections of the mind.

As to the first; If one be in a place where insuperable
impediments, or none at all, are placed in the way of action,
in the first case he gives himself up to despair, in the other
to idleness, and equally in either case does nothing. And, in
fact, the Samoeides and the negroes seem placed in similar
circumstances. If, on the contrary, all the necessaries of life
are uncertain to any one on account of the climate, the soil,
or some other reason, what does he do? Instantly he struggles
to make them more secure by art and industry. He looks out
for cattle. Hence plenty, and with that offspring increase.
Fields have to be cultivated to provide food, and now abundance ensues. And as you will say the desires of the human
mind are not satisfied with this, he adds comfort to necessaries;
then seeks elegance, and lastly luxury. With an increasing
cultivation of life, arts always, and often sciences, increase.
Observe the man, first wild, and then carried to the highest
pitch of cultivation and polish, how much the same man differs
from himself! Look back upon the steps by which he has
progressed. In no two successive steps can a greater exercise
of reason and prudence be observed than in the Samoeide
constructing his hut below the earth against the cold, or in
the negro fabricating an umbrella to protect himself from
the heat.

Besides, sometimes a great difference is seen between men
placed under the same circumstances. What an interval be-

tween Isaac Newton and Bacon, and almost all their contemporaries! And yet they never considered that they were possessed of any particular faculty, which others had not, by which they could comprehend science. They observed nature more accurately, and reasoned better on their observations than others. That was not a natural power, but acquired only by use and custom. What however contributed to form that fortunate habit, no one but themselves could easily say, nor is it necessary to do so; and the matter is so subtle a one, that it might easily escape themselves; since we see every day that many small things create a habit, without those being conscious who are affected by it. In fact, many who have happily promoted the sciences by their labour, confess that they were led by mere accident to give their minds up to it. Since then the force of circumstances is so powerful to excite and amplify the reason, so also the affections of the mind, and especially the desires, are of great influence towards the same end.

What has not been done for science and knowledge, especially in the government and administration of public affairs, through benevolence, or emulation, or envy, ambition, and glory?

No one doubts the important part that education and discipline play in forming and stimulating the mind. But that discipline is by far the best, which not only delivers precepts, but also exercises the faculties of the mind, and compels it as it were to anticipate commands[1]. So also the teachers of youth stimulate the mind to learn by emulation, curiosity, blandishments, and very often by fear. Which influence is the more powerful, let others decide.

Has conformation any thing to do with the increase or diminution of the mental faculties? If the operations of the mind do not altogether depend upon the nervous system, especially the brain, as those think who deny that the mind is anything without matter, still there is no doubt they are most intimately connected with it, and vary with its variations. This is proved by the variations of the mind of the same man,

---

[1] Rousseau, Émil. Liv. III.

according as he is in health, or sickness; sanguine, or depressed. When the skull is broken, or the brain suffers compression, he who previously gave utterance to the most shrewd observations, now seems almost destitute of reason and sense. And who ever doubted, from these instances, that when the condition of the brain is changed, the mind changes also?

It is a question also whether any peculiar condition of this brain, affecting the mind, can be handed down from parent to son? It has been said above that temperament at all events is so communicated. But different temperaments are so connected with different tones and conditions of mind, that, in common parlance, they are referred to mind alone. Therefore, if certain conditions of the brain, from which some operations of the mind proceed, are transmitted by the accident of birth, what is to prevent the peculiar condition of that part of the brain, which is appropriated to reason, being transmitted in a similar way? And this will appear much more probable to one who considers that a diseased condition, like that of madness, is propagated from father to son in the same family for generations.

What has been said goes then to show that something must be attributed to congenital conformation and stamina, but more to exertion, so far as calls are made for it by position, mental affections, and education, in the matter of reason and prudence.

Travellers have exaggerated the mental varieties far beyond the truth, who have denied good qualities to the inhabitants of other countries, because their mode of life, manners, and customs have been excessively different from their own. For they have never considered, that when the Tartar tames his horse, and the Indian erects his wig-wam, he exhibits the same ingenuity which an European general does in manœuvring his army, or Inigo Jones in building a palace.

There is nothing in which men differ so much as in their customs. They are of innumerable origins. Climate[1], soil[2],

---

[1] *Esprit des Lois*, Liv. 14, 15, 16, 17. [2] Ib. Liv. 18.

diet[1], occupations, laws, religion, individual men, government, the institution of monarchy, or a republic[2], with a thousand other things, create and alter their customs in a marvellous way.

As for climate, let me quote the words of a distinguished man. "Under the extremes of heat or of cold, the active range of the human soul appears to be limited, and men are of inferior importance, either as friends or as enemies. In the one extreme, they are dull and slow, moderate in their desires, regular and pacific in their manner of life; in the other, they are feverish in their passions, weak in their judgments, and addicted by temperament to animal pleasure[3]."

Many instances of the effects which come from the causes mentioned are palpable, but my time does not allow me to mention all. And therefore I shall be content with one or two examples, which clearly show how much influence one man may have. The laws and customs of Lycurgus, the former being taken into exile along with him, which were not instituted for pleasure, but for the sake of public and private utility, and to produce an austere virtue, lasted for the space of seven hundred years. So also Peter, justly called the Great, Emperor of the Russians, who bestowed politeness and cultivation on a nation barbarous, rude, and unheard of, or neglected, and, in the teeth of their most deep-seated prejudices, adorned them with customs, amended their laws, and handed down to posterity an empire which is an object of fear to one nation long very powerful, and of suspicion to other peoples and nations, is another splendid instance of the same thing.

However various the causes may be, which create and alter the customs of men, there is but one which can make them lasting, stable and, as it were, eternal. This is imitation, the most powerful principle in man. By this we acquire customs, manners, and almost everything. Sometimes indeed its power

---

[1] *Hist. des Indes,* Tom. 1. p. 66.   [2] *Ib.* Liv. 4, §. 7.
[3] Ferguson's *Essay on the History of Civil Society,* P. III. s. 1.

is such that against our will we are compelled to imitate others. From this source depends the resemblance of customs in the family, the city, or in the whole nation. This was well known to the poet, who had seen through the whole range of the human mind. "*Falstaff.* It is a wonderful thing to see the semblable coherence of his men's spirits and his: they, by observing of him, do bear themselves like foolish justices: he, by conversing with them, is turned into a justice-like serving man. Their spirits are so married in conjunction, with the participation of society, that they flock together in consent, like so many wild geese. It is certain, that either wise bearing or ignorant carriage is caught, as men take diseases, one of another." Shakespeare, *K. Henry IV.*

They are truly few, who judge for themselves what customs are right or wrong, and they are still fewer who, whilst they think for themselves, and differ from the mob, go on to accommodate and alter their customs according to their own opinions.

INDEX OF SUBJECTS.

Africans, 123, 361, 363
Albinos, 132
Algonquins, 121
Alopecides, 73
Americans, 94, 120, 150, 161, 240, 266, 271, 307, 361
Ammonites, 284
Amour, skulls on the, 112
Anthropological Collections, 208, 347
Ape and man, distinction, 168
Arctic animals, 104
Aronuke, 179
Arimaspi, 247
Ass, 78, 101
Astyanax, 380

Baf, 78
Banks, Sir Joseph, 147
Bardeau, 79
Batavians, 115
Belemnites, 284
Belgians, 115
Bertin, 112
Bif, 79
Bimana, 171
Biography of Blumenbach, 1
Biscayan women, 107
Blackened Europeans, 103
Blacks, 371
Borneo, 141
Brain, 392
Brain of ape, 22
Breasts, 125, 247
Bulbs of the hair, 383
Bull, 77
Buttocks in man, 160

Caffres, 110
Cain, 368
California, 83
Callitrichus, 142

Calmucks, 116
Canadians, 110, 121
Canis, varieties of, 363
Cape of Good Hope, 83, 98, 361
Capra revorsa and depressa, 74
Carib, 121
Carinthia, 115
Carolina, 240
Casque, 112
Cat, 75
Cattle, acclimatisation of, 71
Caucasian, 155
Caucasians, 100, 255, 278, 303
Cercopithecus, 177
Chain of nature, 161
Champagne, 67
Chest, 167
Chimpansi, 96, 97
Chin, 383
Chinese, 367
Circassians, 98, 363
Circumcision of female, 126
Classification of man, 99
Climate, influence of, 73, 196
Clitoris, 90, 126, 170
Coccyx, 142
Colchian, 110
Cold, 378
Colour, 203
Colour in man, 106, 367
Colt, modifications in the, 73
Copulation, 75, 169, 182
Cordilleras, 107
Corium, 106
Cow, 77
Creation, mutability in, 280
Creole, 112, 213
Criole, 112
Customs, 392
Cutaneous disorders, 383
Cuticle, 368, 369, 371

INDEX OF SUBJECTS.

Cynamolgi, 257

Darien, inhabitants of, 136
Dauphiné, 60
Degeneration of brute animals, 191, 290
Dentition, 243
Design, 321, 324
Diana monkey, 74
Didactylus ignavus, 91
Diet, 198
Diseases in man, 130, 185
Dodos, 269
Dog, 73, 74
Domestic animals, 72, 291
Duck, 76

Ears, 128, 246
Elevator clavicular, 87
Elk, 73
Embryo, development of, 70
Epholis, 373
Erect position of man, 84, 164
Esquimaux, 99
Ethiopians, 98, 101, 120, 161, 267, 270, 304
Europeans, 101
Exercise, 321
Eye of rabbit, 131
Eyes of man, 225

Fabulous varieties of man, 257
Face, varieties of, 227
Facial line, 235
Feet, 125, 233
Filly, birth of a, 77
Final causes, 361
Fish diet, 376
Foetus, 69, 159
Formative force, 194
Fox, the, 73

Gallus caleouticus, 76
Generation, 346, 358
Generis humani varietate nativa, 65
Genital liquid, 243
Genital organs, 75, 109, 247
Genoese, 116
Giants, 104
Goats, 56
Göttingen, 348
Graafian follicle, 70
Granada, 107
Greenlander, 98
Greenlanders, 99, 118

Griffs, 112
Gunpowder, 370
Guzerat, 110

Hair on man, 124, 127, 159, 173, 192, 224, 354
Hairy men, 68
Ham, 368
Hameln, 87
Hands of man, 86, 159, 251
Heart of man, 179, 377
Heat of sun, 370, 374
Hector, 380
Hemeralopia, 133
Hen, 76
Hereditary peculiarities, 203, 247
Hessian boy, 67
Hinny, 79
Hippocratic macrocephalus, 342
Hog, 292
Homines monstrosi, 129
Homo sapiens ferus, 166, 336
Horn, Cape, 377
Horses, 71, 72, 80, 101, 132, 199
Hungarians, 231
Huaheine, 377
Hybridity, 73, 80, 112
Hybrids, 195, 201
Hymen, 89, 170
Hyaena, 74
Hyponemia, 76

Imads, 257
Imitation, 194
Instincts of man, 82
Intelligent negroes, 302
Intermaxillary bone, 126
Ishmael, 368

Jackal, 74
Jaundice, 368
Jumars, 78
Juvenis bovinus, 337
—— lupinus, 337
—— ovinus, 336
—— ursinus, 337

Kakerlacken, 130, 313

Labrador, 118
Lapps, 99, 116, 231
Languages, difference in, 125
Laughter, 89, 184
Legs, 250, 353
Leprosy, 135

INDEX OF SUBJECTS.   307

Leucœthiopians, 135, 139, 260, 314
Life of Blumenbach,
Linnæus, his classification, 150
Luselho, 133

Macrocephali, 241, 243
Malabar, 110, 136, 137
Malay, 156, 161, 266, 275, 304
Malphigian rete, 126
Mameluck, 112
Man, degeneration of, 293
Man and ape, distinction, 163
Manatee, 61
Mandril, 92, 109
Manual labour, 370
Maro, 77
Marianne, 377
Molatta, 112
Membrana nictitans, 93
Menstrual flux, 90, 192
Mental affections of brutes, 89, 389
Mestiço, 112
Metif, 112
Mice, 132
Molluska, 112
Mongolian variety, 265, 268
Mongolians, 156, 304
Monorchides, 127
Monoculos, 257
Morbific affections, 259
Mulattos, 112, 216
Mules, 101
Mures, 251, 289
Musculus oculi suspensorius, 173
Museum, 155

Nails, 128
Naked condition of man, 69
Natural causes, 390
Natural sciences in Germany, 6
Natural varieties, 224
Nature, chain of, 151
Negroes, 9, 305
New Hollanders, 119, 239
Nocturnal pollutions, 152
Norma verticalis, 237
Nuevalascis, 133
Nymphæ, 90, 170

Obi river, squirrels on, 71
Octaroon, 112
Onagras, 242
Orang utan, 83, 91, 94, 96, 97

Orders, natural, 152
Otaheitans, 119

Pacific Ocean, inhabitants of, 123, 367
Packwax, 84
Panniculus carnosus, 173
Papio, 92, 94
Patagonians, 253
Pathological variation, 140
Peloria, 282
Pelvis in quadrupeds, 83
—— in man, 168
—— in negro, 249
Pentagonist classification of man, 99, 302
Periophthalmium, 93
Persians, 101
Peter von Hameln, 9
Pictures, 152
Pigments, 123
Pimple worm, 289
Pimples, 372
Pineal gland, 179
Plates, explanation of, 66, 162
Plurality of species, 95
Pollutions, nocturnal, 152
Position for copulation, 169
Posticos, 112
Pre-Adamite creation, 253
Premaxillary bone, 92
Primitive world, 283
Puberty, 151
Puella Campanica, 338
—— Transisalana, 338
Pueri Pyrenaici, 339
Puppy, a deformed, 75

Quadrumana, 171
Quarteroon, 112
Quimos, 255

Rabbit, 76
Rabbits, white, 130
Racial varieties of the face, 227
Rams, throats of, 113
Reason, 152
Rete mirabile arteriosum, 175
Reticulum, 113
Retroemingency, 169

Sacrum, 142
Salmo arcticus, 318
Samoeides, 301
Satyr, 97, 141

INDEX OF SUBJECTS.

Scriptures, accuracy of the, 52
Scythians, 119
Semiramis, 60
Senegal, 107
Senegambia negresses, 207
Sexes, part taken by in the generation of the fœtus, 60
Sicilian woman, 134
Simia cynomolgus, 109
—— diana, 74
—— longimana, 97
—— Satyrus, 98
—— troglodytes, 96
Singing birds, 199
Sinuessa, 77
Siron, lizard, 87
Skin, 208, 364
Skin diseases of nun, 134
Skulls, 101, 114, 234
Spartan dogs, 73
Species, 188, 260
Speech, 83
Spotted skin, 113
Squirrels, 71, 73
Stature, 102, 252, 258
Styria, 113
Sun and air, 371
Supreme Being, providence of the, 73
Swedish girl and bear, 80

Tailed men, 142, 243
Tails, 353
Tarsal bones, 167
Tattooing, 129

Tears, 184
Teeth of man, 88, 173, 243
Tehueletæ, 253
Tela mucosa, 180
Temperature, 101
Terceron, 112
Terobratula, 283
Têtes de Boule, 121
Throats of rams, 113
Tierra del Fuego, 103
Transmission, 358
Troglodyte, 97
Typhus fever, 308

Union of man and brutes, 201
Unnatural crimes, 201

Vagina, its direction, 189
Variegated skin, 218
Varieties and species, 190, 264, 332
Vertical scale, 237
Ventrals, 143
Virginians, 110
Vitruvius, 107

White, 371
Wild children, 163
Womb, 377

Yellow fever, 369

Zell, 87
Zephyrea, 70

INDEX OF AUTHORS.

Abildgaard, 246
Ackermann, 223, 241
Actuarius, 133
Adair, 240, 241
Adanson, 307
Adelung, 30
Ælian, 129
Æmilianus, 167
Ætius, 133
Agathemerus, 129
Agricola, 137, 139
Aguirre, 242
Albinus, 78, 101, 106, 115, 143, 210, 222, 364
Aldrovandus, 80, 143, 289
Alefounder, 336
Alexander, 107
Allamand, 261
Alpinus, 248
Alströmer, 122
Anaxagoras, 171
Anderson, 227
Anderson, Jürgen, 25
Andry, 241
Arbuthnot, 60, 335
Argensola, 262
Aristotle, 33, 73, 91, 106, 139, 178, 179, 203, 250
Arrian, 102
Artedi, 19
Arthaud, 262
Asch, de, 156, 157, 158, 230, 241, 349, 354
Attuioch, 271
Attumonelli, 210
Averroes, 136
Avicenna, 124, 130
Aublet, 112, 217, 107
Augustine, St. 226
Aunoy, 248

Bacon, 321
Baldinger, 4, 14, 15, 28, 43, 44
Bancroft, 62
Bankes, 259, 275
Banks, 11, 31, 145, 149, 158, 161, 192, 271, 274, 275, 302
Barbmann, 271
Barbot, 214, 232, 245, 305
Barrère, 105, 210
Barth, 73
Bartolozzi, 310, 336
Bate, 222
Bates, 129
Bauhin, 115, 142
Baumgartner, 211
Baurenfiend, 126, 127
Bayle, 52
Bazin, 21
Beeckman, 104
Begert, 128, 210
Behm, 267
Behrens, 255
Bell, 134
Bellon, 120
Belon, 223
Berchem, 188
Berengarius, 175
Berkel, 273
Bernadotti, 34
Bertin, 88, 115, 175
Bidder, 349
Biet, 223
Billmann, 157, 177
Birch, 104, 244
Blair, 179
Blane, Vincent le, 10
Blanchard, 142
Blane, 21
Bleyswyck, 311
Bligh, 162

INDEX OF AUTHORS.

Blumenbach, 359
Bochart, 73
Boddaert, 262
Boseler, 129
Boerhaave, 108, 122, 308
Bomare, 217, 221, 292
Bonnet, 31, 54, 69, 72, 315
Bontius, 81, 83
Borde, 233
Borgia, 158
Born, 17
Bougainville, 250, 272, 285
Bouguer, 107, 215
Boullay-le-Gouz, 250
Bourguet, 75, 261
Bouterwek, 16
Bowrey, 83
Boxenhard, 253
Brandes, 46
Brasen, 103
Braun, 160
Breton, 241
Breydenbach, 148
Brosses, Dea, 104, 254
Brown, 214
Bruce, 212, 223, 225, 226
Brue, 315
Bruin, 192
Bruin, De, 160, 214
Brun, Le, 122, 127, 128, 129, 135
Bry, De, 122
Bryant, 212, 275
Brydon, 374
Buckman, 244
Buddaeus, 43
Buffon, 52, 53, 76, 78, 87, 90, 133, 187, 189, 210, 218, 245, 252, 254, 262, 277, 331, 362, 365, 367, 370, 373, 381, 382, 383, 384
Büttner, 4, 44, 73, 76, 118.
Buzzi, 281
Byrd, 218

Cadamosto, 245
Cesar, 369
Caldani, 179, 222
Camelli, 136, 140, 262
Camerarius, 126
Camper, 31, 65, 67, 97, 108, 176, 220, 235, 241, 245, 322, 348
Canaegieter, 217
Capetein, 311
Cardan, 71, 77, 81, 107, 121, 136, 138, 139, 243

Carpi, 170
Carteret, 272
Cartwright, 161
Cavendish, 161
Caverhill, 141
Chamberlaine, 170
Chanvalon, 249, 251
Chapman, 132
Chardin, 269
Charlevoix, 121, 127, 242, 283
Chemnitz, 253
Cheselden, 21
Chodowiecki, 160
Christ, 4
Churchill, 78, 245
Clarkson, 310
Clauder, 75
Clavigero, 192, 293
Clayton, 252
Cligny, 256
Clover, 129
Coiter, 91, 114, 177
Collin, 91
Columella, 72, 77
Commerson, 254
Condamine, 185, 242
Connor, 327
Conring, 224
Cook, 122, 160, 214, 257, 262, 313
Correggio, 61
Cossigny, 140, 262
Covolo, 102
Cranz, 162, 104, 108, 118, 214, 231
Cranfurd, 335
Croll, 16
Croix, de la, 267
Cunous, 115
Curtis, 29
Cuvier, 11, 53

Dalrymple, 195, 247, 260, 275
Dampier, 232, 251, 378, 383
D'Anville, 99
Dapper, 136
D'Argenville, 103
Daubenton, 85, 91, 179
Defoe, 232
Deluc, 221
Derham, 28
Descartes, 59
D'Hancarville, 284
Dietz, 44
Dietzmann, 102
Dieza, 247

INDEX OF AUTHORS. 401

Digby, 328
Dilich, 87
Diodorus Siculus, 244
Dobrizhoffer, 273
Doevern, 143
Dornford, 333
Dorville, 253
Duddell, 261
Dürer, 114, 118, 125, 251
Dyck, Von, 311

Ebel, 179
Edwards, 87, 97, 140
Ehrenmalm, 103, 108
Elliotson, 18
Ellis, 104, 118, 251, 257
Elsholtz, 102, 114, 142
Engel, 99, 106, 117, 210, 230, 267
Ernesti, 71
Erxleben, 44, 245
Eustachius, 55, 91, 115, 177

Fabricius, 257, 292
Falconet, 310
Falk, 228
Falkner, 104, 255
Fallopia, 142, 143, 175
Fanton, 106
Fein, 335
Feller, 252, 267
Ferguson, 393
Formin, 113, 125, 217, 247
Festus, 133
Fichte, 18, 62
Fidelis, 80
Filangieri, 339
Fischer, 101, 115, 116, 120, 262
Flourens, 17
Foeqnenbrach, 249
Foes, 133
Fontaine, 62
Fontana, 213, 241, 255
Fontenelle, 55, 82, 136
Fordyce, 195
Forrest, 245, 272
Forster, G., 31, 100, 119, 171, 210, 223, 243, 247, 248, 250, 254, 258, 271, 273, 254
Forster, R., 31
Foucher d'Olsonville, 315
Fourcroy, 213
Franklin, 154
Fremery, 342
Freylinghausen, 137
Frisch, 108, 162

Fuller, 205

Gaertner, 148
Gagliardi, 102
Gainsborough, 310
Galen, 86, 114, 135, 174, 175
Garcilasso, 215, 216, 217
Gebelin, 53
Gentil, 227
George I., 330, 334
Georgi, 249
Gesner, 76, 77, 143, 262, 299
Geuns, 156, 154
Geyer, 337
Giesler, 4
Gily, 216
Girtanner, 212
Glafey, 102
Gleichen, 73
Gmelin, 21, 71, 120, 226, 235, 272
Goethe, 18
Goldsmith, 99, 116, 134, 135, 136, 262
Görz Schlitz, 249
Gordon, 252
Gözo, 322
Gregorina, 306
Gröben, 83, 129, 135, 137, 245
Grotius, 129
Guindant, 141
Gumilla, 218, 219, 220
Günz, 108
Gunner, 262

Hacquet, 224
Haen, 210, 310
Hager, 231
Hahn, 85
Hakluyt, 247
Hall, 134
Haller, 15, 31, 81, 53, 68, 73, 75, 76, 78, 89, 91, 98, 103, 105, 108, 109, 124, 127, 141, 170, 178, 210, 222, 211, 227, 282, 297, 368, 385
Hancarville, 201, 231
Hard, 107
Hardt, 25
Harduin, 133, 139
Hartsink, 215
Harvey, 141, 259
Hauber, 95
Hanterive, 216, 217
Hawkes, 223
Hawkesworth, 127, 128, 140, 143, 215, 246, 250, 252, 302, 315, 368, 371, 377, 351, 383, 354, 355

26

Hawkins, 252
Heiss, 306
Helbig, 141, 258
Heliodorus, 138
Helvetius, 171
Hemmerwam, 112, 123, 127
Henle, 353
Herder, 337
Herissant, 73
Herodotus, 102, 126, 129
Herrera, 203
Hesse, 255
Hesychius, 79
Heyne, 4, 27, 44, 73, 125, 251, 258
Hildan, 102
Hildebrant, 162
Higgius, 344
Hippocrates, 108, 116, 133, 192, 203, 241, 242
Hobbes, 184
Hodges, 160, 216
Hoeven, 353
Hogendorp, 224
Hogg, 11
Högström, 102
Hollar, 160
Hollmann, 310, 320
Home, 94, 103, 116, 272
Honorius, 139
Horace, 30
Hornemann, 22
Howe, 93
Hughes, 94, 126
Humboldt, 22
Humauld, 121
Hunnemann, 161
Hunter, 25, 259, 261, 262, 343
Hunter, Jo., 357
Hunter, Jo. (Gov.), 223
Hunter, W., 70
Hutton, 10
Huschke, 333
Hyde, 112, 215

Ingramias, 114, 115
Insfeldt, 118
Isidore, 124
Istor .Ethicus, 139
Ives, 22

Jacquin, 161
Janson, 183
Jefferson, 252
Jetze, 1

Johnson, 39
Jones, 212
Jonston, 292
Jussieu, 11

Kaempfer, 170
Kaimes, 199
Kaltschmidt, 43
Kampf, 22
Kant, 15, 92, 203, 207, 210, 223, 231, 250, 267, 243
Kästner, 44
Kemble, 60
Kersting, 101, 132
Kettle, 270
Kiug, 174
Klein, 216, 261
Klinkosch, 222
Kluger, 268
Klüppel, 43
Knebig, 129, 142
Köhler, 10
Kolben, 125, 127, 223, 247
Kölreuter, 196
König, 142
Köpke, 141, 259
Kramer, 262
Krascheninikof, 129
Krüger, 332
Krünitz, 210
Kütthardt, 332

Label, 112, 113, 216, 222
Lacepede, 22
L'Admiral, 106
Laert, 107
Laet, 129
La Fosse, 94
Lamothe, 113
Langhan, 113
Langsdorff, 22
Lauitz, 352
Laurenberg, 114, 115
Lavater, 114, 122, 223
Lawson, 241
Le Brun, 134
Le Cat, 89, 95, 97, 106, 130, 139, 210, 231, 261
Ledyard, 262
Leem, 102
Leger, 77
Legnat, 87, 140, 250
Leibnitz, 71
Lenthe, Von, 6
Leonardo da Vinci, 170

INDEX OF AUTHORS.   403

Leroy, 155
Levy, 232, 272
Libavius, 227
Licetus, 80
Lichtenberg and Voigt, 9, 119
Lieberkühn, 103
Ligon, 82
Lind, 389
Link, 11
Linnæus, 13, 51, 54, 57, 73, 84, 90, 93, 95, 98, 125, 129, 142, 150, 152, 163, 165, 172, 173, 191, 198, 226, 249, 255, 267, 281, 297, 331, 337, 338, 361, 370
Linschot, 274
Linschoten, 254
Lischoten, Van, 248
Lithgow, 248
Livy, 73, 129
Lodemann, 28
Long, 196, 217
Lorry, 187, 213, 221
Loubert, 213
Louis of Bavaria, 349
Luc, de, 10, 34, 213
Ludwig, 108, 222
Lucas, 307
Lucian, 302
Lucretius, 81, 287, 323
Ludolph, 135, 306
Lysons, 160

Macrobius, 107
Magellan, 253
Mairè, Le, 307
Malpighi, 200, 289
Marcgrav, 216, 224
Mareion, 174, 215, 223, 232, 241, 245, 257, 272
Martens, 33
Martial, 146
Martini, 129, 141, 142
Mars, 3
Maupertuis, 134, 136, 257, 289
Maximilian, 124
Mayor, 16
Meares, 241
McHenry, 310
Mockel, 213
Moger, 152
Meiners, 269
Molga, 359
Mela, 139
Menule, 16
Menippus, 302

Menizel, 247
Menz, 4
Mercurialis, 125, 251
Meriani, 115, 142, 143
Merk, 31
Merolla, 78
Metager, 268
Meyer, Jurgen, 329
Michaelis, 32, 43, 60, 156, 154
Middleton, 244
Modave, 255
Moler, 210
Molina, 273, 274
Molinelli, 220
Moll, 10, 31
Monboddo, 60, 165, 258, 295, 331, 335
Monneron, 250
Montesquieu, 57, 60
Moreton, 217
Morol, 289
Morgan, 219
Morse, 252
Morton, 319
Moscati, 84, 168
Mothe, 219
Mullen, 94
Müller, 44, 123, 174
Murray, 99, 104, 108
Mycock, 362

Napoleon, 21, 60
Narborough, 222, 252
Naudin, 210
Noorgard, 21
Neoptolemus, 174
Neulaner, 43, 44
Neuwild, 22
Nicolai, 44
Niebuhr, 122, 126, 128, 129, 245, 307
Nipho, 142
Nisbett, 308
Nott and Gliddon, 359
Nux, de la, 262

Observena, 73
Oebme, 310
Oken, 52
Olaus Magnus, 80, 134
Oldendorp, 215, 222, 309
Olearius, 115
Orilavius, 133
Ortega, 274
Osbeck, 17, 25
Oslander, 16

404 INDEX OF AUTHORS.

Ovaglio, 258
Oviedo, 241

Pallas, 72, 102, 117, 164, 193, 201, 250, 252
Papious, 101
Pareus, 60
Paris, 271
Park, 308
Parkinson, 91, 102, 105, 122, 123, 127, 128, 129, 131
Parson, J., 69, 216
Pataki, 152
Paterson, 312
Patot, 181
Pausanias, 221, 258
Pauw, 104, 112, 120, 133, 254, 271, 321
Pavens, 133
Pechlin, 108, 192, 222, 223
Penault, 51
Pennant, 07, 234, 281
Perceval, 251
Pererius, 74
Peter the Great, 393
Petroaius, 125, 251
Peyssonel, 232
Pflug, 118
Plater, 103, 232
Phillies, 241
Phillips, 201
Picart, 234
Pinto, 215, 262
Pistorius, 337
Pliny, 14, 56, 73, 79, 63, 88, 90, 107, 124, 129, 133, 138, 135, 141, 258, 253
Plutarch, 60
Poiret, 214
Pomponius Mela, 128, 139
Porta, 77
Portius, 220
Pownall, 267
Provost, 372, 376, 388
Prichard, 131
Prizelius, 73
Ptolemy, 139, 141
Puento, 247

Quintilian, 10
Quiqueran, 69
Quiros, 275

Ramsay, 251, 308

Rauwolf, 127, 128
Ray, 94, 159, 299, 362
Reaumur, 76
Redeker, 335
Regnard, 271
Reimar, 73, 62
Reinhold, 139
Retzius, 353, 354
Rhodiginus, 102, 107, 124, 125
Rhyne, 249
Richter, 16, 17, 44
Riecke, 243
Riet, 105, 222
Riolan, 91, 249
Robertson, 254, 272, 274
Robinet, 56, 172
Rochefort, 213
Roggewein, 255
Römer, 245
Rondelet, 56
Röntgen, 22
Rosen, 116
Rosinus, 254
Rousseau, 81, 240, 312, 331, 391
Rozier, 73
Rubbi, 254
Rudbeck, 221
Rudolphi, 28, 131
Rueff, 77, 80
Ruhnken, 33
Rusb, 308, 310
Russel, 122, 128, 302
Ruysch, 123
Rytschkow, 141, 258
Rzacynski, 72

Saar, 249
Sabatier, 241
Sagard, 273
Sanders, 23
Sandifort, 183
Santorinus, 106
Sartorius, 34
Saussure, 261
Saxo Grammaticus, 80
Scaliger, 243
Schelling, 18, 62
Schenk, 50
Schilling, 162
Schlözer, 22, 44, 337
Schmidt, 319
Schneider, 52
Schotte, 223, 245
Schouten, 247

INDEX OF AUTHORS.

Schrage, 166
Schreiber, 113, 134
Schreiber, 93
Schroyer, 127, 128
Schröder van der Kolk, 335
Schrötter, 284
Schurigius, 126, 271
Scotin, 96
Sohn, 123
Seetzen, 22
Seneca, 11
Severin, 335
Shaw, 78, 305
Sibthorp, 22
Sickler, 14
Sloane, 214
Smetius, 247
Socrates, 60
Solinus, 10
Sömmerring, 98, 51, 156, 157, 179, 213, 222, 243, 251
Spallanzani, 79
Spanberg, 174
Spangenberg, 335
Sparrmann, 249, 251, 306
Sporen, 262
Spigel, 149, 235, 241, 320
Sprenger, 73
Stahlin, 99
Stel, 140
Steller, 89, 184, 201, 231
Steno, Nicolas of, 172
Stephan, 133, 213
Stieglitz, 78
Storch, 80
Storr, 244
Strabo, 107, 199, 241
Struck, 213
Strahlenberg, 134, 220
Strauss, 278
Stromeyer, 15
Sulz, 132
Sulzer, 93, 97, 262
Swift, 331, 335
Symmonds, 244

Taberranni, 142
Tacitus, 233
Tanner, 44
Tappe, 258
Taitter, 161
Tsarmann, 133
Techo, 271, 273
Teuch, 251, 259

Themel, 262
Thevenot, 127
Thibault, 213
Thibault de Chanvalon, 241
Tigurinus Polyhistor, 77
Torce, 214
Torquemada, 241
Toortaal, 353
Townley, 230
Towns, 210
Trendelnburg, 176
Trithemius, 142
Troja, 17
Tronchin, 126
Tschudi, 340, 353
Tulp, 98, 165, 336
Twiss, 216, 217, 250
Tychsen, 216
Tyson, 84, 87, 91, 92, 93, 95, 97, 141, 175

Ulloa, 124, 251, 273, 305
Unfreville, 257

Vaillant, 256
Valentyn, 216, 262
Vallisneri, 316
Varro, 73, 79
Vasc, 313
Vaugondy, 99, 117, 257
Venette, 78
Verulam, 202
Vesalius, 93, 115, 116, 142, 175, 176, 177, 246, 241
Vesling, 143
Vespucci, 243
Vieq d'Azyr, 176
Virgil, 125, 251
Vitet, 176
Vitruvius, 107
Vogel, 123
Voigt, 9, 43, 165, 191, 203, 244
Volkman, 22
Volney, 231
Voltaire, 56, 57, 66, 134, 136, 250, 270, 281, 339
Vosmaer, 172
Vossius, 135, 137, 140

Wafer, 127, 134, 135, 136, 137, 262
Wagner, K., 31, 103, 105, 132, 262, 347, 349
Walch, 4, 22, 44, 96
Waldeck, 21
Waller, 272

27

Wallis, 103, 215
Walsh, 230, 286
Walter, 226
Warton, 201
Wasse, 182
Wusterns, 141
West, 234
Whang-at-tong, 119
Wheatley, 319
Wieland, 81, 308
Wilson, 210, 272
Winckelmann, 116, 231
Winslow, 117, 244, 245
Winter, 255
Winterbottom, 305
Witsen, 122
Wolff, 137

Wreden, 16
Wrisberg, 138
Wyttenbach, 33

Xenocrates, 22

Yonge, 221
Yvo, 245, 250, 279

Zach, 31
Zachias, 77
Zahn, 88
Zain, 150
Zimmermann, 210, 215, 254, 268, 273
Zingendorf, 59, 331
Zucchelli, 81

THE END.

Plate I.

Fig 1.

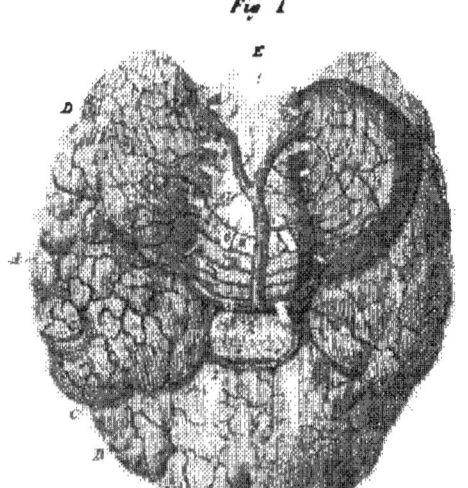

Fig 2.

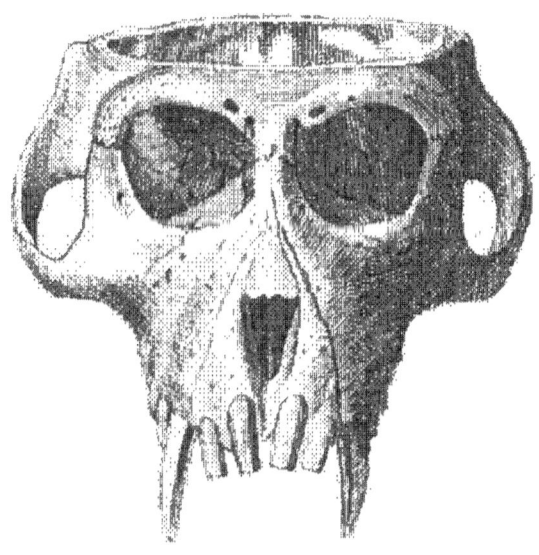

Plate II.

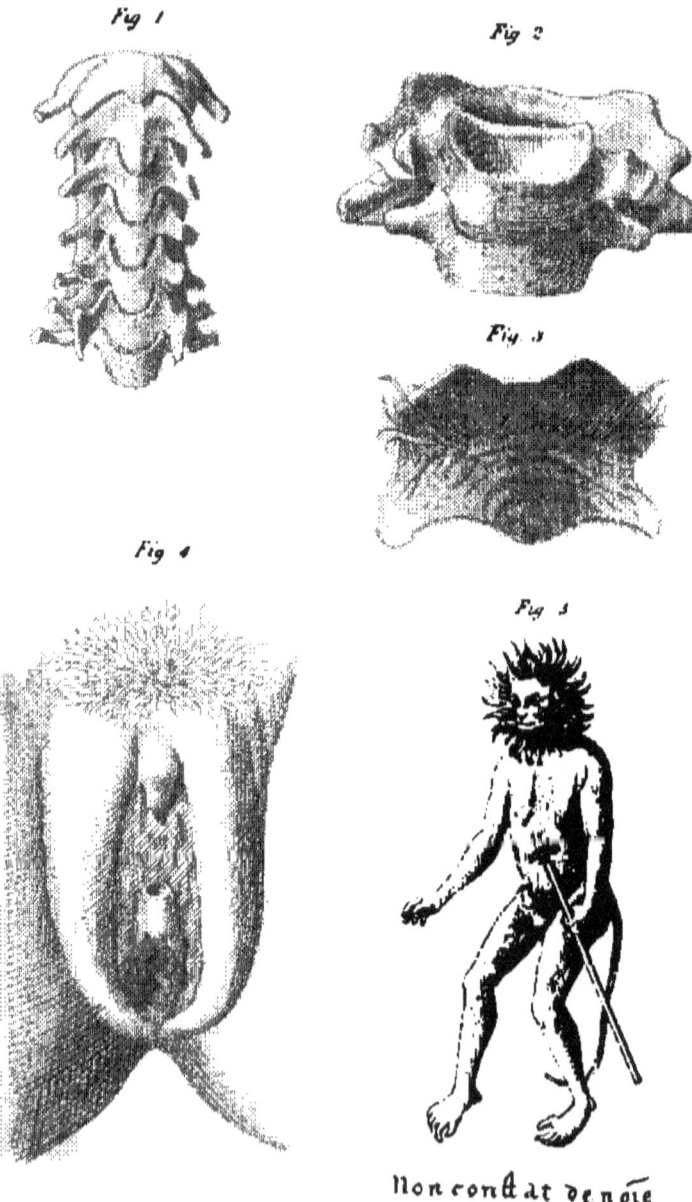

Plate III.

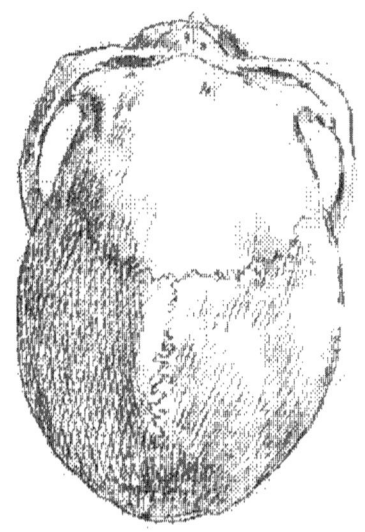

1
Tungusae.

TWELFTH LIST

OF THE

FOUNDATION FELLOWS

OF THE

Anthropological Society of London.

(*Corrected to January 17th, 1865.*)

ANTHROPOLOGICAL SOCIETY OF LONDON.

OFFICERS AND COUNCIL FOR 1864.

President.
JAMES HUNT, Esq., Ph.D., F.S.A., F.R.S.L., Honorary Foreign Secretary of the Royal Society of Literature of Great Britain, Foreign Associate of the Anthropological Society of Paris, Honorary Fellow of the Ethnological Society of London, Corresponding Member of the Upper Hesse Society for Natural and Medical Science, etc.

Vice-Presidents.
CAPTAIN RICHARD F. BURTON, F.R.G.S., H.M. Consul at Santos, etc.
J. FREDERICK COLLINGWOOD, ESQ., F.R.S.L., F.G.S., Foreign Associate of the Anthropological Society of Paris.
BERTHOLD SEEMANN, ESQ., Ph.D., F.L.S., F.R.G.S.
THOMAS DENDYSHE, ESQ., M.A.

Honorary Secretaries.
GEORGE E. ROBERTS, ESQ., F.G.S., Foreign Associate of the Anthropological Society of Paris.
WILLIAM BOLLAERT, ESQ., Corr. Mem. Univ. Chile, and Ethno. Socs. London and New York.

Honorary Foreign Secretary.
ALFRED HIGGINS, ESQ., Foreign Associate of the Anthropological Society of Paris.

Treasurer.
RICHARD STEPHEN CHARNOCK, ESQ., Ph.D., F.S.A., F.R.G.S., Foreign Associate of the Anthropological Society of Paris.

Council.
HUGH J. C. BEAVAN, ESQ., F.R.G.S.
S. E. B. DOUVERIE-PUSEY, ESQ., F.E.S.
CHARLES HARCOURT CHAMBERS, ESQ., M.A.
S. EDWIN COLLINGWOOD, ESQ., F.Z.S.
GEORGE DUNCAN GIBB, ESQ., M.A., M.D., LL.D., F.G.S.
THE VISCOUNT MILTON, F.R.G.S.
GEORGE NORTH, ESQ.
L. OWEN PIKE, ESQ., M.A.
W. WINWOOD READE, ESQ., F.R.G.S., Corr. Mem. Geographical Society of Paris.
JAMES REDDIE, ESQ.
GEORGE FREDERICK ROLPH, ESQ.
CHARLES ROBERT DES RUFFIÈRES, ESQ., F.G.S., F.E.S.
WILLIAM TRAVERS, ESQ., F.R.C.S., L.R.C.P.
WILLIAM SANDYS WRIGHT VAUX, ESQ., M.A., F.S.A., F.R.S.L., President of the Numismatic Society of London.

Curator, Librarian, and Assistant Secretary.
CHARLES CARTER BLAKE, ESQ., F.G.S., Foreign Associate of the Anthropological Society of Paris.

TWELFTH LIST

OF THE

FOUNDATION FELLOWS

OF THE

ANTHROPOLOGICAL SOCIETY OF LONDON.

The names with * before them are those of Fellows who have compounded for their Annual Subscription.

¶ *These Fellows have contributed Papers to the Society.*

| *These Fellows are Members of Council.*

‡ *These Fellows are also Local Secretaries.*

à Beckett, Arthur W., Esq. *17 King Street, S. James's, S.W.*
Adams, Henry John, Esq. *14 Thornhill Square, N.*
Adlam, William, Esq. *Manor House, Chew Magna, Somerset.*
Aley, Frederick W., Esq. *8 Thurloe Place, South Kensington, W.*
Arden, R. E., Esq., F.G.S., F.R.G.S.. *Sunbury Park, Middlesex, S.E.*
Armitage, W., Esq. *Townfield House, Altrincham.*
Armitstead, T. B., Esq.
Arundell, Rodolph, Esq. *34 Upper Montagu Street, Montagu Square.*
Ash, Charles Frederick, Esq., *20 and 21 Upper Thames Street, E.C.*
Ashbury, John, Esq. *9 Sussex Place, Hyde Park Gardens, W.*
Atkinson, Henry George, Esq., F.G.S. *18 Upper Gloucester Place, N.W.*
Austin, Richard, Esq. *Pernambuco.*
Aitken, Thomas, Esq., M.D., Member of the Anthropological Society of Paris. *District Lunatic Asylum, Inverness.*
Airston, William Baird, Esq., M.D. *S. Andrew's, Fife.*
Avery, John Gould, Esq. *40 Belsize Park, N.W.*

* Babington, C. Cardale, Esq., M.A., F.R.S., F.L.S., F.G.S., Sec. Cambridge Phil. Soc., Prof. Botany, Cambridge. *S. John's College, Cambridge.*
Babington, William, Esq. *Hulk "Princess Royal," Bonny River, West Coast of Africa.*
Baker, Benson, Esq., M.R.C.S.E. *6 Cross Street, Islington.*
Baker, J. P., Esq., M.R.C.S. *6 York Place, Portman Square, W.*
Barr, W. R., Esq. *Park Mills, Stockport.*
Barr, Joseph Henry, Esq., M.R.C.S. *Ardwick Green, Manchester.*
Bartlett, Edw., Esq. *8 King William Street, E.C.*
Barton, Alfred, Esq., F.R.G.S. *31 Craven Street, Strand; and Oriental Club, W.*
Beal, The Rev. S., Chaplain Royal Marine Artillery. *Fort Cumberland, Portsmouth.*

Beale, John S., Esq. 4 *Porteus Road*, W.

†Beavan, Hugh J. C., Esq., F.R.G.S. 13 *Blandford Square, Regent's Park, N.W; and Grafton Club*, W.

Beardsley, Amos, Esq., F.L.S., F.G.S. *The Grange, near Ulverstone, Lancashire.*

Beddoe, John, Esq., M.D., F.E.S., Foreign Associate of the Anthropological Society of Paris. *Clifton.*

*†¶ Bendyshe, Thos., Esq., M.A. VICE-PRESIDENT. 88 *Cambridge Street, Pimlico*, S.W.

Benson, W. F. G., Esq. *South Road, Waterloo, near Liverpool.*

Bertram, George, Esq. *Sciennes Street, Edinburgh.*

Best, the Hon. Capt. *Convict Prison, Princetown, Dartmoor, Devon.*

Dingham, H. C., Esq. *Wartnaby Hall, near Melton Mowbray.*

¶ Blake, Charles Carter, Esq., F.G.S., Foreign Associate of the Anthropological Society of Paris, Member of the Comité d'Archéologic Americaine de France. CURATOR, LIBRARIAN, and ASSISTANT SECRETARY. 4 *S. Martin's Place*, W.C.; *and 6 Kingswood Place, South Lambeth*, S.

Blakely, T. A., Capt. 34 *Montpellier Square*, S.W.

Bledsoe, A. T., Esq., LL.D. 33 *Argyll Road, Kensington*, W.

Blonnt, J. Hillier, Esq., M.D. *Bagshot, Surrey.*

†¶ Bollaert, Wm., Esq., Corr. Mem. Ethno. Socs., London, New York and Univ. Chile. HONORARY SECRETARY. 21A *Hanover Square*, W.

Bond, Walter M., Esq. *The Argory, Moy, Ireland.*

Bonney, Rev. T. George, M.A., F.G.S. *S John's College, Cambridge.*

Bosse, Henry S., Esq., M.D., F.R.S., F.G.S. *Clarerhouse, near Dundee.*

‡ Bosworth, The Rev. Joseph, D.D., Trin. Coll., Cambridge, and of Christ Church, Oxford, Prof. Anglo-Saxon, Dr.Phil. of Leyden, F.R.S., F.S.A., F.R.S.L., Corresponding Member of the Royal Institute of the Netherlands, etc., etc. 20 *Beaumont Square, Oxford; and Water Stratford, Buckingham.*

Boulton, George, Esq. 1 *Gordon Square*, W.C.

†¶ Bouverie-Pusey, S. E. B., Esq., F.E.S. 7 *Green Street*, W.

Boruham, W. W., Esq., F.R.A.S. *Haverhill, Suffolk,*

Boys, Jacob, Esq. *Grand Parade, Brighton.*

Brabrook, E. W., Esq., F.S.A. 3 *Parliament Street*, S.W.

Braddon, Henry, Esq. 5 *Dane's Inn*, W.C.

Brady, Antonio, Esq., F.G.S. *Maryland Point, Stratford, Essex.*

Braggiotti, George M., Esq. *New York.* (Care of *Messrs. Corpi and Co., 10 Austin Friars.*)

Brainsford, C., Esq., M.D. *Haverhill, Suffolk.*

Brinton, John, Esq. *The Shrubbery, Kidderminster.*

Brebner, James, Esq., Advocate. 20 *Albyn Place, Aberdeen.*

Brickwood, J. S., Esq. *Claremont House, Tunbridge Wells.*

Brodhurst, Bernard Edward, Esq., F.R.C.S. 20 *Grosvenor St.*, W.

Brooke, His Highness, Rajah Sir James, K.C.B. *Burraton, Horrabridge, Devon.*

Brookes, Henry, Esq. 26 *Great Winchester Street*, E.C.

Brown, Edward, Esq. *Oak Hill, Surbiton Hill, S.*
Brown, E. O., Esq. *Chemical Department, Royal Arsenal, Woolwich.*
Brown, James Roberts, Esq., F.R.S.N.A. Copenhagen. *Sealeby Lodge, Camden Road, Holloway, N.*
Bunkell, Henry Christopher, Esq. 1 *Penn Road, Caledonian Road, Holloway, N.*
Burke, John S., Esq. 4 *Queen Square, Westminster, S.W.*
‡ ¶ Burton, Captain Richard Fenwick, F.R.G.S., H.M. Consul, Santos, Brazil. VICE-PRESIDENT. 34 *Upper Montagu Street, Montagu Square, W.; and Santos, Brazil.*
Burton, Samuel, Esq. *Churchill House, Daventry.*
Butler, Henry, Esq. *Admiralty, Somerset House, W.C.*
*Buxton, Charles, Esq., M.P. 7 *Grosvenor Crescent, S.W.*
Byerley, J., Esq. *Seacombe, Cheshire.*
Byham, George, Esq. *War Office, Pall Mall, S.W.; and Ealing.*

*Cabbell, Benj. Bond, Esq., F.R.S., F.S.A. 52 *Portland Place, W.*
Cameron, Captain, H.M. Consul. *Massouah, Abyssinia.*
Campbell, Henry, Esq. 6 *Claremont Gardens, Glasgow.*
*Campbell, J. *Bangkok, Siam.* (Care of *Messrs. Smith and Elder, Pall Mall.*)
Campbell, Montgomery, Esq. 39A *Wigmore Street, Cavendish Square, W.*
Cannon, Thomas, Esq. 13 *Paternoster Row, E.C.*
Caplin, Dr. J. F. 9 *York Place, Portman Square, W.*
Capper, Charles, Esq. 9 *Mincing Lane, E.C.*
Cartwright, Samuel, Professor. 32 *Old Burlington Street, W.*
Carulla, Facundo, Esq., Honorary Member Manchester Scientific Student's Association. (Care of) *Messrs. J. Daglish and Co., Harrington Street, Liverpool; and 91 Paseo de Julio, Buenos Ayres.*
Cassell, John, Esq. *La Belle Sauvage Yard, Ludgate Hill, E.C.*
† Chambers, Charles Harcourt, Esq., M.A. 2 *Chesham Place, S.W.*
Chambers, William, Esq. *Aberystwith.*
Charlton, Henry, Esq. *Birmingham.*
Chamberlin, William, Esq. 4 *Hervey Terrace, Brighton.*
Chance, F., Esq., M.D. 48 *Errasfield Place, S. Leonard's on Sea.*
† ¶ Charnock, Richard Stephen, Esq., Ph.D., F.S.A., F.R.G.S., F.R.S.S.A., Foreign Associate of the Anthropological Society of Paris, Foundation Member of the Royal Society of Northern Antiquaries, Corresponding Member of the New England Historic-Genealogical Society. TREASURER. 4 *S. Martin's Place, W.C.; 8 Gray's Inn Square, W.C.; and 30 The Grove, Hammersmith.*
Chignell, Hendrick Agnis, Esq. 47 *York Road, Brighton.*
Clare, Rev. Henry, M.A., F.R.S.L. *Crossens, North Meols, Ormskirk.*
Clarendon, The Right Honourable The Earl of, K.G., G.C.B., F.R.S. *Grosvenor Crescent, W.*
Clement, William James, Esq., F.E.S. *The Council House, Shrewsbury.*
Clerk, Lieutenant-Colonel H., R.A. *Royal Arsenal, Woolwich.*
Cock, John, Esq., jun., F.R.H.S., M.S.A. *South Molton.*

Cockings, W. Spencer, Esq., F.E.S.
Coles, Henry, Esq. *Science and Art Department, Kensington*, W.
Collier, J. Payne, Esq., F.S.A. *Maidenhead.*
† Collingwood, J. Frederick, Esq., F.R.S.L., F.G.S., Foreign Associate of the Anthropological Society of Paris. VICE-PRESIDENT. *4 S. Martin's Place*, W.C.; *and 54 Gloucester Street, Belgrave Road*, S.W.
† Collingwood, S. Edwin, Esq., F.Z.S. *26 Buckingham Place, Brighton.*
Cooke, W. Fothergill, Esq. *Electric Telegraph Office, London*
Cooper, Sir Daniel, Bart. *20 Prince's Terrace*, W.
Cory, W., Esq. *4 Gordon Place*, W.C.
Cossham, Handel, Esq., F.G.S. *Shortwood Lodge, Bristol.*
Courtauld, Samuel, Esq. *Gosfield Hall, Essex.*
Cowell, J. Jermyn, Esq. *41 Gloucester Terrace, Hyde Park*, W.
Cox, J. W. Conrad, Esq., B.A. *32 Westbourne Place, Eaton Square; and 4 Grove Hill, Woodford*, N.E.
Cox, W. T., Esq. *The Hall, Spornton, Derby.*
* Cozens, J. F. W., Esq. *Larkhere Lodge, Clapham Park*, S.
Crosswellor, Henry Valentine, Esq. *133 Leighton Road, Kentish Town*, N.W.
Critchett, George, Esq. *75 Harley Street, Cavendish Square*, W.
Crolly, The Rev. J. M., Ph.D. *Trimdon.*
Crowley, Henry, Esq. *Corporation Street, Manchester.*
Croxford, George Rayner, Esq. *Forest Gate, Essex*, E.
* Cuthbert, J. R., Esq. *Chapel Street, Liverpool.*

Daniell, Hurst, Esq. *4 Highbury Park West, Highbury Hill*, N.
Davey, J. G., Esq., M.D. *Northwoods, near Bristol.*
Davies, F. Drummond, Esq. *Hare Court, Temple.*
¶ Davis, J. Barnard, Esq., M.D., F.S.A., Foreign Associate of the Anthropological Society of Paris. *Shelton, Staffordshire.*
Dawson, George, Esq., M.A., F.G.S. *40 Belgrave Road, Birmingham.*
De Horne, John, Esq. *137 Offord Road, Barnsbury Park, London*, N.
Dibley, G., Esq. *72 Malden Road*, N.W.
Dickinson, Henry, Esq., Colonial Surgeon. *Ceylon.*
* Dingle, Rev. John, M.A. *Lanchester, near Durham.*
Dobson, Thomas J., Esq. *Kingston upon Hull.*
Donaldson, Prof. John, Advocate. *Marchfield House, near Edinburgh.*
Dowie, James, Esq. *Strand*
Drake, Francis, Esq., F.G.S. *Leicester.*
Driver, H., Esq. *Windsor.*
Drummond, John, Esq. *The Boyle Court, Gloucester.*
† Du Chaillu, M. Paul Belloni, F.R.G.S., (care of) *129 Mount Street*, W.
Duncan, Peter Martin, M.B., F.G.S., Secretary of the Geological Society of London. *8 Belmont, Lee*, S.E.
Du Val, C. A., Esq. *Carlton Grove, Greenhays, Manchester.*
Duggan, J. R., Esq. *42 Watling Street*, E.C.

*Eassie, William, Esq., F.L.S., F.G.S. 11 *Park Road, Regent's Park*, N.W.
Eeles, Charles William, Esq., R.N. *H.M.S Victoria.*
Evans, E. Bickerton, Esq. *Whitbourne Hall, Doddenham, near Worcester.*
Evans, John, Esq., F.R.S., F.G.S., F.S.A., Secretary to the Numismatic Society of London. *Nash Mills, Hemel Hempstead.*
Ewart, William, Esq. *United University Club*, S.W.
Eyre, Sir Edward John. Governor of Jamaica. *King's House, Jamaica.*
‡¶ Fairbank, Frederick Royston, Esq., M.D., F.E.S. *S. Mary's Terrace, Hulme, Manchester.*
Farmer, Edmund, Esq. 80 *Cheapside, E.C.*
¶ Farrar, Rev. Frederic W., M.A., F.E.S. *Harrow*, N.W.
Fearon, Frederick, Esq. 13 *Pall Mall*, S.W.; *and Maidenhead.*
Ferguson, William, Esq., F.L.S., F.G.S. (Of Kinnendy, Ellon, Aberdeen.) 2 *S. Aidan's Terrace, Birkenhead.*
Firby, Edwin Foxton, Esq. *Gravelthorpe, near Ripon, Yorkshire.*
Firebrace, Frederick, Esq., Lieutenant Royal Engineers. *Shorncliffe.*
Fleming, Captain, 3rd Hussars. *Cavalry Barracks, Manchester.*
Flight, Walter, Esq. *Queenwood College, near Stockbridge, Hants.*
Forrester, Joseph James, Esq. 6 *S. Helen's Place*, E.C.
Foster, Balthazar W., Esq., M.D., Professor of Anatomy at Queen's College, Birmingham. 55 *Calthorpe Street, Edgbaston, Birmingham.*
Foster, M., Esq., M.D. *Huntingdon.*
Fraser, Adolphus Alexander, Esq. *War Office, Pall Mall.*
Freeman, Henry Stanhope, Esq., Governor of Lagos. 27 *Bury Street, S. James's.*
Freme, Major. *Army and Navy Club, St. James's Square*, S.W.
Freuler, H. Albert, Esq., M.D. *North Street, S. Andrew's.*
Fuller, Stephen D., Esq. 1 *Eaton Place*, S.W.
Furnell, M. C., Esq., M.D. *Cochin, Madras Presidency.*

Garrett, William H., Esq. 98 *Guildford Street*, W.C.
Gardner, Charles Henry, Esq. 5 *Clarendon Villas, Loughboro Park*, S.
Georgei, Professor. 18 *Wimpole Street, Cavendish Square*, W.
¦¶ Gibb, George Duncan, Esq., M.D., LL.D., M.A., F.G.S. 19A *Portman Street, Portman Square*, W.
Gibson, G. S., Esq. *Saffron Walden.*
Glaucopides, Spyridon, Esq. 7 *Maitland Park Crescent, Haverstock Hill*, N.
Glennie, J. Stuart, Esq. 6 *Stone Buildings, Lincoln's Inn*, E.C.
Goadby, Edwin, Esq. *Loughborough, Leicestershire.*
Gooch, Thomas, Esq. 63 *London Wall, City.*
‡¶ Gore, Richard Thos., Esq., F.R.C.S., F.E.S. 6 *Queen's Square, Bath.*
Gay, David, Esq. 74 *Cheapside*, E.C.
Green, Sidney Faithhorn, Esq. *Montagu House, Eltham, Kent.*
Gregor, Rev. Walter, M.A. *Pitsligo Manse, Rosehearty, Aberdeenshire.*
Gregory, J. R., Esq. 25 *Golden Square*, W.

Griffits, James Oliff, Esq. 3 *Middle Temple Lane*, E.C.
¶ Guppy, H. F. J., Esq. *Port of Spain, Trinidad.*
Hall, Hugh F., Esq. 17 *Dale Street, Liverpool.*
Hammond, C. D., Esq., M.D. 11 *Charlotte Street, Bedford Sq.*, W.C.
Hancock, H. J. B., Esq. *Duke's Hill, Bagshot.*
Hardman, William, Esq. *Norbiton Hall, Kingston-on-Thames*, S.W.
Harcourt, Clarence, Esq. 2 *King's Arms Yard*, E.C.; *and Cliff Villa, Ladywell, Lewisham.*
Harland, Charles J., Esq. *Madeira Place, Torquay.*
Harlin, Thomas, Esq. *Brook Street, Kingston on Thames.*
Harris, George, Esq., F.S.A., Registrar of the Court of Bankruptcy, Manchester. *Cornbrook Park, Hulme, Manchester.*
Haughton, Richard, Esq. *Ramsgate.*
Hawkins, A. G., Esq. 88 *Bishopsgate Street Without*, E.C.
Hay, Major W. E. 16 *Queen Street, Mayfair*, S.W.
Healey, Edward C., Esq. *Joldwynds, near Docking, Surrey.*
Heath, the Rev. Dunbar I., F.R.S.L. *Esher, Surrey.*
Hepworth, John Mason, Esq., J.P. *Ackworth, Yorkshire.*
Hewlett, Alfred, Esq. *The Grange, Coppull, near Wigan.*
Higgin, James, Esq. *Hopwood Avenue, Manchester.*
† Higgins, Alfred, Esq., Foreign Associate of the Anthropological Society of Paris. HONORARY FOREIGN SECRETARY. 4 *S. Martin's Place*, W.C.; and 26 *Manchester Street*, W.
Hillier, J., Esq. *Sandwich.*
Hobbs, W. G. E., Esq. *The Grammar School, Wareside, Ware, Herts.*
Hobler, F. H., Esq. *Chemical Department, Royal Arsenal, Woolwich.*
Hodge, Thomas, Esq. *South Street, S. Andrew's.*
Hodgson, D. H., Esq. *The Rangers, Dursley.*
Holland, Colonel James. 24 *Princes Square, Hyde Park.*
Horton, W. I. S., Esq., F.R.A.S., F.E.S. *Talbot Villa, Rugeley.*
Hotze, Henry, Esq., C.S.A. 17 *Savile Row*, W.
Hudson, Professor F., F.C.S. 68 *Corporation Street, Manchester.*
Hudson, Henry, Esq., M.D. *Glenville, Fermoy, Co. Cork.*
Hunt, Augustus H., Esq. *Birtley House, Chester-le-Street.*
Hunt, G. S. Lennox, Esq., F.E.S., H.B.M. Consul. *Rio de Janeiro.*
¶ ¶ Hunt, James, Esq., Ph.D., F.S.A., F.R.S.L., Honorary Foreign Secretary of the Royal Society of Literature of Great Britain, Foreign Associate of the Anthropological Society of Paris, Corr. Mem. of Upper Hesse Society for Natural and Medical Science, Honorary Fellow of the Ethnological Society of London. PRESIDENT. 4 *S. Martin's Place*, W.C.; 35 *Jermyn Street*, S.W.; *and Ore House, near Hastings.*
Hunt, John, Esq. 42 *North Parade, Grantham.*
Hutchinson, Jonathan, Esq., F.R.C.S. 4 *Finsbury Circus*, E.C.
Hutchinson, T. J., Esq., F.R.G S., F.R.S.L., F.E.S., Membre Titulaire de l'Institut d'Afrique à Paris, Corresponding Member of the Literary and Philosophic Society of Liverpool. *H.B.M. Consul at Rosario, Argentine Confederation.*

Ioannides, A., Esq., M.D.   8 *Chepstow Place, Bayswater,* W.
Izard, Frederick R., Esq.   141 *High Holborn.*

Jackson, Henry, Esq., F.E.S.   *S. James' Row, Sheffield.*
Jackson, H. W., Esq., M.R.C.S.   *Surrey County Asylum, Tooting.*
Jackson, J. Hughlings, Esq., M.D., M.R.C.P., Professor of Physiology at the London Hospital Medical College.   *5 Queen Square, Russell Square,* W.C.
‡Jackson, J. W., Esq.   39 *S. George's Road, Glasgow.*
Jacob, Major-General Le Grand, C.B.   *Bonchurch, Isle of Wight.*
Jardine, Sir William, Bart., F.R.S., F.L.S.   *Jardine Hall, Lockerby.*
Jarratt, The Rev. John, M.A.   *North Cave, Brough, Yorkshire.*
Jeffery, William S., Esq.   *5 Regent Street, Pall Mall,* S.W.
Jellicoe, Charles, Esq.   23 *Chester Terrace, Regent's Park,* N.W.
*Jennings, William, Esq., F.R.G.S.   13 *Victoria Street,* S.W.
Jenyns, The Rev. Leonard, M.A., F.L.S., F.G.S.   *Darlington Place, Bathwick, Bath.*
Jessopp, The Rev. J., M.A., Head Master King Edward the Sixth's School.   *The School House, Norwich.*
Johnson, Henry, Esq.   39 *Crutched Friars.*
Johnson, Henry James, Esq.   8 *Suffolk Place,* S.W.
Johnson, Richard, Esq.   *Langton Oaks, Fallowfield.*
Jones, J. Pryce, Esq.   *Grove Park School, Wrexham.*
Jones, C. Treasure, Esq., H.M. Consul, Shanghae.   *British Consulate, Shanghae.*
Jones, W. T., Esq.   1 *Montague Place, Kentish Town,* N.W.

Kelly, William, Esq.   28 *Rue Neuve Chaussée, Boulogne-sur-Mer.*
Kemm, the Rev. William Henry, B.A.   *Swanswick, near Bath.*
Kendall, T. M., Esq.   *St. Margaret's Place, King's Lynn, Norfolk.*
Killick, Joshua Edward, Esq.   137 *Strand,* W.C.
‡King, Kelburne, Esq., M.D., Lecturer on Anatomy, Hull; President of the Hull Literary and Philosophical Society.   27 *George Street, Hull.*
Kinlay, W. R. H., Esq., F.R.S.E.   2 *New Smithills, Paisley.*

La Barte, Rev. W. W., M.A.   *St. John's College, Newbury (Berks).*
*¶ Laing, Samuel, Esq., F.G.S.   6 *Kensington Gardens Terrace, Hyde Park,* W.
Lampray, Thomas, Esq.   *Warrior Lodge, The Grove, Hammersmith.*
Lancaster, John, Esq., F.G.S.   *Hindley Hall, near Wigan.*
Land, T. A. Augustus, Esq.   *Bryanston Street, Bryanston Square.*
Langley, J. N., Esq.   *Mowbray Park, Wolverhampton.*
Lawrence, Edward, Esq.   *Brachmount, Aigburth, Liverpool.*
Lawrence, Frederick, Esq.   *Essex Court, Temple,* E.C.
‡¶ Lee, Rd., Esq.   *Wilmot House, Leeds Road, Bradford, Yorkshire.*

Lees, Samuel, Esq. *Portland Place, Ashton-under-Lyne.*
Leitner, G. W., Esq., M.A., Ph.D., F.R.A.S., F.E.S., F.P.S., Professor of Arabic and Mohammedan Law, and Dean of the Oriental Section, King's College, London; Hon. Member and Master of the Free German Hochstift; Examiner in Oriental Languages at the College of Preceptors. *Government College, Lahore, India.*
Levy, W. Hanks, Esq., Director of the Association for Promoting the General Welfare of the Blind; 127 *Euston Road,* W.C.
Lister, John, Esq., F.G S. 28 *Porchester Terrace, Bayswater; and Shebdon Hall, near Halifax, Yorkshire.*
Lockyer, J. Norman, Esq., F.R.A.S., M.R.I. *War Office, Pall Mall,* S.W.; *and* 24 *Victoria Road, Finchley Road,* N.W.
Longman, William, Esq., F.G.S., F.R.S.L., F.R.G.S. 36 *Hyde Park Square,* W.
Lonsdale, Henry, Esq., M.D. *Carlisle.*
Lord, Edward, Esq. *Canal Street Works, Todmorden.*
Lucas, Thomas, Esq. *Belvedere Road, Lambeth,* S.; *and* 10 *Hyde Park Gardens,* W.
Lucy, W. C., Esq., F.G.S. *Claremont House, Gloucester.*
Lukis, Rev. W. C. *Wath Rectory, Ripon.*
Luxmoore, Coryndon H., Esq., F.S.A. 18 *S. John's Wood Park,* N.W.
Lybbe, Philip Powys Lybbe, Esq., M.P. 86 *S. James's Street.*

M'Arthur, Alexander Mc, Esq. *Raleigh Hall, Brixton Rise.*
Macclelland, James, Esq. 73 *Kensington Gardens Square, Bayswater.*
‡ M'Donald, William, Esq., M.D., F.L.S., F.G.S., Professor of Civil and Nat. Hist. in the University of St. Andrew's. *St. Andrew's.*
McCallum, Arthur E., Esq , 39th Madras Native Infantry. (Care of) *Messrs. Smith, Elder, and Co., Pall Mall,* S.W.
McDonnell, John, Esq., F.C.S.L. *Clare Villa, Rathmines, Dublin.*
McHenry, George, Esq. (Care of) 17 *Savile Row,* W.
Mackenzie, Kenneth Robert Henderson, Esq., F.S.A. *Orford House, Chiswick Mall,* W.
Mackintosh, Draper, Esq., M.D. *Gainsborough.*
Mackintosh, Charles F., Esq. *New Cross,* S.E.
Macleay, George, Esq., F.L.S. *Hyde Park Gardens.*
McLeod, Walter, Esq. *Military Hospital, Chelsea,* S.W.
Marsden, Robert C., Esq. 14 *Hanover Terrace, Regent's Park,* N.W.
Marshall, George W., Esq., L.L.B. 119 *Jermyn Street,* S.W.; *and New University Club, S. James's Street,* S.W.
Marshall, Robert, Esq. *Haverstock Villa, Haverstock Hill,* N.
Martin, Sir J. Ronald, F.R.S. 24 *Upper Brook Street,* W.; *and Keydell, near Horndean, Hants.*
Martin, John, Esq., F.L.S., F.G.S. *Cambridge House, Portsmouth.*
Martindale, N., Esq. *The Lodge, Clapham Common,* S.
Mathieson, James, Esq. 1A *Telegraph Street, Bank,* E.C.; *and* 22 *Delitha Villas, Barnsbury Park,* N.

Matthews, Henry, Esq. 30 *Gower Street*, W.C.
Mayall, J. E., Esq. *The Grove, Pinner.*
Mayson, John S., Esq. *Oak Hill, near Fallowfield, Manchester.*
Medd, William H., Esq. *The Mansion House, Stockport.*
Messenger, Samuel, Esq. *Birmingham.*
Michie, Alexander, Esq., F.R.G.S. 26 *Austin Friars*, E.C.; and *Shanghae, China.* (Care of) *Messrs. Smith, Elder, and Co.*
Mill, John, Esq. 1 *Foundling Terrace*, W.C.; and *Gresham House City*, E.C.
Milligan, Joseph, Esq., M.D., F.G.S., F.L.S. 15 *Northumberland Street, Strand*, W.C.; and *Royal Society of Tasmania, Hobart Town.*
Milner, W. R., Esq. *Wakefield.*
†*Milton, The Right Honourable the Lord Viscount, F.R.G.S. 4 *Grosvenor Square*, W.C.
Mirrlees, J. B., Esq. *Sauchiehall, Glasgow.*
Mitchell, Wm. Hen., Esq. *Junior Carlton Club; and Hampstead*, N.W.
Mitchell, William Stephen, Esq. *Gonville and Caius College, Cambridge; New University Club, S. James's Street; and S. George's Lodge, Bath.*
Mivart, St. George J., Esq., F.L.S., M.R.I. (Care of) *Royal Institution, Albemarle Street, and North Bank*, N.W.
Modelier, C. Poorooshottum, Esq. 33 *Western Villas, Blomfield Road, Paddington*, W.
Monk, Frederick William, Esq. *Faversham.*
Montgomerie, F. B., Esq. 2 *Cleveland Row, S. James's*, S.W.; and *Conservative Club, St. James's Street*, S.W.
Moon, the Rev. M. A. *Cleator, Whitehaven.*
Moore, J. Daniel, Esq., M.D., F.L.S. *County Lunatic Asylum, Lancaster.*
Moore, John, Esq. 104 *Bishopsgate Street*, E.C.
Moore, George, Esq., M.D. *Hartlepool.*
Morgan, Fortescue J., Esq. *High Street, Stamford.*
‡Morris, David, Esq., F.S.A. *Market Place, Manchester.*
Morris, J. P., Esq. *Ulverstone.*
Morison, J. Cotter, Esq., F.R.S.L. 7 *Porchester Square, Bayswater*, W.
Morshead, Edward John, Esq. *War Office, Pall Mall*, S.W.
Mortimer, John, Esq. *Pippingham Park, Uckfield*, S.
Mould, The Rev. Joseph, M.A. 16 *Bernard Street, Russell Sq.*, W.C.
Mosheimer, Joseph, Esq. 10 *Alexander Square, Brompton*, S.W.; and 11 *Newton Street, Manchester.*
Müller, Prof. August. *Königsberg, Prussia.*
Murphy, Edward W., Esq. 41 *Cumberland Street, Bryanstone Sq.*, W.
Musgrave, John George, Esq. *Andover.*

Naoroji, Dadabhai, Esq. 32 *Great S. Helen's*, E.C.
Nash, D. W., Esq. 21 *Bentinck Street, Manchester Square.*
‡ Nesbitt, George, Esq. 4 *St. Nicholas Buildings, Newcastle-on-Tyne.*

Newmarch, William, Esq., F.L.S. 17 *Palace Gardens Terrace, Notting Hill*, W.
Newnham, The Rev. P. H., M.A. 9 *Belvedere Terrace, Tunbridge Wells.*
Newton, Henry, Esq. 13 *Hood Street, Newcastle-on-Tyne.*
Nicholson, Sir Charles, Bart., D.C.L., LL.D., F.G.S. 10 *Portland Place,* W.C.
Nicholson, John Pcede Segrave Carington, Esq. *Castle Home, Whittlesea, Cambridgeshire.*
Noel, The Hon. Roden. *Warlies, Waltham Abbey.*
Noldwritt, J. S., Esq. 5 *Water Lane, Tower Street,* E.C.
North, Samuel W., Esq. *York.*
† North, George, Esq. 4 *Dane's Inn,* W.C.

O'Connor, Colonel L. Smyth, Inspecting Field Officer. *Belfast; Union Club, Trafalgar Square; and United Service Club, Pall Mall,* S.W.
Ogston, G. H., Esq. *Mincing Lane,* E.C.
O'Sullivan, The Honourable J. L. (of New York), late U.S. Minister to Portugal. 7 *Park Street, Grosvenor Square.*
Osborne, Major J. W. Willoughby, C.B., F.G.S. *Sehore Residency, India.* (Care of) *Messrs. Grindlay and Co.,* 55 *Parliament Street.*
Owen, Robert Briscoe, Esq., M.D., F.L.S. *Haulfre, Beaumaris.*
Owen, H. Burnard, Esq., F.R.S.L., F.R.G.S. 72 *Gower Street, Bedford Square,* W.C.
Owen, Captain Samuel R. John, P.H. Ass. King's College, London. 113A *Strand.*

Packman, J. D. V., Esq., F.L.S. *Braughing, Ware, Herts.*
‡ Palmer, S., Esq., M.D., F.S.A. *London Road, Newbury.*
Parker, J. W., Esq. *Warren Corner House, near Farnham.*
Parnell, John, Esq. *Upper Clapton,* S.
Parry, Dashwood G., Esq. *Hope, near Wrexham.*
Peacock, Edward, Esq , F.S.A. *Bottesford Manor, Lincolnshire.*
¶ Peacock, Thomas Bevill, Esq., M.D. 20 *Finsbury Circus,* E.C.
Peiser, John, Esq. *Barnsfield House, Oxford Street, Manchester.*
‡ Pengelly, William, Esq., F.R.S., F.G.S. *Lamorna, Torquay.*
Perrin, John Beswick, Esq. *Iry House, Abram, near Wigan.*
Perry, Gerald, Esq., H.M. Consul. *French Guiana.*
Petherick, Horace W., Esq. 2 *Denmark Villas, Wadron End Road, Croydon,* S.
Piesse, O. W. Septimus, Esq., Ph.D., F.C.S. *Chiswick,* W.
† ¶ Pike, Luke Owen, Esq., M.A. 25 *Carlton Villas, Muida Vale,* W.
Pinkerton, W., Esq., F S.A. *Hounslow,* W.
Plummer, Charles. 21 *Old Square, Lincoln's Inn,* W.C.
Prigg, Henry, Esq., jun. *Bury St. Edmunds.*
† ¶ Pritchard, William T., Esq. *Spring Hill, Birmingham.*

Radcliffe, John, Esq. *Oldham.*

Ramsay, A., jun., Esq. 45 *Norland Square, Notting Hill*, W.
Rankin, G. C., Esq. *Conservative Club*, S.W.
Ratcliff, Charles, Esq., F.I.S., F.S.A., F.G.S., F.E.S. *The Wyddringtons, Edybaston, Birmingham.*
†¶ Reade, William Winwood, Esq., F.R.G.S., Corr. Mem. Geographical Society of Paris. *Conservative Club*, S.W.
† ¶ Reddie, James, Esq. *The Admiralty, Somerset House*, W.C.; *and Bridge House, Hammersmith*, W.
Renshaw, Charles J., Esq., M.D. *Ashton-on-Mersey, Manchester.*
Ricardo, M., Esq. *Brighton.*
Richards, Franklin, Esq. 12 *Addison Crescent, Kensington*, W.
Richards, Colonel. *Wyndham Club, St. James's.*
Richardson, Charles, Esq. *Almondsbury, Bristol.*
Riddell, H. D., Esq. *The Palace, Maidstone.*
† ¶ Roberts, George E., Esq., F.G.S., Foreign Associate of the Anthropological Society of Paris. HONORARY SECRETARY. *Geological Society, Somerset House*, W.C.; 7 *Caversham Road*, N.W.; *and 5 Bull Ring, Kidderminster.*
Robertson, Alexander, Esq. *Chantrey Park, Sheffield.*
Robertson, D. B., Esq., H.M. Consul, Canton. *Canton.* (Care of Messrs. Smith, Elder, and Co., Pall Mall.)
Rock, James, Esq., jun. *St. Leonard's-on-Sea.*
Rogers, Alfred B., Esq., L.D.S. *St. John's Street, Manchester.*
† Rolph, George Frederick, Esq., M.A.C.R. *War Office, Pall Mall*, S.W.; *and* 10 *Leinster Square, Bayswater.*
Roussillon, The Duke of. 17 *Weymouth Street, Portland Place*, W.
Routh, E. J., Esq., F.G.S. *S. Peter's College, Cambridge.*
†Ruffières, Charles Robert des, Esq., F.G.S., F.E.S. *Wilmot Lodge, Rochester Row, Camden Town*, N.W.
Ruskin, V., Esq. *Northwich, Cheshire.*
Russell, Captain A.H. *Hawke's Bay, Napier, New Zealand.*

Sanders, Alfred, Esq. 22 *Beaufort Villas, Brixton*, S.
Saint David's, The Right Rev. Connop Thirlwall, the Lord Bishop of, President of the Royal Society of Literature. *Aberywyli Palace, near Carmarthen; and* 1 *Regent Street*, W.
St. John, Spencer, Esq., F.R.G.S. H.M. Consul. *Hayti.*
Salmon, William, Esq., F.G.S. *Ulverstone.*
Salting, William, Esq. 13 *King's Bench Walk, Temple*, E.C.
Sanderson, Alfred W., Esq. 16 *Archibald Street, Bow*, E.
‡ ¶ Schvarcz, Julius, Esq., Ph.D., F.G.S., Corr. Mem. E.S., Member of the Hungarian Academy of Sciences. *Stuhlweissenberg, Hungary.*
Schwabe, E. S., Esq. *Rhodes Terrace, Manchester.*
Scott, The Rev. Robert S., M.A. 7 *Beaufort Terrace, Cecil Street, Manchester.*
Scott, Wentworth L., Esq., F.C.S. 12 *Cornwall Villas, Bayswater.*
†Seemann, Berthold, Esq., Ph.D., F.L.S., F.R.G.S, Adjunct Præsidii of the Imperial L. C. Academia Naturæ Curiosorum. VICE-PRESIDENT. 22 *Canonbury Square, Islington*, N.

Selwyn, the Reverend William, D.D., Canon of Ely, Lady Margaret's Reader in Theology, *Cambridge.*
Seymour, George, Esq. *94 Cambridge Street, Pimlico.*
Sharp, Peter, Esq. *Oakfield, Ealing, W.*
Sharp, Samuel, Esq., F.S.A., F.G.S. *Dallington Hall, Northampton.*
Sharpe, W. J., Esq. *Beulah Spa Villa, Norwood, S.*
Shaw, Alexander Mackintosh, Esq. *Clifford Terrace, Leicester Street, Southport.*
Sheridan, H. B., Esq., M.P. *S. Peter's, Margate.*
¶ Shortt, John, Esq., M.D., Zillah Surgeon. *Chingleput, Madras.*
Shute, Thomas R. G., Esq. *The Rookery, Watford.*
Skene, J. H., Esq., Her Majesty's Consul. *Aleppo.*
Skues, Dr. Mackenzie, Surgeon H.M. 109th Regiment. *Aden.*
Silva-Ferro, Don Ramon de, F.G.S., F.R.G.S., Consul for the Republic of Chile. *21A Hanover Square, W.*
St. Clair, George, Esq., F.G.S., F.E.S. *Banbury.*
Smith, Abell, Esq. *1 Great George Street, Westminster, S.W.*
Smith, Sir Andrew, M.D. *51 Thurloe Square, W.*
Smith, John, Esq., F.E.S. *1 Great George Street, Westminster, S.W.*
Smith, Protheroe, Esq., M.D. *25 Park Street, W.*
Smith, Thomas, Esq., M.D. *Portland House, Cheltenham.*
Smith, T. J., Esq., F.G.S., F.C.S. *Hessle, near Hull.*
Smith, W., Esq. *6 Stockport Road, Manchester.*
Smith, Wm. Nugent, Esq. *Apsley Lodge, Wellington Road, Brighton.*
Smyth, John, Esq., jun. *Milltown, Banbridge.*
Snell, George Blagrove, Esq. *24 Lower Calthorpe Street, Gray's Inn Road, W.C.*
Solly, Samuel, Esq., F.R.C.S. *6 Savile Row, W.*
Southesk, The Right Honourable the Earl of, F.R.S. *Kinnaird Castle, Brechin, N.B.*
Spark, H. K., Esq. *Colliery Office, Darlington.*
Spencer, W. H., Esq. *High Wycombe, Bucks.*
Spencer, Peter, Esq. *Pendleton Alum Works, Newton Heath, Manchester.*
Spooner, The Rev. Edward, D.D., LL.D., Ph.D., M.R.H.S.L., etc. *The Parsonage, Brechin, N.B.*
Spry, Francis R., Esq., Ph.L. *Ashford, Hornsey, N.*
†Stanbridge, W. E., Esq. *Wombat, Victoria, Australia.*
*Stanley, The Right Honourable the Lord, M.P., F.R.S. *23 S. James's Square, S.W.*
Stanley, The Hon. John, Lieut.-Col. *Guards' Club, Pall Mall.*
Stenning, Charles, Esq. *4 Westbourne Park Place, Bayswater, W.*
Stevenson, John, Esq. *4 Brougham Street, Edinburgh.*
Stirrup, Mark, Esq. *3 Withington Terrace, Moss-side, Manchester.*
Stone, Alderman D. H. *33 Poultry, E.C.*
Strachan, John, Esq. *1 Avondale Place, Glasgow.*

Sturman, Edward, Esq. *Camden House, Sydenham Park.*
Sydenham, D., Esq. 104 *Edgware Road*, W.

Tate, A. Norman, Esq. *Ramsey, Isle of Man.*
Taylor, W., Esq. *High Garrett, Bocking, Essex.*
Taylor, W. E., Esq. *Millfield House, Enfield, near Accrington.*
Tenison, E. T. Ryan, Esq., M.D. 9 *Krith Terrace, Shepherd's Bush*, W.
Thin, Robert, Esq. 13 *Hill Place, Edinburgh.*
*Thompson, F., Esq. *South Parade, Wakefield.*
Thompson, Joseph, Esq. *Beech Grove, Bowdon, near Manchester.*
Thurnam, John, Esq., M.D., F.S.A., F.E.S. *Devizes.*
Tinsley, E., Esq. *Catherine Street, Strand.*
Travers, S. Smith, Esq. *Swithin's Lane*, E.C.
† Travers, William, Esq., F.R.C.S., L.R.C.P. *Charing Cross Hospital*, W.C.
Trevelyan, Arthur, Esq., J.P. *Teinholm, Tranent, N.B.*
Trübner, Nicolas, Esq. 60 *Paternoster Row*, E.C.
Tuckett, Charles, Esq., jun. *British Museum*, W.C.
Tylor, Edward Burnet, Esq., F.R.G.S. *Linden, Wellington, Somerset.*

†Vaux, William Sandys Wright, Esq., M.A., F.S.A., F. & Hon. Sec. R.S.L., Pres. Numismatic Society of London. *British Museum*, W.C.
Vernon, George Venables, Esq., F.R.A.S., M.B.M.S., Mem. Met. Soc. Scot., Mem. de la Société Météorologique de la France. *Old Trafford, Manchester.*

¶Wake, Charles Staniland, Esq. 16 *Oxford Road, Kilburn*, N.W.
Walker, Robert, Esq. 42 *Carnarvon Street, Glasgow.*
Walker, Robert Bruce Napoleon, Esq. 10 *Miborne Grove West, Brompton.*
Walsh, Sir John Benn, Bart., M.P. 28 *Berkeley Square*, W.; and Carlton Club, *Pall Mall*, S.W.
Walton, J. W., Esq. 21B *Savile Row*, W.
Warwick, Richard Archer, Esq., M.D., M.R.C.P. 5 *Hill Rise, Richmond*, S.W.
Washbourn, Buchanan, Esq., M.D., M.R.C.P., F.S.S. *East Gate House, Gloucester.*
Waterfield, O. F., Esq. *Temple Grove, East Sheen*, S.W.
Watson, Samuel, Esq., F.E.S. 12 *Bouverie Street*, E.C.
Watts, J. King, Esq., F.R.G.S. *St. Ives, Hunts.*
Westropp, Hodder M., Esq. *Rookhurst, Monktown, Cork.*
Whitehead, J. B., Esq. *Oakley House, Rawtenstall, near Manchester.*
Whitehead, Peter O., Esq. *Holly House, Rawtenstall.*
Whitehead, Thomas K., Esq. *Holly Mount, Rawtenstall.*
Wickes, Henry William, Esq. *Pixfield, Bromley, Kent.*
Wickes, Thomas Haines, Esq. *Pixfield, Bromley, Kent.*

Williams, Eric, Esq. *Newton House, Kensington,* W.
Williams, Thomas, Esq., M.D., F.R.S. *Swansea.*
Wilson, William Newton, Esq. 144 *High Holborn,* E.C.
Windus, Commander, A. T., H.M. late Indian Navy. 14 *St. James's Square.*
Witt, George, Esq., F.R.S. 22 *Prince's Terrace, Hyde Park,* 8.W.
Wittich, Prof. von. *Königsberg, Prussia.*
Wollaston, George, Esq. 1 *Barnepark Terrace, Teignmouth.*
Woodd, Charles H. L., Esq., F.G.S. *Roslyn, Hampstead,* N.W.
Wood, F. Henry, Esq. *Hollin Hall, near Ripon, Yorkshire.*
Wood, the Rev. William S., D.D. *The School, Oakham, Rutland.*
Wright, William Cort, Esq. *Whalley Range, Manchester.*

Yonge, Robert, Esq., F.L.S., Hon. Mem. York Phil. Soc. *Greystones, Sheffield.*

HONORARY FELLOWS.

Agassiz, M. Louis, Professor of Zoology at Yale College, Cambridge, Mass., U.S., For. Mem. G.S. *Cambridge, Massachusetts, U.S.*
Boudin, M., Médecin en Chef de l'Hôpital Militaire St. Martin. 210 *Rue de Rivoli, Paris.*
¶ Broca, M. Paul, Sécrétaire-général à la Société d'Anthropologie de Paris. 1 *Rue des Saintspères, Paris.*
Baer, Von, M. Carl Ernst, Foreign Associate of the Anthropological Society of Paris. *St. Petersburg.*
Boucher de Crevecœur de Perthes, M., Honorary Fellow of the Anthropological Society of Paris, Foreign Correspondent of the Geological Society of London. *Abbeville.*
¶ Carus, Professor C. G., Comes Palatinus, President of the Imperial L. C. Academia Naturæ Curiosorum. *Dresden.*
Crawfurd, John, Esq., F.R.S., Vice-President of the Ethnological Society of London, F.R.G.S., etc. *Athenæum Club.*
Dareste, M. Camille, Sécrétaire de la Société d'Anthropologie de Paris. *Rue de l'Abbaye, Paris.*
Darwin, Charles, Esq., M.A., F.R.S., F.L.S., F.G.S. *Down, Bromley, Kent.*
Eckhard, M., Professor of Physiology at the University of Giessen. *Giessen.*
Gratiolet, M. Pierre, D. M. P., President de la Société d'Anthropologie de Paris. 15 *Rue Guy Labrouse, Paris.*
Kingsley, The Rev. Charles, M.A., F.L.S., F.G.S., Rector of Eversley, Professor of Modern History in the University of Cambridge. *Eversley, near Winchfield, Hants.*
Lartèt, M. Edouard, For. Member G.S. 15 *Rue Lacépède, Paris.*
Lawrence, Wm., Esq., F.R.S., F.R.C.S. 18, *Whitehall Place,* S.W.
Lucae, Dr. J. C. S. *Frankfort.*

Lyell, Sir Charles, Bart., D.C.L., LL.D., F.R.S., V.P.G.S., Eq. Ord. Boruss. "pour le mérite," Hon.M.R.S.Ed., F.S.L., President of the British Association for the Advancement of Science. 53 *Harley Street*, W.

Meigs, Dr. J. Aitken, Foreign Associate of the Anthropological Society of Paris. *Philadelphia.*

Milne-Edwards, Dr. Henry, Member of the Institute, For. Mem. R.S., For. Mem. G.S., Professor of Natural History, Jardin des Plantes. *Paris.*

Nott, Dr. J. C., Foreign Associate of the Anthropological Society of Paris. *Mobile (Alabama, C.S.A.)*

Owen, Richard, Esq., D.C.L., LL.D., F.R.C.S.E., F.R.S., F.G.S., F.L S., Hon. M.R.S.Ed., Hon. F.R. College of Surgeons of Ireland, Eq. Ord. Boruss. "pour le mérite," Foreign Associate of the Anthropological Society of Paris, Chev. Leg. Hon. Institut (Imp. Acad. Sci.) Paris, Director of the Natural History Department, British Museum. *British Museum; and Sheen Lodge, Richmond Park,* S.W.

Pruner-Bey, M., Vice-President de la Société d'Anthropologie. 28, *Place St. Victor, Paris.*

Quatrefages, M. Alphonse de, Professor of Anthropology in the Museum of Natural History, Paris. *Rue Geoffroy St. Hilaire, Paris.*

Renan, M., Membre Honoraire de la Société d'Anthropologie. 55 *Rue Madame, Paris.*

Van der Hoeven, Professor. *Leyden.*

Vogt, Professor Carl, Professor of Natural History. *Geneva.*

Wright, Thomas, Esq., M.A., F.S.A., Hon. F.R.S.L., Corr. Mem. of the Imperial Academy of Paris, Honorary Secretary of the Ethnological Society of London. 14 *Sydney Street, Brompton,* S.W.

CORRESPONDING MEMBERS.

Brücke, Dr. Vienna.
Büchner, Dr. Ludwig. Darmstadt.
¶ Burgholzhausen, Count A. F. Marschall von, For. Corr. G.S., Chamberlain de l'Empereur. Wollzell, Vienna.
Burmeister, Hermann. Buenos Ayres.
Buschmann, Professor. Berlin.
Castelnau, M. de. Paris.
Dally, Dr. E. Paris.
Desnoyers, M. Jules, For. Corr. G.S. Paris.
Dorn, General Bernard. St. Petersburg.
D'Omalius d'Halloy, Professor, For. Mem. G.S. Brussels.
Duhousset, M. le Commandant. (French Army in the) Atlas.
Gervais, M. Dr., For. Corr. G.S. Montpellier.
Giglioli, Professor. Pavia.
Gosse, M. A. L. (père). Geneva.
Gosse, M. H. J. Geneva.

His, Prof. Basle.
Hochstelter, Professor von. Vienna.
Hyrtl, Professor, Vienna.
Kaup, Professor, Dr., For. Corr. G.S. Darmstadt.
Leuckart, M. Giessen.
Martin-Magron, M. 26 Rue Madame, Paris.
Moleschott, Prof. Turin.
Morlot, M., For. Corr. G.S. Berne.
Nicolucci, Prof. Naples.
Pictet, Prof. F. G., For. Corr. G.S. Geneva.
Pouchet, George M. Rouen.
Raimondy, Professor. Lima.
Reichert, M.
Rickard, Major Francis Ignacio, F.G.S., F.C.S. Argentine Republic.
  21a Hanover Square.
Rütimeyer, Professor. Basle.
Scherzer, Dr. Carl von. Vienna.
Schlagintweit, Hermann de. Paris.
Steinhauer, Herr Carl. Copenhagen.
Steenstrup, Professor, Dr., For. Corr. G.S. Copenhagen.
Thomsen, Le Chevalier. Copenhagen.
Uhde, C. W. F. Herr. Berlin.
Vibraye, Marquis de, For. Corr. G.S. Abbeville and Paris.
Welcker, Dr. H., Professor. Halle.
Wilson, Professor Daniel. Toronto.
Worsaae, Professor. Copenhagen.

LOCAL SECRETARIES (GREAT BRITAIN).

BEDFORDSHIRE ......*Higham Ferrars*...Rev. W. Monk, M.A., F.S.A., F.R.A.S.
BERKSHIRE............*Newbury*............J. Palmer, Esq., M.D., F.A.S.L.
CHESHIRE ....*Bebbington*........Craig Gibson, Esq., M.D.
DEVONSHIRE ....*Torquay* ....W. Pengelly, Esq., F.R.S., F.G.S.,
                                                              F.A.S.L., Lamorna, nr. Torquay.
DORSETSHIRE........*Bradford Abbas*, Professor Buckman, F.L.S., F.G.S.
                      near Sherborne.
                 Poole ....Frederick Travers, Esq.
                 Wareham............Charles Groves, Esq.
DURHAM ....*Stockton-on-Tees*...Dr. Farquharson.
GLOUCESTERSHIRE...*Pendock, near* Rev. W. S. Symonds, F.G.S.
                  Tewkesbury.
HAMPSHIRE ....*Isle of Wight* ......Hyde Pullen, Esq.
KENT ....*Chatham* ....Rev. H. F. Bivers, M.A., Luton,
                                                              near Chatham.
LANCASHIRE ....*Liverpool*............W. G. Helsby, Esq., Crosby Green
                                                              New Derby.

LANCASHIRE	...Manchester...	Dr. F. Royston Fairbank, F.A.S.L., St. Mary's Terrace, Hulme.
		David Morris, Esq., F.H.A., Market Place.
NORTHUMBERLAND	...Alnwick...	George Tate, Esq., F.G.S., Secretary to the Berwickshire Naturalists' Field Club, Corresponding Member of the Soc. of Antiq. Scotl.
	Newcastle	George Nesbitt, Esq., F.A.S.L, 4 St. Nicholas Buildings.
OXFORDSHIRE	...Oxford...	The Rev. Joseph Bosworth, D.D., F.R.S., F.S.A., 20 Beaumont Sq.
	Banbury	George St. Clair, Esq., F.G.S., F.A.S.L., F.E.S.
SOMERSETSHIRE	...Bath...	R. T. Gore, Esq., F.A.S.L., F.R.C.S., 6 Queen's Square, Bath.
STAFFORDSHIRE	...Wolverhampton...	Charles Alfred Rolph, Esq., Waterloo Road.
SUSSEX	...Hastings...	Thomas Tate, Esq., F.R.A.S., Essex Cottage, Fairlight.
	Brighton	S. E. Collingwood, Esq., F.A.S.L., 47 York Road.
WARWICKSHIRE	...Birmingham...	W. T. Pritchard, Esq., F.R.G.S., F.A.S.L., Spring Hill.
	Warwick	The Rev. P. B. Brodie, M.A., F.L.S., F.G.S., The Vicarage, Rowington.
YORKSHIRE	...Bradford...	R. Lee, Esq., F.A.S.L., Wilmot House, Leeds Road.
	Hull	Kelburne King, Esq., M.D., F.A.S.L., 27 George Street, Hull.
LANARKSHIRE	...Glasgow...	J. W. Jackson, F.A.S.L., 39 St. George's Road, Glasgow.
FIFESHIRE	...St. Andrew's...	Prof. W. Macdonald, F.L.S., F.G.S., F.A.S.L., Prof. Civ. & Nat. Hist., St. Andrew's.
HEBRIDES	...Islay...	Hector Maclean, Esq., Ballygrant, Islay.
ULSTER	...Belfast...	Brice Smyth, Esq., M.D., 13 College Square.
CONNAUGHT	...Galway...	W. King, Esq., Professor of Geology, Queen's College.

LOCAL SECRETARIES (ABROAD).

AFRICA (West Coast)	Du Chaillu, M. Paul Belloni, F.A.S.L. (care of 120 Mount Street, W.)
ALGERIA	Thomas Callaway, M.R.C.S. (Exam.) 1844, F.R.C.S. (Exam.) 1847, Mem. Fac. Med. Algeria (Exam.) 1862, Mem. Med.-Chir. Soc. Lond. Maison Limozin, Place Besson, Algiers. Care of Montague Gomett, Esq., 4 Coleman St., City.

ARGENTINE REPUBLIC. *Buenos Ayres* ...Facundo Carulla, Esq., F.A.S.L.
AUSTRIA .... *Vienna* ....M. Franciscus Miklosich.
      Hungary............Dr. Julius Schvarcz, F.G.S., F.A.S.L., Member of the Hungarian Acad. Sciences. Stuhlweissenburg.
      Prague ....Dr. Anton Fritsch, Director of the National Museum of Bohemia.
BELGIUM ....*Brussels* ....M. Octave Delepierre.
          John Jones, Esq.
BORNEO .... *Sardwak* ....Edward Price Houghton, Esq., M.D., M.R.C.S.
BRITISH COLUMBIA ....Captain Edward Stamp.
CANADA ....*Montreal*............George E. Fenwick, Esq., M.D.
     Labrador............The Rev. C. Linder.
     Toronto ....Professor Hincks.
CHINA ....   William Lockhart, Esq., M.R.C.S.
         A. G. Cross, Esq., M.R.C.S.
ECUADOR................   J. Spotswood Wilson, F.R.G.S.
EGYPT ....*Alexandria*..........J. Stafford Allen, Esq.
     Cairo ....Dr. Theodor Bilharz.
FRANCE ....*Paris* ....Prof. M. Giraldès, Prof. de Méd. à l'Hôpital des Enfans Trouvées.
     Nice..................Dr. Edwin Lee.
HESSE DARMSTADT...*Giessen* ....Dr. Phoebus.
JAVA ....*Batavia* ....Dr. Wienecke.
     Cocos Islands ......J. G. C. Ross, Esq.
NATAL.....................   The Rev. H. Callaway, M.A.
NEW ZEALAND ......   Captain A. H. Russell, F.A.S.L.
NICARAGUA.............   Commander Bedford Pim, R.N.
OUDE ....   G. Jasper Nicholls, Esq. (H.M. Indian Civil Service). Trekenning House, St. Columb, Cornw.
PRUSSIA ....*Bonn* ....Dr. Schaafhausen.
QUEENSLAND ....   George T. Hine, Esq.
         George W. Brown, Esq.
SAXONY ....*Leipsig* ....Dr. Alfred von Kremer.
SPAIN ....*Gibraltar* ....Captain Brome.
UNITED STATES ......*New York* ....Captain W. Parker Snow.
     San Francisco ...R. Beverley Cole, Esq., M.A., M.D., Ph.D., Professor of Obstetrics and the Diseases of Women in the University of the Pacific.
SWEDEN ....*Stockholm* ....Dr. Retzius.
     Götland ....Dr. Gustaf Lindstrom.
VANCOUVER'S ISLAND........................Edward B. Bogge, Esq., R.N.

www.ingramcontent.com/pod-product-compliance
Lightning Source LLC
Chambersburg PA
CBHW051732300426
44115CB00007B/525